Thematic Approaches for Teaching Introductory Psychology

DANA S. DUNN
Moravian College

and

BRIDGETTE MARTIN HARD
Stanford University

Australia • Brazil • Mexico • Singapore • United Kingdom • United States

**Thematic Approaches
for Teaching Introductory
Psychology**
Dana S. Dunn, Bridgette
Martin Hard

Vice President, General
Manager: Erin Joyner

Product Director:
Marta Lee-Perriard

Product Manager:
Timothy Matray

Content Developer: Liz Fraser

Product Assistant: Katie Chen

Marketing Manager:
Andrew Ginsberg

Manufacturing Planner:
Karen Hunt

Intellectual Property Analyst:
Deanna Ettinger

Property Project Manager:
Erika Mugavin

Art and Cover Direction,
Production Management,
and Composition: Lumina
Datamatics, Inc.

Cover Image Credit:
© stocktributor/Fotolia

For product information and
technology assistance, contact us at **Cengage Learning
Customer & Sales Support, 1-800-354-9706**

For permission to use material from this text or product,
submit all requests online at **www.cengage.com/permissions**
Further permissions questions can be emailed to
permissionrequest@cengage.com

Library of Congress Control Number: 2016948138

ISBN: 978-1-305-88663-6

Cengage Learning
20 Channel Center Street
Boston, MA 02210
USA

Cengage Learning is a leading provider of customized learning
solutions with employees residing in nearly 40 different countries
and sales in more than 125 countries around the world. Find your
local representative at **www.cengage.com.**

Cengage Learning products are represented in Canada by
Nelson Education, Ltd.

To learn more about Cengage Learning Solutions, visit
www.cengage.com

Purchase any of our products at your local college store or at our
preferred online store **www.cengagebrain.com**

Printed in the United States of America
Print Number: 01   Print Year: 2016

Dedicated to Charles L. Brewer and in Memory of Robert C. Calfee

Table of Contents

Big Ideas for Integrating Concepts

Skill Development and Ways of Thinking

Foreword

PHILIP G. ZIMBARDO
Stanford University

TEACHING 2.0: OPTIMIZING THE TRANSFORMATIVE POWER OF TEACHING

Teaching is the most noble of all professions and human activities. When we share our knowledge, we change how the brain functions, how the mind materializes, and how skills and strategies become operational, and that collective wisdom creates and nourishes cultures. Moreover, every teacher is in continual renewal, ever learning and growing as every student seedling matures and flowers.

From my first introductory psychology course as a Yale graduate student back in 1956 to my final lecture at Stanford University some 50 years later, the magical power of psychology continually illuminated my life in endless ways. I do wish I could start all over again because psychology is more exciting now than it ever has been. In the olden days the most boring topic was that of memory, studied with students riveted to memory drums spewing out nonsense syllables to be mastered, while albino rats were figuring out how to get back to the food tray in their Y-maze. Now, the investigation of human and animal memory is amazingly exciting at so many levels of analysis.

We have a great future ahead as we extend the boundaries of our field in both more molar and molecular directions, with something hot for every possible interest. As hot as cognitive neuroscience and behavioral economics are, at the other end of the continuum we have health psychology and peace psychology expanding, and psychologists being involved in human services, the space program, media, environmental sustainability, education, longevity, terrorism, and more. There are no limits to what psychology can offer society and no limits on the potential contributions that the next generation of psychologists can make to our community. What a hot new world is ahead for you neophyte teachers. Please use it all wisely and well.

Now my task at hand is to introduce readers to this very special new contribution to the teaching of psychology. The authors in this delightful volume are all veteran instructors who have honed their teaching skills in the trenches of seminars and/or at the podium of large lectures. Their creative wisdom is offered in ways that can be readily borrowed to tweak parts of a course, jazz up a lecture, or even as the foundation of an entire course for beginning teachers. Graduate teaching assistants can utilize their suggested class activities if their sections involve adding to the corresponding lecture content and also as mental triggers to build out related lecture demonstrations, examples, and exercises. Again, since many intro psych courses provide overviews of most of the substantive areas of psychology, these essays are also a treasure trove to be explored for teachers of the next-level courses in the curriculum. What I really enjoyed most in this manual is the blend of nitty-gritty examples of "try this, do this, consider this alternative" along with the rather profound reflections on essential issues in teaching psychology and also laying out of thematic carpets for broader appreciation.

Finally, my toast to every new and also seasoned teachers is: Live a life of ideas, inspire and transform students, make a contribution to society, be a lifetime student ever curious, ever learning new lessons. And most of all, become shamelessly passionate about your life as a teacher, researcher, and maybe also as a sociopolitical activist. What could be a better way to spend the next four decades of your life?

Preface

The first course that a student takes in psychology goes by many names: General Psychology, Introduction to or Introductory Psychology, Psychology 101, or Psychology One. Whatever the title, the first course in psychology is critically important for many reasons. The course introduces students to the ways psychologists think and talk about human thought, emotion, and action. First, because students are people, who interact with other people, learning psychological ways of thinking can enrich their understanding of everyday experiences and interactions. Such understanding will serve them well in whatever undergraduate major they choose (including psychology itself) and in their postgraduate lives. Second, science is central to psychology, and so the introductory course is also an opportunity to teach students about empirical tools and techniques in the context of content that is memorable and relevant. Learning to think like a psychologist and to appreciate the power and necessity of the empirical method for assessing cause and effect will help students become more reflective of the world they inhabit.

As the discipline of psychology has grown, so have the demands associated with teaching the introductory course. One challenge is the variety of audiences who take the course: prospective psychology majors, those interested in connected disciplines, and those who enroll in the course to complete a general education requirement or out of sheer interest or curiosity. How can instructors provide prospective majors with some sense of the deeper issues of the discipline while giving others a Cook's tour of the science of human behavior?

Besides the many-audience problem, introductory psychology instructors must also contend with the challenges of coverage. Portraying the entire discipline in 10 to 15 weeks is daunting, given the size of introductory books and concomitant expansion of topical research—all reflecting the growth of a vigorous and dynamic field. The burgeoning work in neuroscience, for example, has increased the amount of material in chapters on the brain, sensation, and perception, not to mention the inclusion of social neuroscience findings in the social psychology chapter. Evolutionary psychology, too, touches on both biology and social behavior. Positive psychological research is finding its way into the chapters exploring emotion and personality, and so on.

Instructors of the first course in psychology want to do more than merely cover the material through lecturing or showing PowerPoint slides. They also want to engage students by having them experience the course material in meaningful ways, such as in the aforementioned class demonstrations, writing exercises, targeted videos from the internet, opinion surveys (via clickers or smart phones), and, when possible, critical debate and basic class discussion.

Assessing learning, too, matters. Some instructors develop short writing assignments that encourage students to reflect on course material, including controversial issues or counterintuitive findings. Quizzes and exams need to be designed to allow students to demonstrate what they have learned in significant ways. Opportunities to reflect on and to integrate course material should be part of the assessment process; students should not simply complete recognition-based multiple-choice measures. Cognitive research is clear that deep learning requires active involvement and constructive engagement with a topic.

Both new and veteran instructors feel pushed and pulled in different directions by the distinct demands of running and teaching the introductory course. Some instructors have the support of advanced undergraduate or graduate teaching assistants while others are solely responsible for delivery of their course. Psychologists want to project both rigor and vigor in their classrooms, but they must realistically balance such desires with the limits of their time and resources, as well as other professional demands. For many introductory faculty members, the "center cannot hold." We envisioned this book as a source and resource to help them better navigate and teach the critical first course.

The idea for this book emerged from discussions at the Stanford Psychology One Conference, an annual event dedicated to the teaching of introductory psychology. These discussions inspired the central idea of this volume: teaching introductory psychology by emphasizing one or more key themes throughout the course as a way to unify theoretical and empirical findings and to maintain students' engagement and understanding. In this volume, we present a variety of approaches to doing this. We have asked expert teachers of introductory psychology, representing a variety of institutions and classroom environments, to share a primary theme that they use to teach their course. Each author has been asked to provide a theoretical and practical rationale for their theme: What makes the theme important and of value to students? Each author has also been asked to carefully describe how the theme shapes his or her own course design, content, activities, and assessments.

An initial chapter by Dana S. Dunn highlights the importance of introductory psychology and is followed by three sections that reflect different categories of themes that unify introductory psychology. The first section focuses on broad thematic frameworks that instructors use to guide their approach to teaching the course. Jane Halonen presents a "postmodern" philosophy to teaching the course, which emphasizes active learning. Regan Gurung shares his theme of applications, of making all course content relevant and personal by connecting it to everyday life and real-world problems. Andrew LoGiudice and Joseph Kim present a problem-based learning approach to their course, and finally, Maureen McCarthy shares an approach to teaching the course as part of a study abroad program.

The second section focuses on themes that are overarching concepts or "big ideas" that are explicitly taught to students as a way of integrating content. The authors in this section incorporate many overarching concepts into their courses, but each chapter underscores a specific concept. Ann Nordmeyer, Bridgette Hard, and James Gross highlight the ways that psychology is shaped by interacting forces that are both internal and external to a person. Wayne Weiten describes the inherent subjectivity of experience that is conveyed by content in introductory psychology. Finally, Margaret Lynch argues for evolutionary psychology as a unifying concept for introductory psychology.

The third section explores themes that emphasize specific skills or ways of thinking that can be developed in an introductory psychology course. First, Eric Landrum makes the case for emphasizing skills as a theme of introductory psychology course and explores several skills that are important for students to develop. Jerusha Detweiler-Bedell and Abigail Hazlett describe how to organize a course to develop both written and spoken communication skills. Trudy Loop presents a course theme that emphasizes building resilience, health, and well-being.

Four remaining chapters in this section highlight themes that are connected to the central role of science in psychology. Noland White proposes an introductory course that teaches students the value of using evidence to guide thinking and practice. Erin Hardin presents the theme of training students to see the world "like a psychologist," filled with questions that can be answered scientifically. Neil Lutsky describes how he develops quantitative reasoning skills in his course. Finally, Amy Silvestri Hunter and Susan Teague describe a theme that is focused broadly on developing students' scientific thinking skills.

Contributors to this volume were also asked to present practical tips for designing and teaching introductory psychology. The advice they offer is specific to their themes and also to the specific contexts in which they teach. Our contributors represent a diversity of introductory psychology classrooms, and so their advice is rich and varied.

Some contributors teach courses to hundreds or thousands of students that are primarily lecture-based (Lynch) or with an online learning component (LoGiudice and Kim). Some teach fairly large courses of several hundred students (Hardin), sometimes with smaller discussion-section component led by graduate and undergraduate teaching assistants (Gurung; Nordmeyer, Hard, and Gross). Many teach sections of 20 to 100 students (Detweiler-Bedell and Hazlett; Hunter and Teague; Lutsky; White). One contributor (Loop) teaches AP psychology to high school students.

We hope that this book will inspire those who teach introductory psychology, whether just starting out or rounding out several decades of teaching, to think thematically about the introductory course. What will unify or already unifies your course? Our hope is that our contributors will provide many new ideas and insights that can guide you in designing, redesigning, or revising your existing course.

ACKNOWLEDGMENTS

We are grateful to the Department of Psychology at Stanford, as well as the Stanford Psychology One Conference, for bringing us, the editors, together with our contributors in an intellectually rich setting where the pleasures and challenges of teaching the first course in psychology were discussed. Jon-David Hague, formerly of Cengage, was a champion of the book idea from its inception; we thank him for his enthusiasm in moving the project forward. Tim Matray inherited the project and graciously guided it to completion. We also appreciate the help of Liz Fraser and other colleagues at Cengage as the book went into production. Dana is grateful to Bridgette for her outstanding work ethic and attention to detail, and for her friendship. Hard is likewise grateful to Dana for "showing her the ropes" on this project with his gentle guidance and mentorship. Both agree that working on this project has been a pleasure.

We dedicate this book to two good friends. First, we dedicate this book to Charles L. Brewer, professor emeritus at Furman University, whose influence on the teaching of psychology and on both of us is inestimable. Second, we dedicate this book in memory of our friend and colleague, Robert C. Calfee. Bob was to edit this work with us, but sadly he died just as the project was taking final shape. Bob was a cognitive psychologist and professor emeritus of the Stanford Graduate School of Education and a former dean of the Graduate School of Education at University of California, Riverside. He was a longtime advocate for evidence-based practices in education, an expert in educational technology, and generally a person who brimmed with great ideas. The idea to develop an edited volume based on discussions at the Stanford Psychology One Conference was originally his, and we are so grateful for his influence.

Dana S. Dunn, Bethlehem, PA
Bridgette Martin Hard, Palo Alto, CA

Chapter 1

On the Primacy of Introductory Psychology

DANA S. DUNN[1]

Moravian College

Psychology is the Science of Mental Life, both of its phenomena and of their conditions. The phenomena are such things as we call feelings, desires, cognitions, reasonings, decisions, and the like; and, superficially considered, their variety and complexity is such as to leave a chaotic impression on the observer.
—WILLIAM JAMES (1890, p. 1)

James was a gifted writer and his elegant prose in *The Principles of Psychology* organized the nascent field's observations into a coherent whole for novice students, which then included the first generation or two of psychologists in the United States. In the same way, the first psychology course a student takes now, in the 21st century, should impose some order on the "chaotic impression" James identified. Since the first course is typically introductory psychology, there is certainly the need to create some order and organization for the ever-burgeoning research and pedagogical materials (Stoloff, 2010). Like many tales, psychology's story has grown with the telling. The book you are reading recommends a variety of ways to teach the first course by using some overarching themes to guide the understanding and presentation of theories and findings. A theme, such as *critical thinking* or *evolutionary*

---

[1] I am grateful to Maureen McCarthy and Bridgette Martin Hard for helpful comments on an earlier version of this work.

psychological perspectives, serves as a lens or point of view for categorizing and explaining what might best be described as the core topical areas in the discipline.

Why devote an entire volume to approaches to teaching a single course? My goal here is to discuss reasons for giving pride of place to the first course, whether it is within the curriculum of the psychology major or serving as a general education (or distribution) requirement. Call it what you will; introductory psychology, introduction to psychology, or general psychology is—or should be—an essential part of every college student's undergraduate experience. Implicitly, perhaps, this is already the case, as an estimated 1 million to 1.7 million undergraduates enroll in this course in the United States every year (Gurung, 2013; Steuer & Ham, 2008). Most college students take the course as an elective but some do so as the entry point to the psychology major. But unlike upper-level offerings examining various topics in depth, the introductory psychology course is designed to attract and to serve different audiences of students and to satisfy a wide variety of educational goals, not just those linked to the discipline (Hill, 2006). Thus, there is a certain primacy to the course, as it fulfills many needs.

In this overview chapter, I will discuss factors that promote the course's primacy in psychology curricula and in undergraduate education more generally. These include the fact that the introductory course is often a student's first and last psychology course, that the course encapsulates much of the psychology curriculum, and that it can be taught in myriad ways and is often an arena for showmanship—a place for teachers to work their pedagogical magic. I then turn to a review of the routine challenges facing introductory instructors and close with the view that, despite these challenges, introductory psychology can still provide teachers with the opportunity for pedagogical innovation (for related views, see Stoloff, 2010; Weiten & Houska, 2015).

A SINGLE POINT OF CONTACT WITH PSYCHOLOGY

For most students, introductory psychology is their first and last opportunity to learn about the discipline of psychology in a formal way, as it is likely to be the only psychology course they take. This is an important fact to consider, as it puts pressure on instructors to present material not only factually but also memorably, and to ensure that the breadth of the discipline is well represented. Yet complete coverage of the discipline of psychology is neither possible nor desirable; the field is too big and broad, and now highly specialized, a fact that leads to topical fragmentation (Dunn et al., 2010; Leahey, 2013). These factors compel instructors to make judicious choices about what to present and for how long, as well as what material to necessarily, if regrettably, leave out. Most introductory courses last but one semester—and often occur early in a student's college career—which means that the course must be pitched at a level that is accessible to first-year students. At the same time, the course has to remain interesting to students who postpone their behavioral science elective until later in their college years, as many sections of introductory psychology host a mixed audience of students where collegiate experience or academic sophistication are concerned.

A key factor of introductory psychology's primacy, then, is that the course often represents the *one chance* an instructor and a psychology department or program has to educate the average student, and perhaps the average citizen, about the discipline. Helping students to understand and appreciate that psychology is both a social and a natural science requires some constructive persuasion. Of particular concern is working to undo the biased or naive perspectives about psychology that many college students harbor (e.g., psychologists "read" people's minds, all psychologists are clinically oriented, and a BA in psychology enables one to be a practitioner) (Dunn & Halonen, 2017; Hill, 2006). Some of these uninformed perspectives hail from popular culture and media, ill-conceived pop-psychology books, bogus Internet sites, simple hearsay, or wishful thinking (for further discussion, see Chew, 2006).

To counter the misinformation that many students possess, the introductory course becomes the first (and often last) line of pedagogical defense by repeatedly presenting the logic of experimental design, including crafting clear hypotheses, using randomization, explaining the necessity of control groups, and relying on rigorous testing and replication to identify differences among experimental groups. The focus on experimental methodology has twin goals: to give the "one-course" students a detailed sense of why methodology is crucial to discerning cause and effect while also exposing future psychology majors to learning outcomes and skills that will prepare them for ideas and material they will encounter in advanced courses (APA, 2013). Naturally, students should learn that there are alternative methods available (e.g., correlational approaches, case studies, qualitative methods, survey research) when experimental interventions cannot be employed.

Beyond the needed focus on methodology, what other topical streams should appear in the first course that plays to its primacy? Two other topics should both appear and be reinforced in the class: diversity and ethics. It is important to infuse discussions of diversity throughout introductory psychology because students must be introduced to both the subtleties and the complexities of living in a multicultural society (e.g., Dunn & Hammer, 2014; Littleford et al., 2010; Matsumoto, 2007; Matsumoto & Juang, 2007). Second, students must learn that diversity is not limited to race, ethnicity, or even gender. They will encounter and need to navigate—if they have not already done so—diversity as represented by sexual orientation, religiosity or spirituality, disability, and social class, among other possibilities, in their eventual careers as well as daily lives. A discussion of the role of diversity in the context of research allows students to appreciate the complexity of interpreting the results of research; after all, statistically speaking, life is not just comprised of main effects. Most of our experience is based on complex interactions involving myriad social and psychological variables. For those students who do not major in psychology, the introductory psychology course may be one of the few (perhaps only) courses during their undergraduate experience that tackles multicultural matters head-on (unless their undergraduate institution makes special efforts to do so via cocurricular programs or diversity requirements; cf. Deresiewicz, 2014).

Ethics, in turn, is an important concern that should reappear throughout the course (Handelsman, 2006; LEAP, 2015). Handelsman, for example, argues that as a course topic, ethics is as important as more traditional topics such as perception, social psychology, or learning theory. If students learn about and engage in ethical practices in introductory psychology, they will learn to appreciate the potential ethical pitfalls surrounding studying human and animal behavior, such as privacy, informed consent, and care and housing of laboratory animals, among other issues. Surely, nurturing the ability to engage in ethical reasoning, a form of critical thinking, as Handelsman notes, is a worthy goal for students who enroll in introductory psychology.

If nothing else, helping students to develop ethical, diversity, and methodological awareness, as well as related rudimentary skills, will benefit them in whatever course their lives take. These students will become more savvy consumers of research presented in the media and, one hopes, more open to seeking psychological services, such as counseling or psychotherapy. Perhaps, too, they will be more careful when evaluating various causal claims made in the media or in daily conversation. Naturally, psychology majors will develop broader and deeper perspectives on these issues, but we should not overlook the fact that a well-constructed introductory course encapsulates the content of larger psychology curriculum.

INTRODUCTORY PSYCHOLOGY ENCAPSULATES THE CURRICULUM

In many ways, the introductory course reflects the breadth of the recommended program curriculum for the psychology major. Dunn et al. (2010) urged educators to adopt a core approach to the psychology major, one that corresponds quite well with the content typically taught in introductory psychology. As noted earlier, the heart of any quality introductory course—and psychology curriculum—requires emphasizing the scientific method as a way of knowing (and employing various research methodologies in order to learn about various behavioral phenomena). Similarly, Dunn and colleagues argued that diversity and ethics should be integrated throughout a quality curriculum rather than being the focus of one or two courses (rarely, e.g., are psychology majors required to complete a stand-alone ethics course; Stoloff et al., 2010). We previously considered the utility of having diversity issues and ethical matters revisited throughout the teaching of introductory psychology.

In addition to a foundation in research methods, diversity, and ethics, Dunn et al. (2010) recommended that four content domains—really, core areas—comprise students' course work. Specifically, students should complete at least one course representing the biological bases of behavior (e.g., biopsychology, neuroscience, brain and behavior, animal behavior), developmental psychology (e.g., infancy, child development, adolescence, adulthood and aging, life-span development), sociocultural issues (e.g., social psychology, personality, cultural psychology), and learning and cognition (e.g., cognitive psychology, learning, psychometrics). As you may have noticed, the parenthetical examples of these four areas nicely represent many of the chapter topics found in most introductory psychology texts (e.g., Griggs & Marek, 2001). Thus, a solid program curriculum essentially recapitulates much of introductory psychology (and vice versa).

Beyond a representative course sampling from the four core areas, Dunn et al. (2010) suggested that students should have some type of applied course, where basic theory and results could be examined in terms of their practical or functional value for interpreting behavior. Within a major program, for example, a student might enroll in an industrial/organizational course to learn how research is applied to work settings in order to improve employee morale, well-being, and productivity. Increasingly, introductory psychology courses and textbooks also include one or more chapters dedicated to exploring applied areas of the discipline. For example, stand-alone chapters often include health psychology, psychology and the law, environmental psychology, clinical or counseling psychology, and the psychology of adjustment.

Dunn et al. (2010) urged that a quality undergraduate psychology curriculum should include an integrative experience; however, such opportunities are not typically available in the introductory course. In many programs, students might enroll in a capstone offering, allowing them to use and demonstrate the knowledge and skills acquired in the earlier courses in the major curriculum. Integration is often accomplished in advanced seminar courses dealing with focused research linked to a core area (e.g., infant social cognition in developmental psychology), a history and systems course, or an independent study or honors course. Is there an equivalent integrative aspect to the first course? There can be, especially when an instructor works to point to connections among topics when teaching (e.g., categorization processes not only are essential to cognition but also explain, in part, the origins and dynamics of cognitive accounts of prejudice and discrimination). In a real sense, most of the contributions to this book—individual thematic approaches to teaching introductory psychology—represent an integrative aspect for the first course.

MULTIPLE MODES OF DELIVERY

The introductory course also represents the psychology curriculum because it can be taught in a variety of different ways. The standard or classic approach is the lecture method, where the instructor essentially spends the bulk of each class meeting addressing the class on the day's topical material. Now, of course, the typical lecture is a far cry from the past, as it entails technological innovations, such as PowerPoint slides, screen captures, YouTube videos, clickers for survey student opinion, and open educational resources to engage students.

Many lecturers work to promote active discussion during class time. Such discussion can be fostered by encouraging students to ask questions or by having prepared activities for small group work or demonstration. Some introductory instructors work to illustrate key concepts by replicating experimental demonstrations in the class. Naturally, such demonstrations are often easier to conduct earlier in the term when the material is more focused on sensation and perception (e.g., visual illusions) and memory (e.g., the magic number 7 to illustrate short-term storage) than later, when social psychology, personality, and clinical psychology are reviewed. Nonetheless, presenting brief clips of classic studies (e.g., Milgram's obedience to authority work, Asch's conformity paradigm) or completing quick personality assessments (e.g., the Big Five or OCEAN personality traits) encourage an exchange of ideas between the instructor and the students.

Not all introductory courses are conducted in a face-to-face modality. So-called flipped or hybrid classrooms are becoming more common. In these instances, students complete an activity before coming to class (e.g., watching a video, reading an assignment), allowing faculty to use the face-to-face meeting to engage students in rich discussion.

Finally, of course, some introductory courses are taught completely online, which means that content is delivered virtually, not physically. In online courses, discussion can be synchronous, which means most or all enrolled students are online at the same time and know that they must respond to an instructor's prompts, questions, or observations, as well as comments made by their peers, a given number of times per session or week. In other cases, the course might occur in an asynchronous environment, which means students engage in the class independently and without a live interaction, and the instructor evaluates student performance without direct interaction with the student.

AN ARENA FOR SHOWMANSHIP

The first course has always been the venue for recruiting prospective psychology majors, which means that many psychology programs elect to have their most dynamic teachers lead the course. Thus, the introductory course has always been something of an arena for showmanship, and on some campuses, certain psychology teachers are renowned because of the magic (sometimes literal, sometimes figural) that occurs in their classrooms.

Naturally, it may not be the goal of a given psychology department to recruit more majors—many departments can claim that they have too many majors as it is and with resource constraints (e.g., fewer faculty lines); therefore, increasing program enrollment may not be a goal. However, it is wise to remember that large course enrollments serve as a ready source of research participants for a department's research efforts. Still, there is something to be said for having an intellectually entertaining instructor lead the introductory course because, for many students, the introductory course will be the only exposure they may have to psychology, so conveying the content is both important and partially dependent on the teaching prowess of the instructor leading the class.

ROUTINE CHALLENGES FACED BY
INTRODUCTORY INSTRUCTORS

Teaching introductory psychology typically requires the instructor to deal with a variety of routine challenges. None is insurmountable, but they must be considered when planning and teaching this key course.

Enrollment pressures.   Simply put, the number of students enrolled in an introductory class can influence what happens in the class; teaching a class with 30 students is vastly different than teaching one with 300 students. If an instructor is teaching a larger section, there is little chance that graded writing assignments (e.g., papers, journals) will be required or even feasible, though some in-class ungraded writing might be possible. Student response systems like clickers, for example, may lend themselves to larger classes and can also enhance student experience courses with lower enrollments (e.g., Caldwell, 2007). When it comes to assessing student learning via exams or quizzes, large enrollment classes are apt to rely on multiple choice formats while smaller classes (those with, say, 40 or fewer students) can also have essay questions. Of course, particular classroom dynamics and course requirements are also influenced by the availability of recitation or problem sessions with graduate or undergraduate teaching assistants and graders.

Attending to the mixed audience issue.   As already noted, the general or introductory class attracts psychology majors and minors, as well as students who are curious about the discipline and those who simply want to complete a general education or some other distribution requirement for their own major (e.g., nursing, physical therapy) or to prepare for the revised Medical College Admissions Test. Instructors must be aware of the needs and interests of these multiple groups, so that the course is engaging for the one-time student and substantive enough for those who will go on to take other courses in their major or minor.

Using evidence-based pedagogies when designing the course.   Savvy instructors use evidence-based approaches in their courses in order to increase the opportunities for students to both learn and retain course material. Evidence-based teaching (EBT) relies on empirically validated pedagogical tools and techniques that enhance learning (e.g., Dunn, Saville, Baker, & Marek, 2013). Consider one example, the so-called testing effect, where students are found to recall more information when they are tested in advance on the course materials. Frequent quizzes or tests— whether graded or ungraded—can fit this approach, as data indicate that taking these assessments enhance students' memories (e.g., Karpicke, Butler, & Roediger, 2009). For other EBT approaches that can be integrated into the introductory course, see Ambrose, Bridges, DiPietro, Lovett, and Norman (2010), Brown, Roediger, and McDaniel (2014), and Dunn et al. (2013).

Balancing topical breadth and depth.   There is a tendency among novice introductory psychology instructors to want to "cover it all," a feat that is no longer possible for a variety of reasons including the explosion of information in psychological science and the disparities of topical coverage among the numerous introductory texts. In effect, there is no agreed-upon canonical set of topics or studies. Practically speaking, then, instructors must make some hard choices when preparing lectures and related activities. Certainly, students can be assigned and be expected to read the entire chapter on learning and memory, for example, but if the course meets three times a week for 50 minutes, how much of the material can the instructor cover? The typical introductory instructor—one following a semester model—will cover a chapter a week in order to make a dent in both the textbook and the syllabus within the available 14 or 15 weeks in the semester. Those teaching on a quarter system face a similar problem, though they may meet more frequently and for longer sessions, but compressing 14 or so chapters into approximately 10 weeks is also challenging.

As a result, instructors need to consider how best to convey topical areas with sufficient breadth while being selective regarding what sort of depth matters— particular theories, illustrative or classic experiments, in-class demonstrations, cutting-edge findings, and so on—can reasonably be presented to students. What material must be covered in a quality course on introductory psychology? A reasonable place to begin when planning the course is to adapt the *National Standards for High School Psychology Curricula* (APA, 2011), which are effectively quality principles for teaching a comprehensive introductory course to secondary students. However, these *National Standards* are so useful that some psychology educators encourage their use for college-level offerings of the course (Landrum et al., 2010).

Still, time remains a problem linked with breadth and depth: There is rarely enough time available to accomplish all of the goals instructors set for themselves. Can discussion become a routine part of class, for example, or does the pressure to cover chapters in a timely manner trump such sharing of ideas? To promote collaborative learning, will small group work be possible in the class? Frequent quizzing (e.g., every class meeting or once a week) can be beneficial to student learning but how much active class time will it eliminate? These are all important issues instructors should consider before teaching the course.

Assessment of learning.   Like all faculty members, introductory psychology instructors need to know whether their students are learning the course material and, ideally, applying it to life beyond the classroom. In other words, teachers need to assess student learning and then use their findings to revise future iterations of the introductory course. Assessment in psychology remains an important topic, par- ticularly because of the public's interest in educational accountability: Are colleges and universities doing what they say they do where teaching and learning are con- cerned? There are a variety of resources available for psychology educators interested in learning more about assessment perspectives and practices (e.g., Dunn, Baker, Landrum, Mehrotra, & McCarthy, 2012; Dunn, Mehrotra, & Halonen, 2004), as well as the American Psychological Association's *Assessment CyberGuide for Learning Goals and Outcomes* (2009) and the *Guidelines for the Undergraduate Psychology Major 2.0* (2013).

Ideally, instructors who teach introductory psychology will identify the aspects of the course they want to assess in advance, designing in-class or out-of-class activ- ities and assignments, as well as quizzes or exams, with an eye to discerning whether desired learning goals are being met (e.g., APA, 2013; Dunn, McCarthy, Baker, & Halonen, 2011). For example, if an instructor is interested in how well students understood very basic research methodology, students could be asked to evaluate basic research designs found in accessible sample publications from the field (i.e., identifying independent and dependent variables). Or, if measuring students' abilities to communicate factual knowledge about psychological research is the goal, they could be asked to write a brief review of or op-ed piece on an approachable article dealing with a familiar topic from introductory psychology (e.g., eyewitness testimony in the Memory and Cognition chapter). Another colleague might want to promote students' collaboration skills by assigning a small group project in the course and then assessing its quality as well as the independent contributions of each student. Assessment opportunities abound; the best approach is to decide what will be measured in advance, and how, and to recognize the virtues of assessing a few key learning goals that capture the instructor's goals for the first course rather than trying to evaluate too many.

A PRIMARY POSSIBILITY: OPPORTUNITIES FOR NOVELTY

With planning and practice, the qualities, characteristics, and challenges associated with teaching psychology's primary course can represent opportunities for teachers, just as the course can encourage novel approaches for presenting course material. Indeed, the introductory course may be the best arena in the psychology curriculum for adopting novel approaches to presenting the core topics of the discipline. The content of the class is so rich, diverse, and ever-evolving that there is room for teachers to maneuver, organizing the field and sharing its theoretical and empirical perspectives in many different ways. The diverse and creative approaches taken by the authors of the chapters in this book represent opportunities for novelty in teaching and pedagogy for the important first course. The themes presented in this book afford readers and teachers distinct ways to frame topical material. Providing students with a meaningful framework for construing the broad scope of research areas and findings in psychology will promote a more nuanced understanding and possibly enhance their retention of course material. If nothing else, teaching introductory psychology through a novel, and central, organizing idea—a theme—will help to counter the "chaotic impression," which William James worried that psychology's "variety and complexity" conveyed.

Chapter 2

Introductory Psychology:
A Postmodern Love Story

JANE S. HALONEN

University of West Florida

In the spring of 1969, I fell in love. I was one semester into my undergraduate liberal arts degree as a committed journalism major when my plans for becoming the world's best journalist derailed. My social science elective in general education, introductory psychology, was to blame.

My professor was an engaging lecturer and charismatic character. He opened a new and challenging world for me despite the fact that the classroom climate was a bit chilly. He conducted lectures that offered one-way communication for every class hour. He made no effort to learn student names and did not inspire discussion. Although he had wonderful stories to illustrate the more difficult concepts, the atmosphere he created had a sink-or-swim quality. As he unfolded the facts of psychology, he would often put his feet up on the desk, light a cigarette, and blow smoke rings to emphasize key points. (Yes, it was a very different time.) His multiple-choice tests were an unpleasant necessity, at times including questions from chapters that hadn't yet been assigned, an indication that he reused tests from semester to semester and didn't quite pace himself properly during the class. Despite the hazards in the climate and the evaluation practices, I was hooked. The discipline of psychology spoke to me in a way that no other class ever had. I fell in love with the discipline, changed my major, and never looked back.

For the past 30 years, I have been reexperiencing falling in love with psychology nearly every semester by teaching my own, dramatically different introductory class, which has evolved from lecture-based dominance to something that my former professor wouldn't recognize. I have come to distinguish my professor's lecture-dominated approach to class as "modern" in contrast to my own approach, which I claim is "postmodern" (Halonen, 2014).

Most faculty who completed their advanced degrees in the 20th century came to the teaching of the discipline with some basic modern sensibilities. Once assigned to a course, the modern professor expects to lecture and also expects to exercise a great deal of independence under the protection of academic freedom in how to cover the content and test student achievement. At the end of the course, the modern professor assigns grades to students based typically on test performance and that ends his or her professional obligation. In 1995, Barr and Tagg characterized this approach as "content centered." They argued for a paradigm change that encouraged faculty to become more "student centered," shifting the emphasis from purveying content to designing strategies that would transform students' learning and build their skills.

However, a postmodern approach goes beyond merely being student centered. Barr and Tagg's argument resonated with many faculty who recognized the power of active learning, but the distinction also resonated with various accrediting bodies across the United States. Consequently, at the turn of the century, psychology programs, along with all other disciplines, began to encounter different and more complex demands for the design and delivery of classes. Postmodern faculty tend to incorporate active learning strategies to help students learn content and develop discipline-related skill sets. They design course experiences with an eye toward the role their own courses play in the sequencing and scaffolding of learning in the entire major. They more actively incorporate assessment of student learning outcomes to confirm teaching and learning effectiveness. They may also need to report the results of their shared achievement to the department chair to contribute to a departmental assessment report. In effect, faculty are no longer independent agents attending to their own course assignments but collaborators in building a culture of evidence about teaching and learning effectiveness with their department colleagues.

What sets my introductory course apart is embracing an assessment-friendly stance throughout the course to serve a variety of purposes. My course covers the traditional content of an introductory class but the focus of the course is skill development. The design adheres to both local and national learning outcomes through a sequence of varied assessment strategies. Students emerge from the class with enthusiasm generated by doing psychology. For some, the lure will be great enough to declare the psychology major. For others, they will have experienced psychology as a legitimate liberal arts major.

EDUCATING AS POSTMODERN PROFESSOR

I had the good fortune of being hired for my first academic position at Alverno College, a unique learning environment in which the college's commitment to performance assessment dictated that I experiment with approaches that concentrated on teaching and assessing cognitive skills in parallel with teaching academic concepts. Their pioneering efforts in performance assessment had a profound effect on how I approach any class I teach. My curricular design emerges from this fundamental question: What should students be able to do as a consequence of what they learn in my class?

In 2002, the American Psychological Association (APA) attempted to answer that question by developing national guidelines to assist psychology departments with curriculum design. I had the pleasure of chairing both the task force that developed the original guidelines, passed into policy by the APA in 2007, and the task force that revised the guidelines (*Guidelines 2.0*), which became policy in 2013. Although the most recent guidelines put forth aspirational expectations for achievements at both the two-year and four-year levels, they did not explicitly address what should transpire in introductory psychology.

For the last decade, I have had the luxury of teaching introductory psychology as the honors course offering at the University of West Florida (UWF). By design, UWF honors courses are small (20 or fewer students). I teach the course in a three-hour block, so I can more easily accommodate a range of active learning strategies to support student learning. Accomplishing more than straight lecture is easier when class periods are longer.

Another postmodern reality is that introductory psychology teachers are unlikely to teach committed psychology majors in their courses. Chances are good those students will have taken Advanced Placement Psychology or managed some other strategy for course completion that allows them to enter the curriculum at a higher level once they embark on their major. Consequently, I recognize that not only the majority of students I teach are unlikely to major in psychology but also my course is probably going to be the only exposure they have to the discipline. As such, I announce to my students that I will be working hard to convert those who show talent and have not yet made a commitment to a major in psychology. Therefore, I want my course to be not just informative but engaging and, for some, captivating.

My own course design uses the framework adopted by APA *Guidelines 2.0* (2013) to set forth what students should be able to do as a consequence of taking my course. This strategy involves adopting the five goals proposed by the APA (Content, Critical Thinking, Communication, Ethical and Social Responsibility in a Diverse World, and Professional Development) but articulates what should be expected from those goals at the introductory level. Table 2.1 lists the outcomes around which I build my postmodern course structure for introductory psychology.

TABLE 2.1   Student Learning Outcomes Based on APA's *Guidelines 2.0*

Course Goals

Content

Acquire basic knowledge of theories, concepts, and principles in psychology

- Characterize the development of psychology as a scientific enterprise
- Discuss classic research in psychology including their historical and cultural contexts
- Explain the principles of psychological literacy

Critical Thinking

Apply knowledge of sound research procedures to solve problems

- Use evidence to develop and evaluate claims about behavior
- Evaluate quality of research designs and validity of research claims
- Look for alternative explanations in evaluating the validity of claim

Communication Skills

Refine communication skills related to psychological science

- Begin the use of APA conventions in scientific writing
- Verbally express ideas precisely and persuasively in multiple formats
- Assess strengths and weaknesses on collaborative style as a group member

Ethical Reasoning

Discuss the role of ethical practices in psychology

- Identify relevant ethical issues involved in psychological research and practice
- Discriminate ethical from nonethical practices
- Describe why ethics matters in psychology

Professional Development

Refine skills to complete projects

- Develop strategies for timely completion of assignments
- Evaluate strengths and weaknesses of performance
- Identify applications of psychology that produce career opportunities

THE FIRST SESSION

In modern course design, the professor often regards the first day of class as a throwaway. You meet the students, go over the operational principles found in the syllabus, and then let everyone go home since they haven't had any content yet and students can't be expected to contribute meaningfully to the class. (Similarly, the end of the modern course is also perfunctory; students take a final exam and then disappear into their lives.)

Postmodern sensibilities suggest that not only the first day of class is not a throwaway, but it may be the most important class of the semester because it sets a community-building expectation in which all students will participate. My goals for the first three-hour class are ambitious. I review the syllabus and establish a knowledge baseline in the form of a pretest. I offer a lecture sample about psychology's origins and discuss profitable strategies for taking notes on lecture experiences. I share Bloom's taxonomy (Anderson & Krathwohl, 2002) that introduces how cognitive demands in college will be different than high school. Bloom's taxonomy creates a hierarchy of cognitive skills from low-level skills of memorizing and applying to higher-level skills of analyzing, synthesizing, evaluating, and creating. Understanding the framework will also help students recognize why I'm going to be among their most demanding professors. I also set the tone and expectation that vigorous class discussion will be the norm in my class by having each student describe some of his or her unique personal characteristics and share which human behavior each finds to be most intriguing. Sharing unique features encourages students to compare and contrast their lives and gives me a ready store of student-relevant examples I can use to illustrate concepts in future classes. Although that scope represents a broad range, my three-hour structure easily accommodates those objectives.

I use an e-mail classlist to let students know they need to read the first chapter and to complete a biographical profile before coming to my first class. Because they have demonstrated intellectual competence as students by qualifying to enter the UWF honors program with their high entrance exam scores and high school grade point averages, I feel confident that I can assign homework even before I meet them for the first time. I encourage them to bring their text to class to reinforce the importance of having access to the textbook from the outset of the course.

The biographical profile.   I ask students to complete a fact sheet in the assignment section of the course management system, download and print their answers, and bring the information to class. Appendix 2.1 provides an example of the kind of information I gather. These biographical profiles provide a valuable resource throughout the semester: I reference them periodically to help me select and develop examples that will be personally engaging to students. The profiles also provide an additional memory cue for learning students' names. Some parts of the profile provide data for class demonstrations. For example, I use numerical questions (e.g., How many Harry Potter books have you read?) in a subsequent discussion of psychological statistics. Students can be seduced into thinking statistics can be fun when I derive statistics from their lives. Students explore the average number of speeding tickets the class has achieved and whether there is any correlation to how many times their hearts have been broken. Some of the questions also clarify the importance of good operational definitions for deriving valid research conclusions and underscore the value of precision in research design.

The last two items on the page provide the basis for the first spirited class discussion. Every student must introduce him- or herself to the class by speculating about some way each may be unique from anyone else in the class and also must identify a current behavior about which each is curious. The former disclosure provides additional meaningful cues that help all individuals learn names more efficiently and typically produces some interesting alliances between students who come from large families, have lived overseas, and who don't watch television.

Describing a behavior that inspires curiosity allows me to pronounce whether that behavior will fit the scope of the course content along with some projection of where and when students can follow up on their curiosity. Most comments are typically drawn from contemporary news but occasionally students disclose ideas that can be incorporated into later course activities. (My favorite of all time is "I think it's a funny thing when old people try to dance. People over 40, I mean," which easily can be incorporated into a discussion of prejudice.)

The content pretest.   Because most of the people face postmodern demands for accountability, I elect to conduct a pretest-posttest to demonstrate the representative content expertise gained by being in my class. I constructed a ten-question multiple-choice quiz from the content that I will cover in the next two reading assignments. I ask students to review Social first because it is an area in which they show strong interest and can easily relate to the content. I follow Social with the Methods chapter because of the foundation it provides in how psychologists solve problems. I design the questions to be purposefully challenging because I want to show maximum gains on the posttest, which can then be attributed to their learning in the course. I embed these ten questions in the first examination of the class approximately one month later to assess the value added. Appendix 2.2 provides an example of that quiz along with the performance results for the post-assessment. Not only do I have appropriate data to share with my chair when the call comes for assessment evidence, but also I have clear and telling feedback about how effectively I taught those concepts in that semester. By using the same quiz each year, I can also see improvements in my teaching over time or trouble spots that need additional attention. For example, in one class my students didn't fare well on the posttest question about the role of the IRB (institutional review board). I recognized that the clarity of my lecture could have been a problem. By providing additional examples in the next year, the gain score on the IRB item improved dramatically.

Proof of preparation.   Getting students to read an assignment has always been a challenge. Walvoord (2010) inspired a simple strategy to improve the likelihood that students will prepare for the class by requiring an easy-to-review assignment that demonstrates proof of reading. Using Bloom's taxonomy as a backdrop, I encourage students to write about their reading in one of three forms: (1) a paragraph about what they thought was most interesting concept in their assignment, (2) a question that the reading generated, or (3) a viable multiple-choice question that could be used on a test of that content.

The ideal proof of preparation assignment should be one that professors can easily scan and credit. I count these assignments collectively as 10 percent of the students' grade. Out of the 13 opportunities I offer (I don't expect proof on days that the class is involved in testing), I count the top 10 efforts at 5 points apiece. This leeway allows for absence, illness, and the student learning curve in how to craft a satisfying form of evidence of reading. Appendix 2.3 illustrates the instruction provided on developing appropriate preparation evidence. Although initially students protest having regular homework on their chapter readings, at the end of the class, they routinely, if not a bit grudgingly, admit that the obligation helps most of them stay on task and develop better self-regulation regarding reading assignments.

POSTMODERN ARCHITECTURE AND ASSESSMENT

I divide the course into four distinctive units of effort that involve four very different assessment strategies:

Unit I: What Do Psychologists Do?

This unit includes the obligatory introductory chapter (which I assign students to read prior to their first class), the Methods chapter, and the Social chapter. I want students to feel empowered in their approach to psychology, which is easier to accomplish with these chapters rather than plunging into the hardest dimension, the biological underpinnings of behavior, in the beginning of the course. The assessment is a mix of multiple-choice questions and short essay that offers a strong reality check on how well students are processing the information. The test includes the embedded posttest to harvest a representative sample of how well students are learning and how well I'm teaching.

In addition to the exam performance, I ask students to estimate how many hours of study went into their performance beyond the initial reading of the text. When I return the results, I show the score distribution, review appropriate measures of central tendency (e.g., mean, mode, median), and reveal the correlation between hours of study and course grade. Typically, the correlation not only is a significant positive one but also can include the revealing data points of the person who studied long and hard but scored poorly and the person who studied little and achieved a top grade. For those who do not fare well, I require a more detailed "postmortem" analysis along with the formulation of goals for improvement. The analysis includes reflection on class attendance patterns, completion of reading, typical test-taking results, time management concerns, and a conclusion about whether the results fairly captured what the student had learned. The analysis challenges students to think about what needs to change to be successful in future assessments.

Unit II: How the Body Works

Chapters in this unit include the Biological Bases of Behavior, Sensation and Perception, Consciousness, and Motivation and Emotion. I conclude this section with the chapter on stress and coping, not just because the information in that chapter highlights physiology but also because the stresses of midterm exams provide some contextual grounding that might make the insights from the chapter even more compelling.

For the second assessment, a take-home essay, students must first identify some behavior that they enjoy doing in their leisure time. They are then asked to analyze various dimensions of how their biological capacities support their leisure choices. Appendix 2.4 outlines the questions that I ask and the rubric I use to evaluate student answers. Although it may be a contrast effect with the earlier challenging multiple-choice exam, most students say they not only appreciated the change in assessment form but also recognized that they are unlikely to take for granted the complex inner workings that support their preferred leisure behavior.

Unit III: How We Grow, Develop, Learn, and Think

The quartet of chapters in this unit lend themselves to practical problem-solving: Development, Memory, Learning, and Intelligence. The assessment strategy in this unit involves a group task in which students must identify a behavioral problem and generate a practical solution for that problem that allows them to demonstrate their knowledge from those chapters. Students can select problems that are related to student life or other challenges they might find in day care centers, homes for the elderly, or any other setting that deals with life's developmental stages.

I assign students randomly to groups and allocate some time in the course to getting the group process moving in a positive direction. The quality of the projects appears to be somewhat dependent on how much class time is set aside for group work. Although students may not jettison group members for nonperformance, at the conclusion of their work they do have an opportunity to rate all group members on the caliber of their shared effort along with justifications for any recommended decreases. With this consequence, students report that the practice tends to make their colleagues more accountable and it discourages social loafing.

Projects in the recent past have included the development of a phone app to improve study strategies, a 1950s themed video on successful study strategies, a board game to assist with first-year orientation, and a curriculum to improve parenting skills for individuals struggling with potential abuse problems. Students often invest heavily in the project as it allows for creative thinking as they hone their teamwork skills. Students must document their sources in APA format and deliver a team report to the class to share their creations.

Unit IV: How We Flourish, Fail, and Recover

As a clinician, I save what the students anticipate will be the best for last. Most students eagerly anticipate being able to talk about what is normal and abnormal and many are disappointed that the entire course doesn't focus on this topic. However, following discussion of Personality, Psychological Disorders, and Treatment, the final assessment for the course involves students' conducting as a group a diagnostic interview with a role-playing volunteer. They watch a classic film on schizophrenia to practice making clinical inferences before they conduct their interview. This assessment not only demonstrates some aspects of how clinicians work but also gives students an integrative opportunity to demonstrate psychological literacy.

Appendix 2.5 illustrates the questions asked on the final. On the last day of class, students come prepared to simulate a clinical interview with a faux client. They have had some coaching to develop questions that not only produce a solid interview but can also manifest different orientations (e.g., psychoanalytic, behavioral), in their questions. I typically recruit the faux, client from the theater department from graduate assistants interested in teaching or from past successful students in my course. I ask each faux client to identify a relatively famous deceased individual with recognizable mental health issues. The client then must prepare the life history for a broad range of questions that will ensure comprehensive investigation during the group interview. The students have one hour to cover all the bases that the final entails. The students have three days to complete the profile of the client and assess their comfort level with performing diagnostic tasks. Happily, most students report that the task was much harder than they ever expected from seeing portrayals of psychologists on television. They also find it instructive when there is often little agreement on the diagnostic profile. Their evaluation depends on how well they justify their conclusions from the clinical evidence.

THE LAST SESSION

Modern professors stuff content into every available minute of class time and then use the scheduled final exam as the last contact. Postmodern sensibility suggests that professors have a stronger ritual ending to the course experience (Lutsky, 2010). Consequently, during the scheduled final exam, professors meet the students to review the last unit assessment, straighten out any grade challenges, and revisit the syllabus. Students enjoy the opportunity to defend their diagnostic impressions of the client in an atmosphere that has no further risk of evaluation. The nature of the remaining discussion focuses on students' viewpoints about how well the course produced observable changes in the skills set forth as student learning outcomes. I also gather opinions about ways the course might be improved.

At the conclusion of this final session I offer a post-session to students who may be considering a major or a minor in psychology. I revisit information in the textbook about potential careers related to psychology. I've always thought the detail of various careers in psychology is not pertinent to students who don't plan to major in the discipline. However, having the post-session for those who want to major or minor allows me a unique opportunity to help launch the student in that direction. I emphasize the broad range of employment potential the degree provides upon graduation and also discuss strategies for making the best applications for graduate school (Dunn & Halonen, 2017). I also allow some self-congratulations about sending talented and well-prepared students for their own love affairs with psychology.

CONCLUSION

In *Walden Two* (1948, p. 6), Skinner's alter ego, Professor Burris, lamented that he was often disappointed by his students when he encountered them later in life:

> What distressed me was the clear evidence that my teaching had missed the mark. I could understand why young and irresponsible spirits might forget much of what I had taught them, but I could never reconcile myself to the uncanny precision with which they recalled the unimportant details. My visitors … would gape with ignorance when I alluded to a field that we had once explored together—or so I thought—but they would gleefully remind me, word for word, of my smart reply to some question from the class or the impromptu digression with which I had once filled out a miscalculated hour.

I believe that asking students to wrestle with course content in an encouraging climate helps professors to avoid Professor Burris's fate. A postmodern approach involving an assessment-focused course rich in active learning strategies will facilitate much deeper and long-lasting learning. I sometimes refer to this happy outcome as "velcro learning." Even when the content of psychology becomes fragile in students' memories, their psychological skills should endure.

Appendix 2.1

Introductory Psychology Biographical Profile

1. Have you had a course in psychology before this one? If so, where? What kind of experience was that for you?
2. How much experience do you have in being exposed to others who live differently than you do (e.g., foreign travel, school experiences)?
3. Why did you pick UWF?
4. Is there anything I need to know that might help you be a more effective learner (e.g., sensory deficits, learning difference)?
5. Who is your favorite author?
6. Where do you envision yourself five years from now? (Dream big!!)
7. Answer the following questions (to be used in later lessons on statistics):
    A. _____ How tall are you in inches?
    B. _____ What is your shoe size? (Be exact.)
    C. _____ How many times have you had your heart broken?
    D. _____ How many colds did you have over the course of the last year?
    E. _____ How many hours per day do you spend on Facebook/Twitter?
    F. _____ How many traffic citations have you received?

G. _____ How many stuffed animals do you own?

H. _____ How many hours per week do you watch television?

I. _____ How many Harry Potter books have you read?

8. What grade do you expect to get in this course? How many hours per week do you plan to study?

MOST IMPORTANT

9. Speculate about one way in which you may be unique in comparison to everyone else in the class.

10. What behavior makes you especially curious right now? (Anything happening in the news that makes you scratch your head in wonder?)

Required

I have read the syllabus and understand the terms outlined. I agree to abide by the standards and to enact the Argo honor code: "I will not lie, cheat, or steal or tolerate others who do."

_____   _____

Signature: *Date:*

Appendix 2.2

Pretest-Posttest on Research Methods and Social Psychology with Typical Results

1. Which psychologist pioneered in the experimental study of disobedience to authority?

   a. Watson

   b. **Milgram**

   c. Skinner

   d. Maslow

   e. Piaget

Pretest 23% ➔ Posttest 94%

2. Why should the original disobedience study not technically be classified as an experiment?

   a. The "experimenter" was actually an actor.

   b. No measurable behavior worked as the dependent variable.

   c. No correlations could be determined.

   d. **There was no controlled comparison.**

   e. It wasn't conducted by a certified psychologist.

Pretest 70% ➔ Posttest 90%

3. Which of the following practices should have been present in the design of the disobedience study if it were to qualify as a true experiment?

   a. Participants must be randomly sampled.

   b. **Participants must be randomly assigned to different conditions.**

   c. All experimental staff must be blind to assignment of participant to condition.

   d. Multiple raters must be present to measure participant behaviors.

   e. Participants should have been anonymous.

Pretest 29% ➔ Posttest 94%

4. When Ron accuses a late group member of being lazy before hearing an explanation, he may be committing

   a. a stereotypical error.

   b. the self-serving error.

   d. the self-effacing error.

   c. an illusory correlation.

   e. **the fundamental attribution error.**

Pretest 17% ➔ Posttest 94%

5. Cognitive dissonance studies suggest

   a. attitudes are best changed through peripheral channels.

   b. fear-based information produces optimal attitude change.

   c. cognitive dissonance produces enduring feelings of guilt.

   d. **small monetary incentives can be more effective than large ones in changing attitudes.**

   e. people can be trained to eliminate cognitive dissonance.

Pretest 29% ➔ Posttest 94%

6. Zimbardo's Stanford Prison study

   a. **concluded situational factors have a powerful impact on social behavior.**

   b. established group size is an important factor in conformity.

   c. contrasted the influence of collectivist versus individualist cultures on conformity.

   d. exposed participants to severe stress, resulting in long-term emotional injury.

   e. demonstrated students responded best to authority figures using authoritarian leadership styles.

Pretest 47% ➔ Posttest 100%

7. If you decided to redo the Stanford Prison study, who would need to approve your research proposal?

    a. Zimbardo, the original author

    b. The American Psychological Association

    c. The president of the university hosting the study

    d. **The local institutional review board**

    e. The federal government

Pretest 23% ➜ **Posttest 82%**

8. If I perform the protocol of an experimental study for a second time to see if I can reproduce the results, I have completed a _____ study.

    a. verification

    b. **replication**

    c. duplication

    d. clarification

    e. clone

Pretest 23% ➜ **Posttest 100%**

9. Under what conditions can psychologists use deception in their research?

    a. If the participants agree before the research begins that they can be deceived.

    b. **If the approving bodies agree that the merits of the research outweigh the risks.**

    c. If financial compensation is made available.

    d. If participation will not result in physical harm.

    e. Deception of any kind is no longer tolerated or endorsed by psychologists.

Pretest 17% ➜ **Posttest 76%**

10. Suppose we find a correlation of −.75 between income level and drunk-driving arrests. Which is the safest conclusion?

    a. There is no connection between income and drunk-driving behavior.

    b. Wealthier people tend to drive under alcohol influence more than poor people.

    c. Poverty causes drunk driving.

    d. **Drunk-driving arrests are more likely to take place among poor than wealthy people.**

    e. Drunk driving tends to reduce income-earning potential.

Pretest 29% ➜ **Posttest 82%**

Appendix 2.3

Handout for Proof of Reading and Course Preparation

Higher educators use a framework for "thinking about thinking" called Bloom's taxonomy that was originally created back in the 1960s. Bloom's colleagues, Anderson and Krathwohl, revised his work in 2001. The framework outlines how thinking skills increase in their complexity, especially as you enter college and select a major. Whereas in high school you might have been successful memorizing your way to an A, those strategies only serve as a starting point when the game changes at the university level.

BLOOM'S LEVELS

The first two are often described as "lower-level" thinking skills.

REMEMBER: This level involves memorizing at the most basic level.

Note: You can memorize without understanding what you are learning. Memory skills are usually tested using multiple-choice strategies.

Example: What year was psychology officially founded?

UNDERSTAND: This level involves absorbing the material and being able to explain it accurately. Comprehension skills can be tested using essay questions and multiple-choice exams.

Example: What happens when the corpus callosum is cut?

As you move from lower to higher levels, you will notice that the taxonomy levels build on one another. Each level is increasingly sophisticated and depends on the quality of thinking you accomplished at prior levels. Consequently, testing for higher-level skills involves projects and activities that are more sophisticated than regular tests.

Bloom's "higher-level" thinking skills are as follows:

APPLY: At this level you demonstrate that you can transfer your knowledge to new situations.

Example: What learning principles would you advise a parent to use to interrupt a child's tantrum behavior?

ANALYZE: This caliber of thinking involves breaking bigger ideas into smaller ones.

Example: What variables contribute to sleep disorders?

EVALUATE: This level involves critical judgment. Taking into account all the information available, what choice makes the most sense? This level of thinking also entails providing the rationale.

Example: Which theory best explains language acquisition?

CREATE: The most sophisticated of Bloom's levels addresses creativity. In what ways can you reorganize what is known into new configurations?

Example: How would you design an experiment to test taste sensitivity?

HOW WILL THIS WORK?

Step #1: Read the chapter deeply. Scanning and skimming won't cut it. To be maximally effective, you can't leave your reading to the last minute.

Step #2: Make notes regarding the ideas that intrigue you the most.

Step #3: Allocate some time to reflecting and connecting.

Step #4: Concentrate on making connections: use the internet, examine the news, talk with others, and think about your other courses.

Step #5: Settle on your best idea and write (and rewrite).

Your goal is to persuade me that you have read the chapter, thought deeply about its contents, and will be prepared to discuss it in class.

Criteria for awarding 5 points on homework assignments

_____ clear link specified to assigned chapter

_____ clear and effective writing

_____ content is worthwhile

_____ depth is appropriate

_____ illustrates higher level of Bloom

_____ creativity

Reminder: Outlines of chapters are not acceptable.

Anderson & Krathwohl

Appendix 2.4

Honors Introductory Psychology

EXAM 2—2012

Exam addresses Bio Foundations (chapter 3), Sensation/Perception (4), Consciousness (5), Motivation and Emotion (9), and Stress and Coping (13)

*For this exam process to work, you must select a target behavior that reflects an activity that you enjoy or in which you have developed some expertise. The behavior should involve obvious visible activity for it to work well in your analysis. You may also need to focus on one discrete activity in a complex set of behaviors (e.g., serving a tennis ball) to help with the specifics. All but one question should be linked to your selected behavior so pick your behavior wisely! Each question is worth 5 points. (Hint: Be especially vigilant about paraphrasing properly. Copying text is a bad idea. This exam should give you practice on **paraphrasing**, converting author's ideas and words into your own.)*

1. In a context paragraph, describe the activity and its personal significance to you and your subjective well-being (1 point). Link your observations with two concepts or theoretical frameworks in the Motivation, chapter 9. Which two concepts best explain why you elect to spend time doing this behavior (2 points per concept)?

2. Select one relevant sensory mode and discuss the manner in which *afferent* neural messages travel from stimulus source to the portion of the brain where the information is converted into perception. This question demonstrates

your ability to understanding the underlying physical mechanism of *transduction* presented in chapter 4.

3. Describe a specific motor response connected to your preferred activity (e.g., strumming a guitar, lifting cookies off a pan). Trace the **efferent** neural action from the brain to the specific muscle action. Be sure to identify at least one neurotransmitter that is likely to be involved in achieving the motor behavior. Information for this answer will come primarily from chapter 3.

4. Describe all other parts of the brain that help you accomplish your activity. Strive to be *comprehensive* in addressing all the brain components that help you do what you do, including the contributions made by the lower brain centers. (This answer based on material in chapter 3 should be a long one.)

5. Imagine a circumstance in which an emergency happens while you are doing your behavior. What interior action will transpire? Make a judgment about whether the emergency would interfere with or enhance your ability to perform. (This answer focuses on chapters 3 and 13.)

6. Flip a coin. If heads, fate gives you an abnormality in your left hemisphere someplace. If tails, your abnormality is on the right hemisphere. Speculate about the impact such rotten luck would have on your ability to perform your leisure activity. Be sure to discuss whether there would be an impact on your dominant hand. (You can localize the damaged spot specifically on the hemisphere someplace to help you with your answer.)

7. Select five concepts from the text related to perception. Briefly demonstrate how your preferred activity illustrates each of these concepts. On this question be sure your selected concepts represent the content matter presented in perception, the brain's interpretation of raw data presented in chapter 4. Be careful not to use concepts from the sensation portion of the chapter.

8. Many people believe hypnosis can be used to produce enhanced performance. **Review the arguments in favor and against this position.** Describe whether you think hypnosis could improve the quality of your experience of your target behavior. Be sure to emphasize that you are evaluating and supporting a specific theoretical stance presented in chapter 5 on the effectiveness of hypnosis.

9. Suppose you inadvertently consumed a drug substance that changed your fundamental ability to execute your leisure pursuit. Pick a drug class and describe what the potential short- *and* long-term impacts would be. Be sure to discuss whether the drug would likely have the reported effects if you didn't realize you were taking the drug. Drug effects are discussed in chapter 5.

10. Suppose life handed you some circumstances wherein you could no longer perform your preferred behavior. Offer analysis based on the Stress and Coping chapter about the possible outcomes of your having to forego this behavior. You may include both likely and unlikely scenarios but your

answers should stress a range of possibilities. Your answer should reflect text or lecture material from chapter 13.

Performance criteria

- Uses psychology terminology accurately

- Paraphrases effectively

- Develops answer in sufficient detail to reflecting psychological literacy

  (Hint: Most answers should take at least half a page to answer at the appropriate depth.)

- Follows instruction/answers all parts of the question

- Organizes answers logically and coherently

What would you predict your score will be out of 50?_____

Which criteria reflect your performance strengths?

On which criteria do you need a little more work, if any?

Are you satisfied at this point with how you are managing the challenge of this course? If not, what do you plan to do about it?

Appendix 2.5

Final Exam Honors General Psychology

FALL, 2014

The final exam covers material in the chapters dealing with personality, abnormality, and treatment as well as insights from earlier aspects of the course. Answer each of the nine questions, including all the parts, *in a way that demonstrates your knowledge and your ability to think about problems from a psychological perspective.*

1. Describe five behaviors that are problematic for the client. Stick to observable behaviors, either behaviors that you directly observe or behaviors that the client complains about, but not *inferences* about behaviors. (5 points)

2. Identify five client answers that would help you identify "mental status," or orientation to reality. If questions did not emerge in the interview to establish mental status, describe questions that would produce this information. (5 points)

3. Describe one psychological test you might use to assist you in making decisions about this particular client and defend its use in this situation. Be sure to address the test properties of *reliability* and *validity* in defending your choice. (6 points)

4. Identify an example of a possible defense mechanism that transpired in the interview and discuss why the example qualifies as a defense mechanism. (2 points)

5. Select one personality theory (e.g., Freudian, humanist, cognitive behavioral) and explain the likely derivation of the client's difficulties from that perspective. Be sure to use concepts that are consistent and recognizable using this theoretical approach and provide a sufficiently elaborate description to capture maximum score. (10 points)

6. Speculate about the tentative *Diagnostic and Statistical Manual* profile your client might generate after one visit. You may use the *DSM-5* multiaxial approach or you can focus instead on a multidimensional approach to identify all relevant possibilities, stressors, medical conditions, and global functioning. (10 points)

7. Discuss two treatment strategies that you think would be helpful to the client and justify why you have chosen them from all the options. Describe one treatment strategy you would not use with this client and explain why you would avoid it. (6 points)

8. Describe two ethical principles that you would need to adhere to in executing the treatment plan if you were a psychologist. What is the purpose served by these rules? (4 points)

9. Discuss your comfort level with having to make critical decisions about the client. How easy is the task? How effective were you in responding to the task? What could you have done better? (2 points)

Chapter 3

Give Them Something to Care About: Engaging Students in Introductory Psychology

REGAN A. R. GURUNG

University of Wisconsin-Green Bay

In the classic story of the Trojan horse, the shrewd forces of Greece devise an ingenious scheme to break into the fortified gates of the city of Troy. They build a large wooden horse and wheel it to the city gates under the cover of nightfall. The intrigued Trojans wheel the horse into their walled city. Once night falls again, the Greek soldiers, hidden inside the hollow horse, jump out to open the city gates and allow in their armies, wreaking havoc in the aftermath. Often, teaching large introductory courses seems to mirror the challenges faced by the Greek soldiers. How do we instructors break past the fortifications of student apathy, low motivation, and disinterest, while hoping to create positive havoc in the way they think about psychology?

One answer is making psychology as applicable to student lives as possible and making students see that mastering psychology can actually improve their lives. Playing up the daily application of psychology serves as a Trojan horse for entering their thoughts. Students wheel the discipline past their defenses and into their lives and the theories and content can then emerge. In this chapter, I will discuss how psychology today is well positioned to engage students if it is well presented. Psychology today can easily be constructed into an effective Trojan horse because it is readymade to be applied to students' lives. I discuss how playing up the applications of psychology can increase student engagement and motivation in particular. I review the relevant psychological theories on motivation that support this idea, and then highlight related best practices for engagement. Finally I provide pragmatic ways to make psychology more applied and assess the benefits of the same.

PSYCHOLOGY IS WELL POSITIONED
TO BE APPLIED

Psychological research explores the enormous complexity of human behavior and contributes in important ways to solving a wide range of problems that today's students will confront during their lifetimes (APA, 2014). For example, many pressing contemporary social problems (and likely problems of the next century) reflect, to an appreciable extent, modifiable cognitions, emotions, and behaviors (Zimbardo, 2004). These problems include poverty, global warming, and international conflicts, prejudice and discrimination, exploitation and violence, depression and dysphoria, child neglect and parental divorce, and even rising medical costs: More young people die or become disabled from unfortunate behavioral choices (e.g., drug use, gang violence, drinking and driving) than from all diseases combined (Gurung, 2014a). In addition, many intriguing scientific problems facing humankind correspond to questions students already ask about themselves and others (Zimbardo, 2004). For example: What in the brain and body make thought, emotion, and a sense of self possible? What are the cognitive operations underlying effective problem-solving and optimal decision-making? What are the sociocultural factors that make education effective and enjoyable? How can you best deal with life's stressors? In short, psychology has the tools to change life, and this fact clearly features in the American Psychological Association's *Guidelines for the Undergraduate Psychology Major: Version 2.0* (APA, 2013). *Guidelines 2.0*'s Goal 5 places emphasis "on application of psychology-specific content and skills, effective self-reflection, project-management skills, teamwork skills, and career preparation" (p. 16).

At the same time, psychological science has a demonstrated track record of enhancing human functioning at both the micro and macro levels (e.g., APA, 2005, 2010). The procedures for optimizing human potential, such as successful parenting and aging, athletic and artistic flow, extraordinary memory and reasoning, and maximizing the development of intelligence, and environmental conservation are but a few topics that have received attention in psychological laboratories. These topics can fire a student's imagination; it is almost like providing the student with intellectual superpowers.

Instructors can also make Intro Psych more applicable by more explicitly noting that no one area of psychology fully explains day-to-day life. If students want to really understand why some people procrastinate or why others work hard, they must learn about many different areas of psychology and how they work together. Many of the most exciting advances in psychology today are emerging across traditional training areas within psychology and across disciplines (Cacioppo, 2007). For example, understanding romantic relationships can involve neurochemical (e.g., oxytocin), social (e.g., self-fulfilling prophecies), personality (e.g., traits), and cognitive factors (e.g., automatic thoughts). Comprehensive understanding of the mind and behavior requires a combination of perspectives. One cannot develop a complete and comprehensive understanding of behavior by focusing on only a biological or a social perspective (Cacioppo, 2013). No longer simply a collection of independent domains based on historical or administrative distinctions, psychology in the 21st century has become an integrative multilevel science. Specifically, there has been a trend in the direction of partitioning the science of mind and behavior into different levels of organization (e.g., biological, cognitive, and social), with each contributing to one's understanding a different facet of human behavior. Additionally, there are cross-cutting perspectives that offer invaluable insights into the mind and behavior (e.g., cross-cultural approaches, diversity, individual variations). These cross-cutting perspectives provide the instructor with the ability to pick on any aspect of daily life and show how a combination of psychological factors can be brought to bear on it.

Psychology is unique among all academic disciplines in that it is the study of people—how people think, feel, and act. As such, it is easy to personally relate to the core concepts of psychology in a way that might not be as true of mathematics, astronomy, or supply chain economics. What's more, introduction to psychology is a primer for life, equipping students with a basic understanding of learning, research, emotions, and social interactions that should be useful to them for the rest of their lives. In a field as fascinating as psychology, introduction to psychology is, arguably, the most important course (see Dunn, this volume). For many students it is a first taste that could lead to a lifelong passion for the discipline. For psychology majors, introduction to psychology is the foundation—a broad survey of the most important and interesting scientific findings—that will set the tone for more advanced study. For others, it will be their only contact with psychology and, therefore, their one chance at understanding and learning this science. Given how little students may remember from Intro Psych (Landrum & Gurung, 2013), instructors must prioritize what they will learn and retain.

APPLICATION AS A CORE RECOMMENDATION
FOR INTRO PSYCH

APA's Board of Educational Affairs (BEA) established a Working Group to Strengthen the Common Core of the Introductory Psychology Course. This group examined the common core of the Intro Psych course at the college level, including the content, outcomes, possibility of a laboratory component, and implications for a major versus a nonmajor directed course, and also recommended five action steps to BEA on strengthening the common core (APA, 2014). One of the key recommendations related to the structure of the course.

The Working Group (APA, 2014) recommends that instructors of Intro Psych cover the following:

1. **The scientific method:** Skills involving the development of scientific reasoning and problem-solving, including effective research methods.

2. **Cross-cutting themes:** Cultural and social diversity, ethics, variations in human functioning, and applications (see APA, 2014, for details). For application, instructors are urged to consider questions such as: How does the content of the course apply to everyday life? How can the content of the course contribute to improving one's life and addressing societal problems?

3. **At least two topics** from each of the main pillars of the field (biological, cognitive, development, social and personality, and mental and physical health).

4. **An integration component:** Instructors should design assignments and/or instruction that ties together the different areas of psychology into a coherent whole, again an area where students can apply psychology to their lives. For example, success in the workplace can be better understood by personality characteristics, social or situational factors, developmental histories of coworkers, and underpinning biological factors. It is likely that showing how different areas of psychology interact and are integrated in the study of daily behavior and everyday life may even help students better remember the content.

CAN APPLICABILITY INCREASE RETENTION?

The best scientific evidence available indicates that very little content is retained from the introductory psychology course (Herman, 2010; VanderStoep, Fagerlin, & Feenstra, 2000), a disheartening fact given the hard work of approximately 13,000 psychology instructors around the country. A recent study asked Intro Psych students to voluntarily retake their class cumulative final exam two years after completing the course (Landrum & Gurung, 2013). These scores were compared to the students' own scores the first time they took the class and to senior-level psychology majors enrolled in a Capstone course. As expected, students' retention of Intro Psych information had dropped from an average of 80.6 percent correct score during the course to an average of 56.0 percent two years later. The Capstone/senior-level psychology majors only scored modestly better with 62.7 percent accuracy. The content of introductory psychology has the potential of being vitally important and relevant to students' lives. Without retention of information and a lack of emphasis on the application of psychological principles (especially skills and abilities), the introductory psychology course represents an untapped opportunity for behavior change.

Instructors know very little about what students remember from Intro Psych. It is possible that some topics in Intro Psych are retained better than others. In another study, students were most likely to answer posttest questions correctly about memory and human development, and least likely to answer questions correctly about physiological psychology (McNamara, Williamson, & Jorgensen, 2011). The topics remembered more are likely to be topics that can be made more applicable to daily life. The material in a Memory chapter directly relates to studying and learning in school. The material in a Child Development chapter with its vivid stories of the mistakes kids make as they grow cognitively (e.g., Piaget's conservation demonstration) is easy to relate to. For most students, however, recalling the function of the hippocampus or the location of the visual cortex is a great challenge—they lack a daily context for applying such knowledge; hence, it is forgotten. To make matters worse, some students also lack the motivation to master some concepts (Baneshi, Samadieh, & Ejei, 2015; Bauer, Orvis, Ely, & Surface, 2015).

THE ROLE OF MOTIVATION

It is important to place motivation in the context of teaching and learning. Motivation comes from and is influenced by many different sources. The instructor is also a key player in determining student motivation. Lowman (1995) suggested two key dimensions are important in understanding the interplay between teaching, learning, and motivation:

Dimension 1: Intellectual excitement
> This factor can be influenced by the clarity of instructor presentations (in particular, what material is presented) and the emotional impact on the students (or the way material is presented). Students remember counterintuitive findings or controversial studies. For example, discussing evolutionary psychological studies on mate selection rarely fails to draw attention.

Dimension 2: Interpersonal rapport
> This factor hinges on the awareness of the interpersonal nature of the classroom and suggests a focus on communication skills that enhance motivation and enjoyment of learning and that foster independent learning. Good instructors connect with their students.

Instructors may anecdotally bemoan students' lack of motivation. They may argue that students simply need to be more motivated and underestimate the role that they play in making this happen. The reality is that learning outcomes are dependent in large part on both students and faculty (Hattie, 2015). Yes, students have to want to learn, but there are many strategies faculty can use to make this more likely. Making a course more applicable to daily life may be one major way to motivate students to learn.

There are three commonly used measures of motivation: choice, effort, and persistence (Svinicki & McKeachie, 2011). Students who are motivated to learn choose activities that enhance their own learning; they then work hard, and continue to do so even when there are obstacles to their retention of information. There are many psychological variables linked to motivation. Some students are driven by a high need for achievement, some students are said to be extrinsically motivated (those who study primarily for grades or approval of others), and other students are intrinsically motivated (those who study for the value of the learning in its own right; Jurik, Gröschner, & Seidel, 2014; Ryan & Deci, 2000). Students are generally focused on activities that they value and in which they expect to succeed (expectancy-value theory; Wigfield & Eccles, 2000).

Motivation also directs one toward achieving goals. Some students adopt mastery goals, where the primary desire is to understand and master the material. Other students adopt performance goals, where they focus on their learning outcomes in relation to the learning outcomes of others. The type of goal and the level of motivation that accompanies it may be influenced by the student's mindset (Dweck, 2008). Students who believe intelligence is fixed show different levels of motivation and effort than students who believe that intelligence is malleable (what is called a growth mindset). Each of these different variables relate to motivation and learning (McKeachie & Hofer, 2001; Svinicki & McKeachie, 2011).

Of the different motivational theories that relate to educational success, a number of theories support making Intro Psych material applicable. For example, intrinsic and extrinsic motivation theory (Ryan & Deci, 2000) suggests that teachers tap intrinsic motivation when they arouse student curiosity. For example, instead of being focused on an example grade (e.g., "Study this to do well on the exam"), instructors can introduce concepts in the form of a mystery that needs to be solved or a mission that needs to be completed (e.g., "How would you use what you know about framing to make it more likely your friend will make a healthy behavior choice?"). I design group assignments in class where the goal is to use information from the book and what has just been presented to solve a dating dilemma or a workforce problem.

A different motivational theory, expectancy-value theory, proposes that students direct their energies toward activities they value (Wigfield & Eccles, 2000). Values can be defined either broadly or specifically and include values such as attainment or importance, intrinsic value, and utility values (how useful is the content). By making Intro Psych material more relevant to life, instructors can increase the utility value of the content.

As seen earlier, there are many different theories of motivation in the psychological literature. To help consolidate the different ideas, Svinicki (2004) presented an amalgamated model of motivation, which suggests motivation is influenced by two major factors:

- *Value of the goal*: where a main factor is the perceived need for the knowledge or information and the utility of goal (What use will achieving the goal have?) and

- *the learner's expectation* that the goal can be achieved, influenced in turn by prior experience (How much experience or knowledge does the student have on the topic?).

One of the easiest things an instructor can do to motivate students is to help increase the value of a learning outcome for them. If instructors see students lacking motivation, assessing the extent they value what they are trying to get them to learn is the first critical step to take.

MAKING INTRO PSYCH APPLICABLE

It may appear, at first, as if teaching is a one-size-fits-all endeavor. Although effective teaching techniques often carry over well between large and small classes, large classes present challenges that necessitate special attention. Teaching a large lecture class calls for strategies and techniques and can be seen in the fact that in addition to general teaching tips books (Davis, 2009; Royse, 2001; Svinicki & McKeachie, 2011), there are also books that completely focus on teaching large classes (Heppner, 2007; Staley & Porter, 2002). Whereas some of these books mention the importance of highlighting "application," few instructors direct their attention to this facet of Intro Psych. There are a number of explicit ways to put more application into the classroom (Gurung, 2014b). I will use the example of my class to illustrate some key techniques regarding design, class dynamics, and assessment.

Course Design

I have taught Intro Psych for over 16 years. Some years I taught four sections totaling 500 students. For the last few years I've been teaching sections of 250 students. I have always used a textbook and, so far, have always used a book from a major publisher (although I change the textbook every year in an attempt to find the best book for my students). The next time I teach the class I will use an Open Source book such as the NOBA book with chapters written by content experts such as Elizabeth Loftus and David Buss and available for free to students (www .Nobaprojects.com).

Application can be integrated into every element of course design and one of the first considerations relates to content. If you plan on covering every single page of an Intro Psych textbook, it will probably leave little time to build in good application. I assign most of the chapters in the textbook (9 out of 14) and spend approximately one week on most chapters. I spend extra class periods on difficult material such as biology and learning, and also make sure there are many different ways students interact with the material. Students know (are told) that even if I do not cover some material in class, I may assess their knowledge of it on the exam. Together with four multiple-choice exams (each cumulative, comprising 60 questions, and taken online), students also take an online quiz on each chapter, are assigned to use the textbook technology supplement (e.g., Aplia, PsychPortal, Learnsmart), take part in research for credit, and do in-class group engagement exercises. To facilitate repeated practice (Dunlosky, Rawson, Marsh, Nathan, & Willingham, 2013), students are allowed to take the quizzes as many times as they wish and I count the highest score.

Class design is mapped out in one's syllabus and I take pains to create a student-centric document that illustrates my desire to make psychology applicable. My syllabus for Intro Psych takes into account the fact that the absolute majority of the students are first-year students. In contrast to my syllabi for upper-level courses, my syllabi for Intro Psych speaks more to the student directly. The sub-headings for the course are questions that students commonly ask: How do you show me how much you have learned? (answered with number of exams, quizzes, and other assignments); How do you maximize your grade in this class? (answered with study tips and techniques); How does it all add up? (answered with what each assignment/quiz/exam is worth). I play up the applications of psychology right up-front in answer to the first question, "What is this course about?"

> Psychology is concerned with every aspect of life, including most of the different occupations and jobs one can hold. This course provides an overview of the history and current status of the field and introduces you to the many ways psychology can help you understand and improve your everyday lives. Whether you want to go into business, law, medicine, public service, agriculture, construction, or psychology and its many related fields (e.g., environmental, health, clinical, industrial/organizational, nutritional, exercise/sports), this course will give you the basic theories and knowledge you need to do well in your chosen area. This course will prepare you to appreciate and be better qualified to participate in LIFE, as well as in upper-level courses in psychology and human development.

A key component of course design is assessment and the devil is often in the details. Measuring the effect of applicability directly is difficult. Whereas I would not want to teach a class without application and compare the learning and exam scores to check, I have conducted focus groups with students to assess their impressions of learning. Without fail, students bring up the number of ways they discussed applications in class and see it as something that made them learn the material better.

Going beyond anecdote, I also use application as a form of assessment itself. During the semester I have students do between eight to ten group exercises. I divide the class up into groups of four to five and give all of them real-world scenarios. They then have to generate answers as a group. For example, when teaching Learning, I describe five different everyday situations that feature some form of classical or operant conditioning. Students have to identify the correct concept being used. Whereas this is not a direct test of whether application itself is aiding memory and retention of psychological concepts, it is another way to push application into the classroom.

One of my assessments directly requires application. I often have students write a short three-page paper at the end of the semester. Even with 250 students, I can read over the papers and assign a grade relatively quickly (I do not edit the papers or turn them back), quickly getting a sense of what the students have learned and how well they can apply the material. In short, I ask students to pick a topic from life and apply as much as their knowledge from the course to discussing the topic. Full directions for the assignment are reproduced in Box 3.1.

B o x 3.1 Psychology is Life: Apply Your Knowledge

Why did Facebook become so popular? Why can't Congress work together to pass a federal budget? Why was I not invited to the party last Saturday night? Human behavior has multiple causes, sometimes involving interactions among two or more factors from different areas of psychology. This is the case for everyday behavior and for the big problems facing society today. Pollution, global warming, education, poverty, terrorism, natural resource depletion, population growth, nuclear proliferation, pandemics, social injustice, hunger, and crime, all involve behavioral processes that are shaped by factors moderated by or in interaction with other factors, ranging from biological to sociocultural perspectives. Because human behavior plays such an important role in each of these problems, psychology as an integrated, hub science has much to contribute to their understanding and control. Your challenge in this assignment is to show how different psychological factors or processes, individually or in combination, can influence an issue.

Specifically, your task is to pick a big problem from the list below and indicate theory and research in psychology that describes and explains the role people play in the creation of and solution to the problem. Your paper should be three double-spaced pages. Begin by defining the issue/topic. Look over your notes for the course so far, the chapters you have read, and skim topics in the chapters remaining. Think about the areas of psychology that relate or pertain to your topic. Locate where your topic (or a related topic) is discussed in the text or in your notes. You do not need references beyond your class notes or the textbook.

Think about and include, where applicable, three of these five areas of content that may be interconnected in the overall system of your selected problem.

- *Biological* (e.g., neuroscience, sensation, consciousness, motivation)
- *Cognitive* (e.g., cognition, memory, learning, perception)
- *Social* and individual variation (e.g., social, personality, intelligence, emotion, cultural and gender differences)
- *Biopsychosocial* (e.g., abnormal, health, clinical)
- *Developmental* (e.g., the needs and capabilities of children, adolescents, adults, and the elderly)

Consider the questions below and how ethics, diversity, and applications may influence the resolution of the problem. For instance, what are the major ethical considerations of conducting research or investigating the behavioral aspects of the big problem that you have chosen? What does psychological science have to say about how variations across individuals and roles (including those based on age, gender, sexual orientation, gender identity, race, ethnicity, culture, national origin, religion, disability status, language, and socioeconomic status) contribute to the problem and/or to the solution? What role do the variations you see across individuals (e.g., in terms of their capabilities and vulnerabilities) play in the creation or solution to the big problem you've chosen? How might this big problem affect people's everyday lives if it gets much worse, and how might their everyday lives differ if they were to behave in ways that were to help solve this big problem?

Classroom Dynamics

Beyond assignments and the syllabus, classroom dynamics are important to setting the tone for how you see learning. One of the biggest problems with large classes, especially those with over 60 students, is that students feel that the instructor does not really care about them as individuals. Whereas the size of a class may make it impossible for an instructor to give each student personalized attention, there are still a variety of ways that even a large class can be given the feel of a small class. Perhaps the most consequential day is day one.

The first day of class is extremely important; first impressions are often lasting impressions. Evaluations made after viewing a silent 5-second clip of a teaching assistant on the first day of class predicted how that assistant would be rated at the end of the semester (Ambady & Rosenthal, 1992). I map out how I will use every minute of my initial course meeting. Students in a large class are often expecting to be able to sit back and not have to participate. Many students do not expect the class to be engaging because of its size. If students have not taken a class from me before or do not know anything about me, I know they are going to be curious to see what my style is and to get a feel for what the class will be like. It is likely that students will decide how much effort to give the class based on the first-day impressions and how excited they are by the material. I remind myself that I can set the stage for a good learning experience by having a strong first day.

On day one, I start class with music (even before the period starts) that has a psychological theme and that students should be familiar with (e.g., Aerosmith's Sweet Emotion). Right then and there I discuss how music is often linked to emotions and can adjust one's mood—a psychological phenomenon that will be studied later. I then take the first 30 minutes to provide rich, vivid, examples of areas of life that psychology is relevant. I pick on areas I know students are interested in, such as romantic relationships, sex, drug and alcohol use, stress, and work success. For each of these topics I use full-screen visuals (no words) featuring contemporary people (e.g., celebrities) or situations (e.g., Super Bowl, presentations). Students immediately recognize features of their life, pay attention, and are hooked. I then share the parts of the semester they will hear about each topic.

To highlight applications I also use a life-span approach to situate the different sections of psychology. I work to show students how what feel like discrete chapters are actually part of a single narrative: the story of human experience through life. Before discussing the syllabus at the end of class, I give them a big picture of the semester where I map out the plan for the semester with a narrative. I infuse chapters and domains of psychology within the story of life. I mention the class will start with tools (Research Method), then the biological building blocks that make one human (Brain and Biology, Neuroscience, Sensation), and then start elaborating on human growth and experience. First humans are born and grow (Human Development); they have to learn (Learning), remember (Memory), and then interact with the world (Social) that shapes and is shaped by who they are (Personality). Sometimes things go wrong (Health and Abnormal) and psychology can help fix it (Treatments). I have found that starting class in this way is a much more appealing first day for students who then feel more connected to the class and material.

I also put a key question in front of them: "Why should I care?" I tell students that if they ever find themselves asking this question, they have missed something about the content of the class and psychology. Throughout the semester I aim to make the material as applicable to their lives as possible and repeatedly ask this question and have students answer it in class. This approach is particularly useful early in the semester when students are not sure why they have to study research methods or the biology of the brain and nervous system.

I use many of the strategies that follow on the first day of class and follow through with them later in the semester as well.

- **Try to learn as many names as possible:** Perhaps the single-most powerful way to make a class more personal is to learn students' names. This effort does not need an especially strong memory. Some simple tricks include
  - Take photographs of the students on the first day with them holding cards with their names on it (that they have written/created in class). Use these pictures to memorize a few names before every class. It is well worth your time to spend up to a few hours memorizing names during the first week of school as students greatly appreciate you knowing their names and will work harder in class because of it.
  - Have students sit in the same spots and complete seating charts that identify their names so you can call on individuals in specific spots by name throughout the academic term.
- **Divide students up into smaller groups:** Try to form the students into smaller groups at least once a week. They will get to know more of their classmates and have a chance to talk in a more comfortable environment (i.e., to a small group of two to three peers versus out loud in front of an entire large class).
- **Send out an e-mail** to all your students before the first day of class telling them a little about you and the class, so you can begin to shape their first impressions of you and the class (Legg & Wilson, 2009).
- **After each exam**, but especially after the first one, e-mail each student who fails and try and find out why he or she failed (e.g., did they not study, not understand). Also e-mail the top 5 scorers in class (more if you can). This effort on your part shows students that you do care about their successes and failures and they are not just numbers on your course roster.
- **Arrive at class early and stay after class** so students have an opportunity to talk to you face to face. When you do arrive early, show you are open to questions by setting up your teaching materials quickly and then walking around and talking to students.

- **Use technology to connect students with each other and with you:** Use course management software to have students participate in discussion groups or respond to questions about the class. If you have teaching assistants (TAs), assign each TA to a small group of students from the large class and have the TA be responsible for building a community among his or her group (e.g., hold review sessions or discussion groups on class material).

  - Perhaps form an electronic group for your class online where class members can share videos or news stories they find that relate to material discussed in class or covered in the course. The more opportunities students have to communicate with each other outside of class relative to the course's subject matter, the better their engagement.

Another critical element of course dynamics relates to the delivery of material and how you present information. I use a lot of personal stories in class but also promise students that every story will have a point and relate to class material. Based on the metacognitive concept of self-referencing, my fundamental approach in encouraging students to read is that the basic concepts in psychology are immediately applicable to all humans. Research shows that personalizing a story provides additional memory and retrieval cues for remembering the story details later (Abrahamson, 2006; Barney, 2006). There are universal themes that apply to all people, and in class, I capitalize on those themes—such as changing a romantic partner's behavior, learning a new skill, childhood experiences, and relationships in their many forms (parental, sibling, platonic, romantic). If students see the connections between key psychological concepts and life, they will be more interested in learning about psychology and may retain key ideas long after the course is over. Ultimately, what students remember from introductory psychology are the stories, whether they are told by the instructor or through the textbook. This storytelling approach in the introductory psychology class has been demonstrated to be successful in the past (Fernald, 1989; McAdam, 2002; Ritchey & Bott, 2010). Students will remember material where they can connect the relevance of psychological principles to everyday life—stories engineered to keep them interested in the class from start to finish. I connect these stories to psychological concepts and show how the stories (and the concepts) apply to everyday life. If you can get students to tell stories about their own life using the material, chances are they will remember the concepts even better (Wang, Bui, & Song, 2015).

CONCLUDING THOUGHTS

At the heart of it, the idea in my approach to teaching introductory psychology is to make material applicable, something that effective teachers do intuitively. I weave applications to life and stories in every facet of the course. Not only do the multiple-choice questions feature numerous questions where students have to apply their knowledge (I give them real-life scenarios and questions based on book concepts), but I also start the first class by making the applications a key part of the class. Even if students have to work a little harder to take complex course material and translate it to everyday life, the effort is well worth it. Engaged students make for engaged instructors (and vice versa). Making the material applicable and encouraging students to look for applications of content not only make the course more engaging but stand to make the course material more memorable as well.

Chapter 4

A Focus on Problem-Based Learning

ANDREW B. LOGIUDICE AND JOSEPH A. KIM
McMaster University

THE "REAL WORLD"

It's all too easy to conjure images of that archetypal student in class asking, "*Why* do I need to know this? Does it even apply to the *real world*?" Surely this complaint about practicality surfaces in a variety of contexts, including introductory psychology classrooms. Let's face it—many students perceive introductory psychology material as common sense dressed up in formal terms, and decide memorization is the best course of action. These students go through the motions but lack an appreciation for the pertinence of psychology to their daily lives. Perhaps their disillusion stems from the material appearing far removed from popular psychology (five reasons stress is bad for you) and cutting-edge research (how your brain changes with exercise). After all, to a naive student, Pavlov's dogs may seem more like history than modern psychology, and Treisman's model of attention may seem awfully afield from functional neuroimaging. Therein lies the problem: With large class sizes and limited resources available, how can instructors cover the wide range of foundational content while properly conveying its utility?

We do not claim to have a perfect solution, but we designed the McMaster University introductory psychology (MacIntroPsych) courses with intentions of tackling this pedagogical conundrum. To begin this chapter, we describe an approach called problem–based learning (PBL) and its rationale from a cognitive perspective. Next we outline the rewards and challenges of incorporating PBL into large introductory psychology courses that have large and diverse student bodies. Then, making up a majority of the chapter, we explain how our courses harness PBL to showcase the relevance and utility of the material. We conclude by offering concrete suggestions for how one might incorporate our approaches into their own teaching.

PROBLEM-BASED LEARNING

PBL's History

When the School of Medicine at McMaster was established in 1965, the short-comings of traditional teaching methods became a topic of discussion. Faculty members noted that medical students at other institutions shared a common complaint: They felt what they were learning on paper would serve no benefit in practice (Barrows, 1996). The faculty wished to address this complaint in their new medical curriculum, to the extent that the associate dean claimed "responsibility of experimenting with novel approaches" (Spaulding, 1969). And to the benefit of educators around the world, experiment they did. An American physician and medical educator named Howard Barrows officially joined the faculty in 1971. By virtue of his background in clinical reasoning processes, Barrows believed traditional teaching methods led to shallow and decontextualized learning, explaining why medical students often forgot a worrying amount of foundational material by their junior year (e.g., Levine & Forman, 1973). He argued that medical students should learn by being put in the same context as true practitioners—solving life-like problems—and that this process would refine their clinical reasoning skills (Barrows, 1996). Others added that discussing material-relevant problems in groups might help students elaborate upon prior knowledge (e.g., Schmidt, 1983). These views became hallmarks of the pedagogical approach called PBL.

Six overarching goals of PBL (Barrows, 1996) were highlighted. First, students lay at the center of learning. Instead of explicitly being told what to do, they must discover for themselves how they should seek information to answer questions. Second, students work in small groups because dialog between students is considered integral to learning. Third, trained tutors facilitate discussion. The tutors are not necessarily there to provide new content, but to ask critical questions, thereby helping students structure a vast amount of information. Fourth, students solve novel, challenging, and material-relevant problems to consolidate their learning. More specifically the problems pose novel scenarios such that students' prior knowledge by itself is insufficient to fully comprehend the solution (Figure 4.1). Fifth, the problems must be life-like, allowing students to emulate how professionals apply knowledge in practice. Sixth, and finally, students engage in self-directed learning, regularly seeking out

A 55-year-old woman lies crawling on the floor in obvious pain. The pain emerges in waves and extends from the right lumbar region to the right side of the groin and to the front of the right leg.

FIGURE 4.1 An example of a PBL problem used for medical students. There are no obvious keywords present to indicate what concepts are involved in the solution, encouraging students to not only memorize the material but also understand how it should be applied in different contexts. Obtained from Norman and Schmidt (1992).

new sources of information, discussing findings with peers, and reflecting on progress. This PBL recipe quickly spread when other medical institutions were made aware of it—today an estimated 70 percent of American medical schools employ PBL, albeit to differing degrees (Kinkade, 2005), and elements of the approach have become mainstream in countries around the world (Camp, 1996; Neville, 2008).

But PBL certainly does not end with medical education. It has been adopted in a myriad of fields including (but not limited to) biology, nursing, law, dentistry, business, architecture, and engineering (Camp, 1996). Importantly, this proliferation of PBL spawned many unique variants, leading some to argue that PBL is not a well-defined intervention but instead a broad pedagogical strategy (e.g., Walton & Matthews, 1989). Indeed PBL has been difficult to study due to disputes regarding its implementation and what defines it (Barrows, 1986; Neville, 2008). Nonetheless, an enormous body of literature has been generated to clarify the effects of PBL on learning—searching the PubMed database alone we found over 2,000 abstracts containing "problem-based learning." Exhaustive coverage of PBL literature is clearly beyond the scope of this chapter. Rather, in what follows, we summarize a selection of cognitive research on PBL that encapsulates our rationale for the MacIntroPsych course design.

Cognitive Rationale

Initially PBL was thought to foster flexible problem-solving skills that transferred to other fields of study. But when further work yielded no evidence for such general problem-solving skills (Norman & Schmidt, 1992), focus was shifted toward a more concrete question: How does PBL affect the acquisition and retention of knowledge? The *activation-elaboration hypothesis* offers an explanation by building upon the seminal work of Bransford and Johnson (1972). It posits that when a group is presented with a problem, each individual searches through long-term memory for relevant information, retrieving—and thereby activating—prior knowledge. This activation is in turn thought to facilitate elaboration when new and related information is made available (Schmidt, Rotgans, & Yew, 2011). For illustration, consider an experiment investigating how activation of prior knowledge affects subsequent learning. Participants first studied a passage explaining the properties of waves. One week later, those in the Listen condition watched a video of students discussing waves and how they might relate to radar, whereas those in the Explain condition watched the same video, but with opportunities to verbally address questions arising in the virtual discussion. All participants then studied a final passage explaining how radar works. Comprehension of radar was measured both immediately and after one month. No differences were found immediately, but those in the Explain condition—who activated prior knowledge of waves via discussion before studying radar—retained significantly more information after a month (van Blankenstein, Dolmans, van der Vleuten, & Schmidt, 2011). Other studies have similarly demonstrated that PBL elicits superior long-term retention relative to traditional approaches (Beers & Bowden, 2005; Eisenstaedt, Barry, & Glanz, 1990; Martenson, Eriksson, & Ingelman-Sundberg, 1985; Strobel & van Barneveld, 2009). Together, these findings suggest that prior knowledge is activated when discussing a problem, facilitating subsequent elaboration and retention of that knowledge.

Research on the concept of *transfer* complements the activation-elaboration hypothesis. Transfer refers to the application of knowledge in an unfamiliar context—a task shown to be incredibly difficult for learners (e.g., Quilici & Mayer, 1996). Contary to experts, novices are thought to lack deep conceptual understanding, explaining why they have such difficulty identifying when and how knowledge should be transferred to novel scenarios. The good news is that transfer seems to be poteniated when learners explicitly compare and contrast problems that address the same concepts (e.g., Loewenstein, Thompson, & Gentner, 1999), suggesting that exposure to multiple problems encourages richer conceptual understanding (Norman, 2009). As educators we should not take this lightly. After all, if the educator's goal is to train students to solve novel problems long after a course has ended, transfer of knowledge is paramount.

Another explanation for the apparent success of PBL, and the last we discuss, pertains to student motivation. The *situational interest hypothesis* argues that a challenging problem reveals gaps in understanding and sparks curiosity, leading to increased concentration and a stronger desire to learn (Hidi & Renninger, 2006; Schmidt et al., 2011). Accordingly, students rate their motivation to learn significantly higher when initially presented a problem relative to when the topic is simply discussed (Rotgans & Schmidt, 2011a, 2011b). A problem's relevance to personal experience also seems to influence motivation. In one study, groups of unknowing students received different problems addressing the same concepts. Problems in the "highly relevant" condition were designed to be relevant to students' lives, and problems in the "far-removed" condition were designed to be less relevant. Students in the "highly relevant" condition rated the problems as significantly more relatable to their personal experiences, more interesting, and a better fit with their prior knowledge (Soppe, Schmidt, & Bruysten, 2005). More work is needed in this area, but these present findings suggest PBL is effective because students like a challenge—most notably when they can directly relate to the problem at hand.

REWARDS AND CHALLENGES OF PBL IN INTRODUCTORY PSYCHOLOGY

PBL Emphasizes Practicality

We argue that PBL is particularly well suited for introductory psychology. In our experience, teaching psychology can be a double-edged sword in that students show initial interest because they are familiar with popular psychology and sensational media portrayals, but opt out when they realize psychology is complicated and has gray areas—rendering the material less practical in their eyes. We suggest PBL as a means to break this facade of impracticality. Asking students to solve material-relevant problems in relatable contexts is a straightforward way for students to see how the basics of psychology are applicable to everyday life. Similarly, popular myths or misapplications of research can be presented to demonstrate how the scientific method should be applied to dismiss unfounded claims related to psychology (e.g., the pervasive notion of learning styles in education). Thus, by virtue of its emphasis on practicality, we believe PBL uniquely fits with a field like psychology where students study arguably the most practical topic of all: themselves.

Unfortunately the rapidly changing postsecondary landscape impedes those who wish to experiment with novel approaches. For introductory courses in particular, the most troubling of these changes include larger class sizes, a student body with highly variable academic backgrounds, and more students commuting to campus. Instructors must fill lecture halls with hundreds of students due to high enrollment, tacitly promoting passive learning with verbatim note-taking and minimal processing of course content beyond memorization. Emphasis is put on timely delivery of basic material—usually constrained to three hours per week—such that it becomes an unaffordable luxury to stop and gauge current understanding or execute demonstrations, discussions, and experiments. Inconsistencies between sections may be created inadvertently for larger courses that require multiple instructors. Static schedules are needed for busy students who juggle other commitments or commute to campus; therefore, it becomes tedious to schedule smaller interactive classroom sessions and supervised tests. So grows a propensity toward bland course structures comprising a few lectures per week, one or two high-stakes midterms, and a final exam. Evidently a trade-off exists between feasibility and sound pedagogy in large introductory courses—and feasibility often wins by default. To make matters worse for those eager to experiment more specifically with PBL, its implementation poses further challenges that interact with the general concerns already discussed.

PBL Demands Ample Application and Discussion

Supervised classroom time is limited due to logistical constraints, and so in accordance with PBL, we argue that the precious little time available should be put toward active problem-solving activities rather than delivery of primary course content. However, this means students must have a basic understanding of the material *before* coming to class. Textbooks can provide a good foundation, but passive learning typically ensues due to a lack of engagement. For instance, large-scale surveys administered to college students confirm that rereading and highlighting are pervasive study tactics (Karpicke, Butler, & Roediger, 2009; Kornell & Bjork, 2007) despite their weak impact on learning (Dunlosky, Rawson, Marsh, Nathan, & Willingham, 2013). Therefore, a customizable and user-friendly means of delivering primary course content would be useful, reserving valuable classroom time for higher-level application and discussion.

Critically, the quality of application and discussion are contingent upon the quality of problems encountered. And the quality of a problem from the student's perspective—in terms of clarity, relevance, and ability to stimulate discussion—has been shown to influence the efficacy of PBL (van Berkel & Schmidt, 2000; van den Hurk, Dolmans, Wolfhagen, & van der Vleuten, 2001). This finding poses a challenge because it is time-consuming to create novel real-world problems that stimulate discussion and target specific course concepts, let alone problems that relate to students' lives. To illustrate what we mean, consider the difference between (1) asking students to explain why female peacocks prefer males with larger and more symmetric tails and (2) asking students to explain why it makes sense for women to prefer deeper male voices during the fertile phase of their menstrual cycle. Both problems address sexual selection, but the latter is more relevant to students and arguably more likely to stimulate discussion. In an ideal PBL system for introductory psychology, there would be plenty of these relatable problems available, and an efficient way to refine them from year to year.

PBL Is Difficult to Integrate with Frequent Testing

Students and instructors alike typically view tests as dreaded but necessary tools for assessment, with little or no intrinsic learning value. Yet tests are potent learning tools that enhance retention of information well beyond repeated studying (Karpicke & Roediger, 2008). Indeed frequent testing has been shown to enhance learning in authentic university classrooms (e.g., McDaniel, Roediger, & McDermott, 2007). From a cognitive perspective, these retention benefits seem to be driven by the act of retrieving information from memory; thus, testing is said to be a form of *retrieval practice* (Roediger & Butler, 2011). Related research suggests that immediate corrective feedback increases subsequent retention (Lipko-Speed, Dunlosky, & Rawson, 2014; Butler & Roediger, 2008) and that a delay between testing and feedback leads to even greater retention (Butler, Karpicke, & Roediger,

2007). Too long of a delay, however, will likely reduce the utility of the feedback due to excessive forgetting (Butler & Roediger, 2008). Lastly, in accordance with our previous discussion of transfer, students must receive extensive practice applying concepts to unfamiliar problems, thereby improving the likelihood of transfer later in their careers (Norman, 2009). By this logic, courses need ample test questions and a means of providing customized and delayed feedback, with some questions posing novel scenarios that require application of the material beyond mere recall or recognition memory.

Practically speaking, frequent application-based tests with customized feedback are difficult to employ in large courses. Traditional supervised tests require invigilators and consistent scheduling of campus space, application questions are typically harder to write than simple memorization questions, and a large student body produces many nuanced inquiries. Therefore, an automated testing system would be useful in overcoming these logistical constraints.

THE MACINTROPSYCH BLENDED LEARNING MODEL

So far we have covered the background and rationale of PBL, followed by obstacles impeding its use in large introductory courses. Now we describe our own PBL-inspired approach in detail, specifically addressing how we circumvent each of the aforementioned challenges.

The MacIntroPsych program comprises the two largest courses offered by McMaster University: Psych 1X03 and Psych 1XX3. The 1X03 course is taught in the first semester and covers the history and foundations of psychology, including research methods, classical and instrumental conditioning, language, categorization, attention, memory, and social psychology. Enrollment is around 2,500 students because the course is mandatory for many programs and also a popular elective with no prerequisites. This 1X03 course additionally serves a secondary role as a gateway to the university, because for a majority of students it is one of the first courses with relatively small tutorial sizes that they take after high school. The other course, 1XX3, is taught the second semester. It puts greater emphasis on the biological perspective (introductory biology is a prerequisite), covering topics of development, evolution, neuroscience, vision, color and form perception, audition, hunger, psychological disorders, and psychological treatments. Enrollment for 1XX3 is slightly lower at around 2,000 students because the course is mandatory only for biology-related fields and psychology majors.

With such a large student body it is unfeasible to implement the PBL approach using a traditional course structure. Instead the instructional team adopts blended learning, combining online resources with face-to-face instruction to create the MacIntroPsych Blended Learning Model. Both courses contain 12 major topics taught as week-long units, and each unit is segmented into three steps: (1) primary course content and examples are delivered via an online web module, a courseware guidebook, and an in-class lecture; (2) students attend small tutorial sessions where they apply and discuss course content, solving relatable problems under the guidance of a trained undergraduate tutor; and (3) students complete a timed, online multiple-choice quiz that randomly draws questions from a large question bank, including application-based questions that require transfer. We elaborate on each of these steps in the following sections.

Delivering Primary Course Content via Web Modules and In-Class Lectures

First things first: Students must have a working knowledge of the course content before they can transfer it to novel problems. To this end, a web module is released every week through the university's online learning management system. This approach allows for self-paced learning because students have a week to review the material, take notes, and gain relative mastery of the terms and concepts before they are discussed in class. The web modules present content through audio-narrated slides with timed animations, and the slides are organized in the navigation bar by subtopic (Figure 4.2). Students control how long they want to spend on a given slide and can replay slides as many times as needed. The Menu

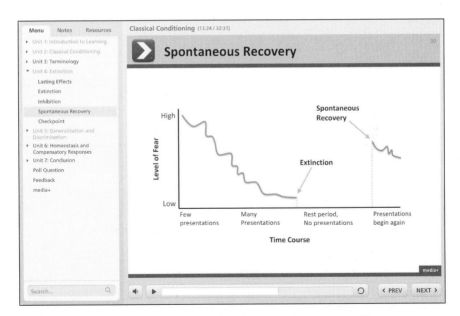

FIGURE 4.2 A slide from the classical conditioning web module. Progress on the current slide is shown at the bottom with the options of pausing or replaying a slide. Although this image is static, portions of the graph in the real web module appear in synchrony with the audio narration, further segmenting the information. Three tabs at the top left can be clicked: Menu opens the outline of the web module, Notes opens a full transcript of the narration, and Resources displays links to supplementary information in the form of videos, articles, websites, and so on. A search function can also be found at the bottom left. For a sample, visit www.intropsych.net.

tab displays an outline of the topic in hierarchical structure, the Notes tab provides a full transcript of the narration, and the Resources tab contains links to selected videos, articles, and other relevant media. A search function allows for quick review such that a student can type in key words and jump to specific parts of the web module. Accompanying the web modules is a hard-copy guidebook containing the course information, key slides from each web module with designated room for notes, practice questions, and a preview of upcoming topics to be elaborated upon in tutorial. The ultimate goal with the guidebook is to provide a central resource that allows students to get the most out of the web modules—specifically by encouraging effective note-taking, the monitoring of self-paced learning, and preparation for upcoming tutorial sessions.

The web modules are designed in accordance with established multimedia principles to maximize learning. Students can pause at any time and review prior material if they wish, segmenting the lesson, so they are better able to integrate the different "chunks" of information (Mayer, 2008). Text on slides is kept minimal to reduce cognitive load, and visuals are synchronized with audio narration to take advantage of both verbal and visual processing channels (Clark, Nguyen, & Sweller, 2011). Checkpoints and polls make the web modules more interactive (Figure 4.3). Checkpoints can be thought of as brief "pause-and-think" exercises that appear after each major section of the web module, consisting of a few questions (e.g., fill in the blank, matching terms, multiple choice) that are not graded for credit but instead serve as informal metacognitive tools. Feedback is immediately provided after an answer is submitted, explaining why the selected answer is correct or incorrect. Incorrect responses provide an opportunity to revise notes and correct misconceptions. Thus these checkpoints promote active learning by

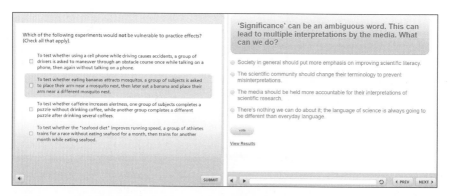

FIGURE 4.3 The web modules include interactive features to promote active learning and help students monitor their self-paced learning. A checkpoint question (left) and poll question (right) from the research methods web module are depicted above. Checkpoint questions are intended to be a metacognitive tool, encouraging students to stop and apply what they have learned before continuing on to new information. Each response option provides customized feedback to correct misconceptions. Polls ask students to comment on contemporary issues related to the topic being discussed, and then reveal the responses from all other students in the class.

motivating students to periodically test their knowledge rather than passively write notes. On the other hand, for polls, a topical question related to the course material is presented and students are able to vote for a response. Upon submitting a vote they are able to see how all other students in the course responded. Finally, students are prompted with a link to an online survey at the end of each web module, allowing them to give feedback on enjoyability and perceived effectiveness. Those who participate are entered into a $250 draw each time feedback is provided, and the prize is administered at the end of the term. With these features in place, the web modules deliver course content in an engaging manner and allow for perpetual collection of feedback within specific topics. Indeed they are consistently viewed as interesting and effective learning tools by students. For example, in the 2014 iteration of 1X03, the average student rating of web modules on a 5-point Likert scale was 4.4, with 90 percent of students selecting either 4 or 5 ($N = 294$).

Web modules offer considerable advantages over traditional lectures when it comes to delivery of primary course content. For starters, students may choose within a one-week time window when they wish to watch the web module and take notes on the material, eliminating the hassles of scheduling three weekly lectures for a large group of students. From the students' perspective, the web module system is convenient because they are able to dovetail their learning into busy schedules—they can even stop a web module to attend another class or complete an urgent task and then return to the module later. This scheduling freedom additionally spares commuters trips to campus. Another challenge of large courses we mentioned earlier is consistency between sections, but again, web modules eliminate this problem because every student has access to the same core material. Catering to a diverse student body, the web modules are fully compatible with screen-reading technology and provide full transcripts of narrations including descriptions of all visuals. The web modules are also self-paced, allowing differently abled students to review parts of the web module whenever and for however long they wish. Lastly, the web modules are permanent resources, available for each student's future reference through the university's online learning management system. In sum, this web module system confers significant advantages over traditional lectures, pertaining to scheduling flexibility, consistency, and accessibility.

The web modules discuss all major concepts from the course, establishing the scaffolding needed for more detailed explanations and examples. But the use of additional examples is essential because, as previously mentioned, it enhances deep processing and transferability of knowledge. To this end students are also assigned supplemental readings (textbook sections or journal articles) and attend weekly in-class lectures. The readings complement the web modules by offering new examples and more in-depth explanations for major concepts. Weekly in-class lectures are similarly designed to elaborate on the course content by connecting it to everyday experiences, current events, and interesting applications. For instance, in one lecture on development students are encouraged to think critically in light of course content, discussing the validity of products designed to enhance infant cognitive abilities. The instructional team feels these more nuanced examples foster comparison and contrast between scenarios, eliciting a deeper contextual understanding of the material.

Consolidating Knowledge via Structured
PBL Tutorials and Tutors

After basic course content is learned via a web module and accompanying courseware, students are ready to apply and consolidate their knowledge through problem-solving activities. This occurs in weekly 50-minute tutorial sessions capped at 25 students to create an intimate small classroom feel. Each tutorial is led by an undergraduate teaching assistant (TA) in the third or fourth year of their psychology degree. The three classrooms currently used for tutorial sections are modestly equipped with a projector, a computer, six whiteboards on the walls, and long tables organized into three islands such that students at an island face each other. As you may have guessed based on this layout, the tutorials are designed to promote peer discussion. Real-life application problems covering the most challenging or integral concepts from the web module are displayed on the projector by the TA. Students then collaborate and apply their knowledge to solve the problems, discussing in small groups at their tables and drawing diagrams on whiteboards. The TA allots time for problems—usually around 3 to 5 minutes for each—and ensures groups are on the right track in their conversations. When time is up, the TA ends the discussions and directs attention to specific groups, asking them to explain their solution and rationale to the class. Groups often debate until more comprehensive solutions emerge. In line with the PBL research discussed earlier, the instructional team believes this collaborative problem-solving process activates prior knowledge and facilitates elaboration, offers practice transferring material to real-world problems, and fosters a motivation to learn.

Some argue that open-ended problems with minimal instruction can be detrimental to learning (e.g., Kirschner, Sweller, & Clark, 2006), so it is important to note that the tutorials are intended to be highly structured. That is, the encountered problems are refined and presented in a logical order such that each tutorial tells a comprehensive "story" about the topic. Here are some sample problems (representing approximately 25 minutes of the classical conditioning tutorial) to make this point more concrete (Figure 4.4). Note the problems occur in a logical sequence. Questions 1 and 2 ask students to map the elements of classical conditioning onto a novel scenario, and then to extrapolate by explaining how classical conditioning works more broadly. Question 3 illustrates stimulus generalization. Questions 4 and 5 force students to compare and contrast the processes of stimulus discrimination and extinction. Question 6 shows how environmental cues contribute to homeostasis via classical conditioning. By imposing this structure, students cover the more conceptually demanding areas of the web module and hopefully leave with a coherent story of the topic.

We stress that knowledgeable, approachable, and well-trained TAs are integral to the success of tutorials. With such small class sizes and emphasis on discussion, it is imperative for TAs to create a safe learning environment by establishing rapport with their students. This arguably makes undergraduate students ideal—they

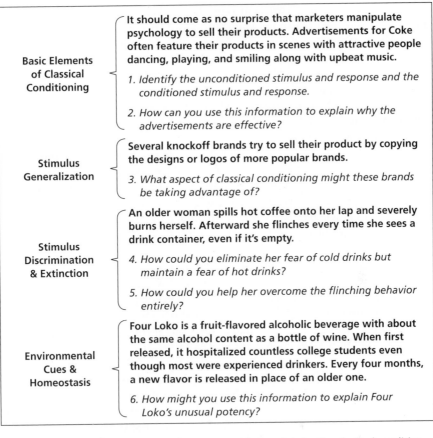

Basic Elements of Classical Conditioning

It should come as no surprise that marketers manipulate psychology to sell their products. Advertisements for Coke often feature their products in scenes with attractive people dancing, playing, and smiling along with upbeat music.

1. *Identify the unconditioned stimulus and response and the conditioned stimulus and response.*

2. *How can you use this information to explain why the advertisements are effective?*

Stimulus Generalization

Several knockoff brands try to sell their product by copying the designs or logos of more popular brands.

3. *What aspect of classical conditioning might these brands be taking advantage of?*

Stimulus Discrimination & Extinction

An older woman spills hot coffee onto her lap and severely burns herself. Afterward she flinches every time she sees a drink container, even if it's empty.

4. *How could you eliminate her fear of cold drinks but maintain a fear of hot drinks?*

5. *How could you help her overcome the flinching behavior entirely?*

Environmental Cues & Homeostasis

Four Loko is a fruit-flavored alcoholic beverage with about the same alcohol content as a bottle of wine. When first released, it hospitalized countless college students even though most were experienced drinkers. Every four months, a new flavor is released in place of an older one.

6. *How might you use this information to explain Four Loko's unusual potency?*

FIGURE 4.4 A set of problems that appeared in tutorials for the classical conditioning unit. Note that the problems address major concepts from the web module, shown in boxes on the left, and their sequence produces a coherent story about the topic.

are generally only two or three years further in their degrees than the first-year students, making them relatable and approachable. Another responsibility for TAs is individually grading students four times throughout the term (i.e., every three weeks) based on tutorial attendance, participation, and preparedness. Students are notified that frequent participation alone is not sufficient to achieve full credit; the *quality* of their input, as determined by the TAs through class discussion, is equally important. The four grades are averaged at the end of the term to make up 10 percent of a student's final grade, classified as "Tutorial Participation." TAs also have out-of-class duties. Online discussion boards operate on the same learning management system as the web modules, and TAs moderate tutorial-specific boards by posting bonus practice questions and giving feedback to students who submit responses. TAs additionally host drop-in office hours in person during the day and through free video chat software in the evenings. To understand how critical TAs are for the course, one needn't look further than the rigorous selection process. Every year the department typically receives over 200 applications for only 20 teaching assistantships. Applications are first filtered based on criteria including grades and academic accomplishments. Those selected for interviews are given presentation design guidelines and asked to deliver a ten-minute lesson. This process reliably yields TAs with ample knowledge, approachability, enthusiasm, and communication skills. And as proof of its success, TAs were rated an average of 4.6 on a 5-point Likert scale by students in the 2014 iteration of 1X03, with 94 percent of students selecting either 4 or 5 ($N = 293$).

In many ways, TAs learn just as much from tutorials as the students do. Incoming TAs enroll in a Teaching of Psychology course taught by the MacIntroPsych professor. Here they discuss contemporary cognitive psychology topics related to education and debate implications for educational practice. Course assessments include major projects aimed at teaching effective presentation design, assessment methods, and knowledge translation. To highlight an example, one major project is to design the problems used in a given tutorial. The class of TAs is split into pairs, and each pair creates and refines problems for a specific week's tutorial (e.g., one pair might develop problems for the classical conditioning tutorial). All TAs, including senior TAs who took the Teaching of Psychology course the previous year, gather every week to review what the designated pair has produced for the upcoming tutorial. Feedback is provided on the perceived clarity and educational value of problems. The pair then makes revisions accordingly and uploads final slides onto the tutorial computers for all TAs to use. If you recall, we mentioned that a steady stream of refined problems is ideal for the PBL approach. The Teaching of Psychology course is the solution because it allows the TAs to generate new problems behind the scenes while gaining valuable teaching experience. Indeed the classical conditioning problems discussed earlier (Figure 4.4) were all recently created by TAs. In this sense the TAs are central to the courses, concurrently studying educational psychology, designing course materials, and applying what they learn to lead effective tutorials. Interestingly, when the Teaching of Psychology course was first in operation, incoming TAs were required to take it and the senior TAs at the time—who never took it—were exempt. Unknowing students were asked to rate the enjoyment and effectiveness of their tutorials, and there seemed to be a preference for TAs enrolled in the Teaching of Psychology course, despite the extra year of teaching experience for the same content accrued by senior TAs (Sana, Pachai, & Kim, 2011; Figure 4.5).

This TA course reflects the philosophy of McMaster's psychology department—the "cascades of knowledge" model. As the name implies, the goal is to have a group of senior students studying a topic in-depth, and then have their expertise spill over to the lower-level students studying the same topic at an introductory level. This approach places emphasis on peer instruction such that students are essentially learning by teaching, hence the use of senior undergraduate TAs leading the tutorials. The product, at least from what the department has observed, is a community where passionate upper-year undergraduates are mentoring newcomers to the program, both in and out of class. It is therefore unsurprising that most TAs report applying for the job because they were motivated by the TAs they had for tutorial two or three years earlier. But the cascade does not

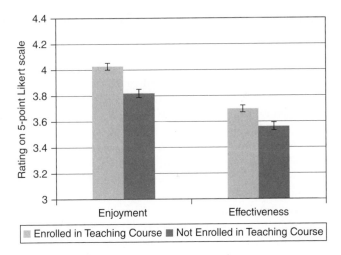

FIGURE 4.5 Comparison of perceived tutorial enjoyment and effectiveness across two cohorts of TAs, as reported by students. One cohort had partaken in the Teaching of Psychology course, and the other cohort consisted of TAs who led tutorials the previous year but did not partake in the Teaching of Psychology course. Data obtained from Sana et al. (2011).

end with undergraduate students; it permeates all the way up to graduate students and postdoctoral fellows in the department, who recruit and train lower-level students to collaborate on their graduate-level research projects. Other courses in the department were recently revamped with this philosophy in mind, and over the past few years, the department has seen a persistent increase in the number of students involved with formal research courses and practicums. Accordingly, the department now offers over 350 independent study courses (e.g., theses, research practicums) each year. Overall the Teaching of Psychology course fits nicely with this "cascades of knowledge" approach, and the instructional team believes it to be an effective pedagogical strategy contributing to the success of MacIntroPsych.

Enhancing Retention via Frequent, Online, Application-Based Quizzes

After basic course content is delivered and tutorials have taken place for the week, students conclude each unit by completing an online assessment. As previously mentioned, it can be challenging to offer frequent testing opportunities with feedback due to logistical constraints. We use the university's online learning management system (the same that houses our web modules and discussion boards) to tackle this problem.

During the week, students are encouraged to integrate self-testing with their study using a sample pre-quiz bank. Although not for credit, the pre-quizzes contain a subset of questions drawn from the larger question bank that is used for the real weekly quiz. Therefore the pre-quizzes provide authentic practice under test-like conditions. Immediately after completion the pre-quizzes are scored, and specific feedback is offered. Pre-quizzes are used for the same reason checkpoints are used in the web modules: to help students slow down and evaluate their understanding before continuing.

For the real weekly quiz, an automated system allows for one attempt within a set 24-hour window. Each quiz is limited to 20 minutes and consists of ten multiple-choice questions randomly drawn from a large question bank. The time limit can be changed on an individual basis, so more time can be allotted to students who require accommodations. Each of the 12 quizzes throughout the term is worth 2.5 percent, summing to 30 percent of a student's final grade. To promote reading of the textbook, students are notified that a few questions on every quiz will draw from examples exclusive to the textbook. The questions themselves are created by instructional staff in accordance with research on best practices in multiple-choice writing (e.g., Haladyna, Downing, & Rodriguez, 2002). Also, stemming from principles outlined in Bloom's revised taxonomy (Krathwohl, 2002), each quiz contains a mix of two types of questions: Recall questions are manageable for students who recognize key terminology and definitions; application questions pose novel scenarios that presumably require transfer, preventing students from relying on key words to deduce correct answers based on familiarity or memorization alone (see Figure 4.6 for juxtaposition of a recall-and-application question). Grades and feedback are released approximately three to four days after the quizzes are completed. Similar to the pre-quizzes, specific feedback is available for each question on the real quiz, explaining why each selected

---

[Recall] What is the purpose of a *t*-test?

A) The *t*-test determines if groups are statistically significant.
B) The *t*-test creates normal distributions, which are used for data analysis.
C) The *t*-test ensures observed differences between groups are due to the dependent variable.
D) The *t*-test indicates the probability that differences between groups are due to random variability.

[Application] A scientist runs a study comparing the lung capacities of musicians and nonmusicians. She compares lung capacity measures from both groups and obtains a *p*-value of 0.01. What does this mean?

A) There is a 1% chance that lung capacity truly differed between the two groups.
B) There is a 99% chance musicians had higher lung capacity due to random variability alone.
C) If no real difference exists between musicians and nonmusicians, the observed difference would occur 99% of the time.
D) If no real difference exists between musicians and nonmusicians, the observed difference would occur 1% of the time.

FIGURE 4.6 A comparison of recall-style (top) and application-style (bottom) questions covering the same concept. Note that students may answer the recall question so long as they remember the basic definition of a *t*-test. However, having only a basic recognition- or recall-level understanding of the *t*-test is insufficient to understand the application question.

response is correct or incorrect. Overall this system allows the instructional team to deliver application-based and low-stakes assessments on a weekly basis, complete with customized, delayed feedback.

Both courses conclude with a final multiple-choice exam worth 60 percent of a student's final grade. Exam questions mostly resemble the application questions encountered in tutorials and on the weekly quizzes, and students are notified of this format to help guide their studying (see Figure 4.7 for a summary of course assessments).

On one hand, the usage of online quizzes raises obvious concerns. First, and perhaps most salient, online assessments allow students to rely on external resources such as the web modules, their textbook, or the internet. In this sense the quizzes are "open book." However, an unprepared student will likely find it overwhelming to search through notes within the 20-minute time limit of the quiz. Indeed most of the questions are designed to pose novel scenarios such that one cannot simply look up the correct answer. Another potential issue with online quizzes is that without supervision, students may collaborate. The instructional team has embraced this since it is not something that can reasonably be prevented. In fact, students are openly told that they may collaborate during their quizzes, but they are explicitly warned that social loafing will deprive them of valuable learning opportunities, and likely lead to poor performance on the larger 60 percent final exam.

On the other hand, using an online platform for quizzes has some perks you may not have originally considered. The current system quickly generates data related to student performance—a convenient tool for any instructor. For example, the instructional team can automatically see the frequency of responses for each specific question. If discrepancy, ambiguity, or low learning value is detected for a particular question, it can be modified and approved by the instructional team before being reentered into the question bank. Another interesting advantage of this system is the ease with which the instructional team measures question effectiveness. As outlined by DiBattista and Kurzawa (2011), simple statistical methods can be used to examine the efficacy of multiple-choice questions. Specifically, based on simple response frequencies, discriminatory power and distractor effectiveness can be calculated for each question. The former measures the extent to which high-performance students

	# Assessments	Style of questions	Final grade percentage
Tutorial participation	4	Recall and application	10%
Weekly online quizzes	12	Recall and application	30%
Final exam	1	Mostly application	60%

FIGURE 4.7 Summary of assessments in MacIntroPsych courses based on quantity, style of questions encountered, and percentage of final grade.

outperform low-performance students on a specific question, and the latter measures the extent to which each incorrect option (i.e., each distractor) teases apart high-performance students from low-performance students. These statistical tools in conjunction with the online platform's data-generation abilities allow the instructional team to quickly and quantitatively infer the effectiveness of each multiple-choice question. In sum, the online system allows the instructional team to take advantage of simple psychometrics, striving toward objectively effective assessments.

There are certainly improvements that could be made to the assessments. One feature currently being worked on is cumulative testing. Research suggests it is beneficial to learn some material, wait for memory to decay over time, then be tested on the material again before it is completely forgotten, and relearn it—a process called *successive relearning* (Bahrick, 1979; Rawson & Dunlosky, 2011; Rawson, Dunlosky, & Sciartelli, 2013). Related research suggests that interleaving test questions enhances learning. For instance, after reading a chapter from a statistics textbook on the ANOVA procedure, you might go to the end-of-chapter questions for practice. However this is not true practice; before beginning the questions you already know they pertain to the ANOVA method you just learned. Thus you are not required to pinpoint the context in which the procedure should be applied, which is just as (if not more) valuable as knowing how to execute the procedure itself. Mixing up questions, such that you are blind to which unit each question belongs to, is therefore a better means of practice. This technique is called *interleaved practice* and has been shown to enhance both motor learning and understanding of mathematical concepts (Bjork & Bjork, 2011; Rohrer & Taylor, 2007; Taylor & Rohrer, 2010). Regrettably the present quizzes do not embrace these findings related to successive relearning and interleaving. Once a module has ended, students do not usually encounter that information again until studying for the final exam. In future years the instructional team aims to rectify this by including questions from multiple units for certain quizzes. With this simple modification both successive relearning and interleaved practice would be harnessed.

A separate line of research researchers are interested in pertains to collaborative testing. As previously described, quizzes are offered online and allow for collaboration among students. Applied studies on collaborative testing typically reveal positive student opinions. More specifically, students report decreased test anxiety (Giuliodori, Lujan, & DiCarlo, 2008; Leight, Saunders, Calkins & Withers, 2012; Zimbardo, Butler, & Wolfe, 2003) and increased perceived learning (Cortright, Collins, Rodenbaugh, & DiCarlo, 2003; Giuliodori et al., 2008; Zimbardo et al., 2003). Nonetheless, the underlying cognitive mechanisms related to long-term retention remain elusive. Some studies report increased retention for concepts tested collaboratively relative to those tested individually (Cortright et al., 2003; Gilley & Clarkston, 2014), whereas others report no difference (Crossgrove & Curran, 2008; Leight et al., 2012). Therefore, before one can be justified in saying that a particular online testing method is effective, more research must be done to measure the effects of collaborative testing on long-term retention.

PRACTICAL ISSUES FOR TEACHING WITH PBL

For those who wish to experiment with the approaches discussed in this chapter, it should be emphasized that it is a worthwhile long-term investment with significant start-up costs. And you need not jump into it all at once. In each following section we describe how instructors might transition from a traditional lecture-style course (or any other course for that matter) to something akin to our approach. Since we realize that the reader may only be interested in particular aspects of our course design, we break it down according to four major features: the web modules, the tutorials, the online assessments, and methods of acquiring student feedback.

Web Module Development

Web modules do not necessarily have to cover a whole course. One could start by creating web modules for limited sections of a course while maintaining a traditional lecture style for the rest. This process may lead to gradual implementation of web modules in the course—perhaps just for one or two topics to begin with. Think of it this way: Have you ever come across a critical topic that you wish you could cover in more detail, but simply cannot due to time constraints in class? This topic would be ideal for your first web module. You may ask students to study the web module before class to get a gist of the topic, reserving lecture time for interesting applications or more detailed analysis. For instance, perhaps there is a particular unit covering statistical methods that normally consumes a lot of class time. Instead of spending class time covering the basics, a web module could be made available so students can access it again and again at their own convenience, and the valuable class time could be devoted to case studies, manipulation of real data sets, and so on. If it is not a good fit, then that could be the extent of your experimentation. But should you decide it works well, you could easily continue this trend by creating more web modules for each new iteration of the course. Overall this graduated approach offers a practical way of experimenting with web modules without the costs incurred all at once.

Tutorial Development

Another significant start-up cost is developing tutorial sessions and their constituent problems. Scheduling is probably the least concerning obstacle because even large introductory courses can usually find a way to schedule smaller classroom sessions in some form or another. The selection of TAs and the designing of problem sets, however, pose bigger obstacles. The PBL approach requires engaging and well-rounded tutors to facilitate discussion during the tutorials. Therefore we stress that significant effort be put into TA interviews and the selection process. Of course the process itself will vary from instructor to instructor based on individual preferences, but we recommend having some formal presentation component to accurately gauge each applicant's knowledge, approachability, enthusiasm, and communication skills. In terms of developing problem sets encountered in tutorial, within our department we have the Teaching of Psychology course where TAs design and refine new problems each year. But this system is not necessary. So long as a solid set of problems is created, it can be recycled for each iteration of the course, perhaps with yearly changes based on student and TA feedback. We also suggest that some type of weekly meeting be set for TAs and instructors to review the upcoming tutorial material, as this helps drastically with TA consistency and preparedness. Altogether, we are convinced that such tutorials are a solid addition to any course as long as there is rigorous TA selection process, a set of thoughtful problems, and weekly meetings to prime TAs and any other instructional staff.

Online Assessment Development

Another large start-up cost to the approach is the online quizzes. There has to be a sufficiently large question bank when instructors are dealing with large courses, otherwise students will stagger their quizzes, relying heavily on the previous quiz attempts of peers to boost their own grades. Obviously this is an undesirable feature. The current solutions, albeit imperfect, have been to substantially increase the size of the question bank over time, and to delay feedback so that it is released at least three days after quizzes are completed. The enlargement of the question bank has been done with the help of experienced TAs who excelled at a multiple-choice writing project in the Teaching of Psychology course. But it must also be noted that writing effective quiz questions is easier said than done. Established principles (e.g., Haladyna et al., 2002) should be followed to minimize extraneous cognitive load—an important consideration when strict time limits are enforced—and to ensure that quizzes measure both basic memorization and deeper conceptual understanding. Based on a system that has worked well for us, we recommend three steps: (1) ask instructional staff or other qualified individuals to review literature on the effective use of multiple-choice questions; (2) have them write questions for each major topic of the course; and (3) designate someone with a thorough understanding of the content to review and refine questions as needed. We also suggest that online quizzes be slowly integrated into a course over time, much like the approach we suggested for web modules. For example, instructors may wish to create quiz questions for a particular topic and assign them merely as practice, probing for student feedback on the effectiveness of the questions. If the online quiz approach proves compatible with the course, the question bank can gradually be expanded over time in partnership with TAs. The aforementioned statistical methods then provide objective feedback to guide the refinement of each question.

Student Feedback

As a final note, although it may sound trite, feedback is of the utmost importance. It is no secret that our first web modules were disliked. Only by intently reviewing feedback was the instructional team able to find what was perceived best by students. On that note, most university courses offer students a formal opportunity to voice their feedback at the end of a course, but in our opinion this is insufficient. Oftentimes the feedback forms are generalized because they cover all varieties of courses, and so specific aspects of the course are not pinpointed. We therefore suggest that students be given the opportunity to provide formal feedback not once but frequently throughout the course, and that all feedback be as specific as possible—instead of asking students how much they liked the web modules or the tutorials, ask them to rate how effective and interesting *each* web module is, or the extent to which problems from a *specific* tutorial generated discussion. When such frequent and specific feedback is acquired, it quickly becomes clear what elements of the approach need improvement.

CONCLUSION

In summary, we offer bird's-eye view of the course as if you were the student. Each week you watch a web module at your convenience using the guidebook to take notes and gauge your understanding of the material, read about new examples in the textbook or a scholarly article, and attend a lecture to see how the material connects to your everyday life. You then participate in a small tutorial session to discuss the material, elaborating on your knowledge by applying it to novel scenarios under the careful guidance of a like-minded tutor. To evaluate your understanding and further practice transferring concepts to new contexts, you complete an online quiz with refined questions either alone or with a group of friends. Four days later you receive specific feedback on your quiz and correct any misconceptions. You then shift gears toward the next topic and begin the process anew. By the end of the course, you gain a better grasp of the material, and hopefully—just hopefully—an appreciation for how pertinent the foundations of psychology are to that enigmatic place called the real world.

Chapter 5

Ciao! Translating Introductory Psychology into a Study Abroad Experience

MAUREEN A. MCCARTHY[1]
Kennesaw State University

Introductory study abroad courses in psychology are delivered using a variety of formats ranging from courses as short as two weeks to those that span an entire 16-week semester to reflect a more comprehensive study abroad experience. In some instances, courses may be offered in a format that includes classroom time prior to departure, or in other instances, lectures and field trips may all occur in the study abroad setting. Increasingly, the introductory psychology course is being offered during study abroad experiences in a variety of countries to fulfill a general education core requirement and is often paired with a set of courses that might be delivered through a study abroad program.

Study abroad programs offer exciting opportunities for teaching introductory psychology in a unique setting, thus allowing for innovative approaches. In this chapter I will offer suggestions for structuring the content, activities, and student learning outcomes, along with practical suggestions for an immersion experience through a study abroad program. Although most of the chapter will reflect experiences from a study abroad program in Italy, study abroad programs generally offer students an opportunity to experience the culture of the country they

[1]I wish to thank Mary Kite, Department of Psychological Science, Ball State University, for her helpful comments and suggestions.

are visiting and to fully apply the principles of psychology to a unique cultural experience.

Study abroad programs may span a full semester, a special mini session, or, more commonly, during an abbreviated summer session. Considering how to organize the scope of content typically covered in an introductory course therefore presents significant challenges. Because the study abroad programs are usually abbreviated, it may be useful to consider a more thematic approach to teaching the course. For example, using the common core framework for introductory psychology (American Psychological Association [APA], 2014), the course can be organized around the five pillars – biological, cognitive, development, social and personality, and mental and physical. This integrated streamlined model provides a topical approach that incorporates the critical content typically comprising the introductory course, and at the same time ensuring that the breadth of the discipline is adequately addressed. Coincidently, the study abroad course that is offered through the Georgia consortium spans a five-week period, so the pillar model of psychology is a useful framework for organizing the content of the course. I will use the five-pillar model throughout this chapter as an organizing framework.

One of the most important things to consider is how to incorporate the cultural dimension of the international setting to capitalize on the study abroad opportunity. Although this cultural experience is critical, for students who may never have left their small region of the United States, the sudden immersion into another culture may be unnerving. So, providing students with the necessary scaffolding to allow them to adjust culturally, along with learning the content of the course, can be achieved by linking the familiar to the unfamiliar. Linking common everyday experiences from the students' home country to comparable experiences in the host country will help students to begin to apply even the most basic of psychological concepts. For example, as students begin their visit, it is helpful to introduce students to a setting that is common in both countries (e.g., grocery store, public transportation, pharmacy) to help them begin to gain an understanding of both the similarities and differences between cultures.

Providing students with an understanding of their place amid the larger world is a useful first step in helping students become oriented. So, I like to begin the course by helping students to understand where they are geographically and how their new location may compare to their home. For example, students may not fully grasp the scale of the size of Italy (the country spans 116,000 square miles) without a specific reference to their personal sense of geography. Placing Italy into perspective relative to their home state will help students to understand the size of the country relative to their own frame of reference. For example, in my home state of Georgia, I explain to students that their own state, 59,000 square miles, is almost half the size of the entire country of Italy. Students can then get a sense of how their home compares to the country they are visiting.

In addition to providing students with a sense of location, it is important to provide a historical context or a relative understanding of the discipline of psychology in the larger scheme of things. For example, the United States is relatively young, especially in comparison to European nations, yet students often have a limited understanding of global history. In other words, the oldest reference students might have made to the past spans approximately 100 years, rather than the thousands of years that are reflected in European nations, and it is difficult for students to grasp entire centuries as a relative span of time. As a second example, drawing on the introductory content of the history of the psychology, the origins of the discipline began in 1879 (Myers & Dewall, 2015). In relative terms, the discipline has been in existence for a little over 100 years. Yet the scientific foundations of the discipline can be traced to the philosophical origins of the discipline, and the beginnings of the science of the world have been studied for centuries before (e.g., Plato, Aristotle, Galileo). When considering the parallels of history, some of the oldest modern structures in the United States are merely 100 years old, closer to the age of the discipline of psychology, while the oldest remaining structure in Italy (Pantheon) was built almost 2,000 years ago. Students will typically visit many historical sites throughout the study abroad experience (e.g., Colosseum, Pantheon, Assisi, Pisa), and it is helpful to remind students of the historical perspective they are experiencing. This comparison of the discipline of psychology relative to the broader field of science may help students grasp the sheer magnitude of a much earlier time. In the following sections of this chapter, I will provide information about how to incorporate field trip experiences and activities with the traditional content of psychology.

PREDEPARTURE PLANNING

To fully be able to grasp cultural differences, it is useful to communicate with students several times prior to departure to prepare the students for a vastly different cultural experience. As indicated earlier in this chapter, it is important to provide students with not only the necessary context for learning but also practical details about travel to a new country. In many instances, a study abroad office may provide this information to students, thus alleviating the need for the faculty member to provide this level of detail. In other cases, individual faculty may be responsible for providing the details about traveling that will help the students make a smooth transition. In either case, it is important to ensure that students are provided with basic information about international travel in order to make their trip safe and enjoyable.

In addition to preparing students to travel, instructors must provide students with appropriate information specific to the course in introductory psychology. So, using the five-pillar format (APA, 2014), predeparture assignments can be developed to provide students with a general overview of the content. For example, prior to departing for the trip, students may be required to complete assignments that allow them to become familiar with the broad structure of the discipline. For example, students may be asked to read the text associated with the biological aspects of behavior (pillar 1), and after reading the chapters they may be asked to complete an assignment about the central nervous system (Appendix 5.1), perhaps imagining how their central nervous system will operate in the country that they will be visiting. In other words, students are merely asked to consider how the biological bases of psychology might apply in a new setting that is unfamiliar.

If instructors use the pillars model, it may be useful to construct a predeparture assignment related to the content of cognition and learning. Students can use the information they have gleaned from reading these chapters prior to departing on the trip, to begin imagining their experience in the study abroad location. For example, students may be required to write a short paper indicating how they will use memory techniques to remember specific locations in their upcoming study abroad experience (Appendix 5.1).

Students often struggle to understand the relative importance of development (pillar 3) as a lifelong process that influences their current daily life. Providing students with a predeparture assignment that helps them reflect upon their early experiences growing up will give them a perspective that they can use as they plan for their study abroad experience (Appendix 5.1). For example, students may be required to reflect on their own personal development and how their experiences may shape their willingness to experience a new environment. Requiring a short essay that links development to an anticipated experience abroad helps students to begin thinking about how the developmental process may influence their travels.

The social and personality pillar provide a rich set of content that students can use to begin thinking about their study abroad experience. For example, students might want to consider how social psychology principles may play a role in how they negotiate an unfamiliar country with a new set of student colleagues (Appendix 5.1). So, students may be asked to write a short paper describing how social loafing may help or hinder the overall travel experience. Asking students to apply terminology from the social psychology domain will help them to incorporate the basic aspects of psychology and provide them with ideas for how to use the content to solve problems they may encounter during the study abroad experience.

Finally, as students prepare for their study abroad experience, they can benefit from readings on stress on health (pillar 5). After reading the assigned chapters, students may be assigned a short paper asking them to consider the role of stress on the immune system as they prepare for the study abroad trip. At the very least, the content associated with stress and health will help students consider the steps they will need to take to have a more productive study abroad experience. It would also be useful to ask the students about their perceived view of positive stress. An additional example may require them to reflect upon the positive aspects of the traveling experience and to explain how positive stress may affect the immune system.

CAPITALIZING ON THE CROSS-CULTURAL OPPORTUNITIES

Although students will complete predeparture assignments that help to prepare them for travel and the study abroad experience, the transition to another culture will be a difficult process for many of the students. A basic orientation to the culture, the daily activities of life, transportation, language, transactions, and other basic skills should also be addressed in orientation sessions prior to departure. Students should also be provided with basic information about cultural mores and expectations about how to navigate an unfamiliar culture prior to departure.

Introducing students to cultural differences prior to departure provides students with the practical information they need to travel and an introduction to discussions surrounding cross-cultural differences. Cross-cultural psychology has evolved as a central element in the undergraduate psychology curriculum. In the initial version of the undergraduate guidelines (APA, 2007), one of the ten goals specified sociocultural and international awareness as critical to the curriculum. In the revision of the guidelines (2013), cross-cultural awareness is infused across each of the five goals for the undergraduate major. So rather than devoting a single goal to cross-cultural issues, the emphasis is on incorporating the role of culture as a central element to the discipline (Dunn et al., 2010) across each of the five undergraduate goals.

A parallel evolution has occurred in the introductory psychology course. Keith (2011) noted that introductory textbooks 50 years ago included very little in terms of cross-cultural psychology. Today the influence of culture is referenced in almost all chapters of most introductory psychology texts. With this increase in references to cross-cultural psychology, the study abroad experience also provides an opportunity to emphasize the cultural aspects of the discipline within an entirely different cultural milieu. For example, when discussing the topic of emotion, it might be possible to ask students to conduct observations of individuals in a public setting during a field trip when students are studying abroad. Asking students to record the emotions that they see expressed in the public setting in a country such as Italy may help them to understand that there are basic emotions that extend across cultures. In other words, a study abroad experience provides an opportunity to more fully realize the cross-cultural elements of psychology through a rich immersive experience.

STUDYING ABROAD

Thus far I have discussed the planning and activities that might be useful in preparing students to embark on the travel abroad experience. Upon reaching the study abroad location, each program operates in a slightly different manner, but field trips, or visits to important cultural sights, are common. For example, in my university we hold a traditional class lecture two days a week and we take students on field trips two days each week. The entire experience lasts five weeks and provides students an opportunity to experience the daily activities of living in a rural Italian community. The field trips include cultural and historical sites that are important for any traveler to visit and in all likelihood the study abroad program will schedule visits for the entire group. In our case, we typically visit several United Nations Educational, Scientific, and Cultural Organization (UNESCO) World Heritage sites (e.g., Rome, Siena, Assisi, Pisa) that could reasonably be reached from the study abroad base. Some sites are critical to an understanding of the larger culture of the country and are important regardless of the specific course content (e.g., Colosseum, Vatican, Uffizi).

However, it is not always possible to link visits to cities as directly to psychological content as other courses (e.g., history, art). But it is possible to link the content of psychology in everyday life to the cultural experience of visiting cities in the study abroad locations. For example, I provide students with the basic principles of psychology using a lecture or seminar format. During the typical classroom time I discussed with students how these principles translate to experiences in real life. Then I select lesser known but related areas of the respective cities that would allow for discussion of the principles. For example, cemeteries offer opportunities to discuss cultural practices in the range of developmental psychology. So, we visited the typical mausoleums that are present in some of the well-known cities (e.g., Rome, Assisi, Pisa), a cemetery for local townspeople, and the Capuchin crypt of the Franciscan monks (Rome). These visits provide a range of cultural experiences that are intriguing to students and provide a rich opportunity for discussion.

Regardless of the field trips that might be planned, I retain the pillar framework of organization to guide the course throughout the time we are traveling. Short assignments are assigned each week to help students engage with the material. Appendix 5.2 includes example assignments that can be used during the study abroad experience.

Beginning with pillar 1 (biological), I provide students with short lectures and ask them to build on their predeparture assignment relating the central nervous system to functioning in an entirely new environment. Sensation and perception are natural extensions of this basic biological content. So, it is possible to use some of the typical activities from a traditional classroom experience and employ them in the study abroad setting. For example, I asked students to navigate a steep uneven path and to describe the various elements of the brain that were operating as they navigated the streets of Montepulciano, Italy.

If one considers the scientific nature of the discipline as a broad discipline that includes psychology, artifacts of science are present in various European locations, thus providing many opportunities to link field trips to the discipline. For example, although not a psychologist, Galileo developed scientific methods and created tools for the study of math, physics, and astronomy. So, one possible field trip might entail visiting the Galileo museum in Florence, Italy, and discussing the role of science and methodologies to the more specific study of psychological science. In advance of visiting the museum, it is possible to find information through online sources or from in-depth travel guides.

It may also be possible to ask students to engage in an activity that capitalizes on the sensation and perception processes. Many European countries are replete with important art works and Italy is no exception. Although art collections may not be explicitly psychological, if one thinks in terms of a general humanities course, artistic works offer a host of opportunities to discuss perception in a unique setting. For example, I ask students to identify the monocular and binocular depth cues that they use to perceive the ornate elements of art in several of the basilicas in cities across Italy. With the help of my colleagues in the arts, I also discussed with students why early art that did not incorporate monocular depth cues (e.g., texture gradient) did not seem to reflect the correct perceptual dimensions that were present in later works of art.

Students may also have the opportunity to consider the research on cultural differences in the perception of basic elements of color or depth perception. For example, Phillips (2011) provides a comprehensive analysis of perceptual differences between cultures. He reviews the cultural differences that exist with regard to color, thus students can benefit from considering the cultural differences that influence perception. For example, people from African cultures performed better on the Müller-Lyer illusion than did Europeans or Americans. Similarly, individuals who grew up in rural cultures (e.g., Guam, Morocco) performed better than Americans on the Ponzo illusion task. Conversely, people with formal schooling are able to interpret 3D images better than people from cultures with limited formal schooling. In other words, students can be encouraged to consider cultural differences that may influence perception across cultures.

Cognitive psychology, the second introductory psychology pillar, offers many opportunities to discuss a cross-cultural influence on what might otherwise be perceived as uniform mental processes. First, it is important to provide students with a basic introduction to each of the areas of cognition (i.e., cognition, memory, perception). The study abroad experience also provides an opportunity to introduce the role of culture in shaping cognitions. Students could begin by reflecting on the cultural perspective (collectivistic versus individualistic) of the country they are visiting and then reflect on how their personal reality may shape their perceptions of the culture they are experiencing. For example, Italy is primarily an individualistic culture in which individuals work to address their personal versus collective needs. Working with the historians that comprised the team of scholars teaching during the study abroad session, students learned that Italians were similar to Americans in this particular respect. Students may also consider the prominent role of Catholicism in the culture of the Italian community. Almost every town has a duomo (an Italian church or cathedral) located near the heart of the town. This strong religious presence is influential in virtually all of the customs and activities of the town.

Cole and Packer (2011) review a number of studies that highlight the differences in cognition that are largely due to different systems of thought that are reflective of cultures. For example, discussion of change or inattentional blindness is a popular topic frequently taught in introductory psychology. In essence, this phenomenon occurs when an observer fails to notice a change in a visual stimulus (Simons & Chabris, 1999). Cole and Packer suggest that research indicates that Asians more accurately detect changes in the background, which is the element of change blindness that regularly tricks entire classes into missing the dancing gorilla. Students might wish to consider how a specific cognitive psychology principle may differ across cultures.

Although physical development occurs in a somewhat predictable pattern (i.e., aging), context and culture significantly affect overall development throughout the life span. If using the predeparture assignments, students may have been encouraged to think about their personal experience growing up relative to the parenting styles of their caregivers. Then during the study abroad experience, students can begin to consider the cultural differences that might influence development in the country they are visiting. For example, Molitor and Hsu (2011) suggest that attachment theory and, by extension, parenting styles may not be universal constructs. Students may want to observe parental interactions during the study abroad experience in a public forum as a way of evaluating the role of culture on the developmental process. For example, during a field trip to a public market or similar venue, students might be encouraged to develop an operational definition of maternal proximity to toddlers. Recording these data for both native members of the culture and visitors might yield differences that could be discussed as possible contributors to attachment.

Pillar 4, social psychology, offers the widest range of options for discussing the role of cultural diversity in an introductory study abroad course. Cultural and social norms are quite different. Early in the trip it is important to begin orienting students to the specific cultural mores of the region. For example, a period of "reposo" occurs every afternoon in many parts of Italy, so students need to be prepared for this time of rest each afternoon because stores are closed and it will not be possible to complete business transactions. Merely shopping for basic supplies is also quite different. For example, shopkeepers will not allow people to touch produce, and this same prohibition is in place at grocery stores. If someone wants to select produce, they must place a plastic glove on their hand to make the selection. Thus a basic orientation to cultural traditions offers an opportunity to discuss the basic principles of social psychology.

More specifically, students learn that people ascribe behaviors to attributions that they make about people and behaviors. Introductory psychology courses often discuss these attributions as the basis for a host of social psychology principles including fundamental attribution error, stereotyping, social loafing, or self-serving bias. It is important to note that Koenig and Dean (2011) suggest that cultural differences exist in how someone makes an internal or external attribution. Further, they suggest that these differences are multifaceted rather than merely the result of individualistic versus collectivistic in dimension. To help students begin to understand the cultural dimensions that might play a role in attribution theory, students might be asked to consider the actions of an individual in a public setting during a field trip. For example, in larger cities it is common for people to rush in ahead of others. It can be useful to ask students to consider why this type of behavior is common and whether it is an internal or an external attribution.

Individual differences and heritability of traits were among the key debates that were popular in the 1860s. Cimino and Foschi (2014) in their historical chronicle of Italian psychology describe the tensions between the northern and southern Italians during this era. Thus it is possible to link some of the current stereotypes associated with regionalism in the United States to similar phenomena that have historically occurred in Italy. In fact some of these same stereotypes persist in the Italian culture today with northern Italians eschewing southern Italians.

Health psychology, pillar 5, offers an opportunity for students to consider their personal worldview and their future of physical and psychological health. It is important to educate students about the similarities that all humans share and that some emotions are universal (Matsumoto & Hwang, 2011) in nature (i.e., anger, disgust, fear, joy, sadness, surprise). A discussion of emotion and health allows for a broader exploration of the underlying reasons for expression of emotion. Students may also be able to identify the cross-cultural differences that might be beneficial in their own health and well-being. For example, walking is a primary mode of transportation in many locations around the world. Not only does exercise promote better physical health, but also the endorphins produced by exercise contribute to greater cognitive health, physical health, happiness, and generally improved functioning. In a sense, this final discussion allows students to begin to integrate the content from across the five pillars into a more global understanding of human behavior. It may also be possible to ask students to compare and contrast the definition of "la dolce vita" or good life between the American and Italian cultures.

TRANSITIONING HOME

Students participating in a study abroad program have almost always described their experience as transformative. Although it is important to teach about the principles of introductory psychology, the study abroad context provides students with an opportunity to develop an appreciation for the global world in which they live. This kind of growth does not emerge simply as a result of the content that is taught during the study abroad experience, but more likely as a result of being immersed in a culture very different from their own. It is important to help students realize this growth.

Instructors frequently create activities to put closure on a course. One way to bring closure to the study abroad experience, along with encouraging students to begin the transition back to their home campus, is to ask them to reflect on the differences in daily activities between the cultures. For example, students might be asked to read Bill Bryson's (1999) chapter in *Coming Home*, and reflect on the differences. Students might write a short paper that will help them to identify the differences and how these differences affected their ability to assimilate into the new culture.

In sum, the study abroad experience is an opportunity of a lifetime. Not only do students learn about the discipline, but they also enjoy a rich cultural experience that cannot be gained any other way. Thus faculty must make every effort to thoroughly immerse the students in the culture of the host country and in the reintegration to the home campus (Berdan, 2015).

Appendix 5.1

Predeparture Assignments

ASSIGNMENT ONE (BIOLOGICAL PSYCHOLOGY)

Read the chapter on biological psychology. Think about your arrival in the city of Montepulciano, Italy. Explain how each of the structures of the brain will work to assist in your initial experience in this new environment. Be sure to identify each of the brain structures and explain how they will work in the context of the new environment.

ASSIGNMENT TWO (COGNITION AND MEMORY)

Read the chapter that pertains to memory and learning. Then using the Atkinson and Shiffrin model (Myers & Dewall, 2015), explain how memory actually works. Consider the experiences you will have in Rome, Italy. Using the model presented in the text, explain the process that would need to take place in order for you to remember key aspects of the Vatican. Be sure to identify each of the processes in your explanation.

ASSIGNMENT THREE (DEVELOPMENT)

Read the development chapter. Consider your experience as a child and the type of parenting style that you parents may have used. Identify the parenting style you experienced and provide evidence of the parenting style. Then explain how the parenting style may influence your study abroad experience.

ASSIGNMENT FOUR
(SOCIAL AND PERSONALITY)

Read the social psychology chapter. Consider the planning that will need to occur for a weekend excursion with a group of colleagues while on the study abroad experience. Explain how you will maximize social facilitation, minimize social loafing, and minimize groupthink. Explain each of the terms in your answer and link the explanations to the terms.

Imagine you become separated from the group. Using psychological principles, what strategies might you use to become reunited with the group. Do not limit your responses to the content from a single chapter of the text.

ASSIGNMENT FIVE (MENTAL AND
PHYSICAL HEALTH)

Read the stress and health chapter. Consider the stress that your colleagues may be experiencing while on this trip. Write an essay for your colleague that describes the role of stress on the immune system. Provide suggestions for ways in which stress can be alleviated.

Appendix 5.2

On-Site Assignments

ASSIGNMENT ONE (BIOLOGICAL BASES)

Imagine that you at your sitting on the piazza in Montepulciano. Out of the corner of your eye, you spot someone that you are seriously attracted to. Describe what happens to your body as you experience the excitement (i.e., parasympathetic and sympathetic nervous system).

Eventually the person of interest leaves the piazza and you decide to complete this assignment. What are the "older brain structures"? Provide a brief description of what each structure is doing in your brain as you sit there typing. What does each lobe of the cerebral cortex do? How is each lobe operating as you record your responses?

ASSIGNMENT TWO (LEARNING AND COGNITION)

Part One: Identify an operant conditioning experience that you have observed while on the trip to Assisi or Pisa. Describe the example with the specific psychological terminology and the type of reinforcement.

Part Two: Identify a problem that you encountered during one of the field trips. Using cognitive psychology terminology, explain how you might employ strategies to solve the problem.

ASSIGNMENT THREE (DEVELOPMENT)

What do twin and adoption studies tell us about the relative roles of nature and nurture on who a person is? Explain the role of nature and nurture in the development of a person who is a native of Italy but is adopted in the United States. For example, explain the developmental behaviors that are likely to be constant across cultures and those that are likely to be distinct.

ASSIGNMENT FOUR (SOCIAL)

Explain the concept of fundamental attribution error. Identify a particular experience that you have had during this travel abroad trip and explain how you may have engaged in a fundamental attribution error. Be sure to clearly identify each of the internal and external attribution features. How does the fundamental attribution error differ across cultures?

ASSIGNMENT FIVE (STRESS AND HEALTH)

Think about a stressful experience that you encountered while on this trip. Briefly describe what happened, and then explain how the general adaptation syndrome applied to your experience. Explain how you dealt with the stressful experience (e.g., Did you experience fear paralysis? Did you see the tend-and-befriend response?).

Identify five strategies that can be used to deal with stress. Explain how you might employ each strategy to deal with a stressful experience in the future. For example, is there a particular cognitive strategy that you might regularly employ in your life in the future?

Chapter 6

Using Integrative Concepts as a Theme in Introductory Psychology

ANN E. NORDMEYER, BRIDGETTE MARTIN
HARD, AND JAMES G. GROSS
Stanford University

Introductory psychology courses differ in many ways. Some take place over a ten-week quarter, while others are two semesters long. Some are offered as large lecture courses with hundreds of students and a rigid timetable of topics, whereas others are small and intimate with plenty of flexibility. Some are general education courses that are intended to be accessible to all students, while others are honors-track courses designed for prospective psychology majors. In many ways, two students at different institutions might have very different experiences taking introductory psychology.

Despite these important differences, one common feature of nearly all psychology courses is the relatively wide range of topics they cover in a short period of time. In the span of just a few months, students learn concepts from most or all of the major subdomains of psychology. Although some instructors choose to eliminate some subset of topics from their syllabus (e.g., developmental psychology, social psychology), many aspire to cover the "entire field" of psychology, recognizing that, for many students, this course will be their only contact with the discipline. Because concepts from psychology have applications to a variety of fields both inside and outside of academia, including medicine, law, business, product design, education, and many others, it seems important for instructors to share with students as much as they can from the full breadth of the field. Thus, when students take an introductory psychology course, they are exposed to a level of intellectual diversity that they may experience in few other courses.

This breadth of content is an appealing aspect of psychology for many students, but it can be overwhelming as well. One common approach to reducing this overload is to segment content according to major subfields, spending a few lectures each discussing biological, cognitive, affective, developmental, social, personality, clinical, and health psychology. This segmentation is encouraged by the standard structure of textbooks (see Griggs & Jackson, 2013) and seems sensible, given that it breaks down the vast amount of information that instructors convey to students, organizing knowledge into more manageable units. This segmentation also previews the likely topics of higher level psychology courses that students might take.

One downside of this approach, however, is that it can give students the misleading impression that subfields of psychology are conceptually separate entities. Rather than coming to appreciate the unity of the field of psychology, students may come to see the field as a collection of unconnected subfields that have little to say to each other. This approach may lead them to miss the relevance of a study they have learned about in a "memory" context to issues surrounding "development" (or culture, etc.). As "experts" in psychology, instructors know how richly interconnected psychology's subfields are, and appreciate the value in being able to think about psychology in an integrative way. Understanding connections across domains allows psychology experts to generate novel hypotheses and richer explanations for psychological phenomena (Ceci & Liker, 1986; Chase & Simon, 1973; McKeithen, Reitman, Reuter, & Hirtle, 1981).

To help students see content the way that they, the experts, do, instructors need to explicitly teach them the connections that we perceive between different subfields. Doing so has several benefits. Helping students to recognize connections that experts perceive between different areas of psychology can improve students' ability to retain specific content. Evidence suggests that people who learn an interconnected set of facts have an easier time recognizing those facts compared to people who learn a set of unrelated facts (Bradshaw & Anderson, 1982; Smith, Adams, & Schorr, 1978). Furthermore, to the extent that recognizing connections leads to a more abstract understanding of content, teaching students to recognize connections may also augment their ability to transfer their understanding to new problems. In a relevant study, students who were given more abstract explanations of a task showed greater transfer of knowledge when asked to solve a similar task, even though these abstract explanations were initially more confusing to them (Hinds, Patterson, & Pfeffer, 2001). Thus, when students understand the relationship between different subfields of psychology, they may be more likely both to retain material and to transfer their understanding to new domains.

Psychology experts can help their introductory psychology students build connections between different subfields of psychology with a course "theme" of integrative concepts that connect content across multiple domains. These integrative concepts are overarching ideas that are illustrated in multiple subdomains of psychology. We use many different integrative concepts in our introductory

TABLE 6.1   Sample Integrative Concepts Used in Psychology One at Stanford University

1. Human thoughts, feelings, and behaviors are determined in part not only by inner forces but also by outer forces, and finally by the interaction of inner and outer forces.

2. Much of who a person is is determined by forces outside of that person's awareness or control.

3. Human minds construct reality, and because the minds are flexible, humans have the power to change their reality.

4. Just because something about human behavior is "natural" does not mean it is necessarily good or even adaptive. Most psychological processes are adaptive in some situations but maladaptive in others.

5. Malfunctions or breakdowns in thinking, feeling, and behavior illuminate how psychological systems work.

psychology course at Stanford University (commonly called "Psychology One"). Table 6.1 presents a few of these concepts.

Integrative concepts correspond to important takeaways or what McTighe and Wiggins (1999) described as "enduring understandings." These are ideas that students will ideally retain long after the course has ended, because they change the way that students think about their everyday experiences. We hope that students will leave our course with an appreciation of the role of psychology in their everyday lives, and a new perspective on their own and others' thoughts and behaviors. By introducing these integrative concepts, our goal is to synthesize content in a way that will make it easier for students to carry these ideas with them beyond the classroom.

TEACHING INTEGRATIVE CONCEPTS

There are several ways to organize a course around integrative concepts. Because these concepts are implicitly present in many different areas of psychology, one approach is to teach a course without mentioning these concepts explicitly, and hope that students identify them on their own. At the other extreme, these integrative concepts can be used to guide course design from the very beginning. Instructors might select a collection of integrative concepts to be used as learning goals, and use these goals to guide the selection of course content, readings, and other assignments. In our Psychology One course at Stanford, we take an intermediate approach. By selecting integrative concepts that arise naturally out of the content that we teach, we can incorporate these concepts by simply drawing students' attention to them as they come up throughout the course. This approach allows integrative concepts to be incorporated into most traditional introductory psychology courses without a complete course overhaul.

In the sections that follow, we will explore the teaching of integrative concepts in detail by focusing on one concept in particular as a case study of our approach. This is a concept that we find to be central to psychology and that we make central to our course: Psychology is determined in part not only by what is inside of people but also by what is outside of them, and most importantly by how those two things interact. First, we will lay out the logic and value of this integrative concept. We will then discuss ways to draw out a concept like this one in lectures and in smaller group settings.

The Importance of the Integrative Concept
of Internal-External Interaction

In the field of psychology, experts often discuss the role of internal forces (e.g., implicit/unconscious processes) and external forces (e.g., the situation/context/culture) in shaping one's thoughts, feelings, and behaviors. It is important for students to realize that these forces are not mutually exclusive; that is, both internal and external forces are simultaneously involved in producing thoughts, feelings, and behaviors, and if students want to understand the mind, they must understand how these forces interact with each other.

This integrative concept connects with much, if not most, of the content in psychology. Indeed, there are psychological phenomena and classic studies that illustrate this concept in every subarea of psychology (see Table 6.2). This concept is present when we discuss the relationship between nature and nurture in shaping how people develop and change across time. It is also present when we discuss the relationship between the *person* and the *situation* in determining how people will think, feel, or behave in any given moment.

This integrative concept has practical relevance to students' everyday lives. Because this concept relates to the internal and external forces that govern students' own behavior, as well as that of others around them (e.g., classmates, parents, roommates), it has the potential to enhance self- and other-awareness long after students have received their final grades. This feature makes this integrative concept what psychologists would call an "enduring understanding," according to McTighe and Wiggins (1999).

Often, students are unaware of many of the internal forces that shape the way they and others think, feel, and behave. For example, specific beliefs or "mindsets" about the nature of intelligence can shape how people interpret academic challenges, and changing these implicit beliefs can influence academic outcomes. In an intervention designed to change students' beliefs about intelligence, students who were encouraged to see intelligence as a malleable trait (instead of fixed and unchanging) received better grades in a math class compared to students in a control group (Blackwell, Trzesniewski, & Dweck, 2007). Similarly, internal expectations about healing can interact with external medical treatments to make them more effective (i.e., the placebo effect; Benedetti et al., 2003). Recognizing how these internal factors shape one's behavior and interact with situations can be quite illuminating.

Students also underestimate or are unaware of the influence of external forces on thoughts, feelings, and behavior. Indeed, it is known that people make common errors in their perception of other people, and even of themselves. The fundamental attribution error (Ross, 1977) describes the tendency to assume that behavior is caused by internal influences, and to ignore the potential role of

T A B L E 6 . 2 Examples of Lecture Content Connected to the Theme of Internal/External Interaction (see Table 6.1, point 1)

Topic	Concept	Specific Examples
Research methods	Task demands	The classic story of "Clever Hans," which demonstrates the potential for an "experimenter" (Hans's owner Wilhlem Von Osten) to inadvertently influence the outcome of an experiment if the situational context is not carefully controlled.
Evolutionary psychology	Sex differences in mate selection	Although men and women differ in their overall level of choosiness and desired qualities in a mate, culture can exaggerate or minimize these differences (e.g., Kasser & Sharma, 1999).
Brain/nervous system	Neural plasticity	London taxicab drivers have greater hippocampal volume the longer they have been driving (Maguire et al., 2000).
Sensation and perception	Perceptual illusions	The Müller-Lyer illusion is stronger or weaker depending on cultural context (Segall, Campbell, & Herskovits, 1966).
Learning: classical and instrumental conditioning	Biological constraints on learning	The Garcia effect, or taste aversion learning, illustrates that animals (including humans) are predisposed to associate certain events (a particular flavor) with certain outcomes (getting sick; Garcia, Lasiter, Bermudez-Rattoni, & Deems, 1985).
Memory	Misinformation effect	Human memories are actively constructed based on their subjective, internal experience of an event. But their memories are additionally shaped by information that comes from the social world, including information supplied by their friends who shared in an experience, and even *misinformation* supplied by tricky experimenters (e.g., Loftus & Palmer, 1974).
Language	Perceptual narrowing of phonemes	From birth, infants are able to discriminate between a wide variety of different phonemes, but as they get more experience with their native language, they become more sensitive to differences that are meaningful in that language and less sensitive to differences that are not meaningful in that language (Werker & Tees, 1984).
Emotion	Two-factor theory of emotion	People interpret their internal physiological arousal differently in different contexts, suggesting that emotional experience depends on assessing both one's internal state and also on external factors (Dutton & Aron, 1974).
Social psychology	The fundamental attribution error	The fundamental attribution error is the tendency to assume that another person's behavior is caused by internal influences, ignoring the potential role of external/situational influences (Ross, 1977). This assumption is more common in individuals from Western cultures (Miller, 1984).
Development	Attachment	Internal factors (temperament) and external factors (maternal responsiveness) interact in the development of different attachment styles. Intervening on maternal responsiveness leads to increased secure attachment in high risk infants (Van den Boom, 1994).
Psychopathology	The diathesis-stress conception	Mental illness is argued to arise from an interaction of a *diathesis*, or predisposition (often genetic) and environmental stress. For example, a study by Caspi et al. (2003) found that risk for developing depression could be predicted based on the interaction of particular alleles and number of stressful life events.

external or situational influences. Students living in a Western cultural context are especially likely to make this error in explaining their own and others' actions (Miller, 1984). For these students, learning about the power of situational forces and their capacity to interact with internal forces can be a real "a-ha!" moment. By forcing them to consider that others' actions can be dramatically shaped by situational forces, students may experience greater compassion and willingness to help others, as well as more positive attitudes toward negatively stereotyped groups (Vescio, Sechrist, & Paolucci, 2003). Furthermore, this concept can help students become aware that surrounding contexts influence their own behavior, sometimes without their awareness, and to recognize ways that they can change their situation to maximize effective behaviors.

An additional reason that this integrative concept is so important is that it can guide students in thinking critically about empirical research. Psychological science often aims to reveal or explore some internal process that drives behavior, independent of context. But of course the cultural context in which a study is conducted can dramatically affect the results. Due to the convenience of collecting data in a university setting, much of psychological research is based on studies that focus on W.E.I.R.D. —Western, educated, industrialized, rich, and democratic—cultures (Henrich, Heine, & Norenzayan, 2010). Instructors can ask their students to consider the generalizability of this research. Additionally, the experimental setting is itself a context that can influence behavior (i.e., task demands), sometimes in unintended ways. Does a person's behavior in the lab necessarily reflect how people act in the real world? Critical consumers of scientific research should consider how the cultural context and the experimental context might affect people's behavior and color the interpretation and generalizability of experimental findings.

Critical consumers of research should also consider individual differences. Some research is aimed at identifying or exploring particular contexts and their influence on behavior. In these studies, individual differences due to internal factors (e.g., biological sex, age) can interact with the effects of particular contexts. Does the same context influence men and women equally? What about older and younger adults? Instructors can create more critical consumers of scientific research by encouraging students to apply this integrative concept when evaluating evidence.

Drawing Out the Internal-External Interaction
Concept in Lecture

In Psychology One, we weave multiple integrative concepts throughout a fairly traditional course structure. Students meet for three 75-minute lecture periods each week. Each lecture focuses on content from a specific subfield of psychology and corresponding chapter in a textbook. Within each lecture, we work to connect specific content to one or more integrative concepts as they emerge throughout the course. In this way, we draw on a wide variety of content and use many different integrative concepts to show students the connections between different subfields.

In our course, lectures necessarily cover a small percentage of the content found in the students' textbook (and in psychology at large). Deciding which content to include in lectures can be quite daunting, and instructors use many factors to guide their decisions. We have found that integrative concepts make it easier to make content choices. When selecting between two possible ideas or studies to present in a lecture, we prioritize the one that connects to one of the integrative concepts that we highlight in our course.

When we teach content relevant to an integrative concept, we make sure to explicitly draw students' attention to that concept. Let us consider again the integrative concept of internal–external interaction. In all cases, we try to highlight the importance of both internal and external forces, but either internal or external forces might take center stage, depending on students' preconceived beliefs about how a particular aspect of psychology works. In some cases, we highlight the unexpected influence of external forces in processes that students think of in everyday life as being mostly driven by internal forces. In others, we emphasize the surprising role that internal forces play in a process students think of as largely externally driven. And in all cases, we try to highlight *interactions* between the internal and external forces: How internal forces will determine behavior *depends* on what is going on in the environment and the situation, and vice versa. Let us expand on a few examples.

First, in teaching students about the human brain, something we do in lecture within the second week of the quarter, we necessarily convey the universality in basic brain structures (e.g., the cortical lobes, structures of the subcortex) and their general functions. The remarkable similarity in brain structure and function across humans is, largely, internally caused by the genetic and evolutionary history that all humans share. Students are accustomed to thinking of biological structures, like the brain, in this way, and they are often bombarded by news headlines proclaiming that some psychological process is "hard wired." Given that students will readily assume that the human brain is largely shaped by internal, genetic forces, we also take care to underscore the brain's plasticity—its ability to respond and adapt to different experiences. One study we describe to illustrate this point is Maguire et al.'s (2000) study of London taxicab drivers, in which drivers with the most experience navigating circuitous London streets were found to have the largest volume in the posterior hippocampus, a region believed to be responsible for storing spatial representations of environments. This example can help students recognize the important role that experience plays in shaping the brain, disabusing students of the notion that the brain's capacity is entirely driven by unchanging internal forces.

A second example comes from the study of attachment, which is usually presented in a lecture on social development. After presenting students with the basic structure of the strange situation test and different attachment styles (Ainsworth & Bell, 1970; Ainsworth, Blehar, Waters, & Wall, 1978), we typically ask students what they think might drive differences in the quality of attachment that children develop. Students typically jump to possible external causes, namely parenting and especially parental responsiveness. We present some research confirming this intuition by Johnson, Dweck, and Chen (2007) that is consistent with the view that securely attached infants expect their parents to be more responsive than infants with insecure attachment styles.

Next we encourage students to think about factors besides parenting that might matter, and share the fact that infants with irritable temperaments, who tend to have a lower threshold for getting upset (largely due to genetics), are at greater risk for developing an insecure attachment style with a primary caregiver. Van den Boom (1994) hypothesized that temperament (an internal factor) predicts poorer attachment, depending on how it interacts with the environment (an external factor): Irritable infants get upset more often and are more difficult to soothe, leading to reduced responsiveness, an environmental factor that, as we have seen, correlates with insecure attachment style. The researchers tested whether intervening at the level of the parents' responsiveness could prevent an infant's temperament from leading to insecure attachment. The researchers identified 6- to 9-month-old infants with irritable temperaments. The mothers of half of these irritable infants were randomly assigned to receive extra training in responding sensitively to their infants. Months later, when the infants' attachment styles were measured, twice as many infants in the experimental condition developed a secure attachment compared to infants in the control condition who did not partake in the intervention. In fact, the irritable infants developed secure attachments at rates similar to average infants. This example helps students recognize the intertwined nature of internal and external factors in development, and in particular raises questions about how psychologists can intervene on those factors to change outcomes.

A third example comes from the Schachter-Singer model of emotion processing (Schachter & Singer, 1962). The Schachter-Singer theory posits that there are two factors involved in the processing of emotions: the physiological response and the subjective interpretation of that response based on the surrounding context. In lecture, we teach students about the famous "bridge study" (Dutton & Aron, 1974), in which male participants were approached by a female experimenter while crossing either a frightening suspension bridge or a more stable and less frightening bridge. Participants filled out a survey and were told that they could contact the experimenter if they had further questions. Male participants who were on the frightening bridge (and therefore experienced more physical arousal) were more likely to contact the experimenter than participants who were on the less frightening bridge, presumably because they interpreted their physiological response as being due to their attraction to the experimenter, rather than fear from being on the bridge. This example demonstrates to students how internal factors (the physiological response) and external factors (the surrounding context) interact to produce familiar emotions.

Drawing Out the Internal-External Interaction Concept in Section

We also use weekly discussion sections as an opportunity to connect specific content to integrative concepts. Students meet weekly in small groups of about 12 students for a 50-minute discussion section. In these discussion sections, a trained teaching fellow (either an advanced undergraduate or a PhD student) leads students through discussion and activities that give students an opportunity to experience lecture and textbook content in a hands-on way and to apply course content to new situations and problems. Teaching fellows are encouraged to develop section plans that enhance content covered in lecture, rather than simply reviewing content. One way that section leaders can enhance content is by helping students identify and reflect on integrative concepts. Next, we focus again on the theme of internal-external interaction to highlight how a discussion section can be used to draw out multiple aspects of an integrative concept.

In a discussion section that occurs the same week that students learn about the Schachter-Singer (1962) theory in lecture, students are led through activities and discussions that allow them to connect course content to the integrative concept of internal-external interaction and see its *usefulness* in analyzing and solving new problems. Section leaders might begin with an engaging demonstration of the "facial feedback hypothesis." In this activity, half of the class is asked to hold a pen in their mouth with only their teeth touching the pen (inducing a smiling facial expression), and the other half of the class is told to hold a pen in their mouth with pursed lips (inducing a frowning facial expression). Students then watch a funny clip (e.g., a short comedy skit) and are asked to rate how amusing they found the clip. Replicating findings from Strack, Martin, and Stepper (1988), students who hold the pen in a way that forces their face into a smile tend to rate the clip as funnier compared to the frowning students. This activity provides a platform for students to review the different theories of emotion and reflect on how their own internal states (feeling their facial muscles in a particular configuration) interacted with context (the video being watched), influencing their feelings of amusement.

After discussing the results of the demonstration, section leaders broaden the discussion by asking "Could you, on purpose, change how you are interpreting your internal state in relation to the surrounding context and thereby change your emotional experience?" This question allows students to reflect on moments in their own lives that they could reappraise their emotional state. Students often suggest that smiling more even when they are feeling sad or anxious might lead them to feel happier/less stressed, a direct application of the facial feedback demonstration. If students do not generate additional examples on their own, instructors could prompt them to think about different contexts: What if you are feeling anxious about an exam? Could you reinterpret the physical feeling of stress to help yourself get "pumped up" to study? How do you think this would affect your performance on the exam? At the end of section, discussion leaders could introduce students to scientific studies that have examined these questions (Jamieson, Mendes, Blackstock, & Schmader, 2010), helping to link students' intuitions to experimental evidence. Activities and discussions like this are intended to show students the relevance and power of the integrative concept: Understanding the nature of the internal and external causes of their experience can give them the power to change their experience.

After this discussion, section leaders might coach students to apply their understanding of internal-external interaction in emotion to solving a practical problem. Section leaders accomplish this by transitioning to a discussion of the Storms and Nisbett (1970) study of participants with insomnia. In this study, participants were given placebo pills and were told that the pills would either increase or decrease arousal. Their counterintuitive results were in line with the Schachter-Singer (1962) theory of emotion: Participants who were told that the pills *increase* arousal reported *decreased* difficulty sleeping, presumably because they were able to attribute their feelings of arousal to a different cause than their insomnia, which reduced feelings of worry and helped them fall asleep faster. Participants who were told that the pills should *decrease* arousal reported a worsening of their insomnia, because they expected their physiological arousal to be reduced by the drug and were even more concerned than usual by their level of arousal. Thus, understanding the particular internal and external forces that drive emotional experience gave experimenters the power to change emotional experience to help those suffering from insomnia.

The discussion section can also be a place for students to use the integrative concept to connect different content areas in the course. After discussing the Storms and Nisbett (1970) study, the section leader can help students apply their new understanding to other subfields of psychology, such as intelligence and the experience of stereotype threat (e.g., people who are reminded of a negative stereotype about a group that they belong to experienced increased anxiety leading to lower performance on the stereotyped task [Steele & Aronson, 1995]). After briefly reviewing these concepts from a previous lecture, the section leader can help students integrate these ideas by asking: "Could you design a study that applies the logic of the insomnia study to try to reduce the experience of stereotype threat?" When students have brainstormed methods to study this, the section leader can tell them about a real study that did just this (Ben-Zeev, Fein, & Inzlicht, 2005), allowing students to compare their designs to a real study. This activity gives students a chance to review content from another topic and practice experiment design and provides a concrete example of how the integrative concept unifies different areas of psychology.

ASSESSING INTEGRATIVE CONCEPTS

How do instructors know that students are learning anything about integrative concepts? What assessments can they use to test their understanding? Psychology One is a large lecture course with a "traditional" exam structure. Students complete two midterms, composed of about 50–60 multiple-choice questions and one or two written answer questions. They also complete a final exam, composed of about 60 multiple-choice questions and a final essay.

Midterm Exams

We work to build several opportunities into our exams for students to reflect on integrative concepts and support them using their own choice of evidence from the course. A sample exam question is shown in Figure 6.1. In this question, students are asked to reflect on the role of context in psychological processes, which is an important aspect of the concept of internal-external interaction.

We have seen many times in this part of the course that context (e.g., the immediate situation, environment, culture) plays a role in a number of psychological processes. *Choose only FOUR* of the topics listed below, and for each, *give an example of a study, finding, or concrete example* from class (from lecture, section, or the textbook) that illustrates how context can shape a person's thoughts, behaviors, or abilities.

1) Memory

2) Thinking

3) Language

4) Intelligence

5) Emotion and motivation

6) Social psychology (social influence, social cognition)

7) Altruism

You do not need to write in essay form; **3–4 *detailed* sentences per example** should be sufficient. Be sure to *describe or define a study, finding, or concrete example* from class and explain the role that context plays; do not just name a psychological phenomenon.

FIGURE 6.1 Sample written answer question on midterm exam.

Note that the question requires students to not only show their understanding of the integrative concept within each example but also choose examples from multiple chapters and lectures, thus forcing them to integrate content from different subareas of psychology. Students do not have to write in essay format on this question, and they usually do well.

Final Exam

At the end of the quarter, students are asked to take a step further in demonstrating their understanding of integrative concepts. On the final exam, students write an integrative essay that counts for 10 percent of their overall course grade. As shown in Figure 6.2, this essay prompts them to do something similar to what they did on the second midterm: To reflect on an integrative concept from the course and to write on the theme using examples from four *different* topics from the course (e.g., sensation and perception, memory, development, social). The difference is that now students must write in full essay format and must fully discuss the integrative concept and work to tie together their examples.

Although students are not told in advance the exact prompt that will be on the exam, they are aware that a large portion of the final exam consists of this integrative essay. We devote part of the final lecture of the course to reviewing these major integrative concepts, which are presented as the "Top 10 Big Ideas" from the course. In this lecture we drive home the integrative concepts of the course one last time, with specific examples of each, and explicitly point out some connections that students may have missed. We also try to show students how specific studies connect to not just one but *multiple* integrative concepts. For example, the Schachter–Singer (1962) theory of emotion described earlier is not only a great example of the theme of internal-external interaction but also a good example of another integrative theme: "Your mind constructs your reality, and because your mind is flexible, you have the power to change your reality." This integrative theme allows us to give a broad review of a course in a way that gives students multiple organizing frameworks as they begin to study for the exam. We explicitly encourage students to study these integrative concepts for the exam, rather than thinking of studying as a task of memorizing many seemingly unrelated terms and concepts.

In a final discussion section of the course, students practice generating integrative concepts with their discussion leader and then practice using the integrative concepts to filter content learned across the course. By asking students to generate these course meta-themes on their own, we encourage them to engage in active learning, which has been shown to have a positive effect on students' understanding and retention of content (see, e.g., Hake, 1998; Prince, 2004). After students have generated several main themes of the course, the discussion leader can choose one and ask students to think of examples of this theme from different topics in the course. This gives students an opportunity to review content while practicing the skills that they will need to write the integrative essay in the exam, while further solidifying their understanding of a specific theme.

The discussion leader also presents a sample question, often containing a variant of the internal-external interaction concept, and allows students to work through it together. This sample question, shown in Figure 6.2, follows the same format as the integrative essay prompt and concerns a variant of the internal-external interaction concept we have discussed.

CONCLUDING COMMENT

When instructors emphasize and integrate multiple integrative concepts in an introductory psychology course, they add depth to the content that they teach. Without integrative concepts to tie multiple areas of psychology together, students may leave the course with a fragmented understanding of psychology, failing to recognize the richness that exists within the field of psychology. This problem can become compounded when students are assigned a textbook to supplement their learning of the content, because textbooks, by necessity, are typically modular in nature. In emphasizing the theme of integrative concepts throughout Psychology One, our hope is that students leave our class with a more unified understanding of the field of psychology. We also hope students will retain and subsequently apply that understanding to other learning domains during their college years and beyond.

We see evidence in our course evaluations that students recognize and appreciate our goal of integration and the specific integrative concepts we teach. On a course evaluation at the end of each quarter, students are asked what their favorite

One of the core themes of this class is the importance of both nature (biological bases and genetic inheritance) and nurture (environment, learning, experiences) for many psychological processes. Discuss how nature and nurture interact to shape at least *four* behaviors, abilities, psychological processes, or outcomes.

Your essay requires an *introduction*, discussion of *four examples*, and a *conclusion*. All four of your examples should come from DIFFERENT categories of psychology (as listed below):

o The brain and nervous system (including cases of brain damage)

o Evolutionary psychology

o Sensation/perception

o Learning

o Memory

o Thinking

o Language

o Intelligence

o Emotion and motivation

o Social psychology (social influence, social cognition)

o Altruism

o Development (cognitive, social, adult)

o Personality

o Morality

o Clinical psychology (diagnosis, psychopathology, and treatment)

o Culture

o Health psychology or happiness

Your essay should include a discussion of the general theme through *clear and detailed* discussions of each example. Each example should describe *specific evidence, studies, theories, or observations from lecture, the text, or your section.* Connect your examples to each other with substantive discussion; do not simply describe four unconnected examples.

FIGURE 6.2 Sample integrative essay question on final exam.

thing about Psychology One is. Students frequently praise the instructor's enthusiasm and fun lectures, as well as the relevance of the content to their lives. But some students share thoughts that point to the integrative nature of the course: "The interconnectedness of all topics introduced and how it can be applied in so many ways to almost any field," and "I enjoyed all the encompassing ideas of the course." Some students point to feeling transformed by what they learned: "All the new things I learned and how it changed me as a person," or "I was able to understand more of myself, and ways in which I can be a better version of myself!"

When we teach Psychology One, we have a number of goals beyond the transfer of content to our students, and integrative concepts support these goals. First, we hope to foster an open-minded yet critical mindset in our students, so that students will leave our course willing to consider new evidence that might contradict their currently held beliefs and able to evaluate that new evidence objectively. The integrative concepts that we teach can guide students toward that goal. As mentioned earlier, when we teach the theme of internal-external interaction, we have many opportunities to challenge students' prior beliefs about the causes of behavior: showing them the role of internal forces where they expect external forces to be primary, and vice versa. These examples provide opportunities to teach students how to revise their thinking in the face of surprising new findings.

Second, we aim to help students think critically about the human condition. What does it mean to be human? Are humans simply the product of their biology, programmed from birth to think and behave in a certain way? Or are they destined to conform to their environment and their culture? Important questions like these rarely have "simple" answers, and may feel impossible to truly understand. Many of the integrative concepts encourage students to recognize and tolerate this ambiguity and complexity, rather than thinking in "either-or" terms—for example, the interaction of internal and external factors on behavior or the adaptive and maladaptive nature of many behaviors. Emphasizing these integrative concepts in an introductory psychology course can help students realize that instead of seeking a "right" or "wrong" answer, they should consider more complex theories. We want students to leave our course with this "enduring understanding," and hope that the lessons embedded within these integrative concepts will help students throughout their lives inside and outside of the classroom.

Chapter 7

The Utter Subjectivity of Human Experience

WAYNE WEITEN

University of Nevada, Las Vegas

I have been an advocate for thematic approaches to teaching introductory psychology for many years. As some readers may know, in 1989 I published an introductory textbook, titled *Psychology: Themes & Variations*, which was built on a foundation of six unifying themes, with a seventh theme added in the third edition. I hoped that the themes would provide threads of continuity across chapters to help students see the connections among various areas of research in psychology. The themes also allowed me to focus a very bright spotlight on crucial insights about psychology and its subject matter—key ideas that I hoped students would remember long after they read my text. As you might guess, I have placed a great emphasis on these themes in my introductory courses over the years.

So, when I was asked to write this chapter, my principal quandary was deciding which of the seven themes to write about. It was akin to selecting a favorite child from among seven cherished offspring. Although I did not have to worry about any hurt feelings from the neglected themes, I was conflicted and the decision required some difficult deliberation. As the title of this chapter reveals, I eventually chose the idea that *people's experience of the world is highly subjective.*

Why this theme? Is it more important than the other six themes? Elevating one theme above the others entails a very subjective judgment (perhaps illustrating the ubiquity of the theme), but I am not prepared to argue that the subjectivity theme is more important than all the others. As I think back about my emphases in the classroom over the years, I have probably attributed more importance to psychology's empiricism and the joint influence of heredity and environment. Upon further reflection I realized that the subjectivity of experience has been something of a favored child from the beginning. When I was making my plans for *Themes & Variations* in the late 1980s, I gathered some informal data regarding which ideas I ought to turn into themes. I had sketched out some tentative plans on my own, but to make sure that I was not wildly out of synch with other introductory instructors, I polled my colleagues at the College of DuPage and attendees at a small teaching conference. Not wanting to sway respondents' suggestions, I posed an open-ended question: "What do you really want students to remember five years from now?" Most of the ideas that I was contemplating were mentioned frequently in the instructors' responses (along with many other worthy ideas), except for the subjectivity of experience. I am not sure that it garnered any endorsements other than my own. Nonetheless, I forged ahead with it as a theme anyway. In retrospect, I think I have always viewed the subjectivity of experience not as the most *important* theme, but as the most *interesting* theme. I have always been fascinated by people's tendency to view the world through their own idiosyncratic and frequently distorted personal lenses. Similarly, I have long been intrigued by how people tend to see what they expect to see, and how the same event or evidence can be viewed in remarkably different ways by different individuals.

In any event, I have been pondering the subjectivity of human experience for decades and I am looking forward to assembling a collage of research and theory on the matter that might help instructors to make this idea the centerpiece of their introductory courses. That said, I should add a caveat. Please note that I have never actually made the subjectivity of human experience the sole, paramount, centerpiece of my introductory courses. Rather, I have always tried to weave a tapestry in which it is one of seven (or more) very important threads of continuity across my introductory course. Given that the subjectivity of experience has always been just one among many themes in my classes, I should note that I have not developed specialized assessments of this specific insight. I will share a few thoughts on assessment issues, but this chapter will focus mainly on research and theory that highlight the subjective nature of human experience.

THE NATURE AND CONTOURS OF SUBJECTIVE EXPERIENCE

Before discussing research and theory, let me expand on the meaning of the assertion that people's experience of the world is subjective. Dictionary definitions of the word *subjective* (e.g., existing only in mind, illusory) tend to emphasize that individuals' perceptions of the world around them may not correspond precisely to external reality. If the complication that external reality may be a little mushier than dictionaries let on is overlooked, this focus on the potentially illusory nature of perception captures one key aspect of the subjectivity of experience. Dictionary definitions (e.g., particular to a given person) also tend to highlight the individualized, variegated nature of personal experience. The point here is that each person has a unique life history and people approach events with different attitudes, different cultural backgrounds, different personalities, and different bodies of knowledge. It is small wonder then that three individuals may experience the same event in three very different ways.

These ideas gleaned from contemporary lexicon give a useful start, but psychological analyses can help instructors to further flesh out *how* experience is subjective and, more importantly *why*. For example, research on visual illusions, reversible figures, perceptual hypotheses, and a host of other perceptual phenomena has shown that there is no one-to-one correspondence between sensory input and perceived experience. The process of perception does not consist of passive reception of incoming signals from the external world. Perception is an active process in which people organize and interpret the information received by the senses. Even the perception of simple objects, such as an apple or a clock, let alone complex events, such as a ballet or a conversation, is to some degree a matter of interpretation. Thus, a key aspect of the subjectivity of experience is humans' tendency to actively construct their personal interpretations of the world around them. Perception is necessarily constructive because people can only assimilate a limited portion of the sensory information that surrounds them, leaving them to test perceptual hypotheses about what is out there in the external world. In other words, perception involves drawing *inferences*, and these inferences are inevitably shaped by past experience.

Although the constructive nature of perception surely contributes to the subjectivity of experience, the reconstructive nature of memory probably makes a far greater contribution, as the malleability of memory seems to dwarf the malleability of perception. Research on memory illusions, the misinformation effect, source-monitoring errors, and so forth has repeatedly demonstrated that individuals' memories are sketchy reconstructions of the past that may be distorted and may include details that did not actually occur. As people go about their business every day, they take in millions of sights, sounds, and events. Their memory systems would be overwhelmed if they stored an exact, detailed record of all this experience. Instead, some sort of compression algorithms must be applied to the details and then they actively attempt to reconstruct the events in their lives as needed. One might think that the reconstructive nature of memory would fuel subjectivity only when individuals need to recall experiences from the "past," meaning last week, last year, or decades ago. But memory reconstruction is pervasive. Even a moment or two after being introduced to someone or seeing a car accident, people rely on reconstructive process to recall their experience. Thus, the fragile, unstable, fallible nature of memory is a huge part of the subjectivity of human experience.

Last, but certainly not least, the subjective nature of human experience includes a wide range of personal biases that cloud individuals' interpretation of events. There are countless forms of bias that can skew individuals' perceptions of themselves, other people, and the events that they encounter. For example, a huge body of research is available on how ethnic stereotypes can warp individuals' perceptions of ethnic minorities. There is an extensive literature on how gender stereotypes can shape individuals' views of males and females. Similarly, research shows that prejudicial attitudes toward gays, the aged, the disabled, and the mentally ill affect individuals' perceptions of these groups. But perceptual biases are not limited to views of other people. Research shows that individuals also display many forms of bias when they turn their view inward and evaluate themselves, reflect on their past, and contemplate their future. And, of course, research reveals that individuals are prone to biased interpretations of events involving their teams, their candidates, their families, their schools, and their decisions. Thus, another key element of the subjectivity of experience is the operation and influence of a host of personal biases.

THE VALUE OF UNDERSTANDING
THE SUBJECTIVITY OF EXPERIENCE

Why do I think it is important to highlight the subjective nature of human experience in the introductory psychology course? I would cite two interrelated reasons. First, I believe that the vast majority of students enter the introductory course with a very limited appreciation of the degree to which their observations, beliefs, and memories are highly subjective. Likewise, I suspect that most students have little awareness of the extent to which their views are colored by various forms of bias. Second, I believe that individuals' lack of insight regarding the subjective nature of their experiences frequently contributes to maladaptive self-deception, misinformed personal decisions, misunderstandings of others' motives and actions, routine disagreements about mundane, everyday issues, as well as contentious social issues of great consequence, and various types of intergroup conflicts.

Is there any empirical evidence to support my claim that students do not understand the extent to which their experiences are highly subjective? After all, there are a variety of popular adages that warn people about the potential subjectivity of experience. Surely students are familiar with the concept of wishful thinking and they have heard that the grass is always greener on the other side of the fence, that love is blind, and that it is all in the eye of the beholder. Perhaps they already appreciate that their views may be colored by their motives, values, and attitudes. The available evidence does not focus on students per se, but on people in general, and it suggests that most individuals have limited awareness regarding the inherent subjectivity of their experiences. Many studies have explored the concept of *naive realism* first described by Ross and Ward (1995, 1996). The central thesis of naive realism is that most people trust their senses, that they assume that they see the world "as it is," and that they are confident that their observations are objective and unbiased. I will get into more of the details and implications later, but the research on naive realism suggests that people *do* embrace the assumption that their views of the world are largely objective (Pronin, Gilovich, & Ross, 2004). As Molouki and Pronin (2015, pp. 396–397) put it, "people are generally unaware that their perceptions are subjective and idiosyncratic … when people perceive any person, event, or social situation, they do not realize that they are framing and interpreting the situation on the basis of the particular context in which they view it."

How about research related to my indictment of subjectivity as a culprit in a diverse array of undesirable or adverse outcomes? In terms of *self-focused phenomena*, one could argue that the subjective nature of experience is a key consideration in the self-serving bias in attribution (Mezulis, Abramson, Hyde, & Hankin, 2004), the better-than-average effect (Brown, 2012), inaccuracy in affective forecasting (Kushlev & Dunn, 2012), distortions in autobiographical memory (Kelley & Jacoby, 2012), false memories of childhood sexual abuse (Loftus, 2000), overconfidence in decision-making (Sieck & Arkes, 2005), unrealistic optimism about personal health (Weinstein, 2003), denial of personal afflictions such as alcoholism (Oltmanns & Powers, 2012), and the cognitive distortions that promote depressive disorders (Beck, 2008). In regard to *other-focused phenomena*, one could argue that subjectivity makes a meaningful contribution to overly favorable evaluations of attractive people (Macrae & Quadflieg, 2010), apparent confirmation of pernicious stereotypes of various groups (Fiske & Russell, 2010), victim derogation (van den Bos & Maas, 2009), interpersonal discord (Kennedy & Pronin, 2008), outgroup derogation (Fiske & Tablante, 2015), the rationalization of prejudice and discrimination (Crandall, Bahns, Warner, & Schaller, 2011), escalating conflicts between groups (Hamilton, Sherman, Way, & Percy, 2015), intercultural misunderstandings (Cohen, 2015), and polarization in the world of politics (Lavine, Jost, & Lodge, 2015).

These are all heavily researched, well-documented phenomena. They are complex matters that reflect many factors and processes besides the reality that one's experience of the world is highly subjective. But many of these phenomena would evaporate if not for the subjectivity of human experience. In sum, I think that there is considerable evidence to support my assertions that students do not fully appreciate just how subjective their views are, and that this subjectivity contributes to many personal, interpersonal, and societal problems.

INTRODUCING THE SUBJECTIVITY OF HUMAN EXPERIENCE

In class, when I first introduce the idea that one's experience of the world is highly subjective I tend to rely on two classic studies from the annals of social psychology. My choices are arbitrary, as one might use countless studies, but I like this pair because they are simple and straightforward, they are easy for students to relate to, and they illustrate different aspects of subjectivity.

The first study that I describe is a groundbreaking examination of person perception by Kelley (1950). In this study, students were told that their instructor was out of town and that their class would be taken over by a new lecturer, whom they would be asked to evaluate. Before the class, the students were given a short description (64 words) of the incoming instructor, with one important variation. Half the students were led to expect a "very warm" person, while the other half were led to expect a "rather cold" one. All the subjects were exposed to the same 20 minutes of lecture and interaction with the substitute instructor. However, the subjects who expected a warm person rated the instructor as more considerate, sociable, humorous, good natured, informal, and humane than the subjects who had expected a cold person. The takeaway messages are that a specific event (the guest lecture) can be viewed in different ways by different people and that people have a tendency to see what they *expect* to see.

The second study that I rely on is one conducted by Hastorf and Cantril (1954). They showed students at Princeton and Dartmouth universities a film of a recent, hard-fought, penalty-riddled football game between the two schools. The students were instructed to watch for rules infractions. Both groups saw the exact same film, but as one might anticipate, the Princeton students "saw" the Dartmouth players engage in twice as many infractions as the Dartmouth students "saw." The investigators concluded that the game "actually was many different games and that each version of the events that transpired was just as 'real' to a particular person as other versions were to other people" (Hastorf & Cantril, 1954, p. 132). In this study, it seems likely that the subjects' perceptions were primarily swayed by their motives, specifically, their favoritism toward their school's team. Although expectations could also have contributed (people may expect their team to not play as dirty as their opponent), I use the results of the study to show how people often have a tendency to see what they *want* to see.

I also use the comment that the game "actually was many different games" to expand on how a single event can yield very different experiences for those who attend the event. I point out that if 5,000 people all go to a specific college basketball game, they tend to assume that they all witnessed the same game. But if one could install hypothetical digital devices that accurately recorded all the sights, sounds, and thoughts experienced by each person during the game, each of the 5,000 digital records of the game experience would be unique. Students often voice skepticism, asserting that, "No, the fans are all watching the same game." To make it more concrete for them I point out that although the fans are in attendance for the express purpose of watching the same game, at any given time many are focused on the messy nachos they are eating, while others are scanning the stands for the beer vendor, relaying new gossip to their companion, complaining about the referees' calls, thinking about an upcoming exam, checking out the attractive person down the row from them, perusing the game program, taking pictures, texting a friend, and so forth. Eventually, most of them seem to begin to understand that there is no single game experience for the attendees, but rather 5,000 highly variegated game experiences. This insight helps them to understand how even a handful of people can come away from a much simpler event with very different sets of experiences.

INTEGRATING SUBJECTIVITY THROUGHOUT THE COURSE

The theme of subjectivity is relevant to most of the major content areas covered in the introductory course. Hence, it is easy to continue to provide compelling examples as one moves from one chapter to the next. To illustrate this reality, I have compiled a list of concepts and phenomena that one might choose to discuss, organized into ten broad content areas. This list, shown in Table 7.1 along with some very brief descriptions of representative findings, is by no means exhaustive, as I limited myself to three examples per area. Indeed, to avoid duplication, the concepts that I will discuss in earnest are omitted from the table. Obviously, in this brief chapter, I cannot discuss subjectivity in all of the relevant areas of psychology, so I will focus on four content areas that are especially rich with potential for demonstrating the subjectivity of human experience: perception, memory, cognition, and social psychology.

Perception

Research on perception has yielded many findings that drive home the subjectivity of experience. In particular, ambiguous or reversible figures that can be seen in two different ways can demonstrate that even the perception of a simple visual stimulus involves interpretation of sensory input. I like to show students the Necker Cube, Rubin's vase/silhouetted faces, and Jastrow's rabbit/duck. My favorite reversible figure is the one originally published in 1915 as a cartoon in a humor magazine under the title "My Wife and My Mother-in-Law." This graphic, first introduced to psychologists by Boring (1930), can be viewed as either a left profile of a young, attractive woman looking over her right shoulder or as a mostly frontal profile of an older, less attractive woman. When I show the graphic in class, I let students spontaneously describe what they see. Sometimes it takes a few minutes before both interpretations are reported. Students who see one interpretation, often experience difficulty seeing the alternate interpretation, so I eventually provide some guidance so that nearly everyone can recognize both interpretations. Finally, I explain that when Leeper (1935) led subjects to expect a young woman or an old woman, they tended to report seeing what they were led to expect. Reversible figures can provide dramatic demonstrations that the same visual input can result in radically different perceptions, and Leeper's findings show that people have a tendency to see what they expect to see.

Studies of inattentional blindness, which involves the failure to see plainly visible objects or events, can also flesh out why people have highly variegated experiences of the world around them. In one influential study (Simons & Chabris, 1999), participants watched a video of three people in white shirts and three people in black shirts passing a basketball. The observers were instructed to focus on one of the two teams and press a key whenever that team passed the ball. Thirty seconds into the task, a woman carrying an umbrella clearly walked through the scene for four seconds. Nearly half (44 percent) of the participants failed to see

TABLE 7.1 Topics Illustrating the Subjectivity of Experience in Various Areas Covered in Introductory Psychology

Area/Concept	Key Insights and Findings
Research Methods	
Placebo effects	Placebo effects, which are largely attributable to individuals' expectations regarding various treatments, are surprisingly strong (Benedetti, 2008). For example, subjects falsely led to believe that they are drinking alcohol show signs of intoxication (Assefi & Garry, 2003).
Social desirability bias	Research subjects tend to give socially approved answers to questions about themselves (Tourangeau & Yan, 2007). Generally, they are not fabricating as much as they are engaging in wishful thinking.
Experimenter expectations and bias	To some degree, experimenters are prone to see what they *want* to see (O'Leary, Kent, & Kanowitz, 1975) and what they *expect* to see (Rosenthal & Fode, 1963).
Sensation and Perception	
Pain perception	The perception of pain is highly subjective, as some people with severe injuries report little pain, whereas others with modest injuries report great pain (Coderre, Mogil, & Bushnell, 2003).
Subliminal perception	Individuals' emotions and attitudes can be swayed by exposure to subliminal stimuli that are not even registered consciously (Massar & Buunk, 2009; Weinberger & Westen, 2008).
Contrast effects	Specific stimuli, ranging from simple to complex, may be perceived differently depending on what they are contrasted with (e.g., the Delboeuf illusion).
Consciousness	
Hypnotic phenomena	Under the influence of hypnosis, some people report seeing and hearing stimuli that are not really there (Spiegel, 2003).
Pseudoinsomnia	Some people report that they get negligible or inadequate sleep, but when monitored in a sleep lab, they manifest sound patterns of sleep (Mitler, Guilleminault, Orem, Zarcone, & Dement, 1975).
Subjective effects of drugs	If people expect a drug to make them feel giddy or serene, their expectations are likely to influence their perceptions of their drug experience (Maisto, Galizio, & Connors, 2004).
Memory	
Distortions of autobiographical memory	Individuals' recall of their personal past is tainted by changes in their attitudes and views (Kelley & Jacoby, 2012). For example, conservative adults recall being conservative in their youth, even when evidence indicates that they were liberal.

(Continued)

Area/Concept	Key Insights and Findings
Imagination inflation	The mere act of imagining an event (that a person had *not* actually experienced) can lead many subjects to believe that they actually experienced the event (Garry & Polaschek, 2000).
Misinformation effect	Individuals' recall of an event they witnessed can be distorted by introducing various types of postevent information, thus demonstrating the reconstructive nature of memory (Loftus, 2005).
Cognition	
Hindsight bias	Once they know an outcome, people tend to revise their interpretation of the past to fit how events actually turned out, thus introducing distortions into memory (Guilbault, Bryant, Brockway, & Posavac, 2004).
Framing	Objectively equivalent situations are viewed differently when choices are structured in superficially different ways (Kahneman & Tversky, 1984).
Illusion of control	People tend to overestimate their ability to influence events that they actually have little or no control over (Thompson, 1999).
Motivation and Emotion	
Subjective well-being	Subjective well-being shows only very modest relations to objective realities, demonstrating that happiness is inherently subjective (Schwarz & Stack, 1999).
Inaccuracy in affective forecasting	People reliably mispredict their future feelings in response to good and bad events, largely because they overestimate the intensity and duration of their emotional reactions (Wilson & Gilbert, 2005).
Mood effects	Manipulations of mood can influence what we remember (Forgas, Goldenberg, & Unkelbach, 2009), how we perceive others (Forgas & Bower, 1987), the perception of pain (Weisenberg, Raz, & Hener, 1998), and many other aspects of personal experience.
Personality	
Self-knowledge	Individuals' perceptions of their personality traits show very modest relations to more objective indicators of their traits, suggesting that self-concepts and self-knowledge are highly subjective (Back & Vazire, 2012).
Better-than-average effect	The vast majority of people believe that they are better than the average person in regard to a host of positive qualities, such as honesty, persistence, driving ability, and managerial skills (Kuyper & Dijkstra, 2009). This bias is so strong that in one case 100% of respondents rated themselves as above average in the ability to get along with others, and 25% reported that they belonged in the top 1% (Myers, 1980).

(Continued)

Area/Concept	Key Insights and Findings
Defense mechanisms	People depend extensively on defense mechanisms to shield themselves from emotional discomfort. Defense mechanisms work through self-deception, allowing people to create illusory views of their motives and actions (Aldwin, 2007).
Stress, Coping, and Health	
Stress appraisals	Appraisals of potentially stressful events are inherently subjective (Steptoe, 2007). Events that are hugely stressful for one person may be routine for another.
Perceptions of physical symptoms	Perceptions of unpleasant physical sensations that might be viewed as symptoms of physical illness depend on individuals' interpretations and vary dramatically (Martin & Leventhal, 2004).
Misperception of health risks	People have a tendency to underestimate the risks of their own health-impairing habits (such as smoking or drinking), even though they view the risks of others' health-impairing habits much more accurately (Weinstein, 2003).
Psychopathology and Treatment	
Cognitive factors in psychological disorders	Rigid, distorted, unrealistic patterns of thinking appear to contribute to the etiology of many disorders, including depression (Christensen, Carney, & Segal, 2006), anxiety disorders (Craske & Waters, 2005), and eating disorders (Williamson, Zucker, Martin, & Smeets, 2001).
Delusions and hallucinations	Hearing nonexistent voices and holding delusional beliefs that clearly are out of touch with reality are extreme manifestations of the subjectivity of experience.
Evaluations of therapeutic progress	Assessments of progress in therapy are highly subjective and biased, as clients want to justify their time, effort, and expense, while therapists want to believe that their interventions are helpful (Luborsky et al., 1999).
Social Behavior	
Illusory correlation	One factor that helps people to preserve their stereotypes of various groups is that people tend to estimate that they have encountered more confirmations of their stereotypes than they actually have (Johnson & Mullen, 1994).
Victim derogation	In an effort to preserve their belief in a just world, people tend to blame victims for their misfortune, so that they feel less likely to be victimized themselves in a similar way (Lerner & Goldberg, 1999).
Idealizing romantic partners	People want their intimate partners to match their ideals regarding traits such as warmth, looks, and dependability (Simpson, Fletcher, & Campbell, 2001). When their partners do not measure up, they often distort reality and make overly favorable evaluations of the partners. Hence, people tend to view their partners more favorably than the partners view themselves (Murray, Holmes, & Griffin, 1996).

the woman. Moreover, when someone in a gorilla suit strolled through the same scene, even more subjects (73 percent) missed the unexpected event! If you show students the gorilla video, which is available on YouTube, they are incredulous that observers could miss the gorilla. Inattentional blindness demonstrates to students that what they see hinges on how and where they focus their attention, which provides yet another reason why a specific event can be experienced in different ways by different people.

My collection of interesting studies that highlight the subjectivity of basic perception has grown in recent years, thanks to the work of Dunning and Balcetis (2013) on *wishful seeing*. In one study (Balcetis & Dunning, 2006), participants were told that a computer would flash a number or a letter to indicate whether they were assigned to a pleasant or unpleasant experimental task. Each of the subjects briefly saw the same ambiguous stimulus, which could be viewed as either a number (13) or a letter (B), and then the computer appeared to crash. When asked what they had seen, subjects hoping for a letter were much more likely to interpret the stimulus as a B, and those hoping for a number were much more likely to view the stimulus as a 13. Another study showed that estimates of distance can be skewed by people's motivational states. Balcetis and Dunning (2010) found that desirable objects (e.g., a bottle of water for thirsty subjects, a $100 bill subjects could win) are perceived to be closer than less desirable objects. Thus, Dunning and Balcetis (2013, p. 36) conclude that, "Although people assume that their visual experiences reflect the outside world as it is, emerging data converge to suggest that, at least in part, they see it the way they want it to be."

Memory

The malleability of human memory makes it a topic that has enormous potential for demonstrating the subjectivity of human experience. One obvious possibility is to focus on the controversy surrounding recovered memories of childhood sexual abuse. I generally do cover the issue of repressed memories, but I do not tend to use recovered memories as an exemplar of subjectivity. Why not, given that false memories of abuse clearly involve subjective distortions of memory (Loftus, 2000; McNally & Geraerts, 2009)? My main reason is that repressed memories seem to strike most students as an exotic phenomenon that has little to do with them and I want students to see the subjectivity of experience as something that has *everything* to do with them, something that permeates their lives. I forego discussing memories of alien abductions (Clancy, 2005; McNally, 2012) as an example of subjectivity for the same reason. I mention these topics because they surely could be used to highlight the subjectivity of human memory, and other instructors might want to harness them for this purpose, but personally, I prefer to focus on more mundane, everyday memory phenomena.

A survey on people's notions about memory found that 63 percent believe that when you retrieve information from long-term memory, you are able to pull up a "mental videotape" that provides an exact replay of the past (Simons & Chabris, 2011). However, countless studies have demonstrated that this is a naive and extremely inaccurate view of memory. My principal goal in covering memory as a topic is to help students understand that their memories are not nearly as accurate, reliable, or complete as they assume. I like to start by discussing how the simple act of retelling a story can introduce inaccuracies into memory (Marsh, 2007). When people retell stories, they tend to make "adjustments" that depend on their goals, their audience, and the social context. They may streamline a story, embellish the facts, exaggerate their role, or omit important situational considerations. When participants in one study were asked to evaluate the accuracy of recent retellings, they admitted that 42 percent were "inaccurate" and that another one third contained "distortions" (Marsh & Tversky, 2004). People may be aware that they are being a little loose with the facts. However, what is interesting is that their intentional distortions can reshape their subsequent recollections of the same events. Somehow, the "real" story and the storyteller's "spin" on it begin to blend imperceptibly. So, even routine retellings of events can contribute to the malleability of memory.

From there, I tend to move on to the retrieval process of *reality monitoring,* in which people reflect on whether something actually happened or they only thought about it happening. This sounds like an odd problem to students. But I point out that people all routinely ponder questions like "Did I pack the umbrella or only think about packing it?" "Did I send that e-mail, or only intend to do so?" I point out that research has demonstrated that individuals often make reality-monitoring errors (Johnson, 2007; McDaniel, Lyle, Butler, & Dornburg, 2008). For example, your e-mail record may show indisputably that you did not send the e-mail that you were absolutely sure you had sent. I wrap up the discussion of reality monitoring by noting that if you cannot be sure about whether you took some simple action two hours ago, how can you be confident that you can accurately remember more complex personal experiences from two days ago, let alone two years ago?

Discussion of reality monitoring leads easily into experimental studies that have shown that it is possible to create "memories" of events that never actually happened. For example, I like to describe the study by Hyman, Husband, and Billings (1995) in which subjects were asked to remember childhood events that had been recounted by their parents. Each subject was asked about a few real events and one that was fabricated. The fabricated events were fairly substantial, such as spilling a punch bowl on the bride at a wedding and being in a grocery store when the fire sprinkler system went off. The researchers managed to create recollections of these fabricated events in 25 percent of their subjects simply by asking them to elaborate on the events. I also like to describe another study (Garry & Gerrie, 2005) in which Photoshop was used to doctor photographs to show participants taking a childhood ride in a hot air balloon. Even with no supportive information supplied, exposing subjects to these bogus photos led 50 percent of the participants to develop "memories" of a balloon experience they never had. Interestingly, subjects in these studies often feel very confident about their false memories, which frequently generate strong emotional reactions and richly detailed "recollections" (Laney & Loftus, 2013).

One can also use the research on the accuracy of eyewitness memory to illustrate the fallibility of human memory. Decades of research have shown that eyewitness testimony is not nearly as reliable or trustworthy as widely assumed (Wells & Loftus, 2013). Although I emphasize that a great many, carefully controlled experimental studies have demonstrated that eyewitness memory can be extremely flawed, this is one of those topics where I think a couple compelling anecdotes can be more convincing than a review of the research. I tend to be fond of the tale of Father Pagnano, a Delaware priest who was accused of a series of armed robberies committed by a perpetrator who was dubbed the "gentleman bandit" because he was unusually polite for a thief (Rodgers, 1982). At his trial, *seven* eyewitnesses confidently identified Father Pagano as the gentleman bandit, but eventually the real culprit came forward and confessed. I ask the students to ponder how could seven people "remember" seeing Father Pagnano commit robberies that he had nothing to do with? How could these witnesses be so confident when they were so wrong? Additional examples of eyewitness misidentifications can be found at the web site for the Innocence Project.

In the final analysis, I emphasize that because humans do not have access to high-fidelity "mental videotapes" they must rely on hazy, frequently distorted reconstructions of the past. This process introduces an enormous amount of "wiggle room" in individuals' recollections of their actions and experiences. The fact that people reconstruct rather than replay their experiences makes an enormous contribution to the highly subjective nature of human experience.

Cognition

Research on thinking, reasoning, and decision-making can also help to clarify why people's subjective views of the same evidence can be very different and can become increasingly different with the passage of time. For example, Nickerson (1998) has described the phenomenon of *confirmation bias*—the tendency to seek and interpret evidence in ways that are supportive of one's beliefs and decisions. Nickerson points out confirmation bias can taint reasoning even when people have no personal interest or partisan view at stake. For example, he reviews how physicians often exhibit confirmation bias in making diagnoses. That is, once they arrive at an initial hypothesis about the likely diagnosis for a patient, there is a natural tendency to mostly look for supporting data rather than to devote serious thought to alternative diagnoses. The key point here is that physicians generally have no vested interest in championing a specific diagnosis other than it happens to be the hypothesis in hand. Moreover, unlike in most political debates, evidence from diagnostic tests or disease progression may eventually provide definitive evidence as to whether their diagnosis was right or wrong. So, in the vast majority of cases (setting aside occasional diagnostic biases motivated by financial incentives), physicians want to make the correct diagnosis. Yet, in spite of their neutrality, they are often victimized by confirmation bias. Thus, I try to emphasize to students that the tendency to seek evidence congenial to one's views seems to be a common cognitive bias that can explain how two impartial observers can review the same evidence and reach contrary conclusions.

Of course, as Nickerson (1998) acknowledges, confirmation bias can also be motivated by a desire to defend beliefs, values, and decisions that people *do* have a personal stake in, such as when people have partisan views on subjects such as abortion, gun control, the regulation of huge banks, or net neutrality. This sort of motivated confirmation bias has been explored in a variety of research paradigms, including work on motivated inferences in the evaluation of ideas (Kunda, 1987), motivated reasoning in the world of politics (Westen, Blagov, Harenski, Kilts, & Hamann, 2006), wishful thinking regarding election outcomes (Babad, 1997), and myside bias in relation to a range of issues and topics (Stanovich, West, & Toplak, 2013).

I prefer to cover the research on *myside bias* with students because this research is especially easy for students to digest. Myside bias consists of the tendency to evaluate evidence in a manner slanted in favor of one's existing opinions, attitudes, and vested interests. For example, in one study (Stanovich & West, 2008), subjects read that "Ford Explorers are 8 times more likely than a typical family car to kill occupants of another car in a crash." They were informed that the German government was considering banning Ford Explorers and asked whether they agreed with the ban. In another condition, similar subjects read that a specific German vehicle was eight times more likely to kill occupants of other cars. They were told that the U.S. government was considering banning the car and asked whether they agreed with the ban. Although the situations were identical, American subjects were significantly more likely to support the ban of the German vehicle than the ban of the American vehicle (Ford Explorer). Similarly, Stanovich and West (2007, 2008) have found that smokers belittle the evidence on the negative effects of secondhand smoke, heavy drinkers are skeptical of evidence on the health risks of alcohol, and highly religious people readily agree that there is a link between religiosity and honesty. Interestingly, research has repeatedly demonstrated that there is no relationship between the tendency to exhibit myside bias and measures of general cognitive ability (Stanovich et al., 2013).

In class, I use the research on confirmation bias and myside bias to make the point that individuals seek information that supports their views; they cling to their beliefs even when confronted with contradictory information; they evaluate evidence from their own idiosyncratic, subjective perspectives; they routinely exhibit a propensity to see what they want to see, and high intelligence conveys no immunity to these biases.

Other lines of cognitive research can provide more innocent, or seemingly harmless, examples of subjectivity in action. For example, Shepperd and McNulty (2002) hypothesized that people judge their outcomes *relative to their expectations*. Hence, the exact same objective outcome, such as earning an "A" in a class, can produce very different reactions depending on whether one was anticipating an "A" or a "C." In a series of elegant experiments, Shepperd and McNulty (2002) found that negative outcomes feel worse when they are unexpected rather than expected, and that positive outcomes feel better when they are unexpected rather than expected.

I also like the practical lessons to be learned from research showing that judgments of the quality of consumer products can be swayed by irrelevant factors such as brand familiarity and price. In one demonstration of this reality, participants tasted wines and rated their quality (Plassmann, O'Doherty, Shiv, & Rangel, 2008). In some cases, they thought they were tasting two different wines. However, it was the same wine presented at two very different prices (such as $10 and $90). As you might guess, the more "expensive" wines garnered higher ratings. Admittedly, wine tasting is inherently a subjective process, but I am confident that price influences the evaluations of all sorts of products, including many that have more objective features related to their quality.

Social Psychology

Perhaps more so than any other area of research, social psychology provides an abundance of material on the subjective nature of human experience. Biases in attribution are a great place to start. I begin by describing *actor-observer differences*— how observers tend to favor internal attributions in explaining others' behavior because internal attributions are simpler and easier, and observers are not privy to actors' perceptions of situational pressures, whereas actors are more likely to explain the same behavior with external attributions because they tend to be aware of the situational factors that have influenced them (Gilbert & Malone, 1995; Krull, 2001). I go on to discuss the *self-serving bias* in attribution—the tendency to make internal attributions for one's successes and external attributions for one's failures (Mezulis et al., 2004). This bias clearly is motivated by self-interest in that it allows people to take credit for their successes and deflect blame for their failures. But the key point that I make is that attributional tendencies result in both actors and observers interpreting the same events in very different ways.

In my coverage of prejudice and discrimination, I emphasize how negative stereotypes of various groups influence individuals' perceptions of these groups because the stereotypes shape their expectations. Evidence shows that people tend to see what they expect to see when they come into contact with groups that they view with prejudice (Dunning & Sherman, 1997). Moreover, prejudicial stereotypes are so pervasive and insidious they often operate automatically, even in people who truly renounce prejudice (Forscher & Devine, 2014). I also note that when people encounter members of a group that they view with prejudice who deviate from the stereotype of that group, they often find ways to discount this evidence (Sherman, Stroessner, Conrey, & Azam, 2005), and that the malleability of memory often leads people to remember actions that are consistent with their stereotypes, while not recalling actions that are inconsistent with their expectations (Fiske, 1998). Obviously, what I try to convey is that prejudice—which represents a major social problem—is rooted to a considerable degree in the subjective nature of person perception processes.

Some instructors may want to expand on this insight and discuss how racial stereotypes can skew perceptions of threat and violence. For example, Duncan (1976) had white subjects watch and evaluate interaction on a TV monitor that was supposedly live (it was actually a videotape) and varied the race of a person who gets into an argument and gives another person a slight shove. The shove was coded as "violent behavior" by 73 percent of the subjects when the actor was black but by only 13 percent of the subjects when the actor was white. This finding readily leads to more recent research on how racial stereotypes can lead people to see a weapon that is not actually there. Laboratory studies have shown that when participants are required to make split-second decisions about the presence of a weapon, they incorrectly report seeing a gun more often in conjunction with black faces than white faces (Payne, 2006). Admittedly, these studies have largely been conducted with civilians rather than police officers, and the simulations are rather artificial approximations of the situations that police officers must confront, but the implications are obvious—they suggest that tragic police shootings of ethnic individuals who turn out to be unarmed hinge on the highly subjective nature of perception. I am hard-pressed to think of a more profoundly important example of the potential consequences of subjective experience in the real world.

In the realm of social psychology, I also like to focus attention on the previously mentioned concept of naive realism, and some of its repercussions. Work on naive realism begins with the observation that individuals generally tend to believe that they view the world "as it is." Hence, they expect others to view the world in much the same way. When others do not view the world in the same way, they need to explain this perplexing disparity. Given that one sees the world as it is, those who see it differently must be uninformed, illogical, or biased (Ross & Ward, 1995, 1996).

Naive realism appears to underlie a number of interesting phenomena that dramatize the subjectivity of human experience. One of these is *false polarization*—the tendency for people on both sides of partisan debates to characterize their opponents as extremists and to overestimate the extent of their mutual disagreement. This misperception stems from people's tendency to assume that the views of those who disagree with them must be distorted by ideology or some other bias, and biased views are assumed to be extreme views. In one study of false polarization, Sherman, Nelson, and Ross (2003) found that proponents of affirmative action overestimated opponents' conservativism and that opponents of affirmative action overestimated proponents' liberalism. The data indicated that the actual (average) attitudes of the two groups were not all that far apart, but people in both groups *assumed* that their opponents held extreme and highly dissimilar views. Obviously, insofar as this subjectively inflated gap in disagreement may be characteristic of political debates in general, it sheds light on (1) why it is often so difficult for opposing sides to bridge the (perceived) gap between them and (2) why people often have such pervasively negative views of their adversaries.

Naive realism also provides the underpinning for the *illusion of asymmetric insight* described by Pronin, Kruger, Savitsky, and Ross (2001). This illusion consists of the tendency for people to believe that their self-knowledge is superior to others' self-knowledge. For example, in one experiment involving college roommates, participants tended to believe that they knew themselves better than their roommates knew themselves. Indeed, in regard to some personal qualities, especially negative ones, such as messiness or susceptibility to flattery, subjects claimed to know their roommates better than the roommates knew themselves. In other words, individuals tend to doubt that others can really understand them, whereas they see others as an open book, and they suspect that others are in denial about their personal shortcomings.

A closely related asymmetry is seen in the *bias blind spot*, which involves the failure to recognize one's own biases (Pronin, 2007; Pronin & Schmidt, 2013). Most people appreciate the fact that a variety of biases may taint the reasoning of people in general, but because biases tend to operate outside of one's awareness, these people fail to appreciate the fact that this insight also applies to them. For example, Pronin, Lin, and Ross (2002) described eight common forms of bias (such as self-serving attributions for success and failure and the tendency to blame victims) and asked subjects to rate the vulnerability of the average American to each bias, as well as their own vulnerability. Participants saw themselves as less vulnerable than others to all eight forms of bias. In a more compelling demonstration of the bias blind spot (Hansen, Gerbasi, Todorov, Kruse, & Pronin, 2014), participants were asked to evaluate the artistic quality of paintings in either an objective manner (by not looking at the artists' names, which included some famous names) or an obviously biased manner (by always checking the names). Before making the evaluations, the subjects who were instructed to use the biased strategy rated it as a relatively biased approach. They then went on to make highly biased ratings based on the artists' names. But afterward, when asked to rate the objectivity of their evaluations, their ratings were no different from the subjects who were instructed to ignore the artists' names. Thus, the subjects were blind to their bias even though they knew they had just used a biased approach in making their evaluations!

False polarization, the illusion of asymmetric insight, and the bias blind spot, all flow from the metacognitive beliefs associated with naive realism. In my estimation, the concept of naive realism can shed considerable light on why interpersonal, societal, and cultural conflicts are so common and so difficult to resolve. Some recent studies have provided a modicum of support for this view. For example, follow-up studies of false polarization suggest that it can fuel and exacerbate conflict in the real world (Kennedy & Pronin, 2012). A study conducted by Kennedy and Pronin (2008) found that individuals' responses to conflict are mediated by the degree to which they perceive the other side as biased. The more people see the other side as biased, the more they tend to escalate the conflict, which often leads the other side to reciprocate, thus creating a spiral of growing conflict. Thus, in situations ranging from marital spats to office feuds to contract negotiations, naive realism may sow the seeds of discord and confrontation.

Working from this assumption, a recent study sought to determine whether making people aware of naive realism and its repercussions might attenuate attitudes regarding a very real, very antagonistic, and long-standing source of discord—the Israeli-Palestinian conflict (Nasie, Bar-Tal, Pliskin, Nahhas, & Halperin, 2014). The researchers point out that in intractable conflicts each side tends to build a collective narrative that tells the story of the conflict from their point of view. Adherence to this collective narrative and dismissal of the other side's collective narrative represent significant barriers to conflict resolution. Nasie et al. (2014) conducted separate studies with Jewish Israeli participants and with Palestinian Israeli participants in which subjects were exposed to brief explanations of naive realism and how it can lead to biased derogation of opposing views. Subsequently, subjects' attitudes toward the other side's collective narrative were measured. In both studies, significant increases in openness to the adversary's narrative were found among the more conservative/hawkish participants. These findings suggest that naive realism is a contributing factor, and perhaps a crucial one, in important real-world conflicts.

ASSESSMENT

As I mentioned near the beginning of the chapter, given that the subjectivity of experience is only one of many themes that I weave throughout my introductory courses, I have not developed any special assessment procedures to determine whether my emphasis on subjectivity results in changed attitudes or enduring insights. My exams include conventional multiple-choice and essay questions that focus on my unifying themes, but I have never analyzed the performance on those questions in comparison to questions related to other content.

Moreover, in regard to the subjectivity theme, even if I went to great lengths to devise elaborate approaches to assessment, I am not sure that I would trust the results. Even if students' exam performance indicated that they had assimilated the idea that one's experience of the world is highly subjective, would I be confident that they would go forward in life largely immune to wishful seeing, confirmation bias, myside bias, self-serving attributions, and the poisonous effects of group stereotypes? Of course not. I would like to think that I have ambitious goals for my introductory classes, but changing human nature is not among them. A certain degree of subjectivity in one's experience of the world is inevitable. Given that people tend to not be cognizant of their personal biases, I suspect that there might be a huge disconnect between how students would respond on exams and how they would respond to actual events and disagreements in the real world.

PRACTICAL THOUGHTS

What sorts of practical thoughts can I offer to those instructors who may be interested in making the subjectivity of experience an organizing theme in their courses? Just a few, which follow. First, students do seem to find the subjectivity of experience to be an engaging line of discourse. Admittedly, I am basing this assertion on my highly subjective impressions and recollections, which are inevitably biased, but I feel like I have had countless lively discussions in classes of the concepts and phenomena that illustrate subjectivity in action. Second, I would not recommend forcing the subjectivity theme into every chapter of introductory psychology. There are some chapters, such as physiology/neuroscience, learning, and developmental psychology, where intriguing examples of subjectivity do not easily come to mind. One could come up with some relevant concepts, but it would be much like forcing a square peg into a round hole. Subjectivity can easily be highlighted in a more than sufficient number of chapters to work as a thematic emphasis, so there is no need to force it upon students when the illustrations are not compelling. Third, as with any theme, topic, or concept, demonstrations and activities can be very useful in driving home the point that experience is subjective. To that end, I have listed published demonstrations related to some of the concepts and phenomena that I have discussed under the rubric of subjectivity in Table 7.2. Fourth, in articulating this theme, the language I use in class is a little different than the language I have used in this chapter, which is intended for a far more sophisticated audience. Although I certainly do use the terminology that "human experience is highly subjective" on a routine basis, that insight sounds a tad abstract to introductory students. What I really try to burn into their brains are the more concrete assertions that "people tend to see what they expect to see and what they want to see, and that they tend to be largely oblivious to their personal biases."

TABLE 7.2 **Demonstrations of Phenomena Illustrating the Subjectivity of Experience**

Phenomenon	Citation
Ubiquity of interpretation	Connor-Greene (2007)
Subjectivity of impression formation (simulation of Kelley, 1950)	Lasswell, Ruch, Gorfein, and Warren (1981)
Illusory correlation	Jackson (2000); Rocklin (1990)
Illusion of control	Dollinger (1990)
Fallibility of eyewitness memory	Charlton (1999); Gee and Dyck (1998)
Implicit memory and subjective judgments	Pierce (1999)
Hindsight bias	Hom, Ciaramitaro, and Valentine (2012)
Better-than-average effect	Nier (2004)
Fundamental attribution error	Howell and Shepperd (2011); Riggio and Garcia (2009)
Actor-observer differences in attribution	Gordon and Kaplar (2002); Kite (1991)
Self-serving attributions	Dunn (1989); Friedrich (1996)
False consensus effect	Kite (1991)

CONCLUSION

In my discussion of assessment, I expressed skepticism about the likelihood that my course theme might reduce students' subjective biases, which seem to be a deeply entrenched feature of human nature. Although that clearly is the most realistic stance to take, I do harbor hopes that hammering incessantly on the subjectivity of experience might chip away, just a little bit, at some of the metacognitive beliefs that foster naive realism. The recent research by Nasie et al. (2014) on changed attitudes regarding the Israeli-Palestinian conflict certainly gives me a newfound glimmer of encouragement. Given the immense importance of some of the phenomena that are fueled by subjectivity (e.g., overconfidence in eyewitness testimony, myside bias, interpersonal discord, the distorting effects of negative stereotypes, polarization on sociopolitical issues), even very tiny increments in students' appreciation of the subjectivity of their experience might yield meaningful benefits. If only a handful of my students come to realize that their view of the world is not the only legitimate view and that their view does not necessarily reflect the world as it is, I will count that as a small step in the right direction.

Chapter 8

Using Evolutionary Theory as an Overarching Theme for Understanding Psychology

MARGARET F. LYNCH

San Francisco State University

When the answer to my persistent question results in an overwhelmingly thunderous response of "survival" from the hundreds of students in class, it is then that I feel a measure of success in driving home the application of evolutionary theory to understanding psychology. The persistent question is, of course, "why?" Why do humans exhibit the behaviors they do? Why do humans have the cognitive processes that they have? The ultimate answer is assuredly for survival: survival for the purpose of successfully passing on one's genes at the individual and/or group level. This ultimate goal of survival is the underlying cause for evolution. The dynamic of evolutionary process accounts for all the biological and psychological processes that make existence possible (e.g., Barkow, Cosmides, & Tooby, 1992; Buss, 2011; Ploeger, van der Maas, & Raijmakers, 2008).

Evolutionary theory provides an extraordinary thread of continuity for understanding the complexity of humans. This thread securely connects and provides cohesion to the vast topics traversed across an introductory course. If students can understand evolutionary theory as an overarching framework, then they can see the separate parts of psychology moving in concert with one another, somewhat like a mobile with all its parts connected into a meaningful piece of art.

The movement of one part directly or indirectly affects the movement of another part because they are threaded together.

As an instructor who embraces using principles of evolution as a unifying theme, I will share with readers the challenges that are inherent in using this concept to hold together all that instructors teach in their introductory psychology class. I would like to first introduce how my course is taught and both the unique and universal aspects of the student population that I am engaged with. Next, I will cover some fundamentals of this theme, evidence from the literature, and ways to use this approach in each subarea of the course. I will also address the challenges inherent in embracing this approach.

MEGA-SECTION GENERAL PSYCHOLOGY AT SAN FRANCISCO STATE UNIVERSITY

The introductory psychology course I teach at San Francisco State University (SFSU) is a traditional lecture course that meets either twice weekly for 75 minutes (spring semesters) or for 50 minutes three times a week (fall semesters). I refer to my course as a "mega-section" because of its size: It enrolls approximately 700 students, generally freshmen and sophomores, per semester and meets in a large auditorium designed as a performance space for creative arts. I am sure some teachers might be thrilled at the chance to "perform" on such a stage, but for me the stage creates an undesired barrier between the students and me. There is no easy way down from the stage except through an offstage stairway and door; thus I cannot walk among the students. Because the room was designed for performance, the acoustics are such that sound travels away from the stage and it is difficult to hear questions and comments coming from the audience. I have solved this by asking student assistants to bring a microphone to students asking questions or making comments.

My classroom is a technology-free environment; there are no electronic devices permitted (with the exception of voice recorders that may be placed on the edge of the stage). The overall prohibition has made distractions far less than in the past. Further, empirical research shows that there is better retention from handwritten notes (Mueller & Oppenheimer, 2014). I encourage students to listen and think and not try to write down everything. A basic outline of the lecture is projected on a large screen and other audio and visual information is presented as appropriate for illustrating concepts. As I suspect is the case at many universities and possibly even some two-year institutions, the very large section format emerged as a way to free up teaching resources for other courses in the discipline. I developed this mega-section format over 25 years ago.

SFSU is a large urban university that is extraordinarily diverse both ethnically and socioeconomically. The undergraduate population at SFSU surpasses 26,000 total (more than 22,000 are full time). Approximately 22 percent of students are the first in their family to attend college. Many students are bilingual or learning English as a second language. SFSU has more than 2,400 international students attending SFSU and it ranks fifth in the nation among master's institutions that host international students. Similarly, it is one of the most ethnically diverse schools in the country. Ethnically, White non-Latino students comprise about 26 percent of the undergraduate population, Asians (Asian, Filipino, Pacific Islanders) about 32 percent, Chicano and Latino about 28 percent, and African Americans about 6 percent. The remainder are designated Native American or "two or more races." The students represent a broad socioeconomic spectrum as well. Basically, SFSU has it all and in large measure.

I often say that SFSU has the very best students in the country, the very worst students, and everything in between. This reality creates not only unique challenges for the faculty but also extraordinary opportunities to engage learners from all walks of life and all educational backgrounds. The delight of teaching psychology is the fact that it does attract students with so many different major objectives. As it is known, students of all kinds are drawn to psychology. Who would not be since it concerns human thought and behavior? The psychology instructors' goal then is to capitalize on students' inherent interest in the topic while providing an organized collection of concepts and ideas which students can grasp. Evolution has certainly proven to me to be a big idea that adds coherence and continuity to these concepts and ideas. Despite being a mega-section, every class has demonstrations or activities that help students inductively learn about and experience concepts and to have fun doing so.

I give four to five multiple-choice tests a semester (spring versus fall) in my course. All are equally weighted and the lowest score is dropped, eliminating the need for "make-up" exams. Students are permitted, and encouraged, to bring a one-page, one-side, handwritten study sheet to the exams. I have found this to be an important pedagogical tool as constructing the sheet necessitates a good deal of studying and effort. Additionally, it is a nice "pony" for students anxious about the exam process. This is especially true when you are packed cheek by jowl in a large classroom (it is worse than coach travel on a crowded airplane).

Because the course is a large lecture-only format without break-out discussion sections, the instructor supports the class with tutoring available throughout the week. SFSU tutors are psychology majors who have excellent academic track records and who receive training through a tutoring course that I teach. The tutors meet with students one-on-one or in small groups. They help students develop good strategies for studying and understanding. They also help students generate examples of concepts and encourage students to see the big picture view: to understand how concepts and information connect to one another.

Additionally, the tutors help with the writing component of the course. This consists of three short papers that are about "research experiential" activities. These activities may involve participating in research, reviewing an empirical research report in a journal, participating in one of SFSU's Student Health Center workshops (the applied side of research), attending the San Francisco Exploratorium (engage in hands-on research-based activities), attending a special lecture or symposium, or being their own subject in an n-of-1 design in which they track data on quitting smoking (SFSU gets about a dozen students per semester who take on this challenge; many of whom report years later that this activity helped them to quit smoking). The tutors help students with their papers as well as locating appropriate journal articles.

It is in this context that I endeavor to impart the concepts of evolution and its application to understanding psychology. I do this by continually asking the question of "how" and "why" a psychological phenomenon exits. This happens as I discuss almost every aspect of psychology with students.

LAYING THE FOUNDATION: TEACHING BASIC PRINCIPLES OF EVOLUTION

To begin to inform students about evolutionary process, it is important to review the basic principles and assumptions. Darwin's (1859) theory of natural selection has a set of three components: variation in the genotype of a species, inheritance of genotype, and differential reproductive success. Only genotypic variations that are heritable can evolve in frequency across generations. Through natural selection, those variations that promote survival and reproduction are increasingly passed on. These products of the process of natural selection are adaptations that solve problems in the environment that can threaten both survival and reproduction. These evolutionary principles have long been applied to other sciences and are an important part of psychology's history. Charles Darwin (1872) himself considered the role of evolution in shaping psychological phenomena, such as emotions. William James's (1890) functionalist approach to understanding psychology made him the first evolutionary psychologist. Responding to and adapting to one's environment is the very function of psychological processes. After all, individuals' evolved biological processes (i.e., brain and nervous system) underlie all of their psychological processes.

If evolution is to provide a thread of continuity and connection for all subsequent material, it is important to present basic principles of evolution early on. A lecture on evolutionary psychology, normally presented at the very beginning of a course, provides the perfect opportunity to build understanding of principles of evolution. It is worth the time and effort to devote an entire lecture to these principles and to allow students to brainstorm and forecast ways in which they think evolution can contribute to understanding psychology across domains. It is good to keep track of their ideas so that they can be addressed again as you come to that specific material. This process allows students to think creatively and to see the advantages of the accumulated knowledge in play as they progress through the material.

Early in the course is also the perfect time to confront specific misconceptions that students might have about how evolution works and how it is applied to psychology. In the following sections, I outline both the basic principles of evolution that I teach and the common misconceptions that students tend to hold.

Tenets of Evolutionary Psychology

The "new" science of evolutionary psychology is in at least its fourth inception, as David Buss's titular work on the topic was first published in 1995 (Buss, 2011). This paradigm for understanding psychological science includes the following basic principles presented by Buss in Dunn et al. (2013, pp. 49–64).

1. All manifest behavior is a function of psychological mechanisms, in conjunction with environmental and internal inputs to those mechanisms.

2. All psychological mechanisms owe their existence at the same basic level of description, to evolutionary processes (scientifically, no other known causal process exists for creating complex organic mechanisms).

3. Natural selection and sexual selection (Darwin's theories) are the most important evolutionary processes responsible for creating psychological adaptations (other evolutionary forces such as genetic drift are too weak to fashion adaptations).

4. Evolved psychological mechanisms can be described as information-processing devices (input, decision rules or other transformation procedures, and outputs).

5. The output of psychological adaptations can be physiological activity, information that serves as input to other psychological mechanisms, or manifest behavior.

6. Psychological adaptations are housed in the brain.

7. Psychological adaptations are functional; that is, they are "designed" to solve statistically recurrent adaptive problems confronted by human ancestors over deep evolutionary time.

Typical Points of Confusion for Students

A basic understanding of evolutionary psychology can help the student in avoiding misconceptions about evolutionary process in psychology. I have seen these misunderstandings limit the ability to see evolution as the overarching concept that keeps all the different subdisciplines hanging together in concert with one another. I outline some of these misunderstandings in the following sections.

What Is an Adaptation?

One point of confusion for students may be in their understanding of "adaptation." The basic tenets of evolutionary psychology as earlier outlined rely heavily on understanding what adaptation is—and is not. The noun "adaptation" has two basic meanings in evolution. Adaptations can be seen as attributes that help a creature survive and reproduce at a given point in time by solving a particular problem. However, in the greater scope of evolutionary theory adaptations are the historical end products of lengthy evolutionary process (Buss, 1995). Psychological adaptations are thus the products of historical evolution, that is, features that were "functionally designed by the process of evolution by selection acting in the past" (Thornhill, 1997, p. 4). Thus, just because a particular ability is helpful or adaptive in the present time does not mean that it was produced by evolution. One example is the currently popular adaptation of reducing saturated and trans fats in individuals' diets to increase personal health. This food-eating behavior could be considered an adaptation (e.g., Schmitt & Pilcher, 2004) in the sense that it promotes survival and reproductive fitness. However, this does not mean that it is the product of historical evolution. So students need to simultaneously appreciate that adaptations occur in the present but are considered "evolved" only if they have been passed down as part of historical evolution. Simply put, if the past becomes the future, evolutionary adaptation has occurred.

What Is Meant by Evolutionary Time?

One of the significant challenges for students is comprehending the concept of "past" as it relates to adaptations. Deep time, that is, evolutionary time, is hard for students to wrap their minds around, maybe even more so, given the techno-logical speed with which people lead their lives today. Adaptations have evolved precisely to solve problems that occur in brief time, that is the immediate and ongoing challenges faced in the seconds, minutes, hours, and days of people's brief lives (Buss, 2010). But evolutionary time is glacially slow (and that is the pace of glaciers before global warming).

I teach about deep time using an approach offered by David Buss (see david-buss.com for extensive material on teaching evolutionary psychology), which involves the analogy of a 100-yard football field to represent the evolution of all life. Once instructors present students with the basic milestone events connected to human evolution, they can overlay these as metaphorical locations on a foot-ball field to provide perspective on deep time. I accomplish this by pointing out that life first emerged 3.7 billion years ago and place this milestone at the starting end of the football field. I remind students that this milestone is supported by empirical evidence and that the science of dating is well established and more than 60 years old. I have had at least one student insist that these findings are merely "tricks of the devil" and have reconciled myself to the fact that there are some people incapable, because of the cognitive barricades they have erected, of changing their thinking. If the evolution of life begins at one end of the football field, then you must travel 99 yards and 2 feet to encounter the genus *Homo*, with Cro-Magnons appearing in Europe only at that point represented by the last tenth of an inch on the 100-yard football field.

Therefore in present time, humans adapt to their environments with a wide array of abilities that have become adaptations over deep time because they enhanced survival and reproductive success. The ultimate cause of thinking and behavior, "survival," is evidenced only in deep time.

Causation

The deep time concept lends itself to students understanding the two funda-mental constructs of proximate and ultimate causality. At the proximate level one can examine the specific ways in which response to environmental demands are executed, that is, adaptation. Ultimately it is survival and reproduction that fuel the change, that is, the adaptive force. It is survival and reproductive success that accounts for the fact that there is still human life on earth and will continue to be with all of its variations. That ultimate dictate of survival is fulfilled by differential reproductive success because of heritable variants. As people like to say, they all have ancestors but they may not all become ancestors.

In teaching about causation, there is the need to continually distinguish between these proximate and ultimate causes. The mechanisms that address the *how* questions are the proximate causes; the ultimate causes, the *why* questions, are always about survival and reproductive success. Though the ultimate cause is broad and consistent, the proximal explanations involve special domain-specific adaptations (Pinker, 1997). This is often a point of confusion for students. Not all adaptations are domain-specific. Some are quite general and allow basic human functioning. These domain-general adaptations are also essential for survival, for example, processing information quickly. At the same time adaptations must be discrete and handle immediate problems presented in the environment. So, for example, quickly processing visual information, a general adaptation, is given relevance by the cognitive processes of perception that occurs in context, a specific adaptation. If I am at a baseball game and something comes flying toward me, I extend my glove hoping to snag a fly ball. If I am at a large field not during a sporting event and something comes flying toward me, I duck assuming the potential for a dangerous hit to the head. In both instances, I have the general capacity to quickly process information and the specific capacity to figure out what it is that is being processed.

Quite simply, beyond the ultimate cause of survival and reproductive success, adaptations need not solve a great sweep of problems. Just as no one physical organ can be expected to do all the functions for the body, no one mental process can fulfill the demands of all mental activity (Buss, 1999, 2011). The human mind is domain-specific, species-typical, and functionally specialized instead of a general problem solver. Thus, evolution is the integrated paradigm that unites the discipline (Barkow et al., 1992; Buss, 1995). Evolution simultaneously can account for the general and the particular aspect of human functioning. This as well accounts for how hypotheses in evolutionary psychology vary in quality and precision and should not be dismissed as merely "just so stories."

"Just so Stories" Misunderstanding

The "just so stories" mythology is a basic misunderstanding that must be laid to rest in conveying the principle of adaptation. The "just so stories" concept derives from the classic Kipling book of the same title. The stories in this book explain the existence and characteristics of all types of creatures in hindsight, without the burden of empirical evidence. A frequent indictment of an evolutionary perspective is that it offers similarly post hoc explanations that are not rooted in evidence. Because evolution occurs over deep time, students may mistakenly believe that the tenets of evolutionary psychology cannot be empirically tested, because to do so would require them to engage in time travel or to track species across millions or billions of years. But evolutionary theory leads to testable hypotheses, and a great deal of evidence has accumulated over the last 20 plus years that has tested such hypotheses. Examples are research on gender differences in mate selection, specific fear response, morning sickness, incest avoidance, specific fears, and men's desire for short-term sexual variety (e.g., Roberts, 2012; Schmitt & Pilcher, 2004).

Adaptation and the Role of Environment

Students may mistakenly think that the environment cannot influence behavior and thought that have resulted from psychological adaptation. This misunderstanding in part occurs from long discarded nature versus nurture perspectives that see biological and environmental forces as separate and pitted against one another, rather than constantly and dynamically interacting. I point out to students that there is absolutely no aspect of human existence that is solely due to one force or the other. All biological determinants (genotypes) are always existing in an environment; even the basic building blocks for a human, sperm and egg, are always in an environment. There is absolutely never one without the other. Environments over deep time provide the pressures for the dynamics of adaptation and it is the environmental input that triggers the adaptive response; without it, nothing would change over time.

Adaptation and the Role of Learning

Buss (2010) points out that another misunderstanding that students have that gets in the way of accepting an evolutionary perspective is the assumption that behaviors are shaped by learning and thus cannot be caused by evolution. Students lose sight of the big picture in failing to realize that human learning is the greatest adaptation. Is this merely a distinction between proximate and ultimate causation? Perhaps, but it tends to create a view that pits evolution against learning. Learning of course requires evolved processes and the value of the ultimate cause is seen in species-specific rates and types of learning. Food aversion is a prime example. Not learning quickly can immediately compromise one's very existence. Nothing emphasizes the need to learn more than the errors that cause a cessation in survival. If humans cease to exist, then adaptation, deep time, and so forth are irrelevant. Again, it all comes down to survival; evolution creates the thoughts and behaviors and changes in the biological structures that underpin them in order for people to survive. Dead is dead; humans all have ancestors but they may not all become ancestors.

Reproductive Success and Fitness

Students consistently come to the course holding misconceptions about the concept of "fitness." They think that fitness refers to traits like size and strength that aid physical survival, rather than traits that aid reproductive success. Helping students understand the true definition of fitness can be achieved with "sexy" (i.e., interesting and provocative) topics like the differences in reproductive strategies between males and females, parental certainty, and the ideas of individual and group fitness. They quickly see fitness more appropriately and as an important aspect of evolutionary theory. It is a wonderful hook to explain fitness to students with these concepts; they have likely never understood fitness in terms of reproductive success; therefore doing so is a valuable foundation for understanding ultimate causality. Dive into this topic; it really will open eyes to a new view.

One can start by explaining that females have an enormous investment in reproductive success, fitness. They give birth to the most altricial young of all mammals. To achieve success, they must care for that offspring for a long time. Males on the other hand can impregnate a near boundless number of females, but unlike the female who actually sees that offspring "spring" from her, there is no certainty of paternity. Nature has balance. These are concepts students have little familiarity with, but there are so many things that can be explained in this framework that students will directly relate to—after all many of them have seen the battles in reproductive investment and parental certainty played out on daytime television (e.g., the antics shown on the Jerry Springer or Maury Povich programs). And, of course, as a grandparent, I can explain that grandchildren are the evolutionary payoff.

CONNECTING EVOLUTIONARY PROCESSES ACROSS TOPICS

Presenting the basic elements of evolutionary theory and principles of ultimate and proximal causality is the essential starting place for weaving the theme of evolution into an introductory psychology course. The next step is to connect the theme to additional topics across the term. I will present here a few ideas for how to weave evolution into every major topic one typically teaches in an introductory psychology course.

I am presenting these topics in the usual order one finds them in a textbook, although I personally change the order of topics from the chapter order in the text (e.g., jumping right to personality and pathology to satisfy the interest of many students at the beginning of the semester). I also do not teach all chapters, and in any given semester, I vary the chapters that I omit. For example, I am usually able to fold in information on therapy with disorders. I often elect not to teach emotion and motivation though clearly they offer easy access to discussing evolution. Heath psychology is covered briefly, mostly focused on stress and coping.

Theoretical Backgrounds

I challenge students to think of ways to evaluate some of the classic theories of psychology with evolutionary processes in mind. It does not take a giant step to reinterpret some of the psychodynamic forces of Freud in an evolutionary context.

What aspects of internal mechanism and the general mechanistic view of human behavior would be consistent with evolutionary psychology? Is the Oedipal complex a contortion of incest avoidance? What is there about oral gratification that is compatible with ultimate cause? So maybe Freud was onto something, but he provided a theory that is nearly impossible to empirically evaluate. Psychodynamic theory is just one of many. In my course, this process of discussing theories begins with different groups of the class discussing among themselves certain theories and then the class comes back together and students share their ideas. I use this technique for many topics. Students are challenged to think about the components of each theoretical perspective that are consistent with an evolutionary theory.

Research Methods

Typically the next topic many of the instructors teach is research methods. At this point, students who have joined the course primarily to learn about personality and pathology are made keenly aware of how individuals come to know what they know. This is the perfect point for a general discussion of scientific literacy: critical thinking and its value in society. After looking at all the different ways instructors rely on empirical evidence, it is useful to come back to the concept of "good theory," or one that is empirically based and testable. It is worth noting that the overwhelming evidence in favor of evolution and the fact that it is the only overarching explanation that holds together all of the discoveries in life sciences and human behavior make it very much a master theory. It is easy to introduce specific research done in an evolutionary psychology context. These studies can be found in a variety of sources (e.g., Buss, 2011). It is good to engage students in thinking about behavior at the different levels of analysis and then speculating about how the proximate causes can be examined. In the end, I bring it back to the ultimate aspects of a phenomenon, despite the nature of the specific empirical strategy.

Biological Foundations of Behavior

The brain and biological foundations for behavior is the typical next topic. No stretch here for discussing evolutionary psychology. Opening with genetics and reproductive strategies further reinforces the platform on which evolutionary psychology is based. A discussion of differential reproductive strategies is easy to get started in any class by having students do something like what Buss (1989) did with his inquiry on mate preference in 37 cultures: I ask students to list what they want in a steady partner. The lists generated will show very different attributes for males and females with females more likely to value financial capacity and males valuing physical attributes. I then discuss with students how the pressures of mortality, infant mortality, reproductive investment, and parental certainty influence these differences. For each, I try to help students understand the organizational concept of balance gained with trade-off.

With regard to the structure of the brain, I emphasize the elegance of specific design in brain structure as well as the advantage of plasticity for maximizing survival. I ask students to consider the adaptive value of the function of different brain structures. What functions do evolutionarily older brain structures handle versus evolutionarily newer structures? Students come to realize that the complexity of being human is the result of the most recently evolved structures.

Consciousness

Consciousness often is the next topic in many introductory texts. I ask students to grapple with the question of how consciousness aids survival. Why would mechanisms evolve to allow awareness of one's conscious state? I try to help students narrow the scope of such a question by focusing on the topic of sleep. I present the different theories of why humans sleep and ask students to evaluate them from proximate (How do people sleep and what occurs when they do?) and ultimate perspectives (How does sleep aid survival?). How do the theories of restoration, problem solving, memory consolidation, and safety offer explanations for why humans sleep and how do they measure up as supporting or not an evolutionary view?

I also share with students an interesting body of literature that has emerged suggesting that prior to the industrial revolution humans did not always sleep in a standard 8 hours per night pattern but rather would wake and be active in the middle of the night and then return to sleep. This pattern is referenced in Chaucer's *Canterbury Tales* as a "first sleep" and a "second sleep" (e.g., Ekirch, 2005, 2015). I challenge students to generate explanations for why humans would sleep in such a pattern. Certainly having sex is something to do if it is cold and dark outside and you have had a bit of rest. I also ask them to consider what environmental pressures have emerged to cause a shift to sleeping through the night.

Sensation and Perception

Sensation and perception easily lend themselves to an evolutionary perspective as these are the very functions that bring in data from the environment that humans make sense of to maximize their survival. Humans have evolved sensory systems that meet the environmental demands required of them. I will briefly touch on a couple of systems that exemplify this.

The chemical senses: Olfaction and gustation.   I describe the sensation and perception of odors and taste as a first signal to potential danger. Human nose literally leads the way. Humans cannot smell as well as their canine companions but they smell as much as they need to survive. Additionally, I present evidence of olfactory communication that influences mate preferences, mother–infant communication, and sexual asymmetry in detection of fear (e.g., de Groot, Semin, & Smeets, 2014). The other chemical sense, gustation, provides a means for both avoiding toxicity and promoting adequate consumption of nutrients. Is the higher concentration of bitter taste buds at the back of the tongue helpful for eliciting a gag response to poisonous things (i.e., many toxic substances are bitter)? Humans later learn to like coffee, gin, and the like, but their natural reaction is to gag as they may be in a class of substances that harms them.

Audition.   Having two ears placed on the sides of the head allows humans to localize sounds that may alert them to danger. I demonstrate sound localization in my class by blindfolding a student and making a click sound above the midline of the student's head from back to front. The sound is very hard to locate, unlike a sound presented more to one side of the head. I then describe how having a brain that automatically coordinates head movements with sound localization (provided by the midbrain structure, the tectum) aids survival by saving time and cognitive processing. A student assistant can make a crashing sound in the hall outside the class and then I point out how the members of the class automatically turned toward the sound (why? it could have signaled danger).

Haptic or cutaneous senses.   Humans can use touch to navigate, to identify good (i.e., not rotten) food to eat, to signal potential harm that comes from pain, and to provide sexual arousal. I ask students to consider why humans have differential concentrations of receptors on different parts of the body (i.e., the hands and the genitals), leading them to understand how sensing in those areas is especially important for survival and reproduction. You can point out how competing signals from the fingertips versus other skin surfaces reach the brain at different rates, based on concentration of receptors and distance. The signal that gets there first and with greater intensity dominates. Handy thing that masturbation would be no fun if you mostly felt your hand.

Learning

Learning typically follows sensation and perception. Here, I emphasize how the principles of learning—classical, operant, and observational—are essential for survival. Not being stuck with simple fixed action patterns as a way of responding to the world allows great flexibility. Organisms that can learn economize on cognitive resources, thus freeing them for more essential demands presented by the environment at any given time. I have students imagine their existence if for each thing they encountered they had to learn anew how to handle it. Basically, everyone would stall out at a very primitive level and not survive. People's superior ability to learn, to think, to remember, and to cogitate is arguably an advantage that humans have over all species (although those species may well have superior abilities in other areas of functioning). Humans are especially skilled at learning through observation. How could one ever put together that Ikea flat pack furniture without watching a YouTube video!

Memory

In any introductory text, learning is followed by memory. What do people remember? How do they remember? Answers to these questions and the evidence of the special design in human memory get individuals to both proximate and ultimate explanations for their memory process. For example, humans are well equipped to remember faces. I ask students what specific structure in the brain makes this possible. The answer is the fusiform gyrus; this is the proximate cause. Next, I ask why this ability has evolved, and what is the advantage gained by learning faces? It is of course survival. There is an advantage of recognizing offspring, partner, and enemy, especially in a species as social as human beings.

I also emphasize an evolutionary perspective on why memory works as it does. Memory is not perfect or exact. The ways that the mind selects and organizes memories, adjusts them with new input, and transforms them for coherence allow individuals to select, retain, and apply previous experiences to new ones; this is essential. Human memory is efficient. It allows economy of their finite mental resources and provides a foundation for problem solving, thinking, and language. Memory gives humans a cohesive record of experiences that facilitates survival.

Intelligence and Cognition

In approaching this material, you can begin by having students think about what intelligence is. Using student-generated definitions of "intelligence," you can point out how intelligence, and cognition more broadly, promotes survival. General intelligence, defined as integrating information from various domain-specific abilities (e.g., spatial reasoning, language), allows for dealing with variant patterns found in nature. Carroll (1993), in a review of the intelligence testing literature, offers ample support for general intelligence consistent with evolutionary psychology. This implies intelligence as a domain-general ability. There is evidence further that speed of processing, working memory, inhibition, habituation, statistical learning (calculating probabilities of events has a survival advantage), associative learning, and metacognition are all considered domain-general abilities. These adaptations facilitate specific functioning and then ultimately facilitate survival. For example, needing to take a long time to think before acting could hardly be adaptive (Ploeger et al., 2008). Once again, it is easy to underscore the conclusion that in addition to understanding the proximate causes of cognitive processes (e.g., the speed at which one can respond to a problem), the ultimate cause is that the function means that it enables us to survive.

Language

What can be more advanced in the evolutionary process than human language? The brain has evolved to commit sizeable real estate to this adaptation. Why might humans have it and other animals not? This is an intriguing question to ask students to ponder. I often ask students to think about it and then present a few theories about why language might have evolved. A recent theory posits that language evolved from tool use by humans and the need to communicate for sharing tools and instructing others in how to use tools (Arbib, 2011). Scientists further speculate that mirror neurons, which are involved in seeing and performing actions and happen to reside in a part of the brain that also serves language functions, allowed for communication through pantomime and then evolved to spoken language; and then the train took off. Having language to teach and communicate with is clearly an advantage for survival.

Health Psychology

Consider discussing the thrifty gene concept as an illustration of the behaviors related to the consumption of high-calorie foods (Wells, 2009). The thrifty gene hypothesis offers an explanation for frugality and thriftiness in the expenditure of energy. Fats, sugar, and high-calorie foods served survival when human ancestors evolved and there was no easy access to such foods. Thus, humans have a brain that evolved to find "bad stuff" especially tasty. Notably, fat, sugar, and high-calorie foods only became bad stuff when human environments shifted to a more sedentary one with a wide availability of food. Thus, many negative health outcomes are thanks to a brain that has been programmed to want fats and sugar … alas!

If survival is so important, then why are humans killing themselves with unhealthy behaviors linked to lifestyle choices? Here is where the concept of deep time provides insight.

Developmental

Developmental psychology is one of the easiest areas to continue the thread of evolutionary psychology, though psychologists have largely set aside the "ontogeny recapitulates phylogeny" (i.e., that the developing embryo mirrors the structural development of lower organisms is human phylum, chordate) as an explicit representation of evolution. One can see, however, in the dynamic changes that occur with development echoes of the evolutionary process. A specific genotype interacts with a broad range of inputs from the environment resulting in a phenotype. Thus, through development a given genotype responds in a dynamic adaptive process with a specific environment. The amazing flexibility of the human child allows its survival in a wide array of contexts. For example, look at the variations in child-rearing across cultures, all successful. The very different child-rearing styles result in survival and ideally create adult humans who will function best in a given culture. What an advantage it is to be human. Humans have an enormous adaptive flexibility to "make it work" in all kinds of circumstances because of generalized and specific adaptions.

Cognitive development also offers good examples of adaptation, both general and specific. Many domain-general cognitive abilities, for example, Piaget's assimilation and accommodation, account for similarities in cognitive development across diverse child-rearing settings. Assimilation and accommodation allow us to handle the environment and to develop lasting ways for understanding it and interacting in it across the life span. Cognition is of course but one aspect of development. The human is essentially very complex and thus is simultaneously developing physically, cognitively, and emotionally. All three domains interact and influence one another in adaptive process.

On the emotional side of development, attachment is a prime example of a human-evolved process that facilitates survival. Many species' offspring have physical abilities (e.g., clinging to mom) that maintain proximity to a life-sustaining caregiver. For humans, the evolved psychological mechanism of attachment serves a similar function. Piagetian adaptation—that is, assimilation and accommodation—and attachment are but two areas of development in which the ultimate goal of survival can be illustrated. Development is full of examples of the dynamics of evolutions.

Personality and Pathology

Personality and pathology are next units of material found in introductory psychology text. As Peter Gray (1996) puts it clearly, many students equate a course in psychology with the study of pathology. According to the National Institutes of Health, more than 18 percent of adults suffer from serious mental illness. This figure likely underestimates the rate of mental health problems because it excludes those with substance addictions. And at some point in their lives, at least 25 percent of people experience a serious mental disorder. How can it be that evolution has created a mind so prone to problems? Is this a consequence of a mismatch of humans' old brains (evolved long ago) with environments of modern creation? This is a provocative question to ask students to consider. Another way I try to help students think about psychopathology is to consider that many pathologies include thoughts, feelings, and behaviors that are adaptive at lower levels of intensity. For example, fear responses, the need for order and regularity, and feelings of sadness serve important functions in people's everyday lives that aid survival. Additionally, many defense mechanisms, ala Freud, may be seen as adaptive ways to cope. For example, hiding one's insecurities or using denial as a "time out" for preparing to handle a significant loss may be seen as adaptive. Considering how overall one's personality develops, Maslow's theory assumes the very basics of evolution—that is, the need for safety and survival is first and foremost before more complex aspects of the human personality develop fully.

Social Psychology

It is sociability that makes human existence possible; alone humans would not survive nor reproduce. Evolutionary principles of natural selection can be seen in all aspects of social psychology and probably most easily in mate selection, aggression, prosocial behavior, and social facilitation. How does the behavior manifest (proximate cause) and how does it aid survival (ultimate cause) are questions that I have found that students have a good deal of ease within social psychology. Maybe this is a consequence of the nature of the material and the fact that it comes at the end of the semester when they have spent a couple of months thinking about evolution as the overarching thread that holds all the areas of psychology together.

Mate selection from an evolutionary perspective can be covered in social psychology. The seminal study of mate selection by Buss (1989) is easy to replicate with a class (see section on biological foundations above). Additionally, prosocial behavior has been investigated from an evolutionary perspective (e.g., Bressan & Kramer, 2015). You can ask students to do a Bogardus-type social distancing scale, rating the likelihood of helping different groups of people. A likely outcome is that students will be more likely to help near relations, demonstrating the notion of kin selection. These are but two examples of how to illustrate the connection of evolution to social behaviors. Whatever individuals choose to discuss or demonstrate in more depth, one can always ask the question of how any of the social behaviors aid survival and reproductive success.

CHALLENGES TO TEACHING EVOLUTIONARY PRINCIPLES TO THE UNWILLING OR MISINFORMED

There are surprising challenges to teaching about evolutionary theory and its application to understanding psychological processes. A 2014 Gallup Poll (Gallup, 2014) revealed that 42 percent of Americans subscribe to a creationist viewpoint: They believe that God created humans in their present form about 10,000 years ago. Many who subscribe to this belief are college-educated: 49 percent have "some college" education and 27 percent are college graduates. Gallup began polling this question in 1982 and the percentage of adherents to the creationist view have not decreased consistently, fluctuating between 40 percent and 47 percent.

So where do instructors begin in "selling" a perspective already eschewed by many of their students? I often begin by making a clear distinction between science and religious beliefs as very different systems of knowledge. The National Academy of Sciences has proposed that the ability to achieve an understanding of the unique ways that science and religion construct knowledge is essential for a scientifically literate citizenry (National Academy of Sciences, 2008). This perspective is reinforced by the literature stressing the importance of understanding scientific process as a unique way of knowing that is distinct from religious beliefs (e.g., Bybee, 2004; Shtulman & Calabi, 2013). When instructors broach religious issues with their students, it is important to acknowledge the value of both religion and science: Both create meaning and understanding in individuals' lives and need not be conflicting.

A discussion of belief versus acceptance of the process of evolution is appropriate in this context (Williams, 2009). I typically explain to students that I am a practicing Episcopalian and that I have found little difficulty in embracing science. In fact, it has deepened my faith. Hokayem and BouJaoude (2008) similarly suggest introducing examples of individuals who have simultaneously and successfully held religious and scientific views, such as the Jesuit scholar Teilhard de Chardin, who dedicated the majority of his life to understanding evolution. I recently visited the Natural History Museum in New York City (site of the *Night at the Museum* movies) and was impressed by a video showing scientists discussing their personal religious beliefs while also stating the absolute, fundamental importance of accepting evolution. The human mind has been shown to be capable of simultaneously holding both religious and scientific views, in part, because their mechanisms for understanding are in fact different. Religious beliefs can guide their decisions about morality and how they live their lives but empirical evidence can provide understanding of why they have the behaviors and mental activity that they do.

Equally important to instructors' efforts to win over those students who are resistant to an evolutionary perspective is to correct misconceptions about evolution that many students hold (Shtulman & Valcarcel, 2012). Thus the challenge is to not only help students learn the correct premises of evolution but also help them unlearn their incorrect suppositions (e.g., each organism producing offspring better adapted than it was at birth). These incorrect suppositions will otherwise cloud students' view of the fundamental principles of evolution (Shtulman & Valcarcel, 2012).

FINAL THOUGHTS

As Walt Whitman (1860) voiced in his extraordinary poem *Song of Myself,* "I am large, I contain multitudes" (p. 52), the human mind allows people to simultaneously hold seeming contradictions. The mind can do this because it is essentially very complex. This complexity of the human mind comprises a large collection of domain-specific, functionally specialized mechanisms (Buss, 1995). It is this complexity that promotes survival. The complexity affords humans many options for adaptive responses to the environment.

My desire is that students not only will enjoy psychology but also be able to apply much of the knowledge to their own lives. Specifically, I also hope that they learn to use the tenets of evolution to understand psychology and themselves as thinking, behaving humans. And when they are asked why a behavior or cognitive process occurs, students not only should be able to explain it in terms of "how" (proximate causality) but also should consistently be able to respond with a fundamental of evolution: the "why" (ultimate causality), which is survival.

Chapter 9

A Skills Theme for the Introductory Psychology Course

R. ERIC LANDRUM

Boise State University

The imparting of skills to students and the assessment of those skills by psychology educators should be a central, core feature of the introductory psychology course. The purpose of this chapter is to convince the reader, and particularly instructors of introductory psychology, that a skills theme is desired for students enrolled in such courses (ideally, as much skills acquisition as possible). Although there are important and interesting debates about what should be the content of introductory psychology (e.g., American Psychological Association [APA], 2013; Dunn et al., 2010), it is my contention that whatever the content, the course should be skills based, because it is the acquisition of skills that can be the legacy for introductory psychology, much more than the memorability of course content (Landrum & Gurung, 2013). To be clear, a skills-based approach in this context means that students actively practice the desired skills and produce products that are the artifacts of skilled performance—such as writing a paper to demonstrate writing skills or giving a speech to demonstrate oral communication skills. Another approach, which is believed to be common, is a content-based approach where introductory psychology instructors grapple with depth versus breadth content issues, and multiple-choice testing is often the method to assessing content retention.

To preview, I begin with a broad overview of the skills necessary for successful college graduates, narrowing to the skills needed by psychology graduates and then addressing potential skills to be practiced in the introductory psychology course. In order for a course to be effective (regardless of content-focused or skills-based), backward course design is recommended, and a brief primer is provided here. The chapter ends with a sample skills-based assignment that demonstrates how instructors might assess multiple skills in one assignment, and be able to do that in a large section of introductory psychology, as the course is often taught in large sections.

SKILLS THAT COLLEGE GRADUATES NEED

On either the national stage or within the discipline of psychology, attention to skills is not new. In 1991, the U.S. Department of Labor formed the Secretary's Commission on Achieving Necessary Skills (SCANS), which in turn issued a SCANS Report highlighting the competencies and foundational skills necessary for success in the workplace (see Table 9.1). Thus, the skills that can be practiced in the introductory psychology course contribute to the accumulated competency of students in these relevant skill areas.

There are certainly other methods by which to organize and characterize the skills needed for successful employment. The Association of American Colleges and Universities (AAC&U, 2004) suggested that the five key outcomes for a liberal education include (a) strong skills (analytical, communication, quantitative,

T A B L E   9 . 1   **Necessary Skills for Workplace Know-How**

Workplace competencies. Effective workers can productively use the following:

- Resources—They know how to allocate time, money, materials, space, and staff.

- Interpersonal skills—They can work in teams, teach others, serve customers, lead, negotiate, and work well with people from culturally diverse backgrounds.

- Information—They can acquire and evaluate data, organize and maintain files, interpret and communicate, and use computers to process information.

- Systems—They understand social, organizational, and technological systems; they can monitor and correct performance; and they can design or improve systems.

- Technology—They can select equipment and tools, apply technology to specific tasks, and maintain and troubleshoot equipment.

Foundation skills. Competent workers in the high-performance workplace need the following:

- Basic skills—reading, writing, arithmetic and mathematics, speaking, and listening

- Thinking skills—the ability to learn, to reason, to think creatively, to make decisions, and to solve problems

- Personal qualities—individual responsibility, self-esteem and self-management, sociability, and integrity

information); (b) deep understanding and applied experiences within disciplines that study nature, society, and culture; (c) collaboration skills and intercultural knowledge; (d) civic responsibility with a proactive approach; and (e) habits of mind that promote integrative thinking and the ability to apply/transfer knowledge and skills from one setting to another setting. In a more recent conceptualization, Pellegrino and Hilton (2012) identified three clusters of 21st-century competencies: cognitive competencies (cognitive processes and strategies, knowledge, and creativity), intrapersonal competencies (intellectual openness, work ethic/conscientiousness, and positive core self-evaluation), and interpersonal competencies (teamwork and collaboration and leadership). Although the skills under discussion are reorganized and re-characterized from time to time, the national data are relatively clear about the importance of skills that all college graduates should possess, as well as data available from employers about the current shortcomings of newly minted college graduates concerning workforce readiness (AAC&U, 2008, 2010; Gardner, 2007).

SKILLS THAT PSYCHOLOGY GRADUATES NEED

There are studies available regarding skills preparation and workforce readiness that are psychology specific (Landrum & Harrold, 2003; Landrum, Hettich, & Wilner, 2010; Perry, Foust, & Elicker, 2013), but these researchers typically focus on psychology graduates rather than students enrolled in a specific course. Advice does exist about assessing skills at the course level, such as the measurement of writing skills (Luttrell, Bufkin, Eastman, & Miller, 2010) in the introductory psychology course (Smith & Fineburg, 2005; Stoloff, 2010) or the research methods course (Thaler, Kazemi, & Huscher, 2009; Tomcho et al., 2009). However, given the popularity of psychology from a national perspective, some empirical work does exist about the role that skill acquisition and development can play in the introductory course. For example, writing skills are often emphasized in introductory psychology (Carroll, 2008; Fallahi, Wood, Austad, & Fallahi, 2006; Jorgensen & Marek, 2013; Madigan & Brosamer, 1990; Nevid, Pastva, & McClelland, 2012), as well as critical thinking skills (Solon, 2007; Wilkinson, Dik, & Tix, 2008), reading comprehension skills (Bell & Limber, 2010; Ray & Belden, 2007), and even juggling skills (Bennett & McKinney, 2000). The introductory psychology course provides a particularly good opportunity to practice skills, in part, due to the sheer volume of students—between 1.2 million and 1.6 million students annually (Steuer & Ham, 2008)—serving as the second most popular course in the United States (the most popular is English composition; Adelman, 2004). Additionally, given that themes presented in introductory psychology can make a real difference in people's lives (e.g., Zimbardo, 2004), the chance to practice skills with information that has everyday applicability to life provides an important opportunity for psychology educators.

A particularly helpful document with regard to encouraging psychology instructors to aspire to a skills-centered approach is the *APA Guidelines for the Undergraduate Psychology Major: Version 2.0* (APA, 2013), hereafter *Guidelines 2.0*.

Although one of the five guidelines is clearly focused on the knowledge base in psychology, the remaining four guidelines center on skills and competencies: scientific inquiry and critical thinking, ethical and social responsibility in a diverse world, communication, and professional development. Although the guidelines are aimed at psychology majors, they are broad enough that their outcomes are desirable regardless of a student's major. Thus, they are useful for all students who take introductory psychology, a course that clearly serves both majors and non-majors. In other words, if an introductory psychology instructor can begin to help students achieve the *Guidelines 2.0* goals for psychology majors in the course, then all students in the course benefit.

DESIGNING A COURSE FOR SKILLS DEVELOPMENT

So how might the introductory psychology course be designed such that a skills focus can be accomplished, especially taking into account that introductory psychology is often a large enrollment course in many parts of the country? How might this course design adequately address the assessment of skills? Quite frankly, teaching skills is not enough; educators must assess skill acquisition and students must also receive feedback about their skills to promote continued improvement. From my perspective, these efforts start with the design of introductory psychology courses, particularly emphasizing a backward design approach.

Experts in course design suggest a sequence of course planning steps that is counterintuitive to many faculty members, hence the label "backward" design (Fink, 2003; Wiggins & McTighe, 1998). In backward design, learning goals are the initial, central focus of the design process. These learning goals must be articulated with clarity and precision (like operational definitions) to be useful in the next step of backward design, which is then to determine the assessment method. *After* the assessment process is in place, the educator designing the course considers the pedagogical approach. Thus, assessment drives pedagogical decision-making. As Wiggins and McTighe (1998) put it, "what would we accept as evidence that students have attained the desired understandings and proficiencies—*before* proceeding to plan teaching and learning experiences" (p. 8; italics in original).

Backward design of the introductory psychology course might push educators out of their comfort zone. For instance, creating learning outcomes first followed immediately by an assessment plan might lead to the conclusion that lecturing is not the optimum pedagogical approach or that a textbook is not necessary. Educators committed to backward design may seek a pedagogical approach that requires additional work on their part. The strength of the backward design approach lies in the articulation of course-relevant learning outcomes. An example of a learning outcome for the introductory psychology course might be "by the end of this course, each student will be able to distinguish a scientific approach from a non-scientific approach, and be able to articulate specific aspects of a psychological science approach." Some educators may not begin their course design or course planning process with learning goals in mind. Learning goals and outcomes may be an individual instructor decision, or they may be controlled by committee decisions or departmental goals. Depending on your departmental or institutional environment, outcomes assessment may be taken seriously or may be taken as a perfunctory task to be completed on periodic basis. Regardless of the local environmental conditions, meaningful assessment data at the course level are vital to faculty members who wish to continually improve their course and their own professional performance. Even in the absence of meaningful departmental learning outcomes, psychology educators should be aware of the five guidelines in the *Guidelines 2.0* materials referenced earlier (APA, 2013).

Some authors use the terms "goals" and "outcomes" interchangeably (Marzano, 2009), whereas others differentiate between goals and outcomes (Suskie, 2009). Learning outcomes are the "knowledge, skills, attitudes, and habits of mind that student take with them from a learning experience" (Suskie, 2009, p. 117). Learning outcomes provide the evidence after the fact, that learning has occurred; it is not uncommon to think about learning outcomes in the context of dependent variables. Learning outcomes are often more precisely defined as learning objectives, where pedagogical approaches are paired with desired outcomes. Well-written learning objectives possess three characteristics (Mager, 1962; Marzano, 2009): performance, conditions, and criteria. First, a learning outcome/objective should describe what the student should know or be able to do after the learning experience. Second, a learning outcome/objective may describe the conditions or context in which the demonstration of knowledge and/or skills is to occur. Third, an acceptable level of performance (criterion) is established to help determine if the learning outcome has been met. For example, if you believe that it is vital for students to be able to understand and articulate the five levels of Maslow's hierarchy of needs, a well-written learning outcome might be: "At the completion of this course, successful students will be able to articulate all of the stages of Maslow's hierarchy of needs and be able to provide a real-life example of each stage." Thus, this learning objective defines what a student should know (Maslow's hierarchy of needs), the context about the demonstration (be able to provide real-life examples), and the acceptable level of performance (all of the stages).

Entire volumes are devoted to providing detailed answers as to how to adequately assess learning outcomes—the scope of this chapter only allows a cursory review of potential methodological approaches. For more depth, I recommend Diamond (2008), Gurung and Schwartz (2009), Maki (2004), Pusateri (2009), Seybert (2002), Suskie (2009), and Walvoord (2004). In fact, there is an entire national organization devoted to the study of learning outcomes assessment on the collegiate level—the National Institute for Learning Outcomes Assessment (www.learningoutcomesassessment.org). Many of these recommendations are relevant at the individual course level.

One rationale for making pedagogical choices would be to follow a developmental process or developmental progression with students (Weimer, 2002). To offer a well-designed introductory psychology course and have students succeed in that course, student motivation plays a substantial role in the level

TABLE 9.2   Strategies to Establish Value and Positive Expectancies for a Course Experience

Strategies to Establish Value

- Connect the material to students' interests.
- Provide authentic, real-world tasks.
- Show relevance to students' current academic lives.
- Demonstrate the relevance of higher level skills to students' future professional lives.
- Identify what you reward and value.
- Show your own passion and enthusiasm for the discipline.

Strategies That Help Student Build Positive Expectancies

- Ensure alignment of objectives, assessments, and instructional strategies.
- Identify an appropriate level of challenge.
- Create assignments that provide the appropriate level of challenge.
- Provide early success opportunities.
- Articulate your expectations.
- Provide rubrics.
- Provide targeted feedback.
- Be fair.
- Educate students about ways individuals explain success and failure.
- Describe effective study strategies.

Strategies That Address Both Value and Expectancies

- Provide flexibility and control.
- Give students an opportunity to reflect.

Source: Ambrose et al. (2010).

of engagement students will have with the course and the instructor. Ambrose, Bridges, DiPietro, Lovett, and Norman (2010) offered research-based suggestions for how to help students value and build a positive expectancy for your course (see Table 9.2).

SKILLS DEVELOPMENT IN THE INTRODUCTORY PSYCHOLOGY COURSE

So what might a skills-based introductory psychology course look like? I am a strong proponent of the "students as producers" movement (Bruff, 2013). What are the characteristics of this movement? The general notion is that students should be the subject of the educational process rather than the object; that is, students need to be producers of knowledge in addition to consumers of knowledge.

When courses are designed with the students-as-producers theme in mind, Bruff (2013) commented that those courses typically have three characteristics: (1) students work on problems that do not have complete answers/solutions; (2) students share their work with others, and do not limit their sharing to the instructor only; and (3) students have some autonomy in the work. Additionally, for the assessment approach to such a course, I strongly favor a behavior-based approach in which students practice the desired skills, and that practice provides artifacts (i.e., products) that not only can be graded but also can yield assessment data that are helpful for my own continued professional development.

As for my own introductory psychology course, I would take a thematic, broad approach. That is, rather than worrying about "covering" all the key topics that one might think need to be covered, I prefer to take deeper dives into serious topics that might positively influence students if they can remember the content and the skills practiced. My five themes would be (1) thinking like a psychologist; (2) improving one's work-life by understanding and applying psychological principles; (3) being psychologically healthy; (4) understanding families, groups, and cultures; and (5) forming and maintaining healthy relationships. Although many of these topics span traditional introductory psychology textbook topics, I would focus on these key themes throughout the course.

Assignments in my introductory psychology course would be centered on skills. Here are some examples of assignments I might use, following by a deeper dive into the "podcast and podcast script" assignment.

APA FORMAT PRACTICE: Multiple assignments in this course require proper and accurate *APA* formatting: (1) proper formatting using MS Word, (2) accurately formatting reference citations, and (3) avoiding/correcting student mistakes. These assignments may be completed as a Blackboard assignment and/or during class sessions. This assignment helps students with writing skills as well as practice in following instructions.

SELF-REFLECTIONS: Part of your introductory psychology experience is to think about the overarching connections (i.e., thematic influences) that you can make concerning the content of this course. Two self-reflection questions are asked at the end of each week on Blackboard: one about the content/YouTube video for a particular week and the other about career preparation and your undergraduate education. Your answers for each question should be about two to three sentences in length (answered Friday–Saturday). This assignment helps with communication skills as well as self-reflection and self-monitoring metacognitive skills.

KNOWLEDGE ABOUT PSYCHOLOGY PRESURVEY AND POST-SURVEY: At the beginning of the course students complete a brief Qualtrics survey about their general knowledge about psychology. At the end of the course, students will complete the survey again. Just do your best to complete the survey honestly. If you complete both surveys by the stated deadlines, you receive full credit (this is a pass/fail assignment). This assignment helps both instructors and students gain insight into students' knowledge state about the course content before and after the course.

SCRIPTED PODCAST: Each student creates an original podcast and records the podcast in one's own voice. The podcast should be a persuasive message about a topic in psychology selected by the student. The statements made in the podcast should be supported by psychological research (evidence-based) and cited by the student in the written script accompanying the podcast. The actual podcast must be at least 3 minutes long but not longer than 4 minutes. Students should upload both the audio podcast file (MP3 only) and the Microsoft Word podcast script directly to Blackboard (use the separate links provided). Prepare your podcast script following *APA* style and include *APA*-formatted references; use a title page (but no abstract). Students are introduced to podcasting best practices during the course and free podcast software. This assignment allows for the practice of verbal and written communication skills, as well as learning a new technology (podcasting) for most students.

POSITION PAPER: Students select one of the five themes that organize the introductory psychology course and write an evidence-based position paper about that topic. Present at least two points of view on the important issue in psychology that you select, and back your claims using an evidence-based approach. Use *APA*-formatted subheadings properly to signpost the different sections of your paper. After presenting (at least) two sides to the issue, conclude your paper with your personal position on the topic, with justification. Include a title page and references adhering to *APA* format. The position paper is a minimum of five pages long, maximum seven pages in length (page count includes the title page and references section). This assignment allows students to demonstrate critical thinking and scientific inquiry skills as well as practice written communication skills.

GROUP PROJECT: The ability to analyze, summarize, evaluate, and create are higher level skills that graduates should possess. Working in groups assigned by the instructor, students create resources and present to the class in one of five content areas: (1) thinking like a psychologist; (2) improving one's work-life by understanding and applying psychological principles; (3) being psychologically healthy; (4) understanding families, groups, and cultures; and (5) forming and maintaining healthy relationships. Your sources may include lecture materials as well as a comprehensive review from various sources (some made available by your instructor). Each student completes a two-page executive summary and groups collaborate to create and deliver a class presentation (with handout). Each group presents its findings to the class; creativity is rewarded. Self- and peer-assessment components are also included. This assignment encourages the development of teamwork and leadership skills, as well as written and oral communication skills.

CLICKER QUESTIONS: I ask clicker questions during the semester, and students respond using a ResponseCard XR (clicker). These questions are worth course points. If I ask an opinion question, students receive a point for any answer. If I ask a factual question (such as those based on the YouTube video to be watched prior to class), students need to answer correctly to earn the point. If a student does not bring his or her clicker to class, he or she cannot earn clicker points that day. Some of the clicker questions will be (1) directly related to the reading and lecture assignments and (2) exploratory in nature to stimulate critical thinking and class discussion. Over the course of the semester, I will ask at least 180 points worth of questions. A maximum of 150 clicker points may be applied to your final course grade. This assignment not only allows for some knowledge comprehension insights but also serves as readiness assurance to encourage students to be prepared for each class session.

RUBRIC DETAILS FOR A SKILLS-BASED ASSIGNMENT

I hope that by sharing these details, some readers will be stimulated to think about the design structure of their own introductory psychology courses. To dig a bit deeper, I want to offer a specific example of one of these assignments described here and how an instructor might take a skills-themed approach in introductory psychology. This scripted podcast assignment and assessment technique is one that I have successfully used in a large enrollment course (more than 100 students). If an educator's learning outcomes were to include a knowledge base in psychology (*APA Guidelines 2.0*, goal 1), critical thinking and scientific inquiry (*APA Guidelines 2.0*, goal 2), and communication (*APA Guidelines 2.0*, goal 4), a scripted podcast assignment like the one described in Table 9.3 is a method by which

TABLE 9.3 Scripted Podcast Assignment Rubric Categories

Podcast (audio file): Your level of achievement on each of the rubric areas described below will be evaluated as novice, competent, or proficient.

Vocal clarity, articulation, and enunciation: Your vocalizations are clear and easy to understand; pacing is not too fast or too slow. Difficult words are clearly articulated; speaker is understandable.

Enthusiasm and persuasiveness: There is variation in the tone of the speaker's voice (not monotone). Speaker sounds interested and passionate about the topic (not bored). Message intends to persuade the listener.

Sound and recording quality: Audio is crisp and clear; no background noises, no crackling of microphone. Volume is appropriate and consistent for the 3- to 4-minute recording. Proper file type and file name used.

Podcast script (Word file): Your level of achievement on each of the rubric areas described below will be evaluated as novice, competent, or proficient.

Complete script provided: The MS Word document provided is the script to the podcast that matches the audio podcast file. File named correctly.

APA Format and Style: Evidence-based statements in the podcast are backed by proper *APA* citations. Script is presented in *APA* format following all page and text presentation rules. Use a cover page first and include the references page last in the document.

these *Guidelines 2.0* goals can be assessed in a behavior-based fashion through a course assignment.

For an introductory psychology course (and other psychology courses), I am a proponent of this type of assessment/assignment for a number of reasons. First, it is a behavior-based assignment, meaning that students must actively demonstrate the skill with an observable outcome, as opposed to a multiple-choice test that might infer a student's knowledge state at one point in time. Second, this assignment allows for the meaningful assessment of at least three of the *Guidelines 2.0* goals, providing the student to demonstrate content knowledge through topics written about in the paper, as well as to practice oral communication skills in the recording of a podcast. It may be that in large introductory psychology courses, there may not be enough time in the semester for every student to give a speech, but using this format, every student's voice can be heard by the instructor via the podcast; thus oral communication and written communication skills are practiced. Carefully constructed rubrics can provide valuable assessment data for instructors to consider as the semester continues and/or for modifications to instruction to be made in future semesters.

When an introductory psychology course is designed (or redesigned) using the principles of backward course design, learning objectives are clarified and assessment techniques are specified. If the aspirational goals of *Guidelines 2.0* are coupled with the informative feedback from employers about the workplace readiness of graduates, then instructors of general psychology can be well prepared to develop behavior-based assignments that demonstrate their students' abilities to be producers of information (in addition to being consumers of information). A skills-based theme to teaching introductory psychology can have benefits that last well beyond the conclusion of the course, particularly when that course is well designed and executed.

Chapter 10

The Purpose and Process of Teaching Communication Skills to Introductory Psychology Students

JERUSHA B. DETWEILER-BEDELL
Lewis & Clark College

ABIGAIL S. HAZLETT
Alteryx, Inc.

Communication begins on day one: As the students filter into the classroom, find seats, and seek out familiar faces, eventually all grows quiet. It is time to begin, and after a brief introduction, the professor prompts each person in the class to tell a brief (sentence-long) story describing the origin of his/her first name. A few say they do not know, but most have a story: *It was my father's name, and his father's before that; It was from a novel, but my parents didn't like the character; My mother wanted to recognize my South African heritage, though people always ask why I'm named "Kenya" rather than "Southafrica."* This seemingly straightforward exercise takes up precious class time, but it is the first time students have the opportunity to communicate with their peers and professor. Telling the story of their name is *what* the students are doing, but of course there is also a *why*. Hearing the story of a student's name increases the likelihood of remembering the name. Later in the semester, this simple first-day exercise can be revisited when the class discusses the methods for enhancing memory. And prompting each and every student to spend a minute talking in front of the class on the first day will hopefully lessen the stress associated with presenting in front of the class later in the term.

In this chapter, we emphasize both *why* and *how* to incorporate communication-based experiences in introductory psychology. As suggested by research on construal level theory (Fujita, Trope, Liberman, & Levin-Sagi, 2006; Trope & Liberman, 2003) individuals mentally represent events in one of two ways: (1) by focusing on the global, superordinate, and temporally distant features of an event (i.e., the purpose of performing a behavior) or (2) by focusing on the local, subordinate, and temporally near features of an event (i.e., the process of performing the behavior). When students learn both the purpose (why?) and the process (how?) of developing communication skills, they acquire greater confidence and are better able to translate what they learn in one particular class to other courses and to life experiences beyond college.

At many institutions, introductory psychology is the most popular class on campus, and it touches the lives of more individuals than any other course. We believe instructors of introductory psychology have an extraordinary opportunity (perhaps even an obligation) to take advantage of the inherently engaging topics of the discipline and to utilize them to propel students forward in their personal and professional lives. As found in a survey of 318 private sector and nonprofit executives, 93 percent of employers agree "a candidate's demonstrated capacity to think critically, communicate clearly, and solve complex problems is more important than their undergraduate major" (Hart, 2013, p. 1). Further, 80 percent of employers surveyed would like colleges to place a greater emphasis on helping students develop written and oral communication skills (p. 8). Introductory psychology is a perfect platform for teaching students *how* to communicate and for demonstrating *why* effective communication is so important.

The value employers place on communication skills is something we have witnessed firsthand. One of us (Abigail) has been an analyst at a company focused on helping students develop the skills necessary for success in college and on giving university administrators information about what helps students succeed so the institution can further enhance students' learning experiences and retention rates. The other of us (Jerusha) has been a liberal arts college professor since 2001. We first met one another when Jerusha was a new professor and Abigail was a first-year undergraduate student taking introductory psychology. Later, Abigail was Jerusha's teaching assistant in this class. When Abigail went on to earn her doctorate in social psychology, one of the introductory psychology classes she taught was to nontraditional college students (full-time working adults). Each of us has seen firsthand that teaching communication skills in introductory psychology benefits our students and capitalizes on expertise we bring from our own professional lives. As coauthors of this chapter we come from a common foundation in our approach to teaching introductory psychology, but we speak from disparate experiences both within and outside of academia.

DESIGNING SYLLABI AND ASSIGNMENTS

Just as we aim to help students develop crucial communication skills, such as knowing one's audience and tailoring one's communication style to best suit that audience, so too do we emphasize the importance of using these same skills as instructors when we design our introductory psychology courses. The sheer popularity of this course means it is taught in a wide variety of educational settings and to a diverse audience of learners. Jerusha teaches in a selective, four-year, residential liberal arts environment where the majority of students are full-time undergraduates, focusing a great deal of their time on their studies. Abigail has taught in similar settings, as well as in an extension school that offers bachelors and associates degrees and continuing education credit to mostly working adults or part-time students with a range of previous educational experiences.

Our approach to course design and syllabus creation has reflected these differences. When teaching in a traditional liberal arts environment, we have built syllabi that emphasize student engagement and time commitment both inside and outside the classroom (e.g., by having discussion questions presented during class time in small groups and by assigning multiple projects outside of class over the course of the semester). When teaching in an extension school environment, Abigail has created a syllabus that allows for participation in and out of class and gives students more flexibility to decide when to complete the bulk of the coursework (e.g., by having discussion questions as part on an online forum and by assigning a single course project with checkpoints throughout the semester).

Cultivating skills in written, verbal, and multimedia communication is one of our central goals when we teach introductory psychology, but we teach these skills somewhat differently than we might in more advanced classes. Yes writing a lengthy literature review is an admirable accomplishment, but how readily does it translate to life after college? And can it be done well in an introductory class? For this reason, we utilize far more focused writing assignments whose purpose is to engage others in a thoughtful dialogue. Yes, completing a senior thesis and presenting one's findings at a conference is a laudable goal, but why wait until senior year to try on the role of an "expert presenter"? Achieving the depth and breadth of a thesis presentation may not be replicable in an introductory psychology class, but learning how to use presentation tools such as PowerPoint or Prezi and overcoming stage fright are just as relevant in an introductory class as in a thesis presentation. And must a student be a media studies major in order to create a compelling short film about a topic of psychological importance? We argue no—this too can be accomplished in an introductory psychology class. The 21st-century students come to the classroom ready to look beyond the more traditional ways of communicating information, and they are open to the challenge of using technology to create persuasive messages.

In the sections that follow, we describe *how* and *why* we teach communication skills the way we do. We teach written communication through the use of thought-provoking questions, oral communication through the use of formal presentations, and multimedia communication through the creation of a brief "mythbusting" video. We include concrete examples of assignments, and we conclude with a brief discussion of some of the practical issues associated with teaching communication skills in introductory psychology.

ASKING AND ANSWERING THOUGHTFUL QUESTIONS: WRITTEN COMMUNICATION

As a discipline, psychology provides students the theoretical and practical foundation necessary to ask good questions. Students of introductory psychology are exposed to a variety of approaches to studying psychological processes, including qualitative and quantitative research methodologies. This exposure is developed further among students who go on to major in psychology through formal study of statistics and research methodology. Additional practice in hypothesis generation and testing leads students to become critical consumers of research—a valuable, life-long skill. An ability to ask and answer good questions is a fundamental communication skill, but students may not initially conceptualize it as such. We believe an introductory psychology course can lay the foundation for this skill for majors and nonmajors alike.

In our teaching, we both have used a variant of an assignment we call "Thought-Provoking Questions" to teach students the skill of asking good questions. The thought-provoking question (TPQ) assignment can be employed in a variety of ways to best suit the needs of the student population and the overarching structure of the course. The core element of a TPQ assignment is to require students to reflect on their weekly readings and pose a series of questions that connect and extend the material they have learned up until that point in time. TPQs are meant to be thought provoking to the audience, as the name suggests, but the author (the student) should find the process of preparing his/her TPQs to be thought provoking as well. TPQs give students practical experience in thinking before asking.

When introducing the TPQ assignment, it is crucial to have a clear outline of the expectations for students so they know what is considered a thought-provoking question (connecting and extending material) and what is not (merely repeating or retrieving material). An example of an excellent, adequate, and insufficient TPQ and a brief discussion of these elements will help to set expectations. Instructor feedback is also important for making certain that students are on the right track with their questions. Depending on the format and size of the course, this feedback can happen in depth at the beginning of the course, or along the way as students submit their assignments. For examples of TPQs, please see Table 10.1.

The general concept of discussion questions will likely be familiar to most students, but we emphasize that asking and answering good questions is a foundational skill students will master by studying psychology. A "good" question is one that provokes serious thought; it is a question that the author finds genuinely interesting; and it is a question that presents a challenging but soluble puzzle. We submit to students that asking thoughtful questions is a skill that will serve them well regardless of the career path they take. We challenge students to name a

TABLE 10.1   Sample Thought-Provoking Questions

Brain Structures	Beginning on page 62, the author explains the varying functions of the cerebral cortex. What are the four lobes (p. 63), and what are their corresponding psychological and physical roles? Later in the chapter, the author lays out the possible effects of injury to these areas, such as the personality changes after damage to the frontal lobe (pp. 67–68). Briefly describe what happened in the famous case study of Phineas Gage. If you were a researcher in the 1800s who had the opportunity to interact with Phineas Gage, what questions would you want to ask him and the people who knew him well before and after the accident?
Consciousness	On pages 73–76, the author discusses consciousness and the sleeping brain. What are the five stages of the sleep cycle? In which stage(s) do we dream? What are some of the reasons why we dream? In the film, *Eternal Sunshine of the Spotless Mind*, there is a firm that specializes in "safely" erasing memories of a given patient by studying the mind of that patient while the patient is sleeping and erasing the specific memories. What do you think we could learn if scientists invented a similar type of machine and used it to examine a person's dreams?
Learning	On pages 160–164, the author discusses learning by observation. What is observational learning? What are the neurons called that seem to be linked to this type of learning? Give examples of how observational learning can be good and how it could be bad. As a child, what kind of TV were you exposed to and how much did you watch it? Do you feel like it has affected your behavior? What impact might the Internet and video games have on behavior learned by observation?
Memory	Throughout the text the author talks about memory and how we encode and retrieve information. On pages 171–184, the author talks about the three-stage model of memory. What are the three stages he discusses? What capacity does the brain have for long-term memory? What did the study of H.M. show about how memory works, and what types of long-term memory was he able to use? If there were a stage of memory that you had to live your life without, what stage would you give up and why?
Judgment and Decision-Making	On pages 216–221, the author discusses mental heuristics. What is the difference between the representativeness heuristic and the availability heuristic? Are these heuristics evolutionarily adaptive? Why or why not? And why are we so likely to base judgments on categorical resemblances? Would the world be a better place if we did not base our decisions (and judgments of others) on heuristics and biases? Why or why not?
Developmental	On pages 274–276, the author discusses the parenting styles associated with different attachment styles. Describe the four types of attachment and four different parenting styles. Which type of attachment and parenting style seems to have the most positive effect on a child's development? How might this answer vary across cultures? What about children who attend day care—Is day care good or bad for the attachment process?
Psychological Disorders	On page 379, the author describes a biopsychosocial explanation of schizophrenia. Specifically, he states that a combination of factors contributes to an individual's disposition and likelihood of developing a schizophrenic condition. Of the factors that contribute to schizophrenia (genetic predisposition, brain abnormalities, and psychological factors), which factors seem to play the most central role? How do societal stigmas against abnormal behaviors impact the individual affected? And in what ways can the symptoms of schizophrenia be accepted in U.S. culture (as many cultures revere those who interact with the nonphysical world)?
Therapy	On pages 390–395, the author focuses on different kinds of therapies that are used to treat many different conditions. What are the four types of therapies described by the author? What are the key characteristics of each type of therapy? On pages 395–396, the author talks about the overall effectiveness of psychotherapy. How might clients' and therapists' beliefs concerning how effective a treatment is influence the outcome of psychotherapy? What advice would you have for a friend or a family member who is trying to find a therapist to help them with a psychological problem?
Social Psychology	The psychology of attraction is described on pages 450–451. What is the mere exposure effect? Briefly describe one study that demonstrates this effect. How do factors that impact our attraction to another person play out in online dating? What would principles of attraction (such as proximity and similarity) suggest for creating an online profile? How could these principles work to your advantage in online dating? What might be some disadvantages?

profession that would not benefit from having a skilled questioner—that is, a person who is intellectually engaged, reflective, stimulating, informed, and effectual. Discussing the long-term, wide-ranging relevance of this skill (the *why*) enhances students' commitment to the TPQ assignment, and providing clear guidelines and corrective feedback (the *how*) maximizes students' success with the assignment.

Peer feedback also helps students develop their question-asking abilities. We ask students to respond to one another's TPQs as a method of peer assessment, because exposure to the responses one's question generated is a powerful way to learn if the question was understood by the audience and was successful in provoking thought. We have incorporated peer feedback on TPQs both with small group discussions during class time and with written responses in an online forum format.

For the in-class discussion variety, students submit their TPQs weekly to the professor and receive a grade for each week completed. In Jerusha's class, students are assigned to prepare a written response to other students' TPQs the week before a test is given (see Appendix 10.1). Students then meet in small groups to participate in a discussion about the responses each member has prepared. The instructor assigns students to answer particular TPQs and to join a specific discussion group so a broad cross-section of class material is covered, offering students the opportunity to use the TPQ discussion as exam review. Because the first test does not occur until several weeks into the semester, students have the opportunity to submit and receive feedback on several TPQs before they meet in small groups, and the instructor has the ability to choose among a broader pool of questions (increasing the quality and scope of questions each student is assigned to answer and discuss).

When teaching introductory psychology in an extension school environment, Abigail has TPQ discussions take place outside of class time. Assigning students to submit their TPQs weekly to an online discussion board available to the instructor and fellow students helps accomplish this objective. Students receive a grade for each question submitted but also are graded on their responses to other students' questions. To encourage broad discussion, it can be beneficial to require students to respond to more than one of their peers' questions. Over the course of a given week, questions and then a series of responses appear on the discussion board as students engage with that week's topic outside of class time. Jerusha took a similar approach when she taught an intensive 6-week-long summer school course. In this context, taking class time for discussion was not feasible, but the online forum proved to be highly effective.

Practically speaking, using the online forum method means the instructor has less control over which questions are answered. However, by ceding some control to students to direct the conversation, the instructor also gains insight into the topics students find most discussion-worthy. Providing early feedback on TPQs to students helps to ensure that the discussions continue to improve over the course of the semester. In addition, incorporating an example TPQ from the past week into an in-class discussion can tie the two forums together, allowing the instructor to provide additional information and to reinforce the elements of a good question by example.

In addition to being a useful method for helping students improve their communication skills, peer feedback also serves to reinforce *why* asking good questions is so important. By hearing peer responses to their own questions and by answering the questions of their peers, students gain firsthand experience with how sharing viewpoints on a topic can shape understanding and retention of information. When students see a test question related to a topic they covered in a TPQ discussion, they not only will have rehearsed that information as part of studying for the test but also will have connected the concept to other experiences and will be more likely to recall the information (Ormrod & Davis, 2004). And when students find that the question is so thought provoking that they share it with others outside of their introductory psychology class, they see this as additional evidence that asking and answering questions is a crucial communication skill.

We would be remiss not to acknowledge that there are many other effective ways to develop question-asking skills in students, including assigning longer term papers that require students to go in depth on a topic. We prefer the TPQ method for introductory psychology because it allows for cumulative development of communication skills throughout the term, gives ample opportunity for students to share ideas with one another, and leaves more room in the syllabus for other substantial assignments, such as oral presentations.

PRESENTING KNOWLEDGE TO AN AUDIENCE: ORAL COMMUNICATION

The experience of taking on an expert role and presenting material to an audience is very powerful. Effective oral presentations require students to use multiple sources, strategically select and organize relevant information, distill the information in a meaningful way to the particular audience, and demonstrate competency as a presenter.

One way to incorporate presentation skills into an introductory psychology syllabus is to assign students to deliver a "mini-lecture" (10 to 15 minutes in length) on a topic within psychology that interests them. This approach worked especially well for Abigail when the short length of a term meant there was material in the textbook that could not be covered in the standard course lectures (e.g., one or two topics that had to be skipped due to time constraints). For the mini-lecture assignment, Abigail assigned students to complete the project as groups of two to three. Practically speaking, this approach minimizes the amount of already-scarce class time needed to get through the presentations. Adding a group component to the assignment also gives students the opportunity to work on interpersonal communication and group problem-solving, skills they will inevitably find applicable regardless of the professional path they take.

When completing the mini-lecture assignment, students practice several valuable communication skills, including selecting and using presentation software, distilling information into the allocated time frame, and finding ways to make the material interesting and engaging to their audience. In order to help students understand how to give effective presentations, the assignment is broken up into a few checkpoints throughout the term. The first part of the assignment is to submit a written outline of the structure and content of the main points they plan to cover. Students receive instructor feedback on this outline and then use it as the basis for creating their presentation. The second part of the assignment, delivering the presentation to the class, is graded against clear guidelines that students see in advance of the presentation date in the form of a rubric (see Appendix 10.2 for an example). The rubric specifies that presentations must be a certain length and include particular elements. It also requires mastery of specific presentational skills (e.g., eye contact, pace) that come from repeated practice. Abigail requires students to include a "who cares?" summary slide that ties the content to the real world, and she requires that each member of the group present part of the content. Additional required elements could include using an audio/visual clip, incorporating an example from a news article or empirical paper, or anything else the instructor wishes students to emphasize. Providing a clear structure for completing the assignment minimizes grading "surprises" for students, and it also provides a scaffold from which students can learn how to create effective presentations: Start with a plan, consider how to make the information engaging to the audience, and assign roles for delivering the presentation.

Presentations need not be lengthy in order to be effective. For example, Jerusha requires each of the (approximately) 40 students in her class to do a 4-minute individual presentation using PowerPoint or Prezi as a presentation tool. For this project, students directly apply the knowledge they have gained from introductory psychology to something of interest in the "outside world." Students choose from a wide range of sources for their outside world project, and some examples are song lyrics, a scene from a movie or television show, a cartoon, or a piece of art. Other students choose to share something they heard on National Public Radio, read in the *New York Times*, saw in a blog, or learned about in a different class. The outside world project begins with a brief written assignment, where the students provide a clear citation of their source, a short summary of the item of interest from the outside world, and a concise yet thoughtful discussion of how the topic is connected to material covered in the lectures or textbook.

Learning *how* to use presentation tools is one of the goals of these assignments. But again, we also expose students to the rationale for *why* they are doing the presentations. One goal for the brief presentation is to give the students an opportunity to practice speaking in front of an audience. At least half of Jerusha's students are in their first year of college, so the outside world presentation provides the opportunity to begin developing presentation skills early on in their college career. Abigail's students come from broader stages of life and many are in school to earn a degree that will help them advance in their career. The mini-lecture assignment serves as an opportunity to practice presentation skills they could take back to the workplace.

Another purpose of the presentation is to demonstrate for students the power of good presentations (or the pitfalls of poor ones) in connecting with an audience and sharing relevant knowledge. How is this accomplished? Like with the TPQ discussion days, the outside world presentations are designed to coincide with material that will be covered on an upcoming test. So, for example, if the upcoming test will cover topics on developmental psychology, then all the outside world presentations will be linked to developmental phenomena. This requires assigning students in advance to topic areas (e.g., neuroscience, social, cognitive) and prompting them to focus their presentation on something they encounter in the outside world that is related. Although the mini-lecture presentations were delivered after the exams had concluded, they still served the purpose of allowing students to share knowledge with their peers. By assigning students to deliver presentations covering a section of the textbook not covered in the lectures, the entire class gained exposure to concepts that would have otherwise failed to make it into the syllabus. This also gave students the power to choose the extra material they wanted to cover. In Abigail's class, students selected topics such as organizational psychology and adolescent development and gave informative overviews of these topics to the entire class, not only increasing their own knowledge but also experiencing the joy of sharing an interest with an audience.

Another outcome of giving oral presentations that serves students well in the future is exposure to the tools necessary for presenting information (e.g., Prezi, PowerPoint). There is a very practical *why* imbedded in the goal of mastering presentation tools, which we make explicit. Students will be asked to give other presentations during the course of their studies, and many of them will be in a position to give presentations in the workplace. Therefore learning to effectively use presentation software will make each successive presentation that much easier. As educators, we also have a slightly longer-term *why* in mind when we assign these types of presentations: Technology moves at breakneck speed and students will undoubtedly be asked to learn many new types of programs throughout their educational and working lives. We believe that practicing the use of a variety of software and other technologies in the process of completing assignments helps prepare students for the lifelong learning they will do as inhabitants of a digital world.

USING DIGITAL TECHNOLOGY TO BUST MYTHS: MULTIMEDIA COMMUNICATION

Access to technologically sophisticated modes of digital communication is no longer limited to experts. Beyond PowerPoint and Prezi are tools such as iMovie and KineMaster Pro. These applications allow novices to edit video footage and include voice-over narration, special effects, and musical accompaniment. Today's students consume most of their media online, and much of that media is in video format. To capitalize not only on student interest but also on the realities of 21st-century communication, we have more recently begun to include an assignment that requires students to research a commonly held psychology-related myth and then to communicate the "truth" in the form of a brief movie presentation.

To set the stage for this project, we give our students a true/false test on the first day of the semester. The test includes items such as the following:

- Most people use only 10% of their brain power.
- Individuals commonly repress the memories of traumatic experiences.
- Ulcers are caused primarily or entirely by stress.
- Only deeply depressed people commit suicide.
- Holding a pencil in your teeth can make cartoons funnier than holding a pencil with your lips.
- Expert judgment and intuition are the best means of making clinical decisions.

When students turn in this true/false test, the professor informs them that almost all the items are, in fact, false. (In the examples included above, the only true statement was about people judging cartoons while holding a pencil in their mouth.) These "myths" are commonplace, and they are addressed systematically in Lilienfeld, Lynn, Ruscio, and Beyerstein's (2009) *50 Great Myths of Popular Psychology* (one of the required books for our classes). Addressing popular myths is a theme that follows the students throughout the semester, and the communication-based project that students complete is to create a compelling, brief video addressing and debunking the myth.

In this assignment, students are asked to explore one myth that Lilienfeld and colleagues (2009) do *not* address in their book. (Conveniently, every chapter ends with a section that lists "other myths.") The students are required to use psychology-related online databases (APA PsycNET and MEDLINE) to track down scientific evidence (peer-reviewed research studies) that helps disprove the myth they have selected. In order to teach the students how to search online databases, we invite our reference librarian to give a hands-on demonstration to the class. Modeling how to try different search terms to debunk the myths is critical (because many of our students have not used these databases before), but if it were not possible to spend class time on such a demonstration, directing students to an online tutorial with specific prompts also would be helpful. We have our students work on this phase of the project individually, and the outcome of their search for evidence is an annotated bibliography of three to five sources. In the annotated bibliography, we ask the students to *summarize* the main arguments of the article, *assess* the source (e.g., its utility, how it compares with the other sources), and *reflect* on how the source has changed the student's thinking about the myth (see Appendix 10.3).

After the students complete their annotated bibliographies and receive feedback, we transition them from individual to group work. We group students in pairs or groups of three, and our aim is to place students together based on shared interests in a myth. It is also useful to assess the students' comfort level with technology and to distribute the more technologically savvy students across groups. That said, the application we use for this project (iMovie) is straightforward, and even novices can become experts quite quickly. (Jerusha was taught how to use it by her 9-year-old son!) Access to the technology necessary to use iMovie (or similar applications) may be easier on some college campuses than others. We were able to apply for and receive a grant to purchase iPads for classroom use, but we quickly found that a number of students already had smart phones and preferred to use their own devices to create film footage and a laptop or desktop computer for video editing.

Once the instructor assigns students to their "mythbusting" groups, the first goal is for students to share their annotated bibliographies with their team members. By this time students will have summarized and evaluated the research articles, and now they must communicate the findings in a meaningful way to their peers. We again make explicit *why* we are asking students to communicate in this way. We remind our students that society is bombarded with information (from the popular press, bloggers, Facebook posts), and the quality of this information is highly variable. Students need to be equipped to track down "expert information" (in this case, scientific data) and to translate this information clearly and concisely to others. After each student communicates the key findings to his or her peers, the group decides which myth to focus on "busting," based on the strength of the evidence. Once the group has chosen its myth, it is time to work on *how* to communicate to a much larger audience in the form of a brief (about 10 minutes long) digital presentation.

We have constructed our assignment so that students learn how to use iMovie as a video-editing tool. As with the other forms of communication we teach, the first step is for students to organize their information and to outline their presentation. But now, rather than writing a paper, participating in a discussion, or giving an oral presentation, students put together the footage necessary for a persuasive communication in the form of a brief movie. Most students use a combination of targeted questions to naive interviewees (e.g., "Will a hypnotized person do anything you ask?"), compelling images and video footage set to music, and a fact-based commentary using voice-over narration. At the end of the semester, each group shows its finished project to the class as a whole.

The assignment also includes an expectation that group members will spend about 5 minutes answering their classmates' questions after showing the video. This gives students the opportunity to be in front of an audience and to practice the skill of talking to a group. Before the semester's end, we believe it is important to solicit students' feedback about their own performance and that of their group members (see Appendix 10.4). An assessment done at the project's completion provides an excellent opportunity for students to reflect not only on the process of completing the assignment (the *how*) but also on the purpose (the bigger picture *why*). In our brief questionnaire, we ask students to describe the challenges they faced and the future opportunities they see for using the skills they developed. Ultimately it is up to each individual to be able to articulate the ways in which a communication-based skill will serve him/her beyond the walls of the introductory psychology classroom.

THE WHY AND *HOW* OF COMMUNICATION SKILLS: PRACTICAL ISSUES

Due to the sheer popularity of introductory psychology, instructors of this course have an opportunity to expose a diverse group of students to the engaging and relevant material that psychology has to offer and to use the course to build foundational skills that will continue to serve students as they move forward in their education and, eventually, their careers. In our own teaching, we emphasize both the *why* and the *how* of building strong communication skills because we believe these skills can have a lasting impact on student success. We also have found that the assignments we describe in this chapter have added incredible richness to our courses and sparked lively, insightful conversations about the wide variety of topics we teach. Thus, focusing on communication skills has enriched not only our students' educational experiences but also the quality of our introductory psychology courses and our enjoyment of teaching them.

What follows is a list of practical recommendations that have grown out of the successes and challenges we have experienced using these communication-based assignments in introductory psychology:

1. *Give feedback early and (ideally) often.* The scope and size of this course can be daunting. There is a great deal of material to cover in a relatively limited amount of time, and for some instructors, the number of students in their classroom is well into the hundreds. But to effectively mentor communication skills, giving feedback is essential. We have prioritized giving feedback early: The first few TPQ assignments and the initial annotated bibliography for the mythbusting assignment receive very close scrutiny in our classes. To the extent that we continue to give corrective and growth-oriented feedback along the way, we see student performance improve not only on the communication-based assignments but also in the course as a whole.

2. *Use grading rubrics and share them with students in advance.* Developing strong communication skills takes time, and most of our students have plenty of room for growth. Yet the grading of these "soft skills" appears more subjective than the right/wrong dichotomy afforded by a multiple-choice test. This reality can produce frustration on the part of both students and instructors. We have found that preparing grading rubrics for the assessment of student performance on these assignments is invaluable and that sharing these rubrics with students ahead of time creates transparency (for a more in-depth discussion of creating a rubric, see Suskie, 2010).

3. *Incorporate peer feedback.* To enhance student learning, we supplement feedback from the instructor with feedback from peers. Especially when teaching communication skills, feedback from peers can be highly informative and relevant to the students. Peer feedback can be more or less structured, depending on the assignment. For the TPQ assignment, we do not ask peers

to provide explicit feedback on the quality of a given student's questions. However, because students are answering one another's TPQs, the feedback comes in a more natural form. If a particular TPQ is difficult to understand or uninspiring to answer, this becomes evident when it is time to discuss the TPQs. For the mythbusting project, we highlighted a peer evaluation that comes at the end of the assignment. However, we also make a point of soliciting peer feedback during the project phase so that challenging situations can be identified and resolved prior to the assignment's due date. Finally, for oral presentations, we rely on questions from the audience as a type of peer feedback. Students learn which parts of their presentation were clear, where more information was needed, and what was of particular interest to the audience during the Q&A portion of the presentation.

4. *Assign group work strategically.* Across a wide variety of career paths, from academia to business, much of the work individuals do is collaborative. To help prepare students to be productive collaborators, many assignments focused on communication skills can include group work. As should be evident from the descriptions of the various projects, we try to intermingle independent and group-based work. For example, the TPQs are written individually, but then they are discussed (online or in person) with a group. The mythbusting annotated bibliography is an individual assignment, but the creation of the video is done in a group. The mini-lecture assignment is group-based, but each individual is expected to produce and present part of the lecture on his/her own. Rather than default to a group project whenever communication skills are involved, we seek to balance individual responsibility with group work within and across our assignments to mimic the expectations students are likely to encounter in their professional lives.

5. *Encourage the use of mixed methods of communication.* One benefit of fostering communication skills in introductory psychology is that it gives students multiple lenses with which to view the content they are learning in class. Although the basic content of introductory psychology is relatively stable, modes of communicating this information are not. Practicing how to move among written work, discussion, and presentations is essential. Even within the assignments we have described, students are asked to use multiple methods of communication: Both the outside world presentation and the mythbusting video also require written communication; the TPQ assignment focuses on writing questions and responses, but the TPQ discussions require oral communication; and many students include multiple forms of media to enhance their outside world presentations and mini-lectures. Flexibility in the use of communication approaches is both an implicit and an explicit goal in our courses.

CLOSING THOUGHTS

As professors, introductory psychology is our first chance to teach students the process of becoming a psychologist, by introducing them to the core topics, varied theoretical perspectives, and fundamental research methods of the discipline;

it is also a terrific venue for exploring the purpose of psychology with students. In teaching students the foundation of the discipline, we get the chance to share the rush of discovery that accompanies studying human thought and behavior. Just as we wish to impart to our students both the process and purpose of the psychological sciences, so too do we believe that emphasizing both the *how* and the *why* of the projects we assign greatly improves student learning as well as our own teaching experiences.

In this chapter we have focused on assignments designed to develop written, verbal, and multimedia communication skills for students taking introductory psychology. We teach these skills by asking students to write and respond to thought-provoking questions, to plan and deliver oral presentations, and to research and correct a psychology-related myth. The assignments we describe represent our own pedagogical approaches to *how* to teach communication skills in introductory psychology, and as such, they are just a sampling of methods that can be applied to this end. We encourage you to adopt, and adapt, these assignments to your own courses as appropriate. Regardless of whether you make use of the particular assignments we have described, we hope you leave this chapter with a strong sense of *why* we emphasize communication skills in our introductory psychology classes.

Educating students to be strong communicators will make them better psychological scholars, to be sure, but communication skills are also broadly applicable for students in their pursuits beyond the introductory psychology classroom. Students will carry the skills they develop in their courses much longer than they will remember the content of the lectures. If instructors arm their students with strong communication skills, then they not only improve the field of psychology, but also improve the fields of business, law, medicine, politics, education, and the many other professions students of introductory psychology choose to pursue.

Appendix 10.1

Thought-Provoking Questions

There are two parts to this semester-long project. The first part takes place *every week* of the semester, and the second part takes place *four times* during the semester.

PART 1: Students are asked to type and turn in one Thought-Provoking Question (TPQ) each week.

*What exactly is a **TPQ**?* A TPQ is an original question set that promotes thought and discussion. Psychological research typically starts with a question about why people think, feel, and behave in certain ways (e.g., How do babies learn language? What triggers good and bad moods? Can a group lead a person to behave uncharacteristically?). The TPQs students turn in need to be related to the textbook material they are reading for that week's class. TPQ can broaden the readings or apply some of the concepts found in the readings to concepts covered in an earlier section of the textbook. They also can relate the textbook readings to other disciplines or to topics of debate in popular culture. Students may find that TPQs highlight a need for future psychological research. Each TPQ incorporates the following key components:

1. A **brief introduction** that provides contextual information and specific page numbers (i.e., What ideas from the text prompted the student to ask the TPQ and where are those ideas located?). Students are asked to imagine

that someone else in the class is going to read and discuss their questions. (This will take place in Part 2 of the project, described below.)

2. At least one **concrete question** (a question that addresses important content from the reading; a question that would be answerable by anyone who reads the text)

3. At least one "what if" or **extending question** (e.g., a question that takes the discussion one step further by suggesting creative applications of the concepts found in the readings; a question that relates the readings to material from other classes or topics of debate in popular culture)

PART 2: There are four tests given in our Introduction to Psychology classes. In the week prior to each test, the class is divided into small groups (of about students per group) and asked to prepare TPQ-related discussion material. The professor chooses and assigns the TPQs to each student. Each individual is responsible for preparing and turning in a typed response to different TPQs, and we make sure that each student is responding to unique (non-overlapping) questions. Student responses to each TPQ are about 200 words, and they turn in one copy to the professor and give one copy to each group member. On the *TPQ Discussion Day* the groups spend a total of (approximately) 45 minutes carrying out brief discussions of each question, with the student who prepared the response rotating in and out of a discussion facilitator role.

Sample *Thought-Provoking Question* Set

Name: Sample Student
Date Completed: Thursday, October 21st
Chapter & Page #s: Chapter 11, pp. 404–444
Text of the TPQ: In Chapter 11, pages 420–424 [**specific page numbers**], the author discusses sleep and sleeping disorders, including the idea that some sleep patterns may be genetically influenced [**brief introduction**]. What are the 4 types of sleep disorders discussed [**concrete question**]? To what extent can sleep disorders such as insomnia be treated by behavioral and dietary changes [**concrete question**]? If a child experiences night terrors (one type of sleep disorder), do you think that child would be more at risk to develop a fear of "monsters in the closet" and/or difficulties falling asleep at night? Why or why not [**extending question**]? If a child you were taking care of experienced a night terror, what would you do [**extending question**]?

Appendix 10.2

Presentation Rubric

RATING

1 = missing   2 = beginning   3 = developing   4 = accomplished   5 = exemplary

PPT/Prezi Presentation

Main points well organized	1	2	3	4	5
Relevant information conveyed	1	2	3	4	5
Conclusion supported by evidence	1	2	3	4	5
Time limit followed	1	2	3	4	5
Overall use of presentation media	1	2	3	4	5

Delivery

Pronunciation and articulation	1	2	3	4	5
Pace and tone	1	2	3	4	5
Eye contact and animation	1	2	3	4	5
Vocalized pauses ("uh" avoided)	1	2	3	4	5
Humor used effectively	1	2	3	4	5
Professionalism	1	2	3	4	5
Informative and credible	1	2	3	4	5

Strengths:	To Improve:

Appendix 10.3

"Mythbusting" Project

This project leads you to explore one of the "other myths" listed at the end of each chapter in Lilienfeld and colleagues' *50 Great Myths of Popular Psychology* book. There are two parts to the project:

PART 1: THE ANNOTATED BIBLIOGRAPHY

You will be assigned one of the myths that the authors list (but that they do not explore in detail). Although you will share this myth with or other students, this phase of the project must be done ***individually***. Your job is to track down scientific evidence (peer-reviewed research studies) that help disprove the myth. Use the library's website to access relevant databases (most likely APA PsycNET and MEDLINE). Search for evidence to support your mythbusting efforts, and find **three to five** relevant peer-reviewed articles. The written material you turn in will take the form of an annotated bibliography. The annotations for each source should be written in paragraph form and each annotation should be approximately 150 words (a total of 450 words for three sources).

WHAT IS AN ANNOTATED BIBLIOGRAPHY?

Information below is excerpted from Dana Bisignani and Allen Brizee's "Annotated Bibliographies" (http://owl.english.purdue.edu/owl/owlprint/614/)

Copyright ©1995-2011 by The Writing Lab & The OWL at Purdue and Purdue University.

All of your sources in the annotated bibliography should be recorded in APA style. See the *APA Style Manual* or visit http://www.apastyle.org/learn/faqs/index.aspx or http://owl.english.purdue.edu/owl/resource/560/01/

Here is a basic example of a peer-reviewed journal article in APA style:

Brehm, B.J., Seeley, R.J., Daniels, S.R., & D'Alessio, D.A. (2003). A randomized trial comparing a very low carbohydrate diet and a calorie-restricted low fat diet on body weight and cardiovascular risk factors in healthy women. *Journal of Clinical Endocrinology & Metabolism, 88,* 1617–1623.

An annotated bibliography **also** includes a summary and evaluation of each of the sources, written in your own words. (NOTE: It is not acceptable to use direct quotes or to "borrow" language from your sources. Be sure to read the source in its entirety and then to write your annotations.)

For the *mythbusting* project, you will annotate **each** of your 3 to 5 sources as follows:

a. Summarize: What are the main arguments? What is the point of the article? If someone asked what this article is about, what would you say?

b. Assess: After summarizing the source, you will evaluate it. How useful is it as a source? How does it compare with other sources in your bibliography?

c. Reflect: Once you've summarized and assessed a source, you need to ask how it fits into your mythbusting research. How does this source help you? Has it changed how you think about your myth? How so?

PART 2: THE IMOVIE PRESENTATION

You will work with one or two other students who were assigned to explore the same myth as you. Together, you will develop a **10-minute** presentation of your mythbusting project. You will use iMovie to create a trailer designed for a general audience. This iMovie trailer should: a) clearly identify the myth, b) question the myth, and c) bust the myth (i.e., present accurate information about the topic). After the presentation, you will be given five minutes to answer questions from the class.

In order to receive full credit, you must (1) help create the iMovie with your group, (2) turn in a 1-page description of the way in which you personally contributed to the creation of the iMovie, (3) present your iMovie and answer questions from the class, and (4) turn in a revised copy of the annotated bibliography you completed earlier in the semester (incorporating the feedback you received from your professor).

Appendix 10.4

Mythbusting Assignment

ALL RESPONSES ARE CONFIDENTIAL

Please comment on your own and your group members' participation.
Use the following scale to complete your ratings (circle one #): **1 = not at all;
7 = extremely**

Name	How involved?	How productive?	How easy to work with?	How dedicated?	How helpful?
1. Self	1 2 3 4 5 6 7	1 2 3 4 5 6 7	1 2 3 4 5 6 7	1 2 3 4 5 6 7	1 2 3 4 5 6 7
2. ____	1 2 3 4 5 6 7	1 2 3 4 5 6 7	1 2 3 4 5 6 7	1 2 3 4 5 6 7	1 2 3 4 5 6 7
3. ____	1 2 3 4 5 6 7	1 2 3 4 5 6 7	1 2 3 4 5 6 7	1 2 3 4 5 6 7	1 2 3 4 5 6 7

Open-Ended Questions:

Describe the greatest challenges you faced in completing each of the following:

a. Annotated bibliography/literature search

b. Working productively with your mythbusting group

c. Completing the iMovie

What aspects of the mythbusting assignment were the most successful?

What aspects of the mythbusting assignment are likely to be most applicable beyond this class?

Chapter 11

Building Well-Being and Resilience with Applications to Everyday Life

TRUDY FREY LOOP*

The Altamont School

Educators feel it is their responsibility to enrich their students' lives by teaching them meaningful lessons that will stay with them past the final exam. There is often no greater reward than having students come back, several years after graduating, to tell instructors how the lessons learned in class have prepared them to lead more positive lives. In teaching an introductory psychology course, there is ample opportunity to enrich students' lives in a meaningful way. In this chapter, I will discuss a method I employ for improving the quality and impact of my department's curriculum, which involves (1) picking a theme with a positive impact you wish to have on your students and (2) designing your course so that as you weave the story of psychology together, students are continuously exposed to material related to this theme. Through continuous reprocessing of the material, students develop greater awareness of the theme in their daily lives and, hopefully, become better equipped to transfer that learning to new situations.

*The author is grateful to Sarah Whiteside, Head of School, for encouragement and support for attending the Stanford One Psychology Conferences and to Michael P. Loop and Chris Thomas for thoughtful suggestions on the revisions. The author sincerely thanks the editors for advice, encouragement, and helpful edits of the manuscript.

I will describe my chosen theme of applications that build my students' well-being and resilience, and how I incorporate this theme into the cognitive, behavioral, and social dimensions of psychology I discuss in my Advanced Placement Psychology course. In the final section of the chapter, I will discuss ways you can integrate beneficial themes into your current curriculum.

The context in which I teach is Advanced Placement Psychology in an intellectually rigorous, yet surprisingly creative and diverse, environment. My class sizes are small, around 15 students each, and because I have the luxury of teaching a year-long course, I can easily mix lecture, discussions, group work, and projects into my course with plenty of time for reflective thought. After graduation, students at The Altamont School enter a variety of college environments across the country and I teach them in their junior and senior years when this major life transition becomes a looming reality. In a world of increasingly competitive college admissions, a course in psychology can provide a reflective interlude between the demands of high school and a future yet unknown. In light of the demands students face during their developmental years, introducing the notion that they can understand and control their reactions and consequently change their mindsets is crucial.

VALUE OF INTRODUCTORY PSYCHOLOGY FOR PROMOTING WELL-BEING AND RESILIENCE

Novotney (2014) reports an increase in the number of students seeking mental health services on college and university campuses over the last decade. The directors of the Association for University and College Counseling Center Directors report that anxiety concerns have risen from about 37 percent in 2007 to 46 percent in 2013, while depression and relationship concerns have stayed about the same (depression: 38 percent in 2007 and 39 percent in 2013 and relationship: about 35.5 percent in 2007 and 35 percent in 2013). One approach to alleviating this situation is to educate those who interact most with students, and adding initiatives to make professors and instructors more aware of psychological distress signals does help to some degree. Another approach to alleviating the situation is to educate students themselves. The question then arises: Where, outside of the counseling realm, can all students be exposed to concepts that might improve their ability to handle tension, stress, anxiety, challenge, decision-making, and, thus, their quality of life?

The answer, I'd argue, is in an introductory psychology course, the second-most popular course on college campuses, reaching approximately between 1.2 million and 1.6 million students annually (Steuer & Ham, 2008), and the approximately 240,000 high school students taking the Psychology AP exam (Myers, 2014). The course contains many concepts that are relevant to developing an understanding of well-being, anxiety, threats, challenges, and decision-making. Introducing these concepts to students is an opportunity to build self-awareness and resilience at a time when they need it most. It is particularly important that the group that spans high school to college freshman be exposed to concepts that give them cause for reflection and provide a navigational map through stressful times.

Having students apply what they learn from the scientific study of mind and behavior to everyday life is a goal that is recommended by the APA's *Guidelines for the Undergraduate Major 2.0* (2013), *National Standards for High School Psychology Curricula* (2011), and *Strengthening the Common Core of the Introductory Psychology Course* (2014). For the themes of well-being and resilience, I have put together intentional focus points of application, hoping that students will be encouraged to make these connections to their lives. My focus points include building academic success, recognizing that stress can be beneficial as well as harmful, understanding emotional conditioning and relaxation techniques, and finally emphasizing decision-making.

BUILDING ACADEMIC SUCCESS

A great starting place for building a theme of well-being and resilience is with applications that directly influence academic understanding, study skills, and motivation in hopes of promoting autonomy and success in my course and beyond. Content in this initial sequence includes memory, self-regulation, metacognitive awareness, mindsets, and problem-solving. The material covered is not only directly relevant to students' performance in my course but also easy to connect back to in later units.

Understanding the Basics of Memory

The topic of memory is an effective starting place to build academic success. Students need to hear evidence-based reasons why some study strategies may be more effective than others. Some topics that can support this understanding include rehearsal (Ebbinghaus, 1885/1964), the spacing effect (Bjork & Bjork, 2011; Ebbinghaus, 1885/1964), the testing effect (Karpicke & Roediger, 2007), and elaborative processing (Craik & Tulving, 1975). Myers (2011) reviews these in his text. The standard forgetting curve (Ebbinghaus, 1885/1964) can be used to make the point that information disappears quickly and then levels off unless rehearsed. Distributing study across multiple sessions is something you can advise students to do, but teaching them about it through research studies has more impact. The testing effect shows that simply asking questions in class, utilizing formative assessment, or having students come up with their own questions helps build enduring memories.

Including specific activities when teaching memory helps students discover the value of elaboration and deep processing. One of the most potent memory demonstrations I've come across targets the use of mental imagery. It is from the *Teacher's Resource Binder to Accompany Myers' Psychology for AP* (Bolt, 2011) and Bolt notes it was originally developed by Don Irwin and Janet Simons. Students are asked to listen to 20 nonsense sentences loaded with potential for mental imagery. An example of a sentence would be: "The green frog jumped into the swimming pool." Half of the class is given instructions to rate how hard it is to form a mental image of the sentence and the other half is given instructions to rate how hard it is to pronounce the words. The students are unaware that they have received different instructions from one another. Following the initial session, students turn the instructions over in order to have an area to write and be free of any contextual retrieval cues. After about a minute, I ask them to answer 20 questions that ask for the subject of the sentences. An example question might be, "What jumped into the swimming pool?" The results are always the same. Those asked to form mental images remember the most words. The students are stunned by the fact that some of them are remembering so many more words than others. It takes a little while for them to either realize or for me to tell them that they were given separate instructions. It is an extremely compelling demonstration of how what you actively do with information influences how you remember it. This demonstration is applicable in classes of any size.

Connecting Memory to Self-Regulation
and Metacognitive Awareness

Interweaving the topic of memory with self-regulation and metacognitive awareness can help students relate what they have learned about memory to planning and implementing best strategies for learning the material. Self-regulation is focused attention on selected goals and coping skills individuals may use to attain them (Lerner, 2002). I encourage students to approach the material in a disciplined manner, taking organized notes, completing assigned readings, building study guides, and creating original quizzes. In my class I refer to these practices as "daily discipline" and this phrase becomes very familiar to students. I try to drive home that there are limited hours in the day, and it is in a student's best interest to learn to use those hours most efficiently and with the most productive results. I stress that planning how one will study for the unit or final exam begins in the very first week of class and that, as evidenced by memory research, utilizing effective strategies such as spacing out the reviews and elaborating on the material increases the likelihood of academic success.

Learning about metacognition and metacognitive awareness encourages students to go back, test themselves, and become aware of what they do and do not know. Studying becomes more of a *system of practice* than a one-time task. The idea of a system takes time to become ingrained, and monitoring one's system of preparation can be helpful. To raise students' awareness of their system of preparation, I periodically include a question at the beginning of tests about techniques students use to prepare for the test. Students receive full credit for simply answering the question and they are incredibly honest, revealing when they are on top of the process and when they are not.

Process-oriented strategies versus outcome-oriented strategies.
I present a study by Taylor, Pham, Rivkin, and Armor (1998) demonstrating how mentally imagining preparation fits into active processing, metacognitive awareness, and daily discipline. In this study, there were three groups of introductory psychology students with an upcoming midterm exam. The control group did not receive special instructions. The second group was instructed to spend 5 minutes a day thinking about a successful outcome (high grade) on the exam and how accomplished they would feel. The third group was instructed to spend 5 minutes a day thinking about the best way to prepare for the exam in order to receive a high grade. Just the sheer imagining of the preparation resulted in exam scores 8 points higher on average than the control group while the group that imagined a successful outcome only saw a 2-point increase. Taylor describes these conditions as process oriented versus outcome oriented. Imagining a process of preparation that gets you to your goal rather than simply the achievement of the goal itself builds success. So, if students focus on how they will prepare, they are more likely to prepare. I drive the point home and again want to impress upon them that studying is a *system of practice* rather than a one-time task.

DEVELOPING A GROWTH MINDSET

Students react differently to challenging work, and some come to us with a sense of perseverance shaped by parents, former teachers, and coaches. I taught a student a couple of years ago who faced and valued challenges. Her ninth-grade geometry teacher (Patricia Bank, personal communication, 2014) took note when she thanked her teacher for the hard, challenging problems because, she said, "It shows you respect me." We've all known students like this. I look out my classroom window early some mornings and see a particular student running on the track alone, building his stamina for next year's cross-country season. Athletes who learn to run or walk long distances know that preparation must be slow and gradual to prevent injury. No one trains for the full distance on the first day. The shorter distances and successes build to the larger ones and changes in ability can sometimes be imperceptible. Academics work the same way. It is educators' responsibility to introduce information at a level that provides incremental moments of success mixed with challenge and sometimes failure.

Why Do People Persist?

Introducing research on mindsets (Dweck, 2007) allows students to consider why there may be individual differences in persistence. I heard Carol Dweck speak on mindsets at a Learning and the Brain Conference (2008). She spoke of how students who come to Stanford all have high SAT scores, but within this pool, there are those who give up quickly and those who persevere. Why does motivation differ in this seemingly homogeneous population? Dweck (2007) describes a fixed mindset as one that sees intelligence as fixed and unchangeable and a growth mindset as one that sees intelligence as malleable or changeable.

I like to introduce students to mindsets by assigning the article "The Secret to Raising Smart Kids" (Dweck, 2007) as a reflective writing assignment aimed at two pages, double-spaced, and followed up by class discussion. One interesting part of the discussion revolves around outcomes for praise for effort versus outcomes for praise for intelligence. The article describes a study in which fifth graders were given puzzles to solve. One group was praised for its effort while the other group received praise for being smart. The students were then given increasingly more challenging problems. It is not surprising that those praised for intelligence gave up the quickest, as the earlier praise rested on the quick ability to solve the problem. If it became hard, their own ego was at stake. The group praised for effort persisted through harder puzzles and seemed to enjoy the work more. The article discusses how a shift in the type of praise individuals receive can encourage a growth mindset. By reading, reflecting on, and discussing this article, students learn to differentiate between a fixed and a growth mindset and how they relate to various walks of life, besides intelligence. Students learn that mindsets can even be situational to a particular class or athletic interest. Someone with a growth mindset on the soccer field may have a fixed mindset when it comes to math class or vice versa. The concept of the growth mindset is important in school, relationships with peers, and relationships with teachers and parents.

Connecting Growth Mindsets to Problem-Solving

I encourage students to continue thinking about the role of mindsets in shaping their perseverance as they transition into learning about cognitive processes like problem-solving. Giving students some challenging classic problems to solve can help them see this. Because the process is enjoyable, with unexpected solutions, the act of solving the problems can be compared to a challenge rather than a threat. Most students love learning about classic problem-solving strategies such as recognizing to solve backward with the water lily problem (Sternberg & Davidson, 1983). The problem goes something like this, "Water lilies double in area every 24 hours. On the first day of summer there is only one water lily on the lake. It takes 60 days for the lake to be completely covered in water lilies. How many days does it take for half of the lake to be covered in water lilies?" The answer is day 59 because the pond will double by day 60.

Another favorite is the one where two strings are hanging from the ceiling far enough apart that one cannot hold one and reach the other. The goal is to tie the two strings together. In the room there is a table, a book of matches, a few pieces of cotton, and a screwdriver. In order to solve the problem, one has to use an object in a manner for which it wasn't designed and, thus, overcome functional fixedness. The solution is for a screwdriver to be attached to one string and used as a pendulum to swing the string so that it comes close enough to grab hold while holding the other string (Maier, 1931). These problems require effortful processing and students can physically feel the engagement, and for the most part they enjoy it. There are a few students who give up easily as well as those who absolutely don't want the answer told until they have figured it out for themselves. This is a classic example of mindsets and an application for encouragement of effort.

Connecting Growth Mindsets to Neuroplasticity

Students can also be convinced to adopt a growth mindset by learning about neuroplasticity: that is, the scientific finding the brain is not fixed and can grow and change with experience. I introduce neuroplasticity with a video segment on amputees from the PBS series, *Secrets of the Mind* (2007), featuring V. S. Ramachandran. The clip follows an amputee who has sensations when touched on the cheek, but experiences these sensations simultaneously in the phantom hand. Because the representation of the hand and face are side by side in the somatosensory cortex, the connections that once came from the phantom hand, but no longer have input, have been innervated by connections coming from the face. The physical brain has changed and adapted to new circumstance.

Students are generally not aware that the brain is constantly adapting to behaviors. One easy way to demonstrate this is through a perceptual adaptation exercise. Utilizing goggles that shift vision 30 degrees to the left (they can be ordered through psychkits.com), a target, and a tennis ball, students see how many throws it takes to adapt to their shifted vision and hit the bull's eye with the tennis ball. Then, after taking the goggles off, students aim at the target again, and realize they have to readjust again to their non-shifted vision. Number of throws can be formally counted and graphed, or students can engage in a competition if so desired. I originally learned of this technique through a former student (Olivia Dure, personal communication, 2011) who carried out a science fair experiment in my classroom using this method.

STRESS—HARMFUL, HELPFUL, OR BOTH?

Stress is omnipresent in student life. Thus, it is important for students to understand the biological underpinnings of stress, how the mindset from which it is viewed shapes its consequences, and ways to alleviate it. The first step is an understanding of the human stress response, both acute and long-term, and the roles of the sympathetic and parasympathetic nervous systems. An effective way to introduce these topics is through the *Scientific American Frontiers* video featuring Robert Sapolsky, "Worried Sick" (2003). The introductory segment explains the fight-or-flight response comparing the reflexive, immediate run of an antelope from a tiger with the more angst-driven social struggles of baboons and humans. Sapolsky notes that chronic stress can have negative health consequences such as high blood pressure and vulnerability to infectious diseases due to a compromised immune system. He points out that human angst, and the resulting chronic stress, is enhanced by advanced cognition. While the antelope simply lives in the present, humans worry about the past and about the future. For the antelope, danger is either realized quickly or is gone and life settles in again. For the baboon or the human, feelings of stress may continue long after the threat has subsided.

Stress Mindsets

A connection can be made, at this point, between how individuals think about their stressors and the amount of stress they feel. Recent work by Alia Crum, Salovey, and Achor (2013) points to a distinction between a mindset that sees *stress as enhancing* and a mindset that sees *stress as debilitating*. She examines the type of mindset as an overarching structure that facilitates certain behaviors and coping mechanisms. In a *stress is debilitating* mindset, the main idea is that stress is inherently harmful. This is the mainstream conception of stress and it can permeate a student's understanding of its effects. This conception encourages coping mechanisms in order to bring stress, viewed as detrimental, under control. Crum comments that coping strategies are not necessarily ineffective in nature and can serve a purpose, but that shifting one's mindset from *stress is debilitating* to *stress is enhancing* can improve health, well-being, and performance on tasks. "The implications of these studies may lead to a more efficient approach—intervening at the level of mindset to provoke a chain of physiological and behavioral reactions which will, in turn, improve health and performance outcomes." In a *stress is enhancing* mindset, coping strategies that help alleviate the stress can certainly be part of the equation, but the primary thought is that stress can be helpful in solving life's problems.

Teaching students about stress mindsets provides an opportunity to talk about academic stressors and whether stress can enhance students' performance. A study by Brady, Hard, and Gross (2016, under review) examined how the way students think about academic stress, manipulated in a simple e-mail reminder about an upcoming exam, could influence performance. One group of students was sent the usual e-mail reminder about the exam while the other group received an extra phrase suggesting the anxiety/arousal they may be feeling could actually help their performance. The results showed the group with the anxiety/arousal phrase performed higher on the midterm. Discussing research on stress mindsets coupled with an understanding of how we frame our own arousal/anxiety can help students face uncomfortable times. Recognizing this connection supports students adopting a holistic outlook when trying to understand their personal stressors.

Having students write about a particular stressor they have encountered in the last year gives them an opportunity to think about how they might respond differently, if at all, to a similar situation in the future. The chosen stressor can be something like applying to college, adjusting to first-semester freshman year, getting assignments in on time, balancing sports and school, and so on. The prompt I often use is: "Explain how you coped when you encountered this stressor before, discussing both emotional and problem-based coping methods you used, and how you might cope if faced with the same stressor again in the future." Many of my students have told me that this assignment helped them face and see their challenges in a different light. A word of caution: Students should be encouraged to pick stressors they must face in everyday life—like balancing academic discipline and extracurricular activities—and not a traumatic stressor they may have endured in the past. Importantly, this assignment is meant to help with problem-solving but is not meant to be a form of therapy.

Exercise as a Moderator of Stress

In addition to teaching students about the potential benefits of stress, I also educate them on ways to lessen physical effects of stress on the body. One way of teaching this is by assigning and discussing an article on the effect of exercise and other healthy lifestyle habits on moderating the effect of chronic stress on DNA. Lu (2014) reports in an interview with Elissa Epel that exercise is a strong antidote to what Epel refers to as "stress soup"—"excessive cortisol, insulin, inflammation, and oxidative stress." Epel explains that telomeres are caps that exist at the end of a strand of DNA and telomerase is an enzyme that replenishes these ends every time a cell divides. Stress can affect the capability of telomerase to replenish the ends, and thus, the telomeres become shortened. Shorter telomeres reflect an acceleration in the aging process. During the interview, Epel refers to the work of Eli Puterman, Lin, Blackburn, O'Donovan, Adler, and Epel (2010) who have studied telomere length in adults and found that exercise has a moderating effect on the length of telomeres. Epel further points out—and this is important for students to hear—that even if we go through a year of unusually high stress, exercise, a healthy diet, and plenty of sleep provide a buffer to the reduction in telomere length.

LEARNING, CONDITIONING, AND RELAXATION

One way to understand the development of a specific fear is through the concept of classical conditioning, where a neutral stimulus (such as a bell) is paired with (presented right before) food, such as in Pavlov's studies (Pavlov, 1927). *Forty Studies That Changed Psychology* (Hock, 2009) includes secondary source articles focusing in detail on the classic learning and conditioning studies. Hock describes the studies in the format of the experimental method so that students have a bridge between reading a technical article and a summary of a study. Watson's Little Albert study (Watson & Rayner, 1920) is presented as a variation of Pavlov's studies where a rat was the conditioned stimulus and a loud clang of a pan was the unconditioned stimulus. By pairing these two together, Watson elicited a specific fear of rats (that generalized to furry animals) in the infant known as Little Albert and showed that fears could be learned. I show original footage of the experiment in the episode "In Search of Ourselves" (1998) from the PBS series, *A Science Odyssey*. Aside from the concept of conditioning, this study provides an excellent entry point into a discussion of ethics in research and how in the present there are institutional review boards where experiments are approved when there is no harm to the subject.

Gradual Exposure to a Stressor Can Reduce Anxiety

The third component in this series of articles (Hock, 2009) I cover is Joseph Wolpe's work (Wolpe, 1961) in overcoming fears through systematic desensitization. The description of Wolpe's study prompts a good discussion that contrasts the origin of a phobia from the psychoanalytic and the behavioral perspectives.

I also underline that all humans have fears and that a phobia is an irrational fear that becomes a problem when it interferes with functioning in normal life. This is a good time to either introduce or link back to a connection already made that both classical conditioning and operant conditioning contribute to the phobia or fear response. The initial association of emotion with a stressor is classical conditioning and the avoidance of the stressor maintains the fear. It is for this reason that gradual exposure to the stressor can be so effective in relieving the fear.

Following this discussion I ask students to identify a specific fear of their own that is minor in nature. In order to further examine the relationship between body and mind, I demonstrate some ways behavioral practices, such as deep muscle relaxation, can help allay cognitive distress. Once students understand the cognitive/physical source of their fears, the next step is for them to create an anxiety hierarchy for their selected fear (the most common fear this year was spiders). I then ask the students to do one round of deep muscle relaxation (Bolt, 2011; Grasha, 1987). Students lie down on the floor on their back, palms down, and are taken through a series of exercises where they tense specific muscle groups and then relax those groups repetitively. For example, they may be asked to make a fist, tense up their right arm for 5 seconds, and then take a deep breath and relax. Rotating through different body parts, such as arms, face, neck, stomach, and legs, students learn deep muscle relaxation techniques and understand how Wolpe would have taken a subject through an anxiety hierarchy with this procedure, only exposing his subjects gradually to their specific fears and what they could endure. Although students understand I am not trying to "cure" a fear but simply trying to demonstrate how Wolpe might have done it, they report enjoying the activity and finding it useful. I encourage students to use deep muscle relaxation as a tool for times of stress by revisiting it throughout the year as a stress break. I have had many students tell me that they implemented the exercise for falling asleep at night.

This activity can be supplemented with other segments from *Scientific American Frontiers*, "Worried Sick" (2003), featuring Herbert Benson on the relaxation response and the work of Janet Kiecolt-Glaser on the ability of the body to heal when under stressful conditions. For medical students in the study presented, this was the time preceding a final exam. She administered surface blister wounds to each subject and then monitored the number of days for healing to occur. One group of medical students received weekly doses of deep muscle relaxation therapy while the control group did not. Students in the experimental group (deep muscle relaxation) were found to heal significantly faster than the controls. This is a concrete, relevant, and dramatic example of the way that practices with the mind can influence the physiology of the body.

PTSD, Classically Conditioned Memories, and
a Calming Emotional Response

For several years I have invited clinicians to class during this unit to talk about topics such as anxiety, PTSD (posttraumatic stress disorder), and cognitive-behavioral and dialectic approaches to therapy. These speakers have explained that therapeutic techniques such as mindfulness (learning to be in the present moment) and behavioral training are healthy ways to learn to deal with stress. One behavioral technique for coping with anxiety that has classical conditioning at its base comes from the pairing of a pleasant emotional memory with a specific smell. Smell is an ancient sense with primary connections linked directly to the emotional limbic system. Dr. Mollie Thomas (personal communication, 2015) suggests to clinical patients suffering from PTSD to identify a favorite scent from childhood and to have that scent with them on their person, in a bottle or a small candle. For example, the smell of vanilla may be associated with feelings of safety and home. Smelling the scent when feeling anxious can then calm the emotional limbic system down. Students find this positive power of classical conditioning fascinating as it relates not only to the clinical treatment of PTSD but to their everyday lives as well.

DECISION-MAKING AND SOCIAL INFLUENCE

So far I have explored three ways of using the introductory psychology course to enhance student well-being. First, how can educators equip students with an understanding of cognitive strategies and a mindset that promotes academic success? Second, how can they increase student understanding of the human stress response and show them how mindsets can influence physiological and behavioral reactions? Third, how can they aid students in understanding conditioned emotional reactions and the powerful behavioral ways exposure to a stressor, deep muscle relaxation, and positive conditioned associations can help alleviate anxiety? The next question shifts to how can they prepare students to recognize factors that contribute to decision-making? In order to make good decisions, it is important they be aware of the human vulnerabilities in judgment, the anxiety associated with cognitive dissonance, the influence of a group on the individual, and the profound influence one individual can have on a group.

Recognizing Cognitive Shortcuts and
Their Influence on Judgment

Cognitive shortcuts or heuristics, which normally work in one's favor, can also make one vulnerable to distortions of facts and it is important students see and understand these. Students need to be aware that situations that seem to involve very logical thinking are often less logical than they appear, and that their judgment can be altered by those who want to influence them. The ability to cognitively and emotionally stop, reflect, and consider seems a crucially important skill for analyzing information.

Encouraging students to seek out multiple perspectives.   Decisions are rarely made in a vacuum and students need to be aware of influences that affect their thinking. This unit is powerful because it shows that people of all ages are prone to cognitive biases and can make irrational choices. Studying the confirmation bias, for instance, makes students stop and reflect on how they collect information to aid them in everyday decision-making (Myers, 2011). Students studying this topic may stop and think, "Do I only look for information that supports my beliefs or do I look at contrasting views as well?" Realizing they are sometimes only receiving half of the story encourages students to seek out multiple perspectives when they encounter a problem in the future.

Recognizing the pitfalls of the availability heuristic.

How aware are students that they are influenced by the media? Typically they have a notion they are affected. Students are generally surprised by the potency of the availability heuristic, a way of making judgments based on the ease with which certain information comes to mind. Fischhoff, Slovic, and Lichtenstein (1977) showed that when subjects are asked to estimate the risk of a dramatic death (such as suicide and homicide) that is more likely to be portrayed in the media versus an actually more common yet less dramatic death (such as stroke and diabetes), the more memorable causes predictably outrank those that are actually more prevalent, demonstrating the way in which viewing media alters the information human minds have on hand. Exposing such a fallacy reminds students to be aware of the information they use to make choices.

A powerful demonstration that shows how framing can affect judgment.

Among the most useful illustrations of the framing effect (Bolt, 2011; Jacowitz & Kahneman, 1995) is an exercise that asks students for the distance of the Mississippi River. Easy enough, right? Most American students have studied the Mississippi River at one point in their lives. However, the way in which the question is posed to students drastically affects their estimates of the river's distance. Interestingly, if you give half the students one prompt—"Is it shorter or greater than 500 miles?"—and the other half a different prompt—"Is it shorter or greater than 3,000 miles?"—you get wildly and predictably different estimates of the length. Students are shown that despite believing they know how long the Mississippi River roughly is, they are still open to influence in their judgment based on the question alone. Students learn that they must think beyond the parameters of a question or debate to remain independent in their judgments.

Cognitive Dissonance and Social Pressure

Hock (2009) explains the concept of dissonance as a state of uncomfortable tension that exists when cognitions and/or behaviors are inconsistent with each other (Festinger & Carlsmith, 1959). In this state, anxiety is produced and the individual looks for a way to reduce the anxiety. When students simply understand that this state exists and have a name for it, it gives a notice to stop, think, and reflect on why they might be feeling anxious. Rather than trying to calm that uncomfortable tension quickly with a rash decision, perhaps they can learn to coexist with the tension long enough to make a more rational choice. The content provided in the judgment and decision-making unit, combined with an awareness of cognitive dissonance and its resulting anxiety, can provide students with the psychological knowledge to make this happen.

An effective way I've found to have students apply their knowledge of cognitive dissonance and other major social psychology concepts is by asking them to view the classic movie or TV version (60 minutes) of *Twelve Angry Men* (2010), and then complete a reflective writing assignment. Students view the film during a class session or on their own. For the writing assignment, I identify key terms and ask students how these terms apply to the movie, followed up later by a discussion in class or extended on an online discussion board. This movie naturally lends itself to topics of prejudice, discrimination, confirmation bias, cognitive dissonance, groupthink, social influence, the fundamental attribution error, and other topics in social psychology. This movie depicts one long continuous moment of uncomfortable tension, competing cognitions, minority influence, and decision-making. The fact that the protagonist can stand firm in his conviction that the evidence be critically evaluated models the ability to tolerate the uncomfortable tension long enough to make an informed decision and influence others.

Tolerating uncomfortable moments takes courage and I want students to know that. Life takes courage. I don't know what difficult moments students are facing now or in the future, but my hope is that a curriculum designed to build strength in and emphasize academic skills, mind/body awareness, and an understanding of decision-making processes will be of help.

TEACHING IN A THEMATIC FRAMEWORK

I've found in this journey that there are three main steps in developing a method for teaching a theme-based application. The first is to pick a theme, the second is to know your context, and the third is to examine your mindset. Choosing a theme may be the most difficult part of applying this method to a curriculum, but it is also the most crucial. Observe your students, interact with them, and listen carefully for potential topics. It can require a great deal of time before arriving at an appropriate theme, but because of the patience and effort exercised in theme preparation, the class will be that much more pertinent to students' lives. Within the array of introductory psychology content, there is so much that can be covered and many resources available. By picking a theme one can revisit during the course, enduring connections can be made in a distributive fashion.

Understanding Your Context

Understanding your context requires reflecting on course content, learning goals, student characteristics, and teacher characteristics (Chew et al., 2010). My context includes Advanced Placement Psychology at the high school level with highly motivated students whose overall goal is to get into college. My class sizes are small, with about 15 students on average, which gives me time to assess in deeper, more elaborative ways than perhaps a large lecture class would provide. The curriculum is strenuous with expectations that all major textbook content will be covered. The APA's *National Standards for High School Psychology Curricula* (2011) addresses the content for a high school psychology course and provides some ideas for application of that content. The College Board maintains a website, AP Central, where expectations of the Advanced Placement (AP) course can be found (see references for link). For the AP course, students are expected to show their knowledge through multiple-choice and free-response questions.

Emphasis on application in Advanced Placement Psychology.   An important piece of the Advanced Placement Psychology context is that students need to be prepared for the free-response essay question on the AP exam. These questions require students to pull together concepts from a wide variety of units and apply them to real life. Questions as well as grading rubrics going back a number of years can be found at the College Board's website for Advanced Placement Psychology (see references for link). I have to prepare my students for this assessment by providing similar ones throughout the course that ask for examples or applications. When the assessment *requires* application rather than memorization, the instructor must teach in a way that supports it, and the student must learn in a deeper, more elaborative way where real-world applications can be produced. Having been an AP Reader for many years, I've seen firsthand the value in good preparation and have witnessed, sadly, when students have not received it.

Content and application at the college level.   At the college level, instructors have more flexibility in what to cover, and are generally not required to cover all units. For example, the APA Board of Educational Affairs Working Group's *Strengthening the Common Core of Introductory Psychology* (2014) recommends instructors select at least two units each from the following "pillars": biological, cognitive, developmental, social/personality, and mental/physical health. Teaching an understanding of research methods is expected to be a foundation for any unit selected. This model encourages instructors to distribute the course content more equitably than perhaps have before. A strong recommendation from the group is to include as elements within each pillar the following: cultural and social diversity, ethics, variations in human functioning, and applications to everyday life. Integration, or making cohesive connections between topics, is strongly emphasized. It's helpful to consider a model such as this one as elements of your potential theme emerge.

Identifying learning goals and teaching strategies.   Another important part of understanding your context is to consider what learning goals and outcomes one is seeking (Chew et al., 2010). If instructors want students to apply psychological science, they need to teach in ways that enable them to do so. Short, reflective writing papers on classic studies read outside of class give students a chance to think and apply before taking part in a class discussion. Having students go out and do a naturalistic observation study can be a great way to find applications, especially for topics like exercise and diet. A discussion of current or historical events and how they relate to certain concepts can be implemented on a recurring basis. When learning goals are well identified, teaching resources can be selected to support the learning process. The resources that come along with introductory psychology textbooks today are vast and valuable. Suggestions for demonstrations, online activities, formative assessments (easily done through technology), and so forth are available and well structured. The real challenge is sifting through all the excellent material available to make a choice.

Examining Your Mindset

Finally, in coming up with a theme-based application, it is important to examine your mindset. Incorporating theme-based applications into your course may require a great deal of effort, but the process can also be highly enjoyable. You have to ask yourself, "Do I have a fixed mindset or a growth mindset about teaching? Do I look for ways to enhance my course? Do I believe that I could be a more effective teacher by discovering and evaluating other methods? Do I have a *stress is enhancing* or a *stress is debilitating* mindset when it comes to feedback?" Crum et al. (2013) found that subjects with a *stress is enhancing* mindset were more interested in receiving feedback on a public speaking exercise. Examining one's own mindset, which can be difficult to do, points the way for growth and improved teaching effectiveness.

Taking a somewhat scientific approach to teaching aligns well with a growth mindset. Approach teaching like you would an experiment (Bernstein et al., 2010). Try something in the classroom and analyze the outcome for student learning. Be willing to experiment and be thoughtful in your analysis of the outcome. I've found that when students know you are passionate about your subject, are willing to take risks, and are interested in their well-being, they will embrace a change and are forgiving when things don't go exactly as planned.

Enjoy your time with your students and fill their toolkits with something they can take into the future, way past the final exam. For many, this will be their only course in psychology, and for others, it may be the spark that influences their career path. Make your course a crossroads where unifying themes that promote synthesis and applications to the real world combine to create lasting memories.

Chapter 12

Using Data to Inform Practice

J. NOLAND WHITE
Georgia College & State University

Instructors of introductory psychology have the good fortune of interacting with students for whom this may be their first exposure to the field, and introducing them to the science of psychology. They stress the importance of the scientific method, teach students about valid sources of information, and warn them against trusting invalid sources. Students are taught about various types of cognitive biases and the kinds of thinking errors people may inadvertently fall prey to.

Teachers need to continually evaluate the methods they use in and outside of the classrooms to determine if students are learning. They also need to model the thinking and behavior they wish for their students to develop. They want to teach students the value of the scientific approach, how to determine and evaluate valid sources of information, and how to apply that information to their own lives. Teachers typically accomplish this by introducing a variety of psychological concepts that are supported by evidence, and then instructing students, or demonstrating to them, the many ways to evaluate the data and potential applications.

However, there is much more teachers can do to really help students understand the value of evidence to support conclusions. They can model the value of evidence by using evidence to inform their teaching practices. They can also build in methods and procedures throughout their course structure that elicit such data. And more importantly, they can incorporate methods and strategies that give their students opportunities to use evidence to guide their own practices.

This chapter focuses on the value of using assessment to gather data, and then using the data gained to inform practice. A key component of this theme centers on the role of formative assessment. This theme applies to teachers and students alike. Teachers can use data to design their courses, evaluate their teaching practices and student learning outcomes, and, where necessary, adjust course methods or strategies. Students can use assessment and data to evaluate their individual learning strategies, topic mastery, and develop skills in metacognition.

FORMATIVE AND SUMMATIVE ASSESSMENT

Amy: I taught my dog to whistle.

Betty: Let's hear it then.

Amy: He can't whistle.

Betty: I thought you said you taught him to whistle.

Amy: I did. He just didn't learn it.

Wiliam, 2011, p. 48

A primary aspect of this theme is taking advantage of various types of assessment methods and strategies, and using them for both *formative* and *summative* purposes. Summative assessment is what many people think of when the term "assessment" is used. It is used to compare individuals and to assign grades. Summative assessment is used to measure achievement and may be applied at the student or program level. Formative assessment is used to inform teaching and learning. It is used by teachers to adjust instruction and by students to adjust learning strategies (Popham, 2008, 2011; Wiliam, 2011). As compared to summative assessment, formative assessment has a greater role as a teaching "tool" and is used to promote learning; it is not simply used to see if learning has occurred. While many teachers make teaching adjustments reactively throughout a given semester, quarter, or period of instruction, a formative assessment approach involves a systematic and planned process in which teachers or students use assessment-based evidence to make adjustments in teaching, or for students to modify their current approaches to learning (Black & Wiliam, 2009; Cizek, 2010; Popham, 2008).

WHY IS EFFECTIVE FORMATIVE AND
SUMMATIVE ASSESSMENT SO IMPORTANT?

Formative assessment strategies have become vital components in all the courses I teach as they fit well with the overall goals I am trying to accomplish. Foremost, I believe that the student's participation and involvement in the learning process is critical. Many teachers hope to have classrooms full of self-initiated learners who work from a base of intrinsic motivation. Reality often reveals a very different picture and one challenge teachers face is the accurate assessment of where each student is (e.g., intellectually, developmentally as a learner, in progressing toward a learning goal) and to provide individualized feedback to each student that is useful and meaningful.

Teachers may have to assist students in recognizing what they have vested in the endeavor, educate them about the importance of their active role in the learning process, and continually emphasize that effective and efficient learning is not a passive activity. Depending on the number of students in a given class, multiplying this challenge by 25, 50, or 100+ times can result in what appears to be a seemingly impossible task. However, if a learning structure or scaffold is established through classes, laboratories, or other planned learning activities, teachers free themselves up so that they can effectively respond to the individual needs of their students.

I strive to serve as a positive model for my students and want to foster a life-long pursuit of learning. At minimum, I hope that students will master the basic knowledge and core skills associated with the discipline of psychology or whatever their major course of study may be. I would like for them to learn how to accurately assess their own levels of understanding along the way, developing both metacognitive skills and reliance on valid assessments. I want them to be informed consumers of information and to respect the process and methods of scientific inquiry, and hope they will be able to synthesize information from various sources as they develop their knowledge base. Lastly, I hope that they can apply their knowledge and experiences in ways that are congruent and respectful of both the scientific method and the recognition of the inherent value and worth of all individuals, or their individual philosophies.

Wherever possible, I try to establish an environment of active learning where I collaborate with students in and out of the classroom. I attempt to work beside them in their active pursuit of information, developing enquiry and dialogue into "established" knowledge, or in taking risks in the pursuit of learning. Students are often uncomfortable when things do not come readily, when they make errors, or when they discover that effective learning requires more time or effort than they may have been accustomed to during earlier educational experiences (e.g., high school, courses that do not have cumulative exams). As such, I teach them about possible misconceptions related to learning, and the role of desirable difficulties and the types of learning strategies that are actually the most effective (E. L. Bjork & Bjork, 2011; R. A. Bjork, 1994; Chew, 2010, 2014; Clark & Bjork, 2014). I challenge them to not rely on studying for recognition and short-term gain through methods like massed practice (e.g., last-minute cramming) and encourage them to use strategies for long-term learning and retention like spaced retrieval practice and interleaving (Carpenter, 2014; Cepeda, Pashler, Vul, Wixted, & Rohrer, 2006; Pyc, Agarwal, & Roediger, 2014; Roediger & Karpicke, 2006). Through the use of a variety of formative assessment methods and strategies throughout the course, I intend to help students to develop an appreciation of the learning benefits that can result from using these strategies far in advance of the summative assessments they will also encounter. Furthermore, students can learn to use the summative assessments in a formative manner if they use the results provided to effectively modify their study and learning strategies.

HOW DO I USE DATA TO INFORM PRACTICE AT THE LEVEL OF MY TEACHING?

Data from both formative and summative assessments are used over the span of my entire course. I access students' misconceptions related to psychology on day one and our last meeting comprises a comprehensive final exam. For any given semester, my current courses are influenced by past data, and current data will inform planning of future courses. Given that many instructors are already intimately aware of the function of summative assessments, I will first elaborate on some key components of formative assessment.

In order for formative assessment to be the planned process it is intended to be, several components are necessary. Foremost is the identification of the desired learning objectives and what concepts or skills will be necessary to assist students to reach that objective, sometimes referred to as *learning intentions* or *learning progressions* (Popham, 2008, 2011; Wiliam, 2011). Assessments are scheduled and used to evaluate student learning at multiple times during the progression and the data are evaluated. The results are shared with students and next steps are planned. If there are any gaps or deficits, necessary adjustments are made to the instructional plan in order to meet the intermediate learning goal, minimize any deficits, and help move student learning along. If students demonstrate successful mastery of the desired concepts or skills, teachers and students can move forward to the next step as they progress toward the desired learning objective.

Effective learning objectives and outcomes give direction for faculty and students alike, focusing on the learning that will come from activities, rather than the activities themselves (Huba & Freed, 2000). The American Psychological Association's (APA) comprehensive learning goals, learning outcomes, and indicators (American Psychological Association, 2013) already provide a framework that instructors of introductory psychology may choose to work from or adapt to their own needs. Additionally, many textbooks have learning objectives or outcomes that are mapped to the APA's learning goals, which can further assist faculty in identifying what specific goals are desired and what interim steps may be required to reach those goals.

For example, for APA's *Goal 2: Scientific Inquiry and Critical Thinking*, one of the learning outcomes is *2.4 Interpret, design, and conduct basic psychological research*, and the foundational indicator is *2.4a Describe research methods used by psychologists including their respective advantages and disadvantages* (American Psychological Association, 2013). A related textbook learning objective may be "Explain the correlational technique and describe its usefulness to researchers" (Ciccarelli & White, 2015).

Other key components of formative assessment are related to the specific assessment strategies and ways in which data will be gathered. Faculty will need to identify the types of assessments that will provide the type of evidence needed to measure a given subskill or core concept. They need to remain mindful of how the interim steps support the desired learning outcome. Furthermore, they should also be clear on what criteria have to be met to indicate "success" and let students and instructors know when students have successfully met that skill or mastered that concept. Assessments may stem from interactions or activities already being used in class, but in general, they should be "no- to low-stakes" as compared to higher-stake activities like summative exams.

Teachers also need to identify what data or finding from a given assessment will prompt a change or modification in their immediate teaching plans. Is it the majority, or a significant portion, of the class getting a set of content-based formative clicker items incorrect? Or is it an obvious incomplete or inaccurate understanding of an identified subskill that is revealed through class discussion? Based on what misunderstanding or deficit is revealed, you should have a plan for what course or learning adjustment will be the most appropriate. Ideally, you will identify possible areas of confusion or the most challenging concepts when you map out the steps required for students to reach a particular learning outcome. Furthermore, by proactively identifying possible student misconceptions during this portion of your overall planning and assessment cycle, you can develop a variety of content- or skill-relevant adjustments or strategies to best assist students.

A final important component of formative assessment is in providing feedback that moves learning forward (Wiliam, 2011). Feedback should reduce the discrepancy between where a learner is and the desired outcome by informing the individual of the identified goal, what their current level of progress is, and where they should go next (Hattie & Timperley, 2007; Hattie & Yates, 2014). Feedback serves a formative function when it prompts the learner to think and is used to improve performance (Wiliam, 2011).

HOW I USE DATA TO INFORM PRACTICE IN MY INTRODUCTORY PSYCHOLOGY COURSE

My most recent and current sections of introductory psychology are taught once a week. The class period is scheduled for 2 hours and 45 minutes during which we take a 10–15 minute break about midway through the period. Introduction to psychology is my favorite course to teach and I believe that students should be exposed to the breadth of topics covered in our field and in their text. I do not omit sections or chapters in favor of teaching others. While many of my students are psychology majors, there are a significant number who are not. This course may be many students' single exposure to the science of psychology. Even for future psychology majors, I do not believe that you can skip *topic x* because they will get it later in their major courses. Hence, a course meeting only once a week and attempting to essentially cover the major areas in psychology and the entire text over the span of a semester place a lot of demands on students. The class structure I describe in the following section has evolved over many years to help students successfully navigate a once-a-week course, to support them in mastering the course content, to assist them in skill development, and to assist me in responding to students' learning needs in and out of the classroom. And while the course structure being described is for my introductory psychology course,

I use similar strategies for all of my other courses, including those that meet more than once a week.

USING DATA TO INFORM COURSE DESIGN

An important component of the class structure is reflected in the attendance policy. There is no differentiation between excused and unexcused absences and students may miss up to two class periods. At three absences, a significant grade penalty is imposed, and if at any time they have two consecutive absences or a total of four absences, they fail the course. Assignment deadlines are also firm with no makeups offered for missed exams or in-class activities, and significant grade penalties for late submissions. Some students view such policies as harsh but I try to convey my belief in student involvement and engagement in the class itself, which they cannot do if they are not present or participating. I remind them they have choices in the courses they take, and in the faculty that offer them. I encourage them to decide early on if they want to remain in my course section and, if they decide to do so, they are entering into an agreement that they understand such polices are part of the current class.

Another intention of having the attendance policy is to assist students in developing their self-regulation skills. To illustrate this, I borrow an analogy from one of my departmental colleagues. I tell students that the attendance policy is a lot like having money in a savings account. However, a single deposit has already been made and you cannot add any more money to the account. You can take money out for something fun (e.g., going to a concert) but if you use all of your savings for fun and leisure, no money will remain when more serious needs arise (e.g., car repair).

While covering the syllabus, I also elaborate on how the course structure has developed over the years. I stress that it is intended to help them be successful and has been shaped by the course goals, student learning outcomes, and student feedback. Likewise, I share how the syllabus and course structure are designed to help them develop critical skills that will allow them to succeed in a future job. I share relevant data on the top reasons new college hires are disciplined or fired to support this point (e.g., Gardner, 2007). In doing so, I am attempting to demonstrate during the very first class meeting how effective assessment and feedback are useful and how they can be used to modify class structure and the learning experience.

USING DATA TO INFORM TEACHING PRACTICES

I try to incorporate multiple tools and methods that will provide accurate data about how effectively students are mastering course material, which will allow me to make any necessary adjustments in my instructional plans. I also try to use methods that allow students to evaluate their own learning and readily see where they are in the learning process. In general, student involvement and engagement are facilitated by lectures, discussions, and a variety of class activities. I also use technology to support both engagement and an active learning environment, with some tools being used in the classroom, and others used outside of class. I take advantage of online homework and study materials and an in-class classroom response system with students using "clickers." While both the online activities and clickers can be used for either formative or summative assessment, in the majority of my classes their primary role is for formative assessment.

Like many faculty, I believe that students will be most successful when they come into the classroom prepared and encourage them to complete their reading and related assignments prior to class coverage of a given topic. I do so by assigning online homework and study materials that have to be completed before the respective class period. While I have created my own assignments and assessments in the past and used the university system's learning management system (LMS) for implementation, I currently use a publisher's LMS to structure these activities. These activities provide multiple pieces of data that are useful for students, and they are very useful for me.

For a given chapter, students have assigned readings and an online study plan that is due prior to in-class coverage of the material. Foremost, students are encouraged to complete their assigned readings before they attempt any portion of the online study plan. The study plan has several components including a pretest, study materials that are assigned based on their individual performance on the pretest, a posttest, and additional remediation materials based on the posttest performance. For example, the pretest is divided into several sections according to content and level of learning. If student A does relatively well but does not meet criteria on a particular section of the pretest, he/she will only be assigned additional study material related to that particular topic. On the other hand, student B may have scored poorly across the board, and in turn will have more study material, covering multiple topic areas, assigned to him/her. Within a couple of days of class coverage of a topic, students are also assigned an online chapter exam and, for some chapters, a brief essay assignment.

It should be noted that I do not use the study plan "pretest" as a true pretest; students are encouraged to read the entire chapter before they complete the respective study plan. In doing so, they can use the results of the study plan pre- and posttest assessments to gauge their current understanding of the assigned material before they ever come to class. They will also only complete assigned study or remediation material relevant to their individual performance. Students can see rather quickly which of their individual study strategies are the most useful, and which may need to be adjusted.

The online pre- and post-assessments on the study plan comprised multiple-choice items, as are the online chapter exams. These are similar to questions they will encounter during the in-class exams. Students are encouraged to complete their online study plans and chapter exams without referring to their text or notes. In doing so, they can use the activities as formative assessments and get an idea of their actual understanding of the assigned content and material, and ability to retrieve the information from memory. By doing so, they can evaluate their ability to retrieve information far in advance of the higher-stake in-class exams and final. They are also engaging in retrieval practice or test-enhanced learning, a strategy that has multiple positive learning effects and promotes long-term learning and is more effective than simply re-reading their text (Dunlosky, Rawson, Marsh, Nathan, & Willingham, 2013; Little & McDaniel, 2015; Pyc et al., 2014; Roediger & Karpicke, 2006).

An important part of my assessment plan is having the chapter study plans due before face-to-face class meeting (see Figure 12.1). This enables me to review the study plan results for a given chapter to get an idea of what topic areas students are grasping, and what areas they are having more difficulty with. I can use that data to modify my classroom presentation or activities for that particular class meeting to best address the needs of those students.

In addition to altering my lecture or activity plan for a given class meeting, I can also modify my formative assessment approaches for that period. I have a set of multiple-choice clicker items for every chapter that are structured by learning objectives that appear in the text, and that I use as a foundation for constructing my summative assessments. I can add more questions to topic sections or learning objectives that students appear to be having more difficulty with, and perhaps not have as many items for those objectives that students appear to be grasping. However, even if the study plan posttest scores indicate that students have a firm grasp of a topic or area, I do not remove all related items from in-class clicker items. I will use some of them during the respective class period, and move some to a future class period, taking advantage of spacing and interleaving to help students further access their ability to effectively retrieve the information (Carpenter, 2014; Cepeda et al., 2006; Clark & Bjork, 2014).

The clicker items used in class provide an immediate appraisal of students' understanding of the material being covered and various levels of items are used. Some are used to evaluate understanding of basic content while others are used to assess comprehension and application. All items are similar in nature to what students may experience during the scheduled summative assessments. They also offer me an excellent way to assess not only what students are grasping but also what errors they are making. While reviewing student responses for a given item, I am able to reinforce reasons why the correct answer is the best choice, and clarify and discuss why a given distractor is not correct or the best answer. Students

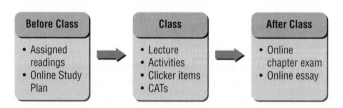

FIGURE 12.1 Flow of chapter assignments and assessments. The sequence of chapter assignments and activities are intended to assist students in assessing their level of understanding throughout the process. The instructor also uses the data to provide feedback, make any necessary adjustments, or modify future course plans and actions.

receive immediate feedback on both their correct responses and the rationale as to why any incorrect response was not the best answer.

In addition to discussion and lecture, other in-class activities provide students with feedback on how well they are mastering content or using psychology concepts in a scientific manner. Students are also able to practice creating their own formative assessments to evaluate not only their own learning but also of their classmates. For example, I use student-created quizzes in class. Students work in pairs to create a set of multiple-choice items and a scoring key covering specific learning objectives from their text. Each item must have a single correct answer and three quality distractors. The quiz items and key are each put on a separate piece of paper, with the quiz authors' names and date at the top of each. They may use their books or notes during their creation but both students have to be involved in the creation of each item; they cannot split them up with each student doing a portion. Discussion is encouraged throughout and they may not simply copy items that appear in their text, or those that were used in the online activities. The time allowed for this part of the activity varies by the number of items that are specified, but I may allow 30 minutes for the creation of 6–8 items. My classes are generally comprised of 40 students so I am able to wander through the class to monitor progress and answer questions. When the quiz from each pair is finished, I will look over the items and answer choices to provide feedback. When all items and quizzes have been created, students exchange quizzes with another pair and I often ask for two exchanges, asking that students do not get their own quizzes back, and to avoid friends exchanging quizzes with each other. Students are instructed to put their names on the quiz they received and are then given time to complete the quiz. They may not use their text or notes during this portion. Again, active discussion with their partner is encouraged and I will give them approximately 1.5 to 2 minutes per item to complete the quiz. Afterward, the original authors score the quizzes and the results are shared with the quiz takers.

This activity has several formative purposes. First, students are able to immediately assess their level of understanding of the current content, based on the ease of creating quiz items. This is not to suggest that creating such items is an easy task, but rather that students having an idea of *what* to assess and the nature of the questions, answers, and distractors they create can reveal aspects of their current understanding of the topic. Second, when students complete the quizzes that were created by others, they are able to further assess their understanding and ability to retrieve information, as they may not use their texts or notes during this time. They can then make changes to their study strategies based on the results. I also review the quiz results after the class meeting and can make any necessary instructional adjustments in future class plans. Lastly, students are encouraged to generalize this quiz-making strategy to their individual study. They can create similar quiz items as they go through the reading assignments and use them in addition to those that appear in the text to assess their understanding and make adjustments in their study approaches. As with any other class or activity, I also encourage them to meet with me outside of class if needed to address questions about content or to discuss possible strategies for modifying their approaches to the material.

PRACTICAL CONSIDERATIONS

As mentioned earlier, students are encouraged to read their text and complete their online study plans and chapter exams without referring to their text or notes, but some students will ignore this advice. Some will focus primarily on the grades for these assignments, and understandably, simply want the highest scores possible. They often want to accomplish this in the shortest amount of time and in a manner that requires the least amount of effort. Through both discussion and activities in class, I try to persuade students to understand the value of my approach. I emphasize that by testing their retrieval of information under conditions similar to the summative assessments they will take in a course (e.g., three in-class comprehensive exams and a comprehensive final exam in my course; see Figure 12.2), and by making the necessary adjustments to their individual learning and study strategies, they will benefit more in the long run than simply scoring an "A" on each of their online study plans and chapter exams.

One of the many ways that the use of these online activities has helped me work with individual students is in responding to the question that goes something like "How can I have only made a 75 (or 70, 60, ...) on your in-class exam when I made 90s or better on all of the study plans and chapter exams?" When students don't use the online activities as suggested, they may see a mismatch in performance between the online activities and in-class exams. While such a mismatch may initially be unsettling, particularly for the student, the information is very informative for me, and can especially be informative for them.

I first ask the student about his or her study habits such as when did he or she start studying for the exam and what methods he or she used. Especially in my introductory psychology course where many of the students are only in their first or second semester, this conversation can reveal many misconceptions, skill deficits, or use of ineffective strategies. For more experienced students, it may be that they have not yet had a course with cumulative and comprehensive exams or their past study methods have largely relied on last-minute cramming or only studying for recognition.

I then explore with them ways in which they use their text and notes during completion of the online study plans and chapter exams. For example, for a given chapter, did they read the entire chapter before attempting the study plan's pretest? Did they complete all of the study assignments that were assigned as the result of their pretest? While completing the study plan pretests and posttests, did they take

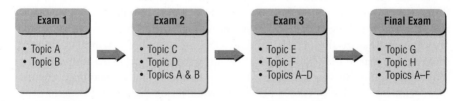

FIGURE 12.2 Summative assessment process. Multiple comprehensive and cumulative summative assessments are used in the course to promote long-term mastery and retention of the topics covered.

them under conditions similar to what they will have during in-class exams or did they look up answers in their book or notes? Based on their responses, I can try to help them identify ways to use effective learning strategies and continually convey the value of using the assignments as they are intended. I try to help them see the value of using them as formative assessments to help them evaluate what they know and what they don't know before the higher-stake in-class exams and to use that data to modify their study methods or strategies.

I also share information about which study strategies are most effective (Dunlosky et al., 2013) and refer them to resources in their text or other materials that illustrate effective study strategies. For example, the *How to Get the Most Out of Studying* video series created by Stephen Chew of Samford University provide an excellent over-view of how students can learn more effectively. These are available at http://www. samford.edu/departments/academic-success-center/how-to-study and on YouTube. Other resources are *Make It Stick: The Science of Successful Learning* (Brown, Roediger, & McDaniel, 2014), and a recent article for students, *Optimizing Learning in College: Tips From Cognitive Psychology* (Putnam, et al., 2016). Both provide an overview of research in cognitive psychology specific to learning and memory that students can readily apply.

In my experience, students tend to be more receptive to the process and rational for using formative assessment strategies if information is offered early in the term about how it will be used in general and how it will affect their indi-vidual experiences. I will also revisit this several times throughout the semester, demonstrating or highlighting examples about how data from a previous assess-ment have been used. Students are asked to share ways in which they have used the results of the formative strategies to modify their approaches to the course content or possibly changed their ways of thinking about or interacting with the information. They are also asked to comment on any adjustments in the way they prepare for summative exams. Often, it is not until after the course that students will realize, or be able to verbalize, ways in which they have incorporated for-mative strategies in their other courses. They may also not be immediately aware of the different ways in which they demonstrate skills associated with reaching a desired goal or learning outcome (e.g., APA Goal 2), or may need assistance in being able to effectively communicate examples of achieving that goal.

With regard to data from online activities, under the best circumstances, the use of data from online study plans completed prior to in-class coverage of material should allow me to tailor a given class lecture or schedule of activities to the partic-ular needs of the class. Students will also benefit the most when they get an accurate appraisal of what they know versus what they don't know. In this circumstance, the online study plans are going to be the most accurate when students complete the activities with sufficient preparation, such as reading the corresponding text mate-rial prior to completing the study plan, and completing the assessments without use of their text or notes. One issue that continually arises is that students either don't always read their text or they look up the answers in their text as they go through the assignments. Classroom demonstrations of interventions based on valid versus invalid or inadequate data may be helpful for some situations.

As indicated previously, formative assessments should generally be relatively "no- to low-stakes" as compared to other class components. In spite of this rec-ommendation, a portion of students may not complete class activities where course credit is not given. For example, when I first started using the online study plans, only the posttests were scored for credit. In doing so, a significant number of students would not complete the pretest or other study materials. The approach I currently take is to assign point values to all of the online and in-class activities that students complete, where some are weighted more than others (i.e., study plan posttests, online chapter exams, and essay items are weighted more) but each activity in and of itself has a minimal impact on their overall course grade.

I continually encourage students to take responsibility for their own learning and to recognize the value of valid data, and encourage them to use the formative assessments to better evaluate their actual current level of understanding. In the attempt to promote use of the assessments, students may retake the study plan posttests and chapter exams multiple times before the posted deadlines. I accept the last score for each posttest, even if not the highest, and calculate the average across attempts for the chapter exams.

With regard to in-class participation and formative assessments, students also have incentives for responding to the clicker items. They can earn one point for each item they respond to, and earn two points for submitting a correct response. I calculate standard scores at the end of the semester, across all clicker items administered during the class. Students performing at the given class's average get full credit, whereas students achieving higher than average can earn extra credit. Only those students who choose not to participate fail to earn full credit for these items.

Beyond the activities already described, data can also be gained from a variety of *classroom assessment techniques*, or CATs, such as background knowledge probes, concept maps, and minute papers (Angelo & Cross, 1993). Additionally, reviewing resources investigating evidence-based teaching or the Scholarship of Teaching and Learning may prove useful for identifying potential assessment strategies and provide additional guidance in selecting assessments and ways in which to evaluate your teaching overall (Ambrose, Bridges, DiPietro, Lovett, & Norman, 2010; Benasi, Overson, & Hakala, 2014; Buskist & Groccia, 2011; Dunn, Baker, Mehrotra, Landrum, & McCarthy, 2012; Gurung, 2014; Gurung & Schwartz, 2009; Gurung & Wilson, 2013).

Lastly, instructors considering the use of such approaches will need to continually be aware of how they approach and frame formative assessment in their classes. Students may initially be taken aback at the apparent level of "testing" that occurs in the course. Even when faculty share aspects of their teaching philosophy and offer information about the differences between formative and summative assessments, students may be hesitant to remain in a particular course section. Other students may choose to stay in the course, but despite the best intentions and efforts of faculty, some students never come to appreciate or at least accept the potential benefits of formative assessment. Some of these students may communicate their negative opinions of such approaches through end-of-term student opinion forms or ratings of faculty effectiveness. Having a knowledgeable department chair or colleagues who are both aware of your efforts and embrace similar approaches can help to mitigate any potential negative effects of such ratings when it comes time for individual faculty reviews. Overall, developing a culture of effective assessment across an entire department can prove beneficial for everyone involved, including students, faculty, and other stakeholders alike.

Chapter 13

Seeing the World Like a Psychologist

ERIN E. HARDIN

University of Tennessee

"I want to change the way you see the world," I tell my general psychology students on the first day of class each semester. I tell students that my modest goal for them is that they leave three and a half months later seeing the world through the lens of psychology. I explain that this means learning how to ask questions about their lives and experiences that can be answered scientifically. I tell them that the science of psychology is relevant to virtually everything people do, and thus if they can learn to see their world like a psychologist—to distinguish questions that can be answered scientifically from those that cannot, to turn real-world issues into empirical questions, and to consider the kinds of evidence that would begin to answer those questions—then they will see the world in fundamentally different ways.

As I will explain in the chapter, seeing the world like a psychologist can, in the short term, help students engage more deeply with the course material and thus learn it more effectively; in the longer term, seeing the world like a psychologist can facilitate students' career and life success by helping them be better consumers of information, think more critically, and make better decisions. In addition, challenging myself to teach introductory psychology in this way has reinvigorated my teaching and inspired me to see my own world differently, too. After providing some context for my teaching, I will explain more fully what *seeing the world like a psychologist* entails and why I believe it is so important, and then describe specific ways I operationalize this outcome in my class and the methods I use to facilitate students' progress toward this goal, before ending with some practical issues about framing one's course around this theme.

PROVIDING CONTEXT

Although I received my B.A. from a small private liberal arts college (which has undeniably shaped my views on undergraduate education), all of my teaching experience has been at large, public state universities. After teaching introductory psychology as a graduate student to class sections of 50–75 students, I spent ten years teaching small (20–30 students) honors sections. In both contexts, I was the sole instructor, with no teaching assistants. With my move to a new university in 2013, I began teaching introductory psychology to classes of ~200 undergraduates. Although my teaching has certainly evolved over time, and the shift from sections of 30 to 200 students necessitated some changes, much of what I describe in this chapter has worked in both the small honors and large regular class contexts (I will note exceptions).

Currently, I teach in a traditional format in which the entire class meets three days a week for 50 minutes. I have a teaching assistant who helps proctor exams, responds to student e-mails, and assists with grading; typically, the teaching assistant and I each grade half of students' work. I use a standard textbook, supplemented with a small number of additional readings. I divide the course into five units: (1) psychology is a science: foundations of scientific inquiry and critical thinking (introduction, critical thinking, and research methods, supplemented with two empirical articles: Mueller & Oppenheimer, 2014; Sana, Weston, & Cepeda, 2013); (2) building blocks of behavior and experience (chapters on memory, biological psychology, sensation and perception); (3) learning and growing (learning, intelligence, human development); (4) person and situation (personality, supplemented by having students complete a series of personality and interest inventories through the campus career center) and social psychology (supplemented by students reading a chapter on aversive racism; Dovidio, Gaertner, & Nier, 2004); and (5) applied psychology: promoting happiness and health and understanding mental illness (health, stress, and coping; sections of the emotion chapter; abnormal; and treatment). After each of these five units, there is a multiple-choice exam, which all together are worth 57 percent of students' grades (in my smaller, honors, sections, exams were primarily short answer and essay). Even in the large sections, the exam for Unit 1 includes some short answer questions, such as asking students to identify pseudoscientific features and violations of critical thinking principles in an actual product advertisement. At the final exam, in both the large and small classes, I ask students to respond to two integrative essay questions that together are worth another 5 percent of their grade.

In my large classes, students are randomly assigned to discussion groups of ~20 students and expected to engage in discussions online (using Blackboard) for each of the five units. Contributions to the discussion boards are graded with a rubric, and together are worth 10 percent of students' grades. The remainder of students' grades is determined by their class engagement (attendance and clicker performance), research experience, and completion of course assessments. Multiple-choice quizzes over each day's assigned readings are available in Blackboard, and students may earn nominal extra credit for completing the quizzes, as well as for completing a syllabus quiz early in the semester. I also make an array of supplemental resources available to students via Blackboard, including copies of my PowerPoint slides (posted by chapter after the completion of the chapter in class); brief video mini-lectures (created with Camtasia) that cover selected material that is not covered in class, but that students are responsible for; and links to relevant videos, articles, and so forth. Despite the large class size, I use as much interaction, discussion, demonstrations, and other activities as possible.

SEEING THE WORLD LIKE A PSYCHOLOGIST: A FUNDAMENTAL ENDURING UNDERSTANDING

The biggest change in my teaching over the past few years has not resulted from moving from class sizes of 30 to 200, but rather from learning about *backward course design* (McTighe & Wiggins, 1999; Wiggins & McTighe, 1998) and being inspired to challenge myself to articulate the most fundamental *enduring understanding* I want students to take from my course. The premise of backward course design is that instructors must first identify what they most want students to learn, then specify the evidence they will accept that they have learned it, and only then think about the specific methods for getting them to that end goal. By placing the emphasis first on identifying and operationalizing essential learning outcomes, instructors are positioned to have a much better sense of what students are really learning. Wiggins and McTighe distinguish three types of learning goals: content that is *worth being familiar with*, ideas or skills that are *important to know and do*, and *enduring understandings*. "The term enduring refers to the big ideas, or the important understandings, that we want students to 'get inside of' and retain after they've forgotten many of the details. Put differently, the enduring understandings provide a larger purpose for learning the targeted content: They implicitly answer the question, Why is this topic worth studying?" (McTighe & Wiggins, 1999, p. 70).

Although there are many important theories and concepts that are worth being familiar with and that are important for students of psychology to know, a majority of students in my introductory courses are not and will never be psychology majors. Why, then, is psychology worth studying? Why is a general education course like general psychology a critical core course for an educated person to be exposed to? As I've challenged myself over the years to think about my course with these questions in mind and to articulate the most fundamental *enduring understandings* that I want all my students, regardless of major, to take from my course, I realized that I frankly don't care if students remember what an unconditioned stimulus is or what Piaget's stages of cognitive development are in 2 months or 2 years or 20 years. But if students can read a headline and ask themselves, *Is that really true? How would I know? What's the evidence?*, then they've learned something important. If, when making a decision, students ask themselves, *What's the evidence?* instead of (or at least in addition to) *What do I feel is true?*, then they have learned what I most want them to in my course. What I strive to do in my course, then, is not simply show students how to apply psychological concepts to their daily lives, but how to apply the process of scientific inquiry to their daily lives. The enduring understanding I want students to leave with is the ability to *see the world like a psychologist*.

WHAT DOES SEEING THE WORLD LIKE A PSYCHOLOGIST REALLY LOOK LIKE?

From the perspective of backward course design, before describing how I try to impart these skills to students, I need to articulate the evidence I would accept that students have, in fact, acquired these skills. In other words, how do I operationalize *seeing the world like a psychologist*? I see three component skills underlying this enduring outcome: distinguishing questions that can and cannot be answered scientifically, turning real-world issues and problems into empirical questions, and considering the kinds of evidence that would address different kinds of questions. When students can read something in their newsfeed or hear a friend make a claim about a social issue or human behavior and ask questions such as *What is the evidence for that claim? Is it consistent with what I know about behavior and experience? What other explanations are there?*, they are seeing the world like a psychologist.

This is exactly what I asked students to do on their final exam in the most recent offering of my course. Students were given this essay prompt:[1]

> From the first day of class, I told you that one of my major goals for you was to help you see the world like a psychologist, which means knowing when and how science can answer real-world questions. Identify one real-world issue, question, event, etc., and approach it "like a psychologist" by (a) creating at least one falsifiable statement or question that is relevant to the issue, (b) explicitly stating your hypothesis, (c) designing a basic research study that would test your hypothesis, and (d) offering an appropriate interpretation of your expected results, based on your research design. In stating your hypothesis, you will need to apply things you've learned in the course to support your specific hypothesis. (For example, if your real-world issue is the effect of MTV on youth, and your falsifiable statement is that adolescents who watch more hours of MTV will be more likely to engage in sexual activity, what have you learned about the effects of media exposure and/or adolescent development that supports your hypothesis?) In describing

---

[1]Later in the chapter, I discuss modifications to this prompt I plan to use in the future.

your research study, be sure to operationalize your variables, identify your research design (correlational or experimental), your independent and dependent variables, control and experimental groups (if you have them), etc. *Note: you may NOT use "the effect of MTV on youth" as your real-world issue. Everything else is fair game.*

Although students independently wrote their answer to this prompt without reference to notes during their final exam time, they were given the prompt almost two weeks in advance and encouraged to work with their peers outside of class to formulate their responses.

One of the most common real-world issues that students chose to address was the shooting of Michael Brown in Ferguson, Missouri, and subsequent unrest that followed both the shooting and the decision not to charge the officer involved.[2] Michael Brown, an unarmed African American adolescent, was killed after a confrontation with Officer Darren Wilson on August 9, 2014 (see Associated Press, 2014), less than two weeks before the first day of class that semester; the grand jury decision not to indict the officer was announced one week before the end of classes (see Davey & Bosman, 2014). Students of all races addressed this very salient real-world issue in many ways: Some wondered about the shooting itself and the question of racial bias in such incidents. For example, some students proposed correlating participants' implicit racial attitudes with their behavior in a shoot/don't shoot video game (similar to the paradigm used by Correll, Park, Judd, & Wittenbrink, 2007, which I had described two and a half months earlier in class). Although one student acknowledged the research on implicit bias that was discussed in class, he hypothesized that race had nothing to do with the incident, with the victim's alleged behavior of lunging at the officer being the primary determinant. He then proposed an experiment in which law enforcement officers would be randomly assigned to interact with either African American or European American actors in a simulation in which all aspects of the situation were controlled to be as identical as possible, with the actors being trained to follow a basic script that always culminated in a physical struggle. His proposed dependent variable was the number of times the officer drew or fired his or her weapon during the simulation. Although this design certainly has its limitations, it nonetheless demonstrates that the student was thinking about the specific kind of evidence that would support his view; rather than simply dismissing claims of racial bias, he demonstrated the ability to take the extra steps to consider what evidence would support (or contradict) his beliefs. Rather than simply saying, "I'm right," he questioned, "How would I know if I'm right?"

Other students wondered about the varying public reactions to the shooting, grand jury decision, and unrest itself. For example, some students hypothesized that differing media portrayals of the events influenced public attitudes. Some offered correlational evidence that would address their hypotheses, proposing to measure quantity and source (i.e., the specific network) of media exposure

---

[2]Although I had referenced these events a handful of times during the semester, I did not spend significant class time discussing them. Thus, students' answers to the essay prompt were not simply summaries of previous class discussions.

along with viewer attitudes. Other students offered experimental evidence, such as randomly selecting adults and then randomly assigning them to watch either one hour of news coverage from a stereotypically conservative media outlet (e.g., Fox News) or one hour of coverage from a stereotypically liberal outlet (e.g., MSNBC), and then comparing viewer attitudes. Still other students were inspired to ask questions about how to effect productive change. One student, for example, wondered whether exposure to positive media messages about African Americans could undo participants' implicit prejudice.

Although there was certainly a wide range in the quality of responses to this prompt, these predominantly first-semester undergraduates were indeed able to take real-world issues, ranging from sexualized fashion shows to marriage equality to the racially charged events in Ferguson, Missouri, and demonstrate an ability to think about them like a psychologist, by breaking the issue down into empirical questions and considering the kinds of evidence that would address those questions. Students did not simply rely on anecdote, intuition, commonsense, or what they wanted to be true; instead, they demonstrated the ability to ask questions about what they suspected to be true and to consider the types of evidence that would help them know. Students did not perceive these real-world events as inexplicable phenomena, but as events that could be parsed and understood—and learned from.

SEEING THE WORLD LIKE A PSYCHOLOGIST:
WHY IT MATTERS

Although giving students the skills to understand and learn from the world around them may be intuitively appealing, there are other reasons that seeing the world like a psychologist is my most critical *enduring understanding*. First, it can help students learn the course content better by encouraging deeper cognitive processing. By framing the goal of the course as teaching students to ask the right questions, I encourage students constantly to ask themselves questions, starting with: *What does this mean for me? How do I see this playing out in my own life?* This questioning curiosity, essential to the process of scientific inquiry, encourages students to apply the material to their unique circumstances. Such application encourages (1) deeper cognitive processing, in terms of Bloom's taxonomy (Krathwohl, 2002) as students link material to their own experiences and (2) greater engagement with the course material as students see the relevance and value of the course concepts for their own lives, both of which enhance motivation and learning (see Chew, 2014; Pintrich, 2003).

Second, seeing the world like a psychologist can make students better writers and thinkers, which in turn makes them more employable. In a recent survey (American Association of Colleges & Universities [AAC&U], 2011), employers were asked what skills colleges should emphasize more; the top three responses, in order, were teaching students to communicate effectively, to think critically, and to apply their knowledge and skills to real-world settings. As already discussed, *seeing the world like a psychologist* provides a vehicle through which students can apply their knowledge and skills to real-world settings. However, the other two outcomes of effective communication and critical thinking are also closely linked to seeing the world like a psychologist.

Critical thinking has been defined in many ways (see Appleby, 2006, p. 58, for one list), including "the use of those cognitive skills or strategies that increases the probability of a desirable outcome" (Halpern, 2002, p. 93) and as "a habit of mind characterized by the comprehensive exploration of issues, ideas, artifacts, and events before accepting or formulating an opinion or conclusion" (AAC&U, n.d., p. 5). Analyzing argument quality by evaluating evidence and "thinking as hypothesis testing" are essential critical thinking skills (Halpern, 2002), as is "selecting and using information to investigate a point of view or conclusion" (AAC&U, 2010, p. 6). As students learn to see the world like a psychologist by distinguishing questions that can and cannot be answered scientifically, turning real-world issues and problems into empirical questions, and considering the kinds of evidence that would address different kinds of questions, they are learning essential critical thinking skills.

These same essential critical thinking skills that are part of *seeing the world like a psychologist* are also essential skills for communicating effectively, particularly in writing. For example, *sources and evidence* are one of the criteria for evaluating written communication in the AAC&U (2010) VALUE Rubric. In addition, learning to see the world like a psychologist involves learning to ask the right questions, which has been identified as an essential foundational subskill of research writing (Bean, 2011). "Asking important, problematic, and significant questions is the heart of engaged research" in any discipline (Bean, 2011, p. 236), yet students rarely see asking questions as part of their role as students and writers; rather, students often believe their role is to unquestioningly summarize and repackage others' ideas. Bean argues that instructors must therefore intentionally teach students how to ask questions and how to distinguish good questions from poor (i.e., naive) questions.

How to ask discipline-appropriate research questions is the first of the seven "difficult subskills of research writing" that Bean (2011) identifies. He advocates a backward design approach to scaffold and sequence the teaching of the seven skills to students. As such, it is particularly appropriate to focus on the initial subskill of asking questions in a foundational level course like introductory psychology. Although learning to ask psychology-appropriate questions is critical for psychology majors, it should also be of value to nonmajors, to the extent that students learn to see question-asking as part of their role and extend such question-asking to other courses. By enhancing students' ability to ask questions and think critically about sources of evidence, teaching students to see the world like a psychologist lays important foundational skills for communicating more effectively.

Finally, seeing the world like a psychologist should be a critical enduring understanding because it has the potential to make students better people and thus to make the world a better place. Landrum (2014) noted that introductory psychology is a "high stakes course [because of its] potential impact of improving lives; psychology represents the academic and professional discipline that has the greatest ability to improve the quality of life worldwide." What psychology offers to the world is a scientific understanding of behavior and experience that anyone can use. All students behave, have experiences, are affected by others' behaviors and experiences, and make decisions based on their understanding of their own and others' behavior and experiences. This is what makes psychology unique— and a critical course for students regardless of major or future career goal. Whether students go on to be stay-at-home parents or law enforcement officers or businesspeople or musicians, *seeing the world like a psychologist* helps them think about themselves and others in new ways and make better decisions.

SEEING THE WORLD LIKE A PSYCHOLOGIST: STRATEGIES FOR TEACHING AND ASSESSMENT

So what happens in the course that facilitates students' movement toward this enduring understanding? The first steps are framing the course in terms of asking questions and setting the stage for students to feel comfortable doing so. Once these norms are established, it is important to help students understand falsifiability, and then to give students ongoing practice throughout the semester in the three critical skills of distinguishing questions that can and cannot be answered scientifically, turning real-world issues and problems into empirical questions, and considering the kinds of evidence that would address different kinds of questions. This practice occurs through a variety of in-class and out-of-class activities, assignments, and assessments. Controversial contemporary issues provide excellent opportunities for such practice.

Framing the course in terms of asking questions.   Early on the first day of class, I ask students to talk in pairs and small groups about what they think psychology is, and then the students and I walk through the definition of psychology together, comparing and contrasting their ideas about psychology with reality. I highlight the topics they raised (e.g., dreams, mental illness, memory, the brain, relationships) and where in the syllabus those concepts will be covered. Importantly, I tell students explicitly that although increasing their understanding of these specific content areas is important, "My overarching goal is to change the way you see the world. I want you to see the world the way a psychologist does, which means asking questions and figuring out which questions could be answered scientifically and which can't."

I explicitly articulate the enduring understanding of *seeing the world like a psychologist* as a fundamental learning goal, and try to model what this means. For example, in the most recent semester, I put up a picture of Michael Brown and briefly described the incident in Ferguson, Missouri. I said, "As a psychologist, I ask myself questions like, *why did this happen? Under what conditions are police more likely to shoot a suspect?*" I then put up a picture of peaceful protestors holding hands at a vigil, and said, "As a psychologist, I wonder why some people think of images like this when they hear the word *Ferguson,* whereas other people think of images like this," followed by a picture of riots and looting. "*How is it that different people can perceive the same events so very differently? Is one perception more or less accurate? How would I decide?* These are the kinds of questions psychologists ask about the world, and the kinds of questions we are going to explore together this semester."

Setting the stage. From the first day of class, then, I frame the course in terms of asking questions. For students to practice this kind of active questioning requires them to be engaged and comfortable participating in class. Thus, I get students asking questions and interacting with each other on the first day of class. I tell students explicitly that I want ours to be a class in which they feel comfortable participating and asking questions, which tends to be more difficult in a room full of strangers, so I ask students to take a few minutes to introduce themselves to each other on the first day of class. I also explicitly discuss my expectation that students' behavior will at all times be respectful, and that although I expect them to actively question each other and the course material, language that is disrespectful based on race/ethnicity, sexual orientation, age, gender or gender expression, religion, ability, social class, or size will not be tolerated. Throughout the semester, I am intentional in using examples, research, and language that incorporate different cultural backgrounds and experiences to promote as many students as possible feeling visible and welcomed.

During the second class session, I engage the students in an empirically supported reciprocal interview activity (Hermann & Foster, 2008; Hermann, Foster, & Hardin, 2010) in which they question each other to clarify their expectations, establish classroom norms, and increase rapport. In smaller classes (~50 or fewer students), the class is broken into groups so that all students participate in asking and answering questions during class. In large classes (~75 or more students), I invite students to share their questions and respond to my questions via online discussion boards in Blackboard outside of class. Several students volunteer through these discussion boards to be spokespeople in the second class session. These spokespeople are responsible for reading the posts from their group and sharing the questions and responses in class. Other students are invited to participate as they listen to the discussion. In both large and small classes, then, the reciprocal interview activity further establishes the norm of question-asking, clarifies expectations, and enhances students' sense of safety and engagement.

Although I encourage questions and discussions throughout the semester even in my large lecture classes, I have also started using student response systems ("clickers") to further engage students in larger numbers and facilitate them thinking about and discussing questions in class (see Mazur, 2009; Smith et al., 2009). Outside of class, students participate in smaller online discussion groups in which they are expected to engage with each other in applying and questioning the course material. Throughout the semester, I use minute papers (Angelo & Cross, 1993; Lom, 2012) at the end of class to elicit students' questions about or applications of the course material (e.g., "What is one question you have from today's class, either something that was not clear, or something you want to know more about, or just something you wondered about?" or "Write down one specific example of X that you thought of today" or "Tell me about a way you've experienced Y in your life"). There are any number of specific techniques instructors can use to foster engagement and participation from students (see Lom, 2012; McKeachie & Svinicki, 2013; Society for the Teaching of Psychology, n.d.), depending on instructors' particular teaching styles; the specific techniques are likely less important than the end goal of actively engaging students with asking questions.

Finally, I model this kind of question-asking at the end of the second class period using an engaging demonstration of my supposed "psychic abilities." The specific demonstration is one I learned from Douglas Bernstein at a National Institute on the Teaching of Psychology conference in the mid-2000s;[3] Timothy Lawson has also described other psychic demonstrations that can be used effectively in classrooms (e.g., Lawson, 2003). After stunning students with my apparent ability to predict where a student will cut a newspaper article, I say, "Isn't that amazing? Aren't you dying to know how I did that? You have until our next class to think about the answer to that question." Not only does this very effectively engage students by creating a mystery for them to solve (see Cialdini, 2005), but also it launches students into the process of scientific inquiry. We begin the following class session by exploring their hypotheses about my abilities, and their intuitive ideas about how to test their hypotheses. I provide them prompts such as, *What evidence would you need before you believed that I am psychic?* and *What would happen if…?* Many of the ideas they generate illustrate essential scientific and critical thinking skills, such as replicability and ruling out rival hypotheses (Lilienfeld, Lynn, & Namy, 2013).

Understanding falsifiability: A key to seeing the world like a psychologist.

This discussion of the ways in which students would go about figuring out how I did the apparent feat of psychic prediction not only further establishes the norm of asking questions but also provides an excellent transition into the research methods chapter. In terms of the course structure, covering research methods first is essential, given that an understanding of research methods underlies students' abilities to understand what an empirical question is and the kinds of evidence that might answer those questions. To this end, I emphasize very early in the course (the third or fourth class session) what *falsifiability* is and why it is important. Using the guiding question of *Is it possible to find evidence that would prove this statement false?*, I go through several examples of statements and practice identifying falsifiable statements.

I then highlight two key reasons why falsifiability is so important. First, if a statement is falsifiable, then it is within the domain of science; if it is not falsifiable, then it is not within the domain of science. Thus, for example, questions about the existence of the divine tend to be outside the realm of science, because it is impossible to falsify a statement such as *God exists*. I state explicitly that just because such questions are unfalsifiable does not mean that they are unimportant; rather, they are questions that are beyond the purview of the psychology class. This discussion provides a nice opportunity both for establishing the boundaries

---

[3]Dr. Bernstein made all audience members promise they would never write down the details of the demonstration, to help ensure the secret remained safe and the demonstration could be used effectively for years to come. For details about this demonstration, you'll have to ask in person!

of the course and for providing a basis on which to respond later in the course when students question the appropriateness of some course content or attempt to rely on nonscientific evidence for a scientific question. The second reason falsifiability is so important is because falsifiable statements are testable hypotheses. Thus, although the statement *God exists* is unfalsifiable, a statement such as *Religious people have higher well-being than nonreligious people* is falsifiable.

Understanding falsifiability in these ways is critical to the two key goals of distinguishing questions that can and cannot be answered scientifically and turning real-world issues and problems into empirical questions. I therefore spend time in class practicing these skills, beginning in either the third or fourth class session. For example, Miley Cyrus's widely discussed sexualized performance at the MTV video music awards in 2013 provided an opportunity to have students consider the sentiment that *MTV is ruining the youth of America!* I asked students in my large lecture to work in pairs to turn that statement into a falsifiable statement, with the hint that they should *think about the kind of evidence you'd expect to see if this is true; the kind of evidence you would need to see before you believed it is true.* Students readily came up with statements such as, *Adolescents who watch more hours of MTV will be more likely to engage in sexual activity/delinquent behavior/substance abuse.* In addition to demonstrating how real-world issues can readily be turned into empirical questions, discussion of their falsifiable statements also provided opportunities to highlight the variety of ways one could operationalize a construct, the importance of clear operational definitions, the need for appropriate comparison groups, and so on.

Ongoing practice seeing the world like a psychologist.   Throughout the semester, I continue modeling the ways in which psychologists ask questions. For example, when introducing social influence, I don't simply mention that the Holocaust inspired research on obedience or that the murder of Kitty Genovese inspired research on the bystander phenomenon; instead, I contrast what I imagine the world's reaction to these events was compared to the reactions of the psychologists. Whereas the world reacted with questions of *How could that happen? Who would do such a thing?* and beliefs such as *I would never do that—they must be evil!*, Milgram and Latane and Darley seem to have reacted with questions such as *Under what conditions would somebody behave in that way?* Thus I model for students ways in which *seeing the world like a psychologist* involves asking different kinds of questions about the world than one might typically ask.

Additional practice distinguishing questions that can and cannot be answered scientifically, turning real-world issues and problems into empirical questions, and evaluating evidence continues throughout the semester using a variety of activities and formative and summative assessments. At the beginning of a new chapter or topic, brief in-class think–pair–share activities (Lyman, 1981, as cited in Lom, 2012) can be used to encourage students to think about the kinds of issues or questions psychologists might be interested in exploring. For example, after discussing what personality is and defining it, students might be asked to get into pairs and spend two minutes generating examples of questions about personality that a psychologist might be interested in, followed by small-group or whole-class discussion of the questions and the extent to which they are falsifiable. During a unit, minute papers might be used to solicit students' questions about the content or to assess students' abilities to create a falsifiable statement from a content-relevant prompt (e.g., *I'm a visual learner* as the prompt during discussion of learning styles). Multiple-choice exam questions can ask students to select the most falsifiable statement, using examples relevant to that particular unit's content. For example:

> *Which of the following is the most readily falsifiable statement?*
>
> a.   *ESP is real.*
>
> b.   *People with ESP can read other people's minds.*
>
> c.   *People with ESP will be able to correctly identify the card someone else is thinking of at rates significantly better than chance.*
>
> d.   *None of the above; ESP cannot be studied scientifically.*

Students also gain practice seeing the world like a psychologist (and give me opportunities to assess their skill acquisition) through participation in online discussion boards. In each of the five units of the course, students are expected to make posts that demonstrate they are applying and thinking about the course content, with particular emphasis on asking questions and thinking about evidence. For example, in addition to posting an example of an application of a concept from a chapter in that unit, students may:

> Pose a question related to a concept in that unit. The question should be the kind of question a psychologist might ask—a question that reframes a problem scientifically and/or that extends information from the class. For example, questions that start with *What evidence would I need to conclude that …? What kind of evidence would strengthen/weaken my position on this issue? Based on what I know about X, what would happen if …?*

Seeing the world like a psychologist by exploring controversial issues.

Controversial topics can provide excellent opportunities to model what *seeing the world like a psychologist* entails, particularly when explored in some depth, as students take a controversial real-world issue and explore the aspects of it that may be addressed empirically (see Dunn, Gurung, Naufel, & Wilson, 2013). I spend an entire class session exploring parenting by same-sex couples, but the basic approach to exploring this issue can be applied to any controversial issue (Hardin, 2013). First, it is essential that the topic is relevant to the course content. My discussion of same-sex parenting occurs during coverage of human development, in the class session for which students have completed the readings over parenting styles, attachment, and children's social and moral development. I begin class by asking students to generate a list of what children need to be happy and healthy, based on what they learned from the textbook. Students invariably offer factors such as adequate nutrition, nurturing and warmth, boundaries and appropriate discipline, healthy peer relationships, stability, and security; they never mention number or gender of parents. I point this out to students and tell them that I will be spending the rest of class discussing parenting by gay and lesbian individuals. I offer the explicit disclaimer that, to the extent their attitudes about same-sex parenting are based on their religious beliefs, those are none of my business. However, to the extent that their attitudes are based on questions about what is in the best interest of children or what benefits or harms children, then that is very much my business, as those are empirical questions that can be addressed with psychological science. I remind students that part of *seeing the world like a psychologist* is recognizing real-world questions that can and cannot be answered empirically, and that although questions about the morality of behavior are outside the domain of science, questions about the *effects* of behavior are falsifiable and thus well within the boundaries of a psychology course.

I next have students generate concerns they have heard expressed about children being raised by gay or lesbian parents, and then we discuss which of those listed concerns could be addressed empirically. Typically, all of the concerns could be, although occasionally we refine a concern to make it so, most often by focusing on how the concern could be operationalized. I then ask the class to choose one of the concerns (e.g., peer relationships), turn it into a falsifiable statement or empirical question (*Are children raised by gay or lesbian parents bullied more than children raised by heterosexual parents?*), and work together to generate a basic research study that would provide relevant evidence. Students discuss the kinds of comparison groups and other controls that would be important, such as controlling for family structure (e.g., single parents) and other demographic factors (e.g., socioeconomic status), controlling for expectancy effects and bias (e.g., by having observers blind to family type rating behavior), and so on. Finally, in whatever time is left, I present the actual research evidence on each of the concerns to the class (see, e.g., Golombok et al., 2003, 2014; Wainright & Patterson, 2008).

This process of exploring a controversial contemporary issue that is directly relevant to the current course content clearly utilizes all three component skills of seeing the world like a psychologist: Students distinguish questions that can and cannot be answered scientifically, turn the real-world issue into empirical questions, and consider the kinds of evidence that would address those questions. I follow up this in class discussion by asking students (1) to think of one question that is left unanswered for them by the research that was considered in class and then (2) to design a basic study that would begin to address their question. This follow-up can be done as an in-class activity in a subsequent class, as an out-of-class homework assignment, or as a short-answer/essay question on the next exam. Not only does this follow-up activity provide students more practice seeing the world like a psychologist (and the instructor additional opportunities to assess students' acquisition of this enduring understanding), but it also communicates to students that unanswered questions remain. This, in turn, seems to reduce defensiveness, as students are given overt permission to express concerns and questions they still have, rather than perceiving that they must agree completely with the evidence presented.

Another approach to exploring controversial issues is to engage students in a debate-style discussion of evidence for and against particular issues. I used this approach regularly in my small honors classes. There are excellent resources for such discussions (e.g., the *Taking Sides* book series from McGraw-Hill), or instructors can readily gather their own. Structured out-of-class assignments or in-class activities can prompt students to think critically about the quality of evidence on each side of the issue, as well as about unanswered questions and the kinds of evidence that would address those questions. Drawing on Halpern's (2014) Making Arguments worksheet, designed to encourage critical thinking, I ask students to offer three pieces of evidence on each side of the issue (arguments and counterarguments), and then to rate the quality of each piece of evidence as *very strong*, *strong*, *moderate*, *weak*, or *very weak*, and then to briefly justify why they made that rating. Adding this step of justifying their ratings forces students to think about their perceptions of the evidence and discourages them from simply rating arguments they agree with as stronger than arguments they disagree with.

After listing and evaluating the evidence on each side of the issue, students articulate their own position. Critically, they then must state one piece of evidence that would strengthen their position and one piece of evidence that would weaken it. This was typically the most difficult part of the assignment for students. Early in the semester, they tended to offer answers such as, "More research like this would make me more confident in my position. Research that found the opposite results would weaken my position." With practice, discussion, and targeted feedback, however, students offered answers that indicated they were better able to think about unanswered questions and consider the kinds of evidence that would address different kinds of questions. For example, a student might suggest that research conducted in a different setting or with a different population or that utilized a longitudinal design would provide new evidence that would support or weaken his or her conclusions. This is the primary change I will make to the integrative essay question prompt I discussed earlier: Rather than simply asking students to offer "an appropriate interpretation of your expected results," I intend to ask students to describe what it would mean for their understanding of the real-world issue if the results supported their hypothesis and what it would mean if the results did *not* support their hypothesis.

SEEING THE WORLD LIKE A PSYCHOLOGIST: MORE THOUGHTS ON ASSESSMENT

In the spirit of backward course design, I have attempted to integrate issues of assessment throughout my discussion of method. To be sure, however, important questions about assessment of this theme remain, the most important of which is, *How do I know that this works?* How do I know that framing my course around helping students *see the world like a psychologist* is effective in this critically important course? Students' contributions to class discussions and responses on minute papers and exam questions certainly provide direct formative and summative evidence about the extent to which they are acquiring the skills I want them to. But other outcomes are important as well. How do I know, for example, that framing the course in this way does make them better thinkers or writers, better people, better able to use psychology in their daily lives? How do I know that framing the course in this way changes the way they see the world? Ideally, I would gather objective data from my students months or years after they complete the course. Even better, I would compare such data to data from students who took introductory psychology with a different theme, or not at all.

The logistical realities of such an endeavor have, thus far, prevented me from obtaining such persuasive evidence. However, there is other indirect evidence supporting the effectiveness of this approach: students' own feedback, both solicited and unsolicited, about the course and the effect it has on them. Every semester, I seek feedback from students at the middle and end of the semester on a formal, anonymous self-designed evaluation. In the most recent semester, 137 students responded at mid-semester and 130 students responded at the end of the semester. On both evaluations I asked students, "To what extent do you feel you are learning … to recognize when psychological principles and scientific methods are relevant in your everyday life?" and "To what extent do you feel you are learning … to ask questions about everyday experiences that could be answered with scientific evidence?" For both questions, students had response options of *very much, a lot, some, a little, not much, not at all*. At the end of the semester, over 92 percent of the students indicated they felt they learned to at least "some" extent to recognize when psychological principles and scientific methods are relevant in their everyday lives, compared to 82 percent on the mid-semester feedback survey; nearly 51 percent indicated they had learned to do this *a lot* or *very much* at the end of the semester, compared to 40.88 percent at mid-semester. At the end of the semester, just over 82 percent of students similarly indicated they learned to at least some extent to ask questions about everyday experiences that could be answered with scientific evidence, compared to 72.27 percent at mid-semester. On this item, 41.53 percent of students at the end of the semester indicated they learned to ask scientific questions about their everyday experiences *a lot* or *very much*, compared to 27 percent at mid-semester. Clearly in future semesters I need to focus more on helping students turn real-world issues and problems into empirical questions; however, the majority of students do at least perceive that they acquire these skills in the course.

Beyond these numbers, students' open-ended comments on the end-of-semester survey offer further evidence that seeing the world like a psychologist has been valuable. For example:

> I feel like I learned a lot by the beginning chapters about when to recognize if something is wrong with a hypothesis or theory. Locating if there is a better source of information, Determining bias, and also just learning that correlation does not cause causation. With these ideas in mind, I have been able recognize whether sources are trustworthy or not or whether I should believe them.

> I find it useful to use psychological principles and the scientific method to determine if a new study or a news report about a study is credible. I use my new knowledge to evaluate other scientific papers and ideas to help myself [develop] better hypothesis and critical thinking skills.

Students' comments on the standard university course evaluation forms also indicate that *seeing the world like a psychologist* is valuable and helps students see the world differently. In the most recent semester, 143 students completed the course evaluation forms; of those, 79 chose to answer the open-ended prompt, "Was this class intellectually stimulating? Did it stretch your thinking?" Although 3 students said *no* and another student responded, "Too much," the remaining 75 students offered an unequivocal *yes*. Moreover, many of these students explained their *yes* by referencing the ways in which they were thinking differently and using psychology in their daily lives. For example:

> Yes, Dr. Hardin was successful in helping me to think like a psychologist.
> Yes. This class ... made me think in a whole new way.
> Yes, the aspect she tries to convey to her classes is that psychology will try to change the way you think about things.
> This class was great in forcing me to think differently and learn about a variety of perspectives that can be present in a given situation. This class has also changed the way I behave to other people and what I think about other people.
> It definitely made me think outside of the box and question things around me.

Students' spontaneous comments also revealed more positive attitudes toward psychology, as well as a sense that they are better people as a result of taking the course. One student, for example, noted: "I also feel like I have learned a lot about my well-being and responsibility as a citizen. Becoming aware of the By-Stander effect and my own personality has just helped me feel like I can be a better person."

SEEING THE WORLD LIKE A PSYCHOLOGIST: PRACTICAL ISSUES

These students' comments suggest that incorporating this theme of *seeing the world like psychologist* into general psychology is possible, effective, and valuable. Fortunately, from an instructor's perspective, doing so is more about framing one's existing course than about constructing a new course. With the exception of intensive, early focus on research methods and the specific issue of falsifiability, instructors are free to include or exclude any topic and to sequence those topics in any order that makes sense to them. Creating a class atmosphere in which students feel comfortable engaging with the material and participating is essential, but the specific techniques by which instructors achieve such an atmosphere are not essential. Once the norm is established and the three skills of distinguishing questions that can and cannot be answered scientifically, turning real-world issues and problems into empirical questions, and considering the kinds of evidence that would address different kinds of questions have been explicitly introduced early in the course, framing the course around *seeing the world like a psychologist* often requires very minor tweaks, as opposed to wholesale restructuring. For example, contrasting the kinds of questions the world asked in response to the Holocaust or the murder of Kitty Genovese in my introduction of social influence added 30 seconds and one slide to my usual approach. Standard class discussion questions and activities can be modified slightly to encourage active questioning and evaluation of evidence.

Even incorporating in-depth discussion of a controversial issue may require little more than adjusting the syllabus to free up one day—or choosing to spend the day on the discussion rather than lecture on the content. Although I typically do present students with summaries of the current research on gay and lesbian parenting, which required me to invest the time to find and read that research, doing so is not essential. The most critical aspect of discussing controversial issues from this framework is engaging students in generating empirical questions and thinking about evidence that would most persuasively address those questions. Actually answering those questions by exploring the existing research can be the job of the students themselves. Students might be divided into groups in class and asked to pull out their laptops and phones to do a literature search on a different question to see what they find; students could also do this work individually or in groups outside of class and then report back on their findings, through class presentations, papers, or responses to exam questions.

Perhaps the most challenging aspect for an instructor in teaching general psychology with this theme of *seeing the world like a psychologist* is intentionally putting on those lenses him- or herself. However, for me, this is also one of the most exciting and rewarding aspects of framing my course around this theme: It has changed the way *I* see the world. As I scroll through my own Facebook feed, or listen to the news as I get ready in the morning, or decide how I will vote on an issue, I find myself thinking about how I would want my students to be thinking in those moments. If they were *seeing the world like a psychologist*, what questions would they be asking? What evidence would they be considering? Considering these questions inevitably forces me to consider the extent to which I'm seeing the world like a psychologist, which in turn leads me to think more critically and engage more fully, both in and out of the classroom.

Chapter 14

Sharing a Full Measure of Psychology: Teaching the Introductory Course to Strengthen Quantitative Reasoning

NEIL LUTSKY

Carleton College

I have a working hypothesis about teaching introductory psychology, loosely tested and supported over 41 years in the classroom. It is this: *If instructors orient their course around significant educational goals and make their justifications explicit for students, both their work and their students' will be infused with energy and meaning.* In this chapter, I will suggest that a particular goal, strengthening students' quantitative reasoning, can readily serve that role. I will argue that addressing quantitative reasoning fits naturally into introductory psychology's educational aspirations and that doing so contributes to students' understanding of psychology's values and practices as well as to students' general education and citizenship.

I will begin by offering a brief on behalf of the importance of quantitative reasoning based on perspectives on psychology education, recent discussions of the goals of higher education appropriate for the 21st century, and psychological research on statistical thinking. In much of the chapter, I will identify specific ideas for instructors of introductory psychology to use to raise attention to quantitative reasoning and to teach students how to employ quantitative reasoning appropriately. I will conclude by identifying five simple strategies for promoting quantitative reasoning in the introductory course. The overarching goal of the chapter is to persuade *teachers* of introductory psychology to embrace and promote quantitative reasoning as an important liberal arts priority so that *introductory students* will do the same in their own work and studies.

SOME BACKGROUND

It may be helpful for readers for me to describe my own background and experience as they relate to the chapter's topic. I have had a long career in psychology at Carleton College, an undergraduate liberal arts college. I have taught introductory psychology for over 40 years, a course rather standard in character. It is 10 weeks in length, relies on a textbook and supplementary readings, covers most but not all chapters in the text, and requires successful completion of two course projects and associated short papers as well as three examinations. In the past, I also offered sections of psychology's required "Data Analysis and Measurement" course. My belief in the importance of the latter body of knowledge not only for psychology majors but also for educated citizens led to my participation 12 years ago in a group at Carleton seeking to promote quantitative reasoning in the general education agenda of the institution. The group wrote a grant— subsequently funded by the U.S. Department of Education's Fund for the Improvement of Postsecondary Education—to support a campus initiative on quantitative reasoning called QuIRK (Quantitative Inquiry, Reasoning, and Knowledge), and I became the first director of the project.

QuIRK funded the development of courses and course modules to involve students in quantitative reasoning across the curriculum, and I began a course for first-year students on the topic. One of the central features of QuIRK was that faculty and staff evaluated how students used, misused, and missed using quantitative information in the presentation of arguments. Instructors did so by sampling papers from mandatory student writing portfolios and coding them (see Grawe, Lutsky, & Tassava, 2009). This evaluation process informed subsequent workshops for faculty and writing staff as well as course development efforts across the curriculum. In conjunction with my involvement in QuIRK, I began participating in a larger community of scholars interested in quantitative reasoning, primarily through the National Numeracy Network (2015; see http://serc.carleton.edu/ nnn/) and its journal, *Numeracy: Advancing Education in Quantitative Literacy* (see http://scholarcommons.usf.edu/numeracy/).

There are two important points for readers I want to make from the above history. The first is that there is a broader literature and community of educators keenly concerned about quantitative reasoning in higher education. I will refer repeatedly in what follows to their contributions. The second point is that my own exposure to the quantitative reasoning movement strongly influenced my teaching of introductory psychology. I had thought, as you might now, that I was already teaching quantitative reasoning as part of my introductory presentations. I talked about correlations; I reviewed basic methodological concepts (e.g., reliability, validity). But teaching quantitative reasoning, I have come to appreciate, involves much more than that. It requires sharing with students why I value quantitative evidence in professional, public, and personal discourses. It has changed how I present material and what I highlight, what I ask of students in assignments and in preparation for examinations, the terminology I use and discuss in class, the issues that evaluating research evidence raises, how I grade, and other key aspects of my instruction. Even though I am teaching introductory psychology, I also make explicit connections between quantitative reasoning in psychology and applications in the wider world (e.g., in media representations of numbers, graphs, and research). I believe this attention to quantitative reasoning has strengthened my teaching and benefited my introductory psychology students. What follows presents background arguments and specific suggestions to allow other introductory instructors to consider whether the same might be true for them.

WHY SHOULD PSYCHOLOGISTS ADDRESS QUANTITATIVE REASONING?

Charles Brewer and colleagues (1993) wrote, "The fundamental goal of education in psychology, from which all the others follow, is to teach students to think like scientists about behavior" (p. 169). One likely meaning of this is that teaching students to think like scientists is important for the sake of students' understanding of contemporary psychology. The Brewer et al. guide implies that familiarity with psychological science, even at the introductory level, involves more than mastery of conceptual vocabularies, major theories, and signal findings; it requires an appreciation of psychology's empirical character and grounding, a basic understanding of research procedures and standards, and encounters with numerical descriptions, measures, and evaluations. If psychology involves thinking scientifically, and if, as the biologist D'Arcy Wentworth Thompson observed, "Numerical precision is the very soul of science" (1951, p. 2), then it follows that encounters with numbers and quantitative reasoning are an essential part of an introduction to psychology. This has long been recognized in major discussions of education in psychology (e.g., Brewer et al., 1993; Cranney & Dunn, 2011; Halpern, 2010).

Teaching students "to think like scientists about behavior" may also have a broader rationale and merit beyond contributing to an understanding of psychology. It may alter how students think about themselves, others, and social and natural phenomena. For example, thinking scientifically may encourage students to evaluate beliefs in the light of evidence-based tests or to state claims more tentatively in the absence of sound evidence. Given that thinking scientifically also entails thinking quantitatively, education in psychology has the potential to strengthen students' quantitative reasoning in everyday life, and this may make a far-reaching contribution to students' general education and lifelong learning.

The mathematician Lynn Steen noted, "The world of the twenty-first century is a world awash in numbers" (2001, p. 1), and developing even a basic faculty for thinking about those numbers is likely to help prepare students for their roles as citizens, professionals, and consumers. As Halpern and Butler (2011) observed, "The constructs of critical thinking and psychological literacy also share considerable overlap with the knowledge and skills required in scientific reasoning .... It is not a set of skills required only for scientists; the general public needs to be wise consumers of research" (pp. 36–37). In other words, there may be general value in reinforcing scientific reasoning and the quantitative reasoning skills that are essential to scientific reasoning in psychology education. Quantitative reasoning can guide encounters individuals have with the numbers that surround and influence them every day; it can provide useful tools for understanding a complex world, and it can contribute to their participation in open discourse about the evidence that may reflect on claims and beliefs.

Consider, for example, a recent article from *The New York Times*, "More Consensus on Coffee's Benefits Than You Might Think" (Carroll, 2015). This is the kind of story a reader would find daily in a major newspaper of record. What background knowledge would someone need to understand the article even at a basic level? The primary findings the piece reports are based on *meta-analyses* of coffee consumption and cardiovascular disease. The article makes reference to *dose-dependent effects* (whether moderate or high levels of coffee consumption are associated with varying outcomes), *significant differences* between certain compared groups and a lack of differences between other groups (e.g., whether coffee consumers differ from nonconsumers on cancer risk—they don't), and *randomized controlled trials* versus *correlational research designs* (an especially important distinction given that almost all the research discussed in the article stems from correlational work). In other words, in order to appreciate a straightforward article on health, a knowledgeable reader would need familiarity with basic quantitative concepts. Of course, these are all concepts that regularly appear in the literature of psychological science.

Psychological scientists know that humans demonstrate cognitive tendencies that limit or bias everyday numerical thinking about phenomena (e.g., Kahneman, 2011). (Later, I will address how one can teach relevant literature to raise student awareness about the need for discipline in quantitative reasoning.) Psychology can help students recognize they may not be inclined to collect and evaluate evidence as systematically as they might assume. For example, research on confirmation bias (see Nickerson, 1998) suggests that, under certain conditions, individuals are less likely to seek disconfirming evidence for beliefs. Well-known work on cognitive heuristics (e.g., Tversky & Kahneman, 1974) demonstrates the insufficient attention individuals may pay to base rate information when judging the likelihood of outcomes. In sum, psychological science itself reminds people of the value of strengthening everyday quantitative reasoning.

Major assessments of the future of higher education further recognize and reinforce the importance of quantitative reasoning as a facet of students' general education. Derek Bok (2006) noted that "certain basic quantitative methods seem applicable to a wide enough range of situations to be valuable for almost all students" (p. 69). The Association of American Colleges & Universities (AAC&U) in its 2007 report "College Learning for the New Global Century" also lists "Quantitative Literacy" as one of its "Essential Learning Outcomes" for higher education across the curriculum. Similarly, the degree qualifications profile developed by the Lumina Foundation for Education (2011) specifies that "quantitative fluency" is a basic intellectual skill that should be strengthened as part of the training students receive during their degree studies, including that for receipt of the associate degree upon graduation from community colleges.

In sum, a broad and compelling case can be made for the importance of addressing quantitative reasoning in undergraduate education. Quantitative reasoning is integral to what it means to be familiar with contemporary psychological science as well as to be prepared for citizenship and work in the 21st century. But should the responsibility to address quantitative reasoning be borne, in part, by instructors of introductory psychology? What follows argues it is both reasonable and attractive for us to do so.

WHY SHOULD INSTRUCTORS ADDRESS QUANTITATIVE REASONING IN INTRODUCTORY PSYCHOLOGY?

Instructors have much to cover in an introductory psychology course, so it is appropriate to ask whether valuable preparation and class time should be dedicated to quantitative reasoning.

Introductory psychology is a popular course. Various estimates (e.g., Cush & Buskist, 1997) suggest annual enrollments in the course are on the order of 1.5 million undergraduates, and this gives psychology instructors access to a majority of America's college graduates (based on extrapolations from the data of the National Center for Education Statistics, 2015). The opportunity for impact is available, but again, what warrants directing that opportunity toward numeracy as an educational goal?

One major reason was introduced earlier: Quantitative reasoning is part and parcel of the contents of introductory psychology. Key findings are presented numerically (e.g., just noticeable differences, the correlation of intelligence or personality test scores of monozygotic twins reared apart), depend on understanding psychometric standards (e.g., the reliability of measurements), rely on understanding the logic of research design (e.g., whether a study is longitudinal or cross-sectional, whether results derive from a true experiment), and involve summaries of a research literature (e.g., meta-analysis of psychotherapeutic outcomes). Introductory texts recognize this and typically cover methodology and statistics in introductory chapters, appendices, and appropriate contexts in content chapters (e.g., reviewing the meaning of correlation in a chapter on intelligence). Students need to understand quantitative concepts like these and gain an appreciation for why psychological scientists rely on quantitative measurements, methods, and representations of findings. The latter helps students to make sense of what they are being asked to learn in introductory psychology and to develop realistic expectations about what further study in psychology entails. Attitudes first established in introductory psychology, for example, may influence whether students approach a statistics requirement in the major as a hurdle to be crossed or as an opportunity to gain essential skills.

Quantitative reasoning appears reliably in lists of the goals of contemporary higher education (e.g., AAC&U, 2007), and institutions increasingly recognize, as Lee Shulman advised, that "authentic and enduring learning … can rarely succeed one course at a time" (1997, p. x). This has been explicitly recognized with respect to quantitative reasoning (Elrod, 2014). Derek Bok (2006), for example, argued, "numeracy is not something mastered in a single course. The ability to apply quantitative methods to real-world problems requires a faculty and an insight and intuition that can be developed only through repeated practice. Thus quantitative material needs to permeate the curriculum" (p. 134). Given this orientation, emphasizing quantitative reasoning in the context of introductory psychology positions that course as making a major contribution to institutional educational priorities. It helps justify investments of resources in such a vital course. Moreover, aligning introductory psychology with broader institutional priorities allows and invites instructors to identify for students ways in which what they are learning in psychology about quantitative reasoning may contribute to larger educational ends.

WHAT ASPECTS OF QUANTITATIVE REASONING SHOULD INTRODUCTORY PSYCHOLOGY HIGHLIGHT?

Instructors may be familiar enough with quantitative concepts, measures, and procedures that arise in a normal introductory psychology course. I want to approach this question from a different perspective, that of the general literature on education in quantitative reasoning. What do treatments of numeracy highlight as most worth mastering in undergraduate education? Are the same quantitative concepts relevant to material typically covered in introductory psychology? Does the more general approach identify topics psychology instructors could consider emphasizing more than they now do?

A good place to start is with a general characterization of quantitative reasoning. Elrod (2014), writing in the AAC&U journal, *Peer Review*, cites the QuIRK definition of quantitative reasoning: "the habit of mind to consider the power and limitations of quantitative evidence in the evaluation, construction, and communication of arguments in public, professional, and personal life." This implies that students need to gain both an appreciation for the potential value of quantitative information and analysis and a sufficient understanding of quantitative information so as to be able to evaluate and use it. Drawing student attention to why psychologists rely on data may be of particular importance to introductory instructors; instructors may, arguably, invest so much time in explaining what a quantitative concept represents (e.g., a correlation) that they fail to highlight why they find that concept informative and useful.

The quantitative reasoning literature contains more specific listings of topics thought to be important to numeracy. Jessica Utts's classic article entitled "What Educated Citizens Should Know About Statistics and Probability" (2003) highlights seven such topics: (1) randomized experiments versus observational studies, (2) statistical versus practical significance, (3) what the absence of statistical significance may or may not mean, (4) sources of bias in surveys and experiments, (5) appreciating chance and coincidence, (6) false positives and confusion of the inverse, and (7) recognizing variability.

Lutsky (2004) developed a set of "10 QR Questions at the Ready" originally for faculty colleagues at Carleton who were interested in learning more about how to think critically and knowledgeably about research-based claims in the media. Most of these faculty either lacked statistical background or lost whatever familiarity with statistics they had due to time, disuse, or retrospective interference. These questions have subsequently become a staple of the quantitative reasoning education literature (Lutsky, 2008). The ten questions, each of which frames more specific component questions specified in the full listing, are the following:

1. What do the numbers show?
2. How representative is that?
3. Compared to what?
4. Is the outcome statistically significant?
5. What's the effect size?
6. Are the results those of a single study or a literature?
7. What's the research design (correlational or experimental)?
8. How was the variable operationalized?
9. Who's in the measurement sample?
10. Controlling for what?

Sutherland, Spiegelhalter, and Burgman (2013) recently offered a list of "20 Tips for Interpreting Scientific Claims," one that emphasizes methodological and statistical issues primarily anchored in biological research. Among the concerns Sutherland and colleagues highlight are the following: "no measurement is exact," "bias is rife," "bigger is usually better for sample size," "extrapolating beyond the data is risky," "controls are important," and "data can be dredged or cherry-picked." Taken as a whole, the list underscores the need for caution when reading research.

A recent report (Zhao, Dowd, & Searcy, 2012) on quantitative reasoning deserves introductory psychology teachers' special attention. This is because the report serves as background for revisions of the Medical College Admission Test (MCAT). The new MCAT is designed to merge "statistical thinking and quantitative reasoning into the assessment of the natural, social, and behavioral sciences content" (Zhao et al., 2012, p. 16), and students interested in medical school are now being advised to take introductory psychology in partial preparation for the exam. In other words, pre-med students are enrolling in introductory psychology both to gain background in behavioral science and, quite specifically, to strengthen their understanding of quantitative reasoning. Zhao and colleagues surveyed faculty and student respondents from medical schools in the United States and Canada to help develop a list of important statistical and quantitative topics for aspiring medical students and organized responses in terms of two groupings: research design and statistical reasoning. The former includes topics such as experimental versus nonexperimental designs, independent versus dependent variables, and research ethics; the latter covers measures of central tendency and variability, statistical association and correlation, and making sense of tables, figures, and graphs. The listings for each are more extensive than these brief summaries, and the interested reader is encouraged to read the full report by Zhao et al. (2014).

What emerges from the above specifications suggests considerable convergence around a picture of the quantitative literate undergraduate. He or she should appreciate the value of numerical thinking and evidence; should understand representations of data in measures of central tendency, variability, and association, and, in basic tables and graphics, should recognize the implications of experimental versus nonexperimental research designs; should gain familiarity with statistical significance and effect size; and should appreciate the importance of research replications and literature (e.g., meta-analysis). Of course, students in introductory psychology, given their likely backgrounds, wouldn't be expected to gain a highly technical understanding of these concepts. Nonetheless, they should be exposed to quantitative matters of these kinds and develop a working familiarity with these basic topics.

None of the above lists, however, emphasizes another aspect of quantitative reasoning relevant to introductory psychology and elementary uses of quantitative reasoning more generally, namely writing with numbers. Students in introductory psychology are commonly called upon to write responses to short answer or essay prompts that may potentially involve quantitative information (e.g., research results). They may be asked to write short papers on topics in psychology that may be framed by descriptive information (e.g., presenting epidemiological information on a disorder) or that may involve summarizing empirical findings. Students may also be required to write up accounts of laboratory or demonstration exercises and their results. Writing with numbers may be an important part of work in introductory psychology, introduces students to a domain of quantitative skill and reasoning they will need to employ should they decide to major in psychology, and again serves greater general education needs. Helping students learn how to write effectively with numbers offers instructors another opportunity to address quantitative reasoning, as discussed later.

HOW CAN INSTRUCTORS HELP STUDENTS LEARN ABOUT QUANTITATIVE REASONING IN INTRODUCTORY PSYCHOLOGY?

Quantitative reasoning is not going to be the focal concern of instruction in introductory psychology, but arguments presented earlier suggest it would be desirable, natural, and useful to strengthen students' appreciations for and background in quantitative reasoning in the context of the introductory course. How might this be achieved? What follows identifies and elaborates possible means for raising attention to quantitative reasoning in introductory psychology. The author has employed most of the suggestions discussed in following sections, but it may be of interest to note that a number of these developed as a consequence of this increased sensitivity to quantitative reasoning concerns. Readers of this chapter may find that they too will notice and alter how they present information, what they discuss, how they grade, and what projects they assign in light of the concerns raised in the quantitative reasoning literature.

Presenting Quantitative Information

Randomly select any class presentation for introductory psychology. Chances are a substantial portion of that presentation will consist of descriptions of the findings of research in psychology. How do instructors convey those findings to students? They can do so by describing findings verbally, as, for example, when they state that, "In the Asch study, individuals often conformed their answers to the general consensus even when their perceptions clearly showed them that the group's answer was incorrect." Alternatively or in addition to that, they can specify the exact results using numbers: "Only 25% of all participants resisted conforming their answers to the group's." Note that the numerical description is more precise and easily leads to questions. Why did a quarter of all participants not conform? How does that level of nonconformity and conformity compare to those obtained in other conditions of the Asch (1951) conformity study? I find that students often overgeneralize research findings in psychology, such as those of the Asch study, and that emphasizing the exact results helps to counter that tendency. It is useful in this regard to draw attention to the numbers, perhaps by asking students to think about them and generate questions based on them. Presenting numerical results also gives the instructor an opportunity to point out the value of precision when conveying information and the usefulness of numbers to communicate with accuracy.

Presenting actual results, such as the means on a dependent variable in experimental versus control conditions, invites a variety of quantitative reasoning discussions. What are independent versus dependent variables, and what were these in the study being presented? How was the independent variable manipulated? How was the dependent variable measured? Is the difference in the means of the two groups statistically significant? How large a difference was found? What do statistical significance and effect size indicate? How much variability was there in the dependent measure, and what other factors might account for that? I'm not suggesting that every time two means are presented an instructor needs to ask students to consider these and other quantitatively relevant questions (or to raise an equivalent set of questions about correlational results). My point here is that presenting findings provides an opportunity to direct attention to key questions that might be useful in elaborating the meaning of the results under consideration and that may help students when they encounter other quantitative claims both within and beyond psychology.

A critical question in this regard concerns the character and logic of true experiments. Students come to psychology with a loose understanding of experimental research design. Not infrequently, students will label any empirical study an experiment or consider any research design that involves the comparison of two groups similarly. Analyses of student writing at Carleton College and of the assignment prompts on which that writing is based have shown that even instructors in other fields may use the term "experiment" to refer to any intervention made in an empirical context regardless of whether the research design within which that intervention was conducted was that of a true experiment. Because understanding the logic of a true experiment is so critical to appreciating what the results of an experimental study may be indicating, it's important for instructors in psychology, a field that relies heavily but not exclusively on experimental research design, to reinforce an appreciation for that logic. I also find it useful to tell students that I will insist they employ the term in a rigorous manner in their usages within the course and to remind them that when they encounter the term "experiment" in other contexts, it may or may not reflect the same rigorous meaning. That is something the research consumer will need to evaluate in light of additional information.

When teaching the meaning of a true experiment, I also link that to the terms "Randomized Controlled Trial" or RCT. The latter terminology is sometimes used in research evaluating psychotherapy effectiveness, but it is generally foreign to psychology. Nonetheless, when students read about medical findings in the newspaper, they are likely to encounter the term "randomized controlled trial" and not recognize they already know what the label signifies: the same research design as a true experiment. I will often prepare a slide with a newspaper medical story that includes a reference to an RCT to show students how what they are learning about research in psychology can inform their understanding of research in the news.

Another means of presenting research findings in an introductory class is to use graphics. I regularly reproduce graphs, figures, and tables from research articles or even from the introductory text on my lecture slides. I can then do one of two things: walk students through an account of what the graphic is showing or ask the students to interpret the findings represented on the graphic themselves. The latter can serve as a rich prompt for a brief interlude of meaningful small group or class discussion even within a large lecture course. Here again opportunities for instruction in quantitative reasoning abound (see Few, 2004; Tufte, 2001). For example, I will regularly remind students to look first at the y-axis in a graph and determine whether it has a zero point. That should influence the impression of the effect represented in the graphic, a concern that generalizes to the public's consumption of graphics in the news, as I show students through egregiously manipulative examples.

A key question about research results presented in the introductory course is whether those are the outcomes of a single study or a replicated line of research. Students may assume that findings I discuss represent robust lines of research, but that may not be the case or instructors may be unfamiliar with work subsequent to classic studies that evaluates well-known findings and their meaning. Moreover, students may encounter media references to "research," and that may refer to a single study, even one that hasn't been peer-reviewed, or the results of a meta-analysis of a substantial literature. A headline indicating "Research Shows ..." or "New Research Shows ..." often isn't interrogated by the reader sufficiently or elaborated clearly in an article to allow a determination of whether the outcome is that of a single study or a research literature. Teachers of introductory psychology can highlight this distinction by drawing attention to it explicitly and by indicating when they present research findings whether those represent robust lines of research and supporting meta-analyses or specific studies. The recent concern for the replicability of major findings in psychology (e.g., Pashler & Wagenmakers, 2012) and in science more generally (e.g., Ioannidis, 2005) underscores teachers' responsibility to exercise caution in making research claims. Related but not identical questions that can be raised about the generalizability of research findings across cultures (e.g., Gergen, Gulerce, Lock, & Misra, 1996; Henrich, Heine, & Norenzayan, 2010; Mitterer, 2012), from the laboratory to the field (e.g., Mitchell, 2012), and across history (e.g., Gergen, 1973) further underscore instructors' need for precision and circumspection when discussing research findings in introductory psychology.

A more basic use of quantitative reasoning in presentations in introductory psychology involves data describing the prevalence of phenomena under consideration. What are the incidence rates for various mental disorders? How are those calculated? How common is intergroup violence? Is distracted driving a major cause of road accidents? Descriptive information of this sort frames discussions of topics in psychology and is often used to suggest how important those topics are in society. Instructors and texts regularly employ statistics to establish the frequency of phenomena, and this gives instructors the opportunity to model sound practices when citing descriptive statistics. Instructors can share with students where they obtained the statistics they cite, why they trust those data (or what complications ought to inform their considerations of the numbers they use), and how the data were initially generated by the source they are using.

Eliciting and Shaping Quantitative Writing

The previous section has highlighted quantitative reasoning topics that introductory instructors can raise as they present information to students, but they, in turn, commonly ask students to present information to them and, sometimes, to their peers or another audience. The instructions and guidance they provide students for their written (or oral) work offers another opportunity for them to address quantitative reasoning. One broad way of doing so is to ask students to anticipate the reasonable questions about their quantitative claims that an educated reader or listener might generate and to respond to the most important of those questions in what they present. As an instructor, I try to shape students' anticipations, reminding students, for example, that readers might be interested in knowing how common whatever it is that they are discussing is (and why readers should trust the figures cited). When I discuss written work on examinations, which in the case of my introductory courses involves short answers and essays (in addition to more common multiple-choice questions), I show students possible responses varying in precision due to uses of ambiguous quantifiers (e.g., "many") as opposed to specific numerical findings. This is an approach modeled from an excellent source on writing with numbers (Miller, 2004), *The Chicago Guide to Writing About Numbers*, where the author presents examples of "Poor," "Better," and "Best" written variations on a topic. When I ask students to grade the examples I share with them, they invariably recognize how impressive and informative precise quantitative information can be.

It is important to reiterate that quantitative information can be used in writing in a variety of ways. At Carleton College, instructors undertook a broad review of quantitative content in student writing, using papers sampled from required portfolios. The coding rubric they developed (Grawe et al., 2009) employed three broad categories of potential relevance: no relevance, peripheral relevance, or central relevance. The last referred to papers in which quantitative evidence was central to the arguments or issues raised in the paper. A typical psychology laboratory report would most likely fit in that category. The "peripheral relevance" category was used for papers where quantitative information could have been used or was used to provide background or useful details for the issues under consideration. A paper describing a new therapeutic technique for treating anxiety, for example, could begin with descriptive data on the prevalence of the disorder. This suggests that even papers in psychology that are not primarily about empirical findings may nonetheless include quantitative information usefully.

Assigning Quantitative Projects in the Introductory Course

A major means I employ to expose students to quantitative reasoning is to assign two small research projects as part of the introductory course. There are many alternatives to this strategy, including involving students in course laboratories and online research activities, reviewing primary research or media presentations on psychological topics, and developing research proposals. I will discuss what I do for illustrative purposes and draw wider observations based on that.

I give a first empirical project assignment to students just after the course begins. I ask students to go online to complete, optionally and anonymously, questionnaires assessing the five factor traits of personality and subjective well-being. (An early version of both modules described is available at this site: http://www.acad.carleton.edu/curricular/PSYC/classes/psych110_Lutsky/. I have moved both to the campus course management system, which, unfortunately, makes them inaccessible to the public.) Students are subsequently told their task is to frame a simple research question that can be addressed by the data set derived from their responses (and those of students from the course in prior years), analyze the data relevant to their question, and write up a brief report of their findings. Students will have read the personality trait section of the text and heard my class presentation on the topic, and I also ask them to study the statistics and methodology appendix to the text as well as a short *Current Directions in Psychological Science* article summarizing a meta-analysis on personality and well-being.

What am I trying to accomplish with this project? First, I want students to see how psychological scientists pose and answer questions using data. Students have the opportunity to see for themselves how data can inform questions of interest to them. Second, I want students to learn about basic statistics—here, correlational data analysis, correlation size, and statistical significance—in a purposive manner. Students need to begin to understand these concepts from the reading, background information on the assignment handout, and my teaching because they will be using and talking about that information. Students will also have their first encounter with a meta-analysis, which allows me to discuss the technique and its strengths and weaknesses. Finally, students will be writing with numbers as they summarize the findings they obtained.

For the second research module in the course, which is scheduled during the consideration of cognitive psychology, I have students take an online version I created of the Jones and Harris's (1967) experiment on correspondence bias (see also Gilbert & Malone, 1995) and then later read individual web pages I wrote, each of which summarizes a study investigating a question about correspondence bias using a variant of the original research paradigm. These pages present simple summary statistics (e.g., the means on the dependent variable for the different conditions of a study) but do not interpret the results. I leave that to the students. After examining this stripped-down version of a literature review, students are assigned the task of designing a study using a variant of the Jones and Harris's paradigm to investigate a question about correspondence bias. My intent here is to show students how research literature pursues questions raised about important findings by altering elements of a basic research procedure. I want students to think in terms of literature rather than an individual well-known study, to recognize how scientists raise questions about basic findings and pursue those in empirical investigations, and to encounter and make sense of actual findings of research studies.

These are the particular assignments I use, but their significance in the current context is that they involve introductory students in data analysis, make learning about statistics and methodology meaningful and important, require students to think about what numbers they encounter mean, and link data to personally interesting research questions. Involving students in research-based assignments also provides a rich opportunity for classroom instruction about quantitative reasoning (e.g., when I explain to students and remind them as they construct their reports why they should not confuse correlation with causation). The culmination of these projects is represented in short papers that students write. Here again, students are called upon to use their knowledge of quantitative reasoning appropriately as they share with others what they did, what they found, and the limitations of their empirical investigations.

The Psychology of Quantitative Reasoning

Instructors covering topical material in introductory psychology will find they have numerous opportunities to draw students' attention to the importance of learning about quantitative reasoning. The historian of statistics, Stephen Stigler, noted, "Statistical concepts are ubiquitous in every province of human thought" (1999, p. 1), and a wide variety of literature in psychology demonstrates this (e.g., Dehaene, 2011; Peters et al., 2006). Instructors also have reason to believe, as psychological scientists, that thinking in a disciplined statistical manner doesn't come easily to human cognition. According to Daniel Kahneman (2011), a fundamental question in cognitive psychology is this one: "Why is it so difficult for us to think statistically?" (p. 13). There are debates about the issue to be sure (Gigerenzer & Gaissmaier, 2011), but these discussions in psychology allow instructors to draw attention to the importance of quantitative reasoning in everyday cognition and to recommend means of strengthening their quantitative reasoning. I regularly share with introductory students New York University philosopher Kwami Appiah's pithy advice to incoming students: "Learn Statistics. Go Abroad" (Appiah, 2005), and I recommend to students that they take a statistics course some time during their undergraduate education. In sum, the very material instructors teach can ground an argument to students that quantitative reasoning is something they should pursue seriously.

FIVE EASY WAYS TO STRENGTHEN STUDENTS' QUANTITATIVE REASONING IN THE INTRODUCTORY COURSE

Although it's possible to invest significant preparation and teaching time for an introductory course in instruction in quantitative reasoning, it's also easy to draw attention to significant quantitative reasoning concerns with little effort but with great benefit for undergraduate audiences. Here are five suggestions, drawn from the discussions presented earlier, that may be worth your consideration:

1. Present findings in class numerically and graphically, and walk students through what they should look for and understand when encountering those findings.

2. Draw students' attention to the value of thinking quantitatively: to the precision it offers, to the information it provides on the magnitude of effects, to the concerns for representativeness it introduces, and to the public discourse about these issues it promotes.

3. Emphasize and reemphasize throughout the course basic quantitative reasoning concerns for experimental versus correlational design, replicability and meta-analysis, and other grounds for thinking knowledgeably and cautiously about research findings.

4. Connect encounters with quantitative reasoning in psychology to applications in other important domains students are likely to encounter, such as research on health or media presentations on statistics.

5. Show students how psychology underscores the importance of training in statistics and methodology, and recommend to students, regardless of their majors, that they seek such training as part of their undergraduate educations.

The need to strengthen undergraduates' quantitative reasoning habits of mind in the service of the lives they will lead as educated professionals and citizens is widely recognized. Teachers of introductory psychology have a natural opportunity to contribute to this important educational goal to enhance education in psychology and more generally, and I hope this chapter has reinforced instructors' commitment to one of the key virtues of psychological science: its responsible and critical uses of quantitative reasoning.

Chapter 15

Infusing Scientific Thinking into Introductory Psychology

AMY SILVESTRI HUNTER
AND SUSAN M. TEAGUE
Seton Hall University

WHY MAKE SCIENTIFIC THINKING A CORE CONCEPT IN INTRODUCTORY PSYCHOLOGY?

Imagine yourself in this situation: You launch into a lecture on psychological research methods in an early meeting of your new Introductory Psychology class. You've carefully chosen studies to illustrate different research designs that you believe will engage students and fuel their interest in psychology. You're hoping to show them that research does, in fact, connect to their everyday lives. You might discuss the classic Schachter (1959) study of anxiety on the need for affiliation, telling students that people who are anxious about an upcoming event prefer the company of others rather than being alone, but *only* if the others around them are feeling uncertain and anxious themselves (i.e., "misery loves miserable company").

Next, for a study you think will really grab their attention, you might recount a dramatic demonstration of gender differences in social cognition (Abbey, 1982). The researcher documented that although men and women participants observed the same interaction between a male–female couple, they perceived the exchange in markedly different ways and made very different attributions about the conversation they witnessed, with male participants perceiving much more flirtatiousness and sexual overtones in the interaction than female participants. For a study that may seem more current and relevant to them, you may describe how people texting or talking on their cell phone avoided walking into a tree with money dangling from it but were unlikely to notice the money itself, demonstrating that we often fail to process important environmental information when we are distracted (Hyman, Sarb, & Wise-Swanson, 2014). Perhaps, we optimistically think, they will be persuaded to not use their laptops for off-task purposes during class when we tell them that not only do participants randomly assigned to a multitasking condition recall less lecture information than their non-multitasking counterparts, but so do participants who simply were in view of the multitasking student (despite their perception that they were not distracted by their multitasking peer; Sana, Weston, & Cepeda, 2013).

From the front row of the classroom, a student waves his hand and loudly announces: "I disagree with the results of that study. I multitask during class all the time and get straight As." You may find yourself at once pleased and discouraged: on the one hand, it's wonderful that the student is engaged and thinking deeply enough to realize that this study might not be *the* definitive investigation of this topic, but at the same time, it's obvious that this student—and likely, most of the rest of the class—hasn't quite gotten the concept of the scientific process and how it works. You might praise the student for thinking deeply enough to have raised the question, and add that skepticism is an essential part of scientific inquiry, and of daily life, for that matter. If we believed everything we read or heard we would be a confused bundle of contradictions. We would also get taken advantage of a lot. But, as you explain to the class, empirical research simply documents the results of observation or testing and the information reported by researchers in their studies is not up for debate: they found what they found, and it isn't legitimate to "disagree" with their results.

If there were ever an appropriate time to use that hackneyed phrase "it is what it is," this truly is the moment. What the "disagreeing" student is missing is an essential component of the empirical approach to psychology. Researchers simply document what they find, and it isn't legitimate to dispute their observations. Certainly, we can justifiably evaluate and criticize the way the study was designed, how it was conducted, or even suggest that important variables were left out, but there's just no debating what was scientifically observed unless some fatal design flaw or confound is present.

In this chapter, we will explore ways in which scientific thinking can be integrated into the Introductory Psychology course. A discussion with your students of issues surrounding scientific thinking can flow organically from the types of questions and comments that they often have, and repetition of these ideas and issues throughout the semester will aid in their understanding. We will also review ways in which their understanding of these concepts can be assessed not only in the Introductory course but throughout the major.

WHAT IS SCIENTIFIC THINKING, AND WHY IS IT SO DIFFICULT TO TEACH?

Scientific thinking encompasses a broad range of topics, including the process of systematic inquiry, experimental control, empiricism, hypothesis testing, and thinking critically about research. Scientific thinking is the primary means by which we as psychologists evaluate information, and most scientists apply this method not only in our professional lives but our personal lives as well. Frequently, our students don't understand how essential scientific thinking is to the way in which psychologists ask and answer questions about behavior, and even after we explain it to them it often seems that they fail to generalize this way of thinking to daily life, other courses, or even other topics within the Introductory course (Stark, 2012). The importance of scientific thinking in the psychology curriculum is not a new concept. However, its integration into the psychology curriculum has become even more relevant with its inclusion as one of the five goals in the American Psychological Association's (APA) *Guidelines 2.0 for the Undergraduate Psychology Major* (APA, 2013).

As professors, we often have a two-pronged battle in our attempts to teach scientific thinking to our Introductory Psychology students. First, we must convince them that—contrary to their belief—psychological knowledge is not generated with the use of intuition or personal experience, but with the scientific method. Second, we need to demonstrate the relevance of the scientific method to their personal and professional lives. Even if our students will not be designing and conducting their own research, should they choose to pursue a helping profession they will typically be relying on evidence-based practice to guide their decisions. This is true not only for fields such as clinical and counseling psychology but also for such diverse areas as medicine, physical or occupational therapy, and education, just to name a few. Integration of this topic into the Introductory course is particularly relevant to our majors, as it sets the tone for the rest of their psychology curriculum. An accurate understanding of the discipline will help enhance student satisfaction with their chosen major. For the majority of our students who are not psychology majors, this may be our only opportunity to refute some of the myths about our field (e.g., it's not all about dream analysis and disorders) and emphasize the applicability of psychology to daily life.

The scientific approach is a logical method of inquiry demonstrated to be maximally productive in building a systematic and comprehensive knowledge base. Advantages of using the scientific process include (1) greater accuracy of data due to obtaining information objectively through empirical methods, which are repeatable and verifiable by others; (2) more efficient identification and correction of errors through the comparison of new information to existing scientific data, with convergence of evidence seen as confirmatory; and (3) establishing the superiority of one hypothesis (or theory) over another through clearly defined comparisons made under systematically controlled conditions (Gould, 2002).

Scientific thinking proceeds systematically in a step-by-step fashion, often starting small by documenting only bits and pieces of the picture, while building toward an understanding of the larger phenomenon in an orderly way. Such a systematic approach is sometimes criticized as reductionistic, but complex phenomena can rarely be accurately understood all at once. Taking their complexities apart to examine the parts separately and then logically putting them together again as each is elucidated is often the most productive way to proceed. The scientific approach is characterized by both "bottom-up" processing, an integrative progression of thinking in which individual observations are used as the basis for broad theories, and features of "top-down" processing, in which broad theories are tested with specific observations (Trochim, 2006). However, not all of our students find this to be an intuitive process. From our own observations it seems that many of them seem to gravitate more toward the use of "bottom-up" processing, in which they use their own observations to draw conclusions about behavior but fail to appreciate the importance of the "top-down" approach of testing theories with careful observations and evaluation.

Empirical research demonstrates that as students progress through the major, their degree of interest in the scientific aspects of the field becomes negatively correlated with practitioner career interests: As practitioner aspirations increase, interest in the scientific approach to psychology diminishes (Holmes & Beins, 2009). Scores on the Need for Cognition scale, which reflect the degree to which an individual enjoys effortful thinking, have been found to be positively correlated with the level of scientific, but not practitioner, interest in undergraduate psychology students (Holmes & Beins, 2009). As Need for Cognition scores are also related to the ability to learn new and cognitively demanding tasks (Day, Espejo, Kowollik, Boatman, & McEntire, 2007), this suggests that understanding and applying the processes of scientific thinking requires more active cognitive engagement—and effort—than many students may be accustomed to expending.

Part of the challenge of education in psychology is to *persuade* students of the value of the more objective, scientific mindset and its relevance to daily life. We use the term "persuade" because according to Holmes and Beins (2009), this is exactly what we need to do to help students appreciate the value of the scientific approach. This is particularly important among students with practitioner aspirations. These researchers documented that the majority of their psychology majors were interested in becoming practitioners and that students characteristically relied on their intuition and experience as a guide toward their understanding of psychology. They simply didn't see the scientific approach as essential to their understanding of psychology or as a key component of their future practice. The "Boulder model" of the scientist-practitioner is often invoked as a guiding principle of education in psychology, but it hardly seems relevant for many majors, as many of them do not seem to appreciate that scientific research provides the basis for practice (Overholser, 2007; Zachar & Leong, 1992).

In addition to its relevance within the field of psychology, a scientific mindset is a valuable tool with which to evaluate the many and varied types of information that confronts each of us every day. In the present era of "too much information," many people don't think very much about where all that information comes from, let alone whether or not it is accurate; it may not even occur to them to question its accuracy, never mind its scientific basis. For all the emphasis on critical thinking skills in education over the past years, it seems that many students (and regular people, too) still lack this fundamental and important ability—or maybe they simply fail to generalize this "academic skill" into their everyday lives.

We should consider, also, that because scientific thinking is a demanding, complex cognitive task, and is relatively novel for most students, even if we are able to persuade them of its importance to their professional and personal lives, they still need practice to become familiar with and skilled in using this approach. Just as athletes repeatedly drill specific moves and sequences of plays to the point that they become automatic, we need to provide our students with the practice they need to become facile at scientific thinking. For example, Thieman, Clary, Olson, Dauner, and Ring (2009) demonstrated that a weekly laboratory component integrated into Introductory Psychology courses provided a plethora of benefits, among which increase in knowledge, interest, and comfort in applying the scientific approach to psychological issues was notable. Practice helps to develop skills, whether in sports or in critically evaluating information we encounter continually. Practice is what our students need, and if we provide all the examples, thereby doing the thinking for them, they will not readily—if at all—learn this set of skills for their own use. Fortunately, there are many ways in which we can incorporate the practice of scientific thinking into our individual courses and even our curriculum as a whole.

WAYS TO EMPHASIZE SCIENTIFIC THINKING IN INTRODUCTORY PSYCHOLOGY

Making changes to your course is always challenging and time-consuming, and many professors have designed their courses in very deliberate ways that are well suited to their own teaching style and their students. Radical departure from "business as usual" has been advocated by many, but practically, there are many barriers to restructuring courses (Lambert, 2012). Scientific thinking can be infused into courses in a myriad of ways: What we offer here are suggestions for various ways in which it can be incorporated into the Introductory course and beyond.

Lecture Examples

An explanation of the concept of scientific thinking with the textbook definition is a fine start. If instructors do this when they introduce the concept of the scientific method, for example, they are likely to explain it as "a set of assumptions, attitudes, and procedures that guide researchers in creating questions to investigate, in generating evidence, and in drawing conclusions" (Hockenbury, Nolan, & Hockenbury, 2015, p. 16). While this is a clear and accurate definition that most students can understand and repeat on an exam, this idea is not likely to be very meaningful to them without spending more time on the concept. Additional class time allocated to explaining and elaborating how the process works and having students engage in active learning exercises to reinforce and enhance lecture material will no doubt be beneficial (Balch, 2012; Steven & Witkow, 2014; Thieman et al., 2009). And, as mentioned previously, practice is essential: A similar approach implemented across a variety of topics is likely to be an effective way to reinforce the utility and applicability of scientific thinking across many domains in psychology (as suggested by Holmes & Beins, 2009).

One way to introduce the importance of the scientific process might be to start with a vivid example. Tell your students that you've already decided upon their final course grades based on where they are currently seated in the classroom. Specifically, based on your previous experiences in which students who sat on the left side of the room earned As while students who sat on the right side earned Ds, you're going to assign those grades now without giving any exams or grading any other assignments. Ask the class whether they're satisfied with this arrangement (those on the left likely will be, but it's a different story for the rest). Next, ask them if this is *fair*. Then go for the clincher: Is your assignment of grades to students on the basis of their location likely to be *accurate*? Aren't there likely to be just as many "go-getters" on the right side of the room as there are "slackers" on the left in this particular class? What happens when we draw conclusions about a particular population based solely on our own experience and in the absence of data (in this case, exam grades and other course work)?

Suddenly, the importance of verifying your beliefs through systematic observation and collection of data will make more sense to them and demonstrate that we cannot form valid conclusions based solely on our assumptions about the way things are, or based on our personal experience. We must put things to the test, and quite literally so in this case. For most courses, the primary way to assess learning is by formulating a set of questions that students should be able to answer if they have learned the course content. Their performance on these questions is used as an indicator of the extent to which they have mastered course concepts and principles. While it would be much more efficient (not to mention less stressful for professors and students alike) to be able to somehow *look at* our students and determine the degree to which they've learned course material, exams are one way to collect verifiable evidence that is based on objective measurement. And we can all agree that this is more accurate than simply assigning grades based on seating pattern!

Another topic in the Introductory course where integration of scientific thinking comes naturally is the section on research methods, a topic that students seem to find uninspiring despite our insistence that it is integral to the discipline. In the context of contrasting the differences between experimental and correlational research, and highlighting the point that "correlation is not causation," students can be asked to think of additional factors that might also be involved in a particular correlation; in other words, get them to identify potential "third variables" that could influence the observed relationship. One example that seems to resonate with our students is a discussion of the correlation between aggressive behavior and watching violent TV, which has been replicated numerous times (for review, see Bushman, Gollwitzer, & Cruz, 2014; Glymour, Glymour, & Glymour, 2008). This correlation is often portrayed in the popular press as a causal relationship in which watching violent TV—or, more likely today, playing violent video games—causes children to behave aggressively. Our first challenge is convincing students that this correlation is "real." Many of them try to discount the relevance of this finding based on personal experience: "I play violent video games all the time, and I would never hurt anyone"; "Everyone knows that TV violence isn't real."

We can use this line of research to demonstrate the probabilistic nature of science; that is, while research can explain patterns of behavior in a population, it does not perfectly predict every individual every time. There will be plenty of individual exceptions to this relationship, but there is no disputing the statistical result that these two variables are, in fact, related. We can also discuss how a correlation does not allow us to infer causation. Even though some individuals may use this finding to support their notion that watching violent TV or playing violent video games causes aggression, the converse may be true: Children who are higher in aggressive tendencies may prefer violent TV. Finally, this example can also serve as a great exercise in identifying "third variables," other factors that may influence or contribute to the observed relationship. Ask students what other factors could lead to a child behaving aggressively and choosing to watch violent TV. Often they are slow to begin to generate ideas, but once they get the hang of it, they are likely to come up with all sorts of variables such as peer influence or discipline style of parents. This example could even lead to a discussion of how an experiment could be set up so as to determine whether there is a causal relationship between these variables, and the necessity of showing temporal precedence to support a proposed causal relationship between variables.

Yet, all too often, results of correlational research are presented in the popular media as if they explain cause and effect. Prior to students' exposure to scientific thinking in Introductory Psychology, they are pretty much used to uncritically accepting whatever they're told. We have found that presenting numerous examples of such misrepresentations in class helps students to develop their evaluative skills and their ability to formulate alternate explanations that might also account for correlational relationships. Some examples are (1) drinking wine daily leads to higher mental acuity in middle-aged women (e.g., Hitti, 2005); (2) daily meals with family reduce teens' chances of abusing drugs and alcohol (e.g., Hendrick, 2010); (3) use of Facebook can improve memory in older adults (e.g., Abrams, 2013); (4) increased temperature increases violent crime (Dahl, 2012); and (5) reading fitness magazines causes young women to develop eating disorders (e.g., Fillon, 2013)—and the list goes on.

Until the obvious flaw in claiming cause and effect in such reports is pointed out to them—and the idea that they even need to question these claims—they all too often passively accept whatever conclusions are presented to them. You can almost see the transformation in their way of thinking once you ask them to question the findings and to generate alternate accounts of these relationships. A strong point in favor of this activity is that you can tell your students from the beginning that there are potentially hundreds of right answers, given the universe of factors that might also explain *cause*. Once students are assured that they're unlikely to be wrong, they are more likely to respond in class, and the class tends to keep generating ideas. For example, the observed relationships between health and both wine consumption and checking Facebook may be related more strongly to maintaining friendships and staying socially active. Similarly, it's likely that there is no special ingredient in mom's lasagna that prevents drug abuse, but family interaction and involvement in a teen's life. In hot weather many people are outside their homes (and may be drinking alcoholic beverages to cool off) and thus may be more likely to be involved in a dispute. Finally, young men and women who have eating disorders are likely to be more focused on fitness publications than those without a disorder. These are just a few of the many alternate explanations that may emerge; there are *many* possibilities.

For additional practice in thinking scientifically, turn the tables on students when they ask the ever-popular question, "Has there *ever* been a study?..." This can seem frustrating at times because it indicates an expectation that we know every study in the field and also requires us to search through our vast memory stores of knowledge to dredge up whatever is most relevant to the specific inquiry. Yet the underlying question reflects the student's curiosity, one of the foundations of scientific inquiry, and this is undeniably a good thing. So the next time you're put between this rock and a hard place, flip the question, if not the whole classroom. Tell them you can't say for certain, but ask them how such a question could be tested scientifically. In other words, have the class generate ways in which the "question in question" could be tested empirically, assuming it is possible. While it's important to acknowledge the scientific curiosity of the student who asked the question, it's just as important to avoid asking that one student to respond to your question—which will likely squelch class discussion for the remainder of the term. Make it a collaborative effort instead. You'll likely have to do some shaping of their study toward the right direction ("you're getting more valid; more valid," as in the old children's game). Along the way, ask for potential problems that might arise from operationalizing your variable(s) in a particular way, what you might have left out, what you need to control for, and then ask what you've forgotten to take into account. Propose results that might be obtained, and why or why not the hypothesis might be supported. If this isn't clear already, we're proposing that you spend a fair amount of class time on this, and not just the usual quick answer to the "Has there ever been a study. . ." with the usual, "Well, not specifically, not that I'm aware of, but it would be interesting..."

Class Activities and Demonstrations

We hope the approaches described so far will provide examples that engage your students as they do ours, but it may not convince them that they, too, are prone to drawing incorrect conclusions when they do so based on their own intuition or experience. Throughout the semester, we can reinforce the idea of the importance of using the scientific literature instead of relying on our own intuition or common sense by providing a brief summary of a study and asking students to predict the results. This approach is also useful as a way for us to model for our students the importance of relying on scientific thinking and drawing conclusions based on data across various topic areas in the field. We can also include demonstrations that have relatively easily identifiable confounds. For example, one great demonstration of the autonomic nervous system is to have students measure their heart rate before, during, and after writing about an emotional event. On average, this results in elevated heart rate while writing as a result of increased emotional arousal (LaVoie, 1987). However, this demonstration is subject to a number of confounds including (but not limited to) lack of a control group, individual variability in the degree of emotionality of the event chosen by each student, and measurement error in recording heart rate.

Analyzing claims made on websites is another way that students can start to identify flaws in critical thinking and has the added advantage of demonstrating the utility of critical thinking in everyday life. A personal favorite of ours is the popular press article indicating that clinical psychology majors have an extraordinarily high unemployment rate (this finding has been reprinted in several places on the web, but one source is Dumbauld [2014]). Of course, there are numerous issues with this finding, not the least of which is the lack of availability of clinical psychology as an undergraduate major. This result can also lead to a discussion on the pros and cons of collecting data via self-report, as was the case in this study. An engaging in-class activity is the "Coke-Pepsi Challenge," introduced in our department by our colleague Susan Nolan and used thereafter to great advantage by many of us. This demonstration affords many possibilities for illustrating different points about scientific inquiry, systematic control, confounding of variables, and even participant bias. For this activity, the instructor comes to class with numerous types of Coca-Cola and Pepsi (e.g., regular, diet, cans, bottles), and announces the need for student volunteers to taste the two types of soda and state their preferences as a way to determine—once and for all—which soda is better. The instructor then pulls out a can of Coke and a bottle of Diet Pepsi and begins to set up the taste test, but pauses to ask the class whether this is a good test. Most obvious to students is the difference between the regular and diet soda formulations and they quickly identify this; the potential effect of packaging differences upon taste is a close second. So corrected by the students, the professor then reveals a "regular" Coke and Pepsi, both in cans, but one is cold and the other is not. "Oh well, how much difference can that make?" the professor asks, and is immediately interrupted by student protests. When cold, canned, and regular Cokes and Pepsis are produced for the "final" test, the professor asks what else might influence tasters' opinions. Expectations based on knowledge of brand names, order of tasting the products, and many other considerations may emerge. But whatever the specifics, this demonstration gets students actively involved in generating their own ideas about the kinds of factors one must consider when making scientific comparisons. Even a simple taste test turns out to be fairly complicated after all!

Individual or Small Group Work

Walking students through examples and demonstrations such as these illustrating the importance of scientific thinking during class is one approach that we have used successfully. However, even though there are many connections between scientific course content and daily life that are obvious to us, students are new to this way of thinking. The integration of techniques that require more active involvement has been demonstrated to result in better outcomes for students (Freeman et al., 2014). Practice—and having some time to reflect and prepare—helps. This practice can take many forms and can include work done alone or with peers either in or out of class.

We start by asking students to generate their own examples of how to utilize the process of scientific thinking in their own personal or professional lives. However, there are some practical issues to consider when attempting this approach. Often, such questions are met with silence and blank looks, or the same bright student in the front row answers *yet again*. In asking the class as a whole to answer a specific question, telling students that there are dozens (or more) right answers to a question tends to boost the rate of responding. Consider a question about the concept of operational definitions, such as, "What actions or outcomes might indicate stress?" As we mentioned previously, if students are told that there are potentially hundreds of correct answers, participation skyrockets; students feel more comfortable playing these odds. Further, if individual students are generating their own responses rather than simply listening to a list of examples from the professor, their more active involvement is likely to increase their comprehension of that concept.

While an instructor-led discussion of scientific thinking with the entire class is a great way to introduce this topic to students and model the process for them, having students generate ideas within pairs or small groups is an effective strategy to increase their involvement while simultaneously increasing their understanding of the scientific process. An added benefit of having students work in small groups to answer a question is that they typically end up referring to and comparing class notes. This comparison of class notes with others is an effective way for students to fill in gaps in their own understanding. But a more beneficial consequence of exposure to the construals of others may be to help sharpen their ability to understand the content of psychology more scientifically. Practice in seeing how others think about such complex principles and processes may help to free students from being bound to their own perspective. In time, their intuitive, subjective approach to understanding principles of psychology may be supplanted by a more objective, scientific point of view.

Active learning strategies that involve entire classes or groups of almost any size also have been devised. For example, the understanding of scientific thinking in individual students can be assessed in class through the use of *one-minute papers* that serve as a concept check, short *reaction assignments* focusing on "the most interesting, important, or surprising idea in class today was…," or *reading quizzes* that may boost the pre-class reading of course materials. These can be set up within an electronic course management system (e.g., Blackboard) and automatically graded, thereby all but eliminating an investment of time on the part of the instructor after the quizzes are set up. Inviting students to *suggest class activities and demonstrations* engages their thinking about concepts to a greater extent than simply passively experiencing the ones you produce for them (Balch, 2012; Thieman et al., 2009). Assignments completed out of class can help students to reflect on complex ideas and solidify their comprehension. Reporting and discussing all students' individual responses during the following class meeting provide deeper processing of content through repetition, reflection, and critical analysis.

Cooperative learning strategies are, by their very nature, active approaches and include such tasks as asking students to *summarize each other's in-class answers or comments*. Asking students to *generate test and/or quiz questions* in small groups is an effective way to focus them on the important aspects of course content. Most *review sessions* consist of a course summary by the professor. A twist on this to enhance scientific thinking is to hold a review session in which students work in small groups to answer questions posed by the professor. If done properly, *role-playing* engages students extensively as they act out the characteristic symptoms of major depression, for example, while others try to identify the disorder. *Panel discussions*, which may or may not involve role-playing as well, may also be used effectively to help students learn complex content. Also, turning course content into games can work in at least two ways: Creating questions from the materials reinforces learning, while playing games hones mastery of the content as well (Duke University Center for Instructional Technology, 2014; University of Minnesota Center for Teaching and Learning, 2008).

This approach to scientific thinking in which students generate their own examples and applications can be implemented in a variety of ways, but it's essential to incorporate some degree of feedback so that students can quickly learn whether or not they are on the right track. This is relatively easily accomplished in a smaller class, in which the instructor can walk around the room providing feedback to small groups. In a larger class, the use of the think-pair-share model, in which students work in pairs to formulate a response to a problem and then offer a response as a team, can allow for instructor comments on at least a few examples volunteered by students. Scaffolding or modeling of the process may be helpful to them. If the instructor deconstructs a concept or skill into its components and then ensures that students understand and learn these parts it may facilitate students' ability to do the same. Through scaffolding, the instructor simultaneously models the steps, skills, and processes required in scientific thinking. By demonstrating each of these to students, the instructor serves as an exemplar for behaviors that students can incorporate into their own thinking and actions.

Out-of-Class Assignments

Of course, in-class activities are great, but class time is always limited—there never seems to be enough time to do everything we want to do! Fortunately, there are many ways in which out-of-class work can help us achieve our goal of giving students practice in applying scientific thinking. Of course, any of the activities we've listed above can also be utilized as out-of-class assignments. However, when completed out of class, these assignments can be more involved and require more application to promote students' ability to connect psychology to daily life. For example, these days it is almost impossible to avoid the claims made by the anti-vaccine movement, with a number of media personalities promoting the claim that vaccines are toxic (e.g., Vani Hari, aka FoodBabe) and cause autism (e.g., Jenny McCarthy). The personal appeals made by these media-savvy individuals are often more compelling than the findings reported in scientific journals, but there has been a pro-science response of late, which has resulted in a number of student-friendly explanations of the science that has consistently failed to demonstrate a link between vaccines and autism. We can provide students with one anti-vaccine and one pro-vaccine popular press style website and ask them to critically evaluate the claims in each. This could even be taken a step further, with students asked what advice they would give to new parents who are confused by the contradictory media messages. The first part of this assignment can be integrated into the research methods section of Intro, with a discussion of how scientists systematically seek answers to questions and why this way of knowing is superior to anecdotes or personal experience, while the second part can be integrated into the section on developmental psychology. Through such activities, the complex abstractions presented in the text and in class seem as if they relate to their lives, after all.

Another possible out-of-class assignment is one used by our colleague Kelly Goedert in response to the often-asked "has there ever been a study" question. If a student asks such a question and you don't know the answer, you can give the entire class the task of doing a PsycInfo search to find the answer to that question and submitting a brief description of the study at the next class meeting. In this way, students are further reinforced for their attitude of scientific inquiry. A few extra credit points can go a long way in providing motivation for this assignment! In this way, responding to the question takes very little class time and students are reinforced for asking and answering such questions with an extra credit opportunity. We can even take a few minutes at the start of the next class to ask students to briefly report on what they found, thereby providing an answer to the original question for the entire class.

While these techniques can be useful, we have all seen times when students fail to generalize a concept from one assignment to another. However, there are other types of assignments that can help enhance transfer of this skill. For example, Holmes and Beins (2009) suggested using strategies of attitude change, such as counter-attitudinal advocacy in which students, regardless of their actual beliefs, would be required to generate reasons that scientific research in psychology is valued, even essential to the discipline as a whole. The logic is that attitude change will occur because students look at the arguments they've formulated and will infer that they must really believe the point of view they've constructed (i.e., self-perception of attitudes). In this way more positive attitudes toward the use of the scientific approach are generated, which is particularly important among students whose goal is to enter into the helping professions.

LOGISTICAL ISSUES IN INTEGRATION OF CRITICAL THINKING INTO INTRODUCTORY PSYCHOLOGY

Of course, the manner in which an instructor chooses to implement the integration of scientific thinking is dependent on many factors, including course structure (mostly lecture, discussion-based, flipped, etc.) and class size. Assignments that are perfectly reasonable for a class of 25 may be untenable for a class of 100, even if one is lucky enough to have help from a teaching assistant. (As a side note, we have found that undergraduates are often eager for the opportunity to serve as teaching assistants, even on a volunteer basis, and can provide valuable course assistance.) However, even in large classes some degree of student interaction and assessment other than multiple-choice exams is desirable, and grading large numbers of written assignments can be made easier with the use of a rubric. Further, a grading rubric made available to students provides guidance for completing assignments and may help to reduce the ambiguity that sometimes "paralyzes" students—especially at the start of an academic term. Beginning students often crave more direction as they figure out "the college game." With practice in the application of scientific thinking, most students will develop their analytical and writing skills sufficiently throughout the semester to make grading their work much less burdensome by the end of the term.

Holmes and Beins (2009) warn ambitious psychology professors that even the cleverest examples and most engaging activities concerning research may not affect students' perceptions of the *importance* of scientific thinking. They frame the issue in motivational terms and state that unless students recognize and invest in this point of view, they will not be motivated to internalize this approach to the discipline or the world. The authors suggest infusing research across all psychology courses—content as well as methods courses—and incorporating it throughout the entirety of the course. In other words, it should not be given cursory treatment at the beginning of the term and then seldom mentioned again. While a detailed treatment of this approach is beyond the scope of this chapter, we can conclude that if we want our students to generalize what they are learning about scientific thinking in Introductory Psychology, we must incorporate as much as of this as possible across the curriculum to reinforce to our students the importance of scientific thinking as a key feature of the discipline.

ASSESSING THE EFFECTIVENESS OF SCIENTIFIC THINKING INSTRUCTION

Assessment in Individual Courses

Clearly, assessment is relatively straightforward when scientific thinking is integrated into individual course activities such as writing assignments or exam questions. Of course, developing new assignments and exam questions is always time-consuming and prone to trial and error, but the supplementary materials used by you or your colleagues for your Research Methods course can be a great source of ideas. The material may need to be simplified to be appropriate for an Introductory Psychology audience, and coordination is necessary with faculty who teach Research Methods to ensure that students are not being given the same assignments, but assignments and exam questions that require the use of critical thinking abound in these materials. For example, students can evaluate the types of claims made by a website promoting an herbal remedy for attention deficit hyperactivity disorder (ADHD) or eye movement desensitization and reprocessing (EMDR) as a treatment for anxiety and can consider how a study could be designed to test these claims (Morling & Smith, 2012). Another source is sample multiple-choice and free-response questions from old Advanced Placement (AP) Psychology exams, which are available (with scoring criteria!) on the College Board website (College Board, 2015). For example, a free-response question in 2013 provided students with a sample experiment and asked them to identify an operational definition, an ethical flaw, and a research design flaw and explain how the flaws could be corrected.

One caveat here is to make sure one "closes the loop," so to speak, by providing students with feedback on their performance and possibly making additional changes to the way in which course material on scientific thinking is presented to ensure that students understand the concepts.

Assessment Across the Curriculum

Given the importance and integration of scientific thinking within Introductory Psychology, a single assessment measure—or even multiple measures completed during the Introductory course—may be desirable. However, assessment within only one course fails to address the broader goal of having students habitually use scientific thinking processes across multiple courses as well as outside the classroom. In fact, many of us would agree that the optimal assessment of scientific thinking would be whether or not students use this approach in their daily lives. Practically speaking this presents some difficulty, but it is feasible to assess scientific thinking at various points during a student's undergraduate career.

The APA's *Guidelines for the Undergraduate Psychology Major* (2013) have suggestions for relevant standardized tests with national norms. These include (but are not limited to) the California Critical Thinking Skills Test (Insight Assessment, 2013), the Halpern Critical Thinking Assessment (Halpern, 2010), and the Psychological Critical Thinking Exam (Lawson, 1999). Although these are labeled critical thinking, not scientific thinking, it is clear that many of the concepts assessed in these measures overlap with scientific thinking, broadly defined.

There are many ways in which the use of nationally normed tests is beneficial, not the least of which is the ability to make comparisons between students nationally and those at a particular institution (e.g., Pliske, Caldwell, Calin-Jageman, & Taylor-Ritzler, 2015). This also reduces the time necessary for the creation of such tests and provides ready-made validated and reliable assessments, thereby saving valuable time and resources. However, the use of such tests is not without potential issues. Perhaps first among these is implementation, including whether or not to require students to complete such a test and, if so, how to motivate them to perform to the best of their ability. There are a variety of models for such testing, including requiring a certain score for graduation or making it a required component of a capstone course. Another consideration is the cost to purchase and score the assessment and whether that should be borne by the department or the student.

In light of these considerations, it might be more desirable for a department to develop an in-house assessment of scientific thinking. This can take several forms. For example, students in our department who do research with a faculty member also enroll in a three-credit course titled Laboratory Research Experience. This class meets once per week and students discuss a variety of issues related to research, practice reading primary journal articles, and give brief presentations on the research in their laboratory. Students' grades in the course are determined by both their lab and course performance. As such, students in this course would be an ideal population within which to assess scientific thinking. In particular, pre and post assessments could be done at the start and end of the semester to assess changes in scientific thinking that occur as a result of the research experience. Another possibility is the use of a scientific thinking rubric when grading class presentations to determine the extent to which students have acquired specific scientific thinking skills. A similar assessment could be done in other courses ranging from Introductory Psychology to Research Methods to a capstone course to assess changes over the students' undergraduate career.

Another possibility is the use of a process analogous to the scoring of written AP exam responses by a committee of experienced course instructors. Papers already assigned in upper-level courses might be evaluated by the general faculty or an "assessment committee" for student proficiency in the principles of scientific thinking. A comprehensive rubric would facilitate evaluation of the scope of students' grasp of scientific psychology. Once again, the key to success with such a technique is feedback to instructors regarding areas in which students struggle so that relevant material can be emphasized in specific courses.

Our department has recently implemented a requirement that all our majors maintain an electronic portfolio (see Vigorito, 2011, for a discussion of the creation of electronic portfolios). Students add assignments from required core psychology courses (e.g., Orientation to the Psychology Major, Research Methods, Senior Seminar) as well as any other artifacts they believe reflect skills they have acquired throughout the course of their undergraduate career. For example, students in our department may include a reflection piece from Internship, in which they explore what they've learned about themselves and their career path from their internship experience; a PowerPoint presentation describing an ongoing study to which they are contributing in Laboratory Research Experience; or a literature review demonstrating their skills in reviewing and summarizing the literature on a particular topic. It is our hope that this portfolio serves a dual purpose: Not only can we use it for assessment, but our students can create a repository of their work demonstrating their skills and abilities that will be useful as they transition to full-time employment or graduate school. As we have just begun the e-portfolio program we have not conducted any assessment of its contents but we plan to do so in the near future.

In response to the changes being implemented on the 2015 Medical College Admissions Test, which will now include items on social and behavioral sciences, there is likely to be increased interest in efficient and effective means by which to integrate scientific thinking skills into the Introductory Psychology course. In a recent investigation, students in Introductory Psychology were exposed to a course module utilizing active learning techniques to address scientific thinking (Stevens & Witkow, 2014). At the end of the semester, these students showed superior performance on final exam questions related to scientific reasoning as compared to students in a standard Introductory Psychology course. Not only do these findings demonstrate that scientific thinking can be taught successfully in Introductory Psychology, but also they provide a means by which to assess these skills. The integration of a single course module on scientific thinking and its assessment could be repeated in courses typically required for psychology majors, thereby underscoring the importance of this skill for our students. Inclusion of such a module would likely be more beneficial to them, in big-picture terms, than the more conventional and typically superficial rehash of research methods in every course.

INCORPORATING SCIENTIFIC THINKING INTO A CROWDED CLASS CALENDAR

Of course, all of these activities, assignments, and assessments take time: they fill precious class time and can require substantial modifications to our courses, adding to our already overburdened professional lives. While we can offer no suggestions for the problem of what seems to be ever-increasing responsibilities on the part of faculty, we can attempt to address the concern regarding use of class time and make suggestions regarding how to organize class meetings with a greater emphasis on scientific thinking.

The struggle instructors have between choosing breadth versus depth of coverage in the Introductory course is not new. However, experts in psychology teaching and learning are generally of the opinion that there are substantial benefits to emphasizing depth over breadth. As an example, in an interview psychology teaching expert Jane Halonen admits to having struggled with striking a balance between covering the breadth of course content and taking the time to help students learn how to think scientifically (Irons, 2007). She reports that it used to be difficult for her to give up class time spent dealing with the vast territory that comprises Introductory Psychology, but that the enduring skill of thinking deeply and critically (i.e., scientifically) is much more beneficial to students than learning current "facts" in the discipline that will change over time. The scientific mindset—and skill set—endures long after the known facts at any given time are modified by new information. We can teach students "the facts" or we can teach them how to discover and think about "the facts"; the latter is, no doubt, more valuable in the long run. Halonen says that she would "rather invest class time in activities that will promote enduring learning on a narrower range of content than fool myself into thinking that because I've covered the content I've done a good job of teaching and the students have done a good job of learning" (Irons, 2007, p. 265). In addition, it is worth pointing out that psychology majors and minors will take specialized upper-level courses that will expand upon content areas in the field.

As dedicated students of psychology ourselves, we likely chose to continue our education in the field partly out of interest: it's all fascinating to us! Over the years we have refined our lectures and activities to produce the best outcomes for our students. We know which topics most interest them and which are a struggle to teach, and research methods is often in the latter category. The Introductory course is our opportunity to explain to potential majors what the field is (and is not) about, and for nonmajors it may be our only opportunity to do so. In light of all that, what material should we drop from our course in favor of a greater emphasis on scientific thinking?

We suspect that most of us —especially those with control issues—are not quite ready to give up all of our "professing" in the classroom; not quite yet anyway, but we can at least reprioritize our classes. We know that it's scary going "off script" and that change in something so central as one's customary teaching practices is difficult, no matter how adventurous we may believe ourselves to be. Our integration of student-centered scientific thinking activities into classes has increased over time, and primarily been a shift in emphasis. My experience (ST) has been that not much course content had to be omitted to accommodate the changes, as I have typically taken a hands-on approach to class meetings, incorporating demonstrations, video clips, and discussions interspersed throughout. I found that increasing integration of scientific thinking activities required more deliberation. It's not something easy to do spontaneously—at least for me. I found that more structured activities and assignments were necessary as a foundation for conducting classes in this way. At present, I devote approximately half of most class meetings to the students' participatory learning, but can't see myself ever getting to the "no more lecture" stage advocated by some (Lambert, 2012).

Here is a kind of "play by play" of a typical class meeting that would occur fairly early on in a semester as an introduction to psychological research methods. I would briefly (in 10 minutes or so) introduce the topic of research methods in a broad overview at the beginning of a class meeting and then have the students participate in the "Coke-Pepsi Challenge" (described previously). Throughout the demonstration I ask for student input about whether the numerous comparisons that I propose makes sense from a scientific perspective; that is, does it give us information obtained through systematic, controlled, and unbiased means? After several minutes of this discussion, I travel around the classroom, asking students (not at random, per se, but not waiting for volunteers) for responses to my questions about relevant terms and concepts. I might start with definitions of independent variables (IVs) and dependent variables (DVs), then ask others for examples of IVs and DVs, ask whether or not specific research questions can be tested via manipulation of IVs, segue into the issue of the nonexperimental nature of some interesting topics, and then introduce various nonexperimental research techniques. I would frequently pause for concept checks both by soliciting questions and by "randomly" asking questions to check students' understanding. I make certain to circulate throughout the entire auditorium—sitting in the back row will not protect you in my classroom. (In fact, you may get special attention if you try to hide.) Depending on how time goes, I might ask students to work together in small groups (of five or so) to propose a study of a topic that interests them. We have groups report their ideas to the larger class, who is asked to play devil's advocate to critique weaknesses of proposals. I make sure to emphasize that criticisms are to be based solely on scientific grounds; it is not "our job" to criticize ideas or interests. And because students may propose some outlandish methods from time to time, this makes an interesting platform from which to launch a discussion of the ethics of research. Toward the end of the class meeting, I take 5–10 minutes to throw out major terms and concepts and inform students that they are responsible for knowing and understanding these. I let them know that this is their best chance to ask questions of me (aside from office hours, of course). At this point, we're out of time—and energy, most likely—but we can honestly say that for those who have engaged with the material, learning has happened.

I follow pretty much the same procedure for each topic covered during the semester, but have not found it necessary to decrease the number of topics that I am able to incorporate across the semester with this structure. Instead there has been more of a shift in priorities from transferring information to the more challenging goal of achieving student understanding and assimilation of course content. Because many of our Intro classes have enrollments of 80 students or above, it sometimes seems that my primary role in these class meetings is more or less to control the chaos by keeping things on task during student-led activities. However, I firmly believe that students come away from these classes both with a more genuine understanding of the particular topic of study that day and most certainly with a better understanding of, and greater appreciation for, the scientific basis of psychology. Most importantly, they are getting the *self-generated practice* they need to make scientific thinking a more automatic—even default—way of construing their world. This ability will be invaluable to them across time and domains for the rest of their lives.

We need to teach our students to adopt a scientific mindset: to be able to discern critical information to be evaluated more fully, and not simply accepted as true—especially within the domain of psychology. It is critical that students understand the quality and limits of research reported in the popular media—what it can and can't tell us—and how to evaluate it accurately for themselves. Most students have learned through experience to be skeptical consumers of products and services; we need to help them to become skeptical consumers of ideas and "facts" in the same way. For all the emphasis on critical thinking skills in education over the past years, it seems that many students (and lots of regular people, too) still lack this fundamental and important ability—or they may simply fail to generalize this "academic skill" into their everyday lives. They need this kind of specialized training in multiple courses across the curriculum to help them "internalize" it by the time they graduate. The lasting beauty of teaching scientific thinking is that it is truly applicable to any topic within the field of psychology, which provides multiple opportunities to have our students practice its application. By reinforcing this skill we are giving our students tools to become better psychologists and better consumers of information, which will benefit them throughout their lives.

So start as small as you need to, but we strongly advise you to try this approach and to give it a reasonable chance. It will likely be difficult at first, as it was for us. Our integration of student-centered scientific thinking activities into classes was quite gradual. In fact, we first committed to using only a small part of one class meeting per week for more student-based activities during class time, while increasing relevant out of class assignments. But as with everything else (like scientific thinking for students), it will come more naturally with practice. But we believe that, as we found, even your trial efforts will be sufficiently reinforced by the obvious results you will begin to see in your students' understanding, and in the improved quality of your classroom meetings. If you've ever wished for more involved students—and who hasn't—this is the way to make it happen. Take a chance; we believe that your efforts will be abundantly rewarded!

References

Abbey, A. (1982). Sex differences in attributions for friendly behavior: Do males misperceive females' friendliness? *Journal of Personality and Social Psychology, 42,* 830–838. doi:10.1037/0022-3514.42.5.830

Abrahamson, C. E. (2006). Motivating students through personal connections: Storytelling as pedagogy in introductory psychology. In D. S. Dunn & S. L. Chew (Eds.), *Best practices for teaching introduction to psychology* (pp. 245–258). Mahwah, NJ: Erlbaum.

Abrams, L. (2013). *Study: Facebook may improve memory.* Retrieved from http://www.theatlantic.com/health/archive/2013/02/study-facebook-may-improve-memory/273439/

Adelman, C. (2004). *The empirical curriculum: Changes in postsecondary course-taking, 1972–2000.* Washington, DC: U.S. Department of Education.

Ainsworth, M. D., & Bell, S. M. (1970). Attachment, exploration, and separation: Illustrated by the behavior of one-year-olds in a strange situation. *Child Development, 41,* 49–67.

Ainsworth, M. D., Blehar, M. C., Waters, E., & Wall, S. (1978). *Patterns of attachment: Assessed in the strange situation and at home.* Hillsdale, NJ: Erlbaum.

Aldwin, C. M. (2007). *Stress, coping, and development: An integrative perspective* (2nd ed.). New York, NY: Guilford Press.

Ambady, N., & Rosenthal, R. (1992). Thin slices of expressive behavior as predictors of interpersonal consequences: A meta-analysis. *Psychological Bulletin, 111,* 256–274. doi:0033-2909/92

Ambrose, S. A., Bridges, M. W., DiPietro, M., Lovett, M. C., & Norman, M. K. (2010). *How learning works: 7 research-based principles for smart teaching.* San Francisco, CA: Jossey-Bass.

American Association of Colleges & Universities. (2011). *The LEAP vision for learning: Outcomes, practices, and employers' views.* Retrieved from http://www.aacu.org/sites/default/files/files/LEAP/leap_vision_summary.pdf

American Association of Colleges & Universities. (n.d.). *VALUE rubrics*. Retrieved from https://aacu.org/value-rubrics

American Psychological Association. (2007). *APA guidelines for the undergraduate psychology major*. Retrieved from http://www.apa.org/ed/resources.html

American Psychological Association. (2009). *Assessment cyberguide for learning goals and outcomes*. Retrieved from http://www.apa.org/ed/governance/bea/assessment-cyberguide-v2.pdf

American Psychological Association. (2011). *National standards for high school psychology curricula*. Retrieved from http://www.apa.org/education/k12/national-standards.aspx

American Psychological Association. (2013). *APA guidelines for the undergraduate psychology major: Version 2.0*. Retrieved from http://www.apa.org/ed/precollege/undergrad/index.aspx

American Psychological Association. (2014). *Strengthening the common core of the introductory psychology course*. Washington, DC: American Psychological Association, Board of Educational Affairs. Retrieved from www.apa.org/ed/governance/bea/intro-psych-report.pdf

American Psychological Association. Presidential Task Force on Enhancing Diversity. (2005). *Final report of the task force on enhancing diversity*. Retrieved from http://www.apa.org/pi/oema/resources/taskforce-report.pdf

American Psychological Association. Presidential Task Force on Psychology's Contribution to End Homelessness. (2010). *Helping people without homes: The role of psychologists and recommendations to advance research, training, practice, and policy*. Retrieved from http://www.apa.org/pi/ses/resources/publications/end-homeless-ness.aspx

Anderson, L. W., & Krathwohl, D. R. (Eds.). (2001). A taxonomy for learning, teaching, and assessing: A revision of Bloom's taxonomy of educational objectives. Boston, MA: Allyn & Bacon (Pearson Education Group).

Angelo, T. A., & Cross, K. P. (1993). *Classroom assessment techniques: A handbook for college teachers* (2nd ed.). San Francisco, CA: Jossey-Bass Publishers.

Angler, J., Huntley, D., & Reinherz, L. (Writers, Directors, Producers). (2003). Worried sick [Television Series episode; DVD]. In Chedd Angier (Production Company), *Scientific American Frontiers*. United States: Connecticut Public Television.

AP Central—The AP Psychology Exam. (n.d.). Retrieved from http://apcentral.collegeboard.com/apc/public/exam/exam_information/2088.html

Appiah, K. (2005). College makeover: "Learn statistics. Go abroad." *Slate*. Retrieved from http://www.slate.com/articles/news_and_politics/college_week/2005/11/college_makeover_7.html

Appleby, D. C. (2006). Defining, teaching, and assessing critical thinking in introductory psychology. In D. S. Dunn & S. L. Chew (Eds.), *Best practices for teaching introduction to psychology* (pp. 57–69). Mahwah, NJ: Lawrence Erlbaum associates, Inc.

Arbib, M. A. (2011). From mirror neurons to complex imitation in the evolution of language and tool use. *Annual Review of Anthropology, 40*, 257–273.

Asch, S. E. (1951). Effects of group pressure upon the modification and distortion of judgment. In H. Guetzkow (Ed.), *Groups, leadership, and men* (pp. 177–190). Pittsburgh, PA: Carnegie Press.

Assefi, S. L., & Garry, M. (2003). Absolut® memory distortions: Alcohol placebos influence the misinformation effect. *Psychological Science, 14*, 77–80.

Associated Press. (2014, August 25). Guide to developments in Ferguson police shooting. *The New York Times.* Retrieved from http:/www.nytimes.com

Association for University and College Counseling Center Directors. (2013). *Association for University and College Counseling Center Directors annual survey.* Retrieved from http://files.cmcglobal.com/AUCCCD_Monograph_Public_2013.pdf

Association of American Colleges & Universities. (2007). *College learning for the new global century.* Retrieved from http://www.aacu.org/leap/documents/GlobalCentury_final.pdf

Association of American Colleges and Universities. (2004). Our students' best work: A framework for accountability worthy of our mission. *Peer Review, 7*, 25–28.

Association of American Colleges and Universities. (2008). *How should colleges assess and improve student learning?* Washington, DC: Hart Research Associates.

Association of American Colleges and Universities. (2010). *Raising the bar: Employers' views on college learning in the wake of the economic downturn.* Washington, DC: Hart Research Associates.

Babad, E. (1997). Wishful thinking among voters: Motivational and cognitive influences. *International Journal of Public Opinion Research, 9*, 105–125. doi:10.1093/ijpor/9.2.105

Back, M. D., & Vazire, S. (2012). Knowing our personality. In S. Vazire & T. D. Wilson (Eds.), *Handbook of self-knowledge* (pp. 131–156). New York, NY: Guilford Press.

Bahrick, H. P. (1979). Maintenance of knowledge: Questions about memory we forgot to ask. *Journal of Experimental Psychology: General, 108*, 296.

Balcetis, E., & Dunning, D. (2006). See what you want to see: Motivational influences on visual perception. *Journal of Personality and Social Psychology, 91*, 612–625. doi:10.1037/0022-3514.91.4.612

Balcetis, E., & Dunning, D. (2010). Wishful seeing: More desired objects are seen as closer. *Psychological Science, 21*, 147–152. doi:10.1177/0956797609356283

Balch, W. (2012). A free-recall demonstration versus a lecture-only control: Learning benefits. *Teaching of Psychology, 39*, 34–37.

Baneshi, A. R., Samadieh, H., & Ejei, J. (2015). Achievement goals and academic performance: The mediating role of achievement and self regulated emotions. *Journal of Psychology, 18*, 381–392.

Barkow, J. H., Cosmides, L., & Tooby, J. (1992). *The adapted mind: Evolutionary psychology and the generation of culture.* New York, NY: Oxford University Press.

Barney, S. T. (2006). Capitalizing on the self-referencing effect in general psychology: A preliminary study. *Journal of Constructivist Psychology, 20*, 87–97. doi:10.1080/10720530600992915

Barr, R. B., & Tagg, J. (1995, November/December). From teaching to learning: A new paradigm for undergraduate education. *Change, 27*, 12–25.

Barrows, H. S. (1986). A taxonomy of problem-based learning methods. *Medical Education, 20*, 481–486.

Barrows, H. S. (1996). Problem-based learning in medicine and beyond: A brief overview. *New Directions for Teaching and Learning, 1996*, 3–12.

Bauer, K. N., Orvis, K. A., Ely, K., & Surface, E. A. (2015). Re-examination of motivation in learning contexts: Meta-analytically investigating the role type of motivation plays in the prediction of key training outcomes. *Journal of Business and Psychology, 31*, 33–50. doi:10.1007/s10869-015-9401-1

Bean, J. C. (2011). *Engaging ideas: The professor's guide to integrating writing, critical thinking, and active learning into the classroom* (2nd ed.). San Francisco, CA: Jossey-Bass.

Beck, A. T. (2008). The evolution of the cognitive model of depression and its neurobiological correlates. *American Journal of Psychiatry, 165*, 969–977. doi:10.1176/appi.ajp.2008.08050721

Beers, G. W., & Bowden, S. (2005). The effect of teaching method on long-term knowledge retention. *The Journal of Nursing Education, 44*, 511–514.

Bell, K. E., & Limber, J. E. (2010). Reading skill, textbook marking, and course performance. *Literacy Research and Instruction, 49*, 56–67.

Ben-Zeev, T., Fein, S., & Inzlicht, M. (2005). Arousal and stereotype threat. *Journal of Experimental Social Psychology, 41*, 174–181.

Benasi, V. A., Overson, C. E., & Hakala, C. M. (2014). *Applying the science of learning in education: Infusing psychological science into the curriculum.* Retrieved from the Society for the Teaching of Psychology website: http://teachpsych.org/ebooks/asle2014/index.php

Benedetti, F. (2008). *Placebo effects: Understanding the mechanisms in health and disease.* New York, NY: Oxford University Press.

Benedetti, F., Maggi, G., Lopiano, L., Lanotte, M., Rainero, I., Vighetti, S., & Pollo, A. (2003). Open versus hidden medical treatments: The patient's knowledge about a therapy affects the therapy outcome. *Prevention & Treatment, 6*, 1a.

Bennett, D. J., & McKinney, V. M. (2000). Juggling topics in introductory psychology: Applying newly learned concepts to a newly learned skill. *Teaching of Psychology, 27*, 121–122.

Berdan, S. N. (2015, April 17). Study abroad could be so much better. *The Chronicle of Higher Education,* p. A52.

Bernstein, D. J., Addison, W., Altman, C., Hollister, D., Komarraju, M., Prieto, L., … Shore, C. (2010). Toward a scientist-educator model of teaching psychology. In D. F. Halpern (Ed.), *Undergraduate education in psychology: A blueprint for the future of the discipline* (pp. 29–45). Washington, DC: American Psychological Association.

Bjork, E. L., & Bjork, R. A. (2011). Making things hard on yourself, but in a good way: Creating desirable difficulties to enhance learning. In M. A. Gernsbacher, R. W. Pew, L. M. Hough, & J. R. Pomerantz (Eds.), *Psychology and the real world: Essays illustrating fundamental contributions to society* (pp. 55–64). New York, NY: Worth Publishers.

Bjork, R. A. (1994). Memory and metamemory considerations in the training of human beings. In J. Metcalfe & A. Shimamura (Eds.), *Metacognition: Knowing about knowing* (pp. 185–205). Cambridge, MA: MIT Press.

Black, P., & Wiliam, D. (2009). Developing the theory of formative assessment. *Educational Assessment, Evaluation and Accountability, 21*, 5–31. doi: 10.1007/s11092-008-9068-5

Blackwell, L. S., Trzesniewski, K. H., & Dweck, C. S. (2007). Implicit theories of intelligence predict achievement across an adolescent transition: A longitudinal study and an intervention. *Child Development, 78,* 246–263.

Bok, D. (2006). *Our underachieving colleges: A candid look at how much students learn and why they should be learning more.* Princeton, NJ: Princeton University Press.

Bolt, M. (2011). *Teacher's resource binder to accompany Myers' psychology for AP.* New York, NY: Worth Publishers.

Boring, E. G. (1930). A new ambiguous figure. *American Journal of Psychology, 42,* 444–445.

Bradshaw, G. L., & Anderson, J. R. (1982). Elaborative encoding as an explanation of levels of processing. *Journal of Verbal Learning and Verbal Behavior, 21,* 165–174.

Brady, S., Hard, B. & Gross, J. (2016). *Reappraising test anxiety increases academic performance for first-year college students.* Manuscript under review.

Bransford, J. D., & Johnson, M. K. (1972). Contextual prerequisites for understanding: Some investigations of comprehension and recall. *Journal of Verbal Learning and Verbal Behavior, 11,* 717–726.

Bressan, P., & Kramer, P. (2015). Human kin detection. *Wires Cognitive Science, 6,* 299–311.

Brewer, C. L., et al. (1993). Curriculum. In T. V. McGovern (Ed.), *Handbook for enhancing undergraduate education in psychology* (pp. 161–182). Washington, DC: American Psychological Association.

Brown, J. D. (2012). Understanding the better than average effect: Motives (still) matter. *Personality and Social Psychology Bulletin, 38,* 209–219. doi:10.1177/0146167211432763

Brown, P. C., Roediger, H. L., & McDaniel, M. A. (2014). *Make it stick: The science of succesful leanring.* Cambridge, MA: The Belkap Press of Harvard University Press.

Bruff, D. (2013, September 3). Students as producers: An introduction. *Center for Teaching, Vanderbilt University.* Retrieved from http://cft.vanderbilt.edu/2013/09/students-as-producers-an-introduction/

Bryson, B. (1999). Coming home. In *I'm a stranger here myself: Notes on returning to America after twenty years away* (pp. 1–8). New York: NY: Broadway Books.

Bushman, B. J., Gollwitzer, M., & Cruz, C. (2014). There is broad consensus: Media researchers agree that violent media increase aggression in children, and pediatricians and parents concur. *Psychology of Popular Media Culture,* advance online publication. doi:10.1037/ppm0000046

Buskist, W., & Groccia, J. E. (Eds.). (2011). *Evidence-based teaching: New directions for teaching and learning* (Vol. 128). San Francisco, CA: Jossey-Bass.

Buss, D. M. (1989). Sex differences in human mate preferences: Evolutionary hypotheses tested in 37 cultures. *Behavioral and Brain Sciences, 12,* 1–49.

Buss, D. M. (1995). Evolutionary psychology: A new paradigm for psychological science. *Psychological Inquiry, 6,* 1–30.

Buss, D. M. (2010). Why students love evolutionary psychology and how to teach it. *American Psychological Association Education Directorate, 20,* 1–9.

Buss, D. M. (2011). *Evolutionary psychology: The new science of the mind* (4th ed.). Boston, MA: Pearson.

Buss, D. M. (2013). Seven tools for teaching evolutionary psychology. In D. S. Dunn, R. R. Gurung, K. Z. Naufel, & J. H. Wilson (Eds.), *Controversy in the psychology classroom: Using hot topics to foster critical thinking* (pp. 49–64). Washington, DC: American Psychological Association.

Butler, A. C., & Roediger, H. L. (2008). Feedback enhances the positive effects and reduces the negative effects of multiple-choice testing. *Memory & Cognition, 36*, 604–616.

Butler, A. C., Karpicke, J. D., & Roediger, H. L., III. (2007). The effect of type and timing of feedback on learning from multiple-choice tests. *Journal of Experimental Psychology: Applied, 13*, 273.

Bybee, R. W. (2004). Evolution and the nature of science. In R. W. Bybee (Ed.), *Evolution in perspective* (pp. 15–24). Arlington, VA: National Science Teachers Association Press.

Cacioppo, J. T. (2007). The structure of psychology. *Observer, 20*, 3, 50–51.

Cacioppo, J. T. (2013). Psychological science in the 21st century. *Teaching of Psychology, 40*, 304–309.

Caldwell, J. E. (2007). Clickers in the large classroom: Current research and best-practice tips. *CBE Life Sciences Education, 6*, 9–20.

Camp, G. (1996). Problem-based learning: A paradigm shift or a passing fad? *Medical Education Online, 1*, 1–6.

Carpenter, S. K. (2014). Spacing and interleaving of study and practice. In V. A. Benassi, C. E. Overson, & C. M. Hakala (Eds.), *Applying the science of learning in education: Infusing psychological science into the curriculum* (pp. 131–141). Society for the Teaching of Psychology. Retrieved from the Society for the Teaching of Psychology website: http://teachpsych.org/ebooks/asle2014/index.php

Carroll, A. E. (2015). More consensus on coffee's benefits than you might think. *The New York Times.* Retrieved from http://www.nytimes.com/2015/05/12/upshot/more-consensus-on-coffees-benefits-than-you-might-think.html

Carroll, D. W. (2008). Brief report: A simple stimulus for student writing and learning in the introductory psychology course. *North American Journal of Psychology, 10*, 159–164.

Carroll, J. B. (1993). *Human cognitive abilities: A survey of factor-analytic studies.* Cambridge, UK: Cambridge University Press.

Caspi, A., Sugden, K., Moffitt, T. E., Taylor, A., Craig, I. W., Harrington, H.,… Poulton, R. (2003). Influence of life stress on depression: Moderation by a polymorphism in the 5-HTT gene. *Science, 301*, 386–389.

Ceci, S. J., & Liker, J. K. (1986). A day at the races: A study of IQ, expertise, and cognitive complexity. *Journal of Experimental Psychology: General, 115*, 255–266.

Cepeda, N. J., Pashler, H., Vul, E., Wixted, J. T., & Rohrer, D. (2006). Distributed practice in verbal recall tasks: A review and quantitative synthesis. *Psychological Bulletin, 132*, 354–380. doi: 10.1037/0033-2909.132.3.354

Charlton, S. (1999). Do you see what I see? Examining eyewitness testimony. In L. T. Benjamin, B. F. Nodine, R. M. Ernst, & C. B. Broeker (Eds.), *Activities handbook for the teaching of psychology* (Vol. 4, pp. 194–199). Washington, DC: American Psychological Association.

Chase, W. G., & Simon, H. A. (1973). Perception in chess. *Cognitive Psychology, 4*, 55–81.

Chew, S. L. (2006). Seldom in doubt but often wrong: Addressing tenacious student misconceptions. In D. S. Dunn & S. L. Chew (Eds.), *Best practices for teaching introduction to psychology* (pp. 211–223). Mahwah, NJ: Erlbaum.

Chew, S. L. (2010). Improving classroom performance by challenging student misconceptions about learning. *Observer, 23*, 51–54.

Chew, S. L. (2014). Helping students to get the most out of studying. In V. A. Benassi, C. E. Overson, & C. M. Hakala (Eds.), *Applying science of learning in education: Infusing psychological science into the curriculum* (pp. 215–223). Washington, DC: Society for the Teaching of Psychology. Retrieved from http://teachpsych.org/ebooks/asle2014/index.php

Chew, S. L., Bartlett, R. M., Dobbins, J. E., Hammer, E. Y., Kite, M. E., Loop, T. F., … Rose, K. C. (2010). A contextual approach to teaching: Bridging methods, goals, and outcomes. In D. F. Halpern (Ed.), *Undergraduate education in psychology: A blueprint for the future of the discipline* (pp. 95–112). Washington, DC: American Psychological Association.

Christensen, B. K., Carney, C. E., & Segal, Z. V. (2006). Cognitive processing models of depression. In D. J. Stein, D. J. Kupfer, & A. F. Schatzberg (Eds.), *Textbook of mood disorders*. Washington, DC: American Psychiatric Publishing.

Cialdini, R. B. (2005). What's the best secret device for engaging student interest? The answer is in the title. *Journal of Social and Clinical Psychology, 24*, 22–29.

Ciccarelli, S. K., & White, J. N. (2015). *Psychology: An exploration* (3rd ed.). Boston, MA: Pearson.

Cimino, G. & Foschi, R. (2014). Northerners versus southerners: Italian anthropology and psychology faced with the "southern question." *History of Psychology, 17*, 282–295.

Cizek, G. J. (2010). An introduction to formative assessment. In H. L. Andrade & G. J. Cizek (Eds.), *Handbook of formative assessment* (pp. 3–17). New York, NY: Routledge.

Clancy, S. A. (2005). *Abducted: How people come to believe they were kidnapped by aliens.* Cambridge, MA: Harvard University Press.

Clark, C. M., & Bjork, R. A. (2014). When and why introducing difficulties and errors can enhance instruction. In V. A. Benassi, C. E. Overson, & C. M. Hakala (Eds.), *Applying the science of learning in education: Infusing psychological science into the curriculum* (pp. 20–30). Society for the Teaching of Psychology. Retrieved from the Society for the Teaching of Psychology website: http://teachpsych.org/ebooks/asle2014/index.php

Clark, R. C., Nguyen, F., & Sweller, J. (2011). *Efficiency in learning: Evidence-based guidelines to manage cognitive load.* San Francisco, CA: John Wiley & Sons.

Coderre, T. J., Mogil, J. S., & Bushnell, M. C. (2003). The biological psychology of pain. In M. Gallagher & R. J. Nelson (Eds.), *Handbook of psychology: Biological psychology* (Vol. 3, pp. 237–268). Hoboken, NJ: John Wiley & Sons.

Cohen, D. (2015). Cultural Psychology. In M. Mikulincer, P. R. Shaver, E. Borgida, & J. A. Bargh (Eds.), *APA handbook of personality and social psychology, Volume 1: Attitudes and social cognition* (pp. 415–456). Washington, DC: American Psychological Association. doi:10.1037/14341-014

Cole, M., & Packer, M. (2011). Culture and cognition. In K. D. Keith (Ed.), *Cross-Cultural psychology: Contemporary themes and perspectives* (pp. 133–159). Malden, MA: Wiley-Blackwell.

College Board. (2015). *AP central: The AP psychology exam.* Retrieved from http://apcentral.collegeboard.com/apc/public/exam/exam_information/2088.html

Connor-Greene, P. A. (2007). Observation or interpretation? Demonstrating unintentional subjectivity and interpretive variance. *Teaching of Psychology, 34*, 167–171. doi:10.1080/00986280701498541

Correll, J., Park, B., Judd, C. M., & Wittenbrink, B. (2007). The police officer's dilemma: Using ethnicity to disambiguate potentially threatening individuals. *Journal of Personality and Social Psychology, 83*, 1314–1329. doi:10.1037//0022-3514.83.6.1314

Cortright, R. N., Collins, H. L., Rodenbaugh, D. W., & DiCarlo, S. E. (2003). Student retention of course content is improved by collaborative-group testing. *Advances in Physiology Education, 27*, 102–108.

Craik, F. I., & Tulving, E. (1975). Depth of processing and the retention of words in episodic memory. *Journal of Experimental Psychology-General, 104*, 268–294. doi:10.1037//0096-3445.104.3.268

Crandall, C. S., Bahns, A. J., Warner, R., & Schaller, M. (2011). Stereotypes as justifications of prejudice. *Personality and Social Psychology Bulletin, 37*, 1488–1498. doi:10.1177/0146167211411723

Cranney, J., & Dunn, D. S. (Eds.). (2011). *Educating the psychologically literate citizen: Foundations and global perspectives.* New York, NY: Oxford University Press.

Craske, M. G., & Waters, A. M. (2005). Panic disorders, phobias, and generalized anxiety disorder. *Annual Review of Clinical Psychology, 1*, 197–225.

Crossgrove, K., & Curran, K. L. (2008). Using clickers in nonmajors- and majors-level biology courses: Student opinion, learning, and long-term retention of course material. *CBE-Life Sciences Education, 7*, 146–154.

Crum, A. J., Salovey, P., & Achor, S. (2013). Rethinking stress: The role of mindsets in determining the stress response. *Journal of Personality and Social Psychology, 104*, 716–733. Retrieved from http://psycnet.apa.org.fetch.mhsl.uab.edu/index.cfm?fa=-search.displayrecord&uid=2013-06053-001

Cush, D. T., & Buskist, W. (1997). Future of introductory or general psychology course each year. *Teaching of Psychology, 24*, 119–122.

Dahl, J. (2012). *Hot and bothered: Experts say violent crime rises with the heat.* Retrieved from http://www.cbsnews.com/news/hot-and-bothered-experts-say-violent-crime-rises-with-the-heat/

Darwin, C. (1872). *The expression of the emotions in man and animals.* London, UK: John Murray.

Darwin, C. (1959). *The origin of the species by means of natural selection.* London, UK: John Murray.

Davey, M., & Bosman, J. (2014, November 24). Protests flare after Ferguson police officer is not indicted. *The New York Times.* Retrieved from http://www.nytimes.com

Davis, B. G. (2009). *Tools for teaching.* San Francisco, CA: Jossey-Bass.

Day, E., Espejo, J., Kowollik, V., Boatman, P., & McEntire, L. (2007). Modeling the links between the need for cognition and the acquisition of a complex skill. *Personality and Individual Differences, 42*, 201–212.

De Groot, J. B., Semin, G. R., & Smeets, M. M. (2014). Chemical communication of fear: A case of male–female asymmetry. *Journal of Experimental Psychology: General, 143*, 1515–1525.

Dehaene, S. (2011). *The number sense: How the mind creates mathematics.* New York, NY: Oxford University Press.

Deresiewicz, W. (2014). *Excellent sheep: The miseducation of the American elite and the way to a meaningful life.* New York, NY: The Free Press.

Diamond, R. M. (2008). *Designing and assessing courses and curricula: A practical guide* (3rd ed.). San Francisco, CA: Jossey-Bass.

DiBattista, D., & Kurzawa, L. (2011). Examination of the quality of multiple-choice items on classroom tests. *Canadian Journal for the Scholarship of Teaching and Learning, 2,* 4.

Dollinger, S. J. (1990). The illusion of control. In V. P. Makosky, C. C. Sileo, L. G. Whittemore, C. P. Landry, & M. L. Skutley (Eds.), *Activities handbook for the teaching of psychology* (Vol. 3, pp. 170–171). Washington, DC: American Psychological Association.

Dovidio, J. F., Gaertner, S. L., & Nier, J. A. (2004). Contemporary racial bias: When good people do bad things. In A. G. Miller (Ed.), *The social psychology of good and evil* (pp. 141–167). New York, NY: Guilford Press.

Duke University Center for Instructional Technology. (2014). *Active learning.* Retrieved from http://cit.duke.edu.get-ideas/teaching-strategies/active-learning/

Dumbauld, B. (2014). *Which college majors have the lowest (and highest) unemployment rates?* Retrieved from http://www.straighterline.com/blog/college-majors-lowest -highest-unemployment-rates/

Duncan, B. L. (1976). Differential social perception and attribution of intergroup violence: Testing the lower limits of stereotyping of blacks. *Journal of Personality and Social Psychology, 34,* 590–598.

Dunlosky, J., Rawson, K. A., Marsh, E. J., Nathan, M. J., & Willingham, D. T. (2013). Improving students' learning with effective learning techniques: Promising directions from cognitive and educational psychology. *Psychological Science in the Public Interest, 14,* 4–58. doi:10.1177/1529100612453266

Dunn, D. S. (1989). Demonstrating a self-serving bias. *Teaching of Psychology, 16,* 21–22. doi:10.1207/s15328023top1601_6

Dunn, D. S., Brewer, C. L., Cautin, R. L., Gurung, R. A. R., Keith, K. D., McGregor, L. N., . . . Voigt, M. J. (2010). The undergraduate psychology curriculum: Call for a core. In D. F. Halpern (Ed.), *Undergraduate education in psychology: A blueprint for the future of the discipline* (pp. 47–61). Washington, DC: American Psychological Association.

Dunn, D. S., & Halonen, J. S. (2017). *The psychology major's companion: Everything you need to know to get where you want to go.* New York, NY: Worth.

Dunn, D. S., & Hammer, E. D. (2014). On teaching multicultural psychology. In F. L. Leong, L. Comas-Díaz, G. C. Nagayama Hall, V. C. McLoyd, & J. E. Trimble (Eds.), *APA handbook of multicultural psychology, Vol. 1: Theory and research* (pp. 43–58). Washington, DC: American Psychological Association. doi:10.1037/14189-003

Dunn, D. S., Baker, S. C., Landrum, E., Mehrotra, C. M., & McCarthy, M. (Eds.). (2012). *Assessing teaching and learning in psychology: Current and future perspectives.* Belmont, CA: Cengage.

Dunn, D. S., Brewer, C. L., Cautin, R. L., Gurung, R. A., Keith, K. D., McGregor, L. N., . . . Voight, M. J. (2010). The undergraduate psychology curriculum: Call for a core. In D. F. Halpern (Ed.), *Undergraduate education in psychology: A blueprint for the future of the discipline* (pp. 47–61). Washington, DC: American Psychological Association.

Dunn, D. S., Gurung, R. A. R., Naufel, K. Z., & Wilson, J. H. (Eds.). (2013). *Controversy in the psychology classroom: Using hot topics to foster critical thinking.* Washington, DC: American Psychological Association.

Dunn, D. S., McCarthy, M. A., Baker, S. C., & Halonen, J. S. (2011). *Using quality benchmarks for assessing and developing undergraduate programs.* San Francisco, CA: Jossey-Bass.

Dunn, D. S., Mehrotra, C., & Halonen, J. S. (Eds.). (2004). *Measuring up: Educational assessment challenges and practices for psychology.* Washington, DC: American Psychological Association.

Dunn, D. S., Saville, B. K., Baker, S. C., & Marek, P. (2013). Evidence-based teaching: Tools and techniques that promote learning in the psychology classroom. *Australian Journal of Psychology, 65,* 5–13. doi:10.1111/ajpy.12004

Dunn, D., Baker, S. C., Mehrotra, C. M., Landrum, R. E., & McCarthy, M. (2012). *Assessing teaching and learning in psychology: Current and future perspectives.* Belmont, CA: Cengage Learning.

Dunning, D., & Balcetis, E. (2013). Wishful seeing: How preferences shape visual perception. *Current Directions in Psychological Science, 22,* 33–37. doi:10.1177/0963721412463693

Dunning, D., & Sherman, D. A. (1997). Stereotypes and tacit inference. *Journal of Personality and Social Psychology, 73,* 459–471. doi:10.1037/0022-3514.73.3.459

Dutton, D. G., & Aron, A. P. (1974). Some evidence for heightened sexual attraction under conditions of high anxiety. *Journal of Personality and Social Psychology, 30,* 510–517.

Dweck, C. (2008). *Mindset: The new psychology of success.* New York, NY: Ballantine.

Dweck, C. S. (2007). The secret to raising smart kids. *Scientific American Mind, 18,* 37–43.

Dweck, C. S. (2008, February). *Mindsets: Impact on brain processes, motivation & learning.* Paper presented at Learning and the Brain Conference, San Francisco Airport Marriott Hotel.

Ebbinghaus, H. E. (1964). *Memory: A contribution to experimental psychology.* New York, NY: Dover. (Original work published 1885.)

Eisenstaedt, R. S., Barry, W. E., & Glanz, K. (1990). Problem-based learning: Cognitive retention and cohort traits of randomly selected participants and decliners. *Academic Medicine, 65,* S11–S12.

Ekirch, A. R. (2005). *At day's close: Night in times past.* New York, NY: Norton.

Ekirch, A. R. (2015). Sleep we have lost. Retrieved from http://www.history.vt.edu/Ekirch/sleepcommentary.html

Elrod, S. (2014). Quantitative reasoning: The next "across the curriculum" movement. *Peer Review, 16,* 5–9.

Fallahi, C. R., Wood, R. M., Austad, C. S., & Fallahi, H. (2006). A program for improving undergraduate students' basic writing skills. *Teaching of Psychology, 22,* 171–175.

Fernald, L. D. (1989). Tales in a textbook; Learning in the traditional and narrative modes. *Teaching of Psychology, 16,* 121–124.

Festinger, L., & Carlsmith, J. M. (1959). Cognitive consequences of forced compliance. *The Journal of Abnormal and Social Psychology, 58,* 203–210. doi:10.1037/h0041593

Few, S. (2004). *Show me the numbers: Designing tables and graphs to enlighten.* Oakland, CA: Analytics Press.

Fillon, M. (2013). *Fitness magazines and eating disorders: Is there a relationship?* Retrieved from http://psychcentral.com/lib/fitness-magazines-and-eating-disorders-is-there-a-relationship/000285

Fink, L. D. (2003). *Creating significant learning experiences: An integrated design approach to designing college courses.* San Francisco, CA: Jossey-Bass/Wiley.

Fischhoff, B., Slovic, P., & Lichtenstein, S. (1977). Knowing with certainty: The appropriateness of extreme confidence. *Journal of Experimental Psychology: Human Perception and Performance, 3*, 552–564. doi:10.1037//0096-1523.3.4.552

Fiske, S. T. (1998). Stereotyping, prejudice, and discrimination. In D. T. Gilbert, S. T. Fiske, & G. Lindzey (Eds.), *The handbook of social psychology* (4th ed., Vols. 1 and 2, pp. 357–411). New York, NY: McGraw-Hill.

Fiske, S. T., & Russell, A. M. (2010). Cognitive processes. In J. F. Dovidio, M. Hewstone, P. Glick, & V. M. Esses (Eds.), *The Sage handbook of prejudice, stereotyping, and discrimination* (pp. 115–133). Los Angeles, CA: Sage.

Fiske, S. T., & Tablante, C. B. (2015). Stereotyping: Processes and content. In M. Mikulincer, P. R. Shaver, E. Borgida, & J. A. Bargh (Eds.), *APA handbook of personality and social psychology, Volume 1: Attitudes and social cognition* (pp. 457–507). Washington, DC: American Psychological Association. doi:10.1037/14341-015

Forgas, J. P., & Bower, G. H. (1987). Mood effects on person-perception judgments. *Journal of Personality and Social Psychology, 53*, 53–60. doi:10.1037/0022-3514.53.1.53

Forgas, J. P., Goldenberg, L., & Unkelbach, C. (2009). Can bad weather improve your memory? An unobtrusive field study of natural mood effects on real-life memory. *Journal of Experimental Social Psychology, 45*, 254–257. doi:10.1016/j.jesp.2008.08.014

Forscher, P. S., & Devine, P. G. (2014). Breaking the prejudice habit: Automaticity and control in the context of a long-term goal. In J. W. Sherman, B. Gawronski, & Y. Trope (Eds.), *Dual-process theories of the social mind* (pp. 468–482). New York, NY: Guilford Press.

Freeman, S.., Eddy, S. L., McDonough, M., Smith, M. K., Okoroafor, N., Jordt, H., & Wenderoth, M. P. (2014). Active learning increases student performance in science, engineering, and mathematics. *PNAS Proceedings of the National Academy of Sciences of the United States of America, 111*, 8410–8415. doi:10.1073/pnas.1319030111

Friedrich, J. (1996). On seeing oneself as less self-serving than others: The ultimate self-serving bias? *Teaching of Psychology, 23*, 107–109. doi:10.1207/s15328023top2302_9

Fujita, K., Trope, Y., Liberman, N., & Levin-Sagi, M. (2006). Construal levels and self-control. *Journal of Personality and Social Psychology, 90*, 351–367.

Gallup, June 2, 2014. In U.S., 42% believe creationist view of human origins. Retrieved from http://www.gallup.com/poll/170822/believe-creationist-view-human-origins.aspx

Garcia, J., Lasiter, P. S., Bermudez-Rattoni, F., & Deems, D. A. (1985). A general theory of aversion learning. *Annals of the New York Academy of Sciences, 443*, 8–21.

Gardner, P. (2007). *Moving up or moving out of the company? Factors that influence the promoting or firing of new college hires.* Collegiate Employment Research Institute, Michigan State University (Report 1-2007). East Lansing, MI: Michigan State University.

Garry, M., & Gerrie, M. P. (2005). When photographs create false memories. *Current Directions in Psychological Science, 14*, 321–324. doi:10.1111/j.0963-7214.2005.00390.x

Garry, M., & Polaschek, D. L. (2000). Imagination and memory. *Current Directions in Psychological Science, 9*, 6–10. doi:10.1111/1467-8721.00048

Gee, N. R., & Dyck, J. L. (1998). Using a videotape clip to demonstrate the fallibility of eyewitness testimony. *Teaching of Psychology, 25*, 138–140. doi:10.1207/s15328023top2502_18

Gergen, K. J, Gulerce, A., Lock, A., & Misra, G. (1996). Psychological science in cultural context. *American Psychologist, 51*, 496–503.

Gergen, K. J. (1973). Social psychology as history. *Journal of Personality and Social Psychology, 26*, 309–320.

Gigerenzer, G., & Gaissmaier, W. (2011). Heuristic decision making. *Annual Review of Psychology, 62*, 451–482.

Gilbert, D. T., & Malone, P. S. (1995). The correspondence bias. *Psychological Bulletin, 117*, 21–38.

Gilley, B. H., & Clarkston, B. (2014). Collaborative testing: Evidence of learning in a controlled in-class study of undergraduate students. *Journal of College Science Teaching, 43*, 83–91.

Giuliodori, M. J., Lujan, H. L., & DiCarlo, S. E. (2008). Collaborative group testing benefits high- and low-performing students. *Advances in Physiology Education, 32*, 274–278.

Glymour, B., Glymour, C., & Glymour, M. (2008). Watching social science: The debate about the effects of exposure to televised violence on aggressive behavior. *American Behavioral Scientist, 51*, 1231–1259. doi:10.1177/0002764207312020

Golombok, S., Mellish, L., Jennings, S., Casey, P., Tasker, F., & Lamb, M. E. (2014). Adoptive gay father families: Parent–child relationships and children's psychological adjustment. *Child Development, 85*, 456–458. doi:10.1111/cdev.12155

Golombok, S., Perry, B., Burston, A., Murray, C., Mooney-Somers, J., Stevens, M., & Golding, J. (2003). Children with lesbian parents: A community study. *Developmental Psychology, 39*, 20–33. doi:10.1037/0012-1649.39.1.20

Gordon, A. K., & Kaplar, M. E. (2002). A new technique for demonstrating the actor-observer bias. *Teaching of Psychology, 29*, 301–303. doi:10.1207/S15328023TOP2904_10

Gould, J. (2002). *Concise handbook of experimental methods for the behavioral and biological sciences*. Boca Raton, FL: CRC Press.

Grasha, A., (1987). *Practical applications of psychology*. Upper Saddle River, NJ: Pearson Education, Inc.

Grawe, N. D., Lutsky, N. S., & Tassave, C. J. (2009). A rubric for assessing quantitative reasoning in written arguments. *Numeracy, 3*, article 3. Retrieved from http://scholarcommons.usf.edu/numeracy/vol3/iss1/art3

Gray, P. (1996). Incorporating evolutionary psychology into the teaching of psychology. *Teaching of Psychology, 23*, 207-214.

Griggs, R. A., & Jackson, S. L. (2013). Introductory psychology textbooks: An objective analysis update. *Teaching of Psychology, 40*, 163–168.

Griggs, R. A., & Marek, P. (2001). Similarity of introductory psychology textbooks: Reality or illusion? *Teaching of Psychology, 28*, 254–256. doi:10.1207/S15328023TOP2804_03

Guilbault, R. L., Bryant, F. B., Brockway, J. H., & Posavac, E. J. (2004). A meta analysis of research on hindsight bias. *Basic and Applied Social Psychology, 26,* 103–117.

Gurung, R. A. R. (2013). Introduction. In S. Afful, J. J. Good, J. Keeley, S. Leder, & J. J. Stiegler-Balfour (Eds.), *Introductory psychology teaching primer: A guide for new teachers of PSYCH 101* (pp. 3–5). Retrieved from the Society for the Teaching of Psychology website: http://teachpsych.org/ebooks/intro2013/index.php

Gurung, R. A. R. (2014). Assessing the impact of instructional methods. In V. A. Benassi, C. E. Overson, & C. M. Hakala (Eds.), *Applying the science of learning in education: Infusing psychological science into the curriculum* (pp. 185–193). Society for the Teaching of Psychology. Retrieved from the Society for the Teaching of Psychology website: http://teachpsych.org/ebooks/asle2014/index.php

Gurung, R. A. R. (2014a). *Health psychology: A cultural approach* (3rd ed.). Belmont, CA: Cengage.

Gurung, R. A. R. (2014b). *Discover psychology: Instructor's manual* (digital edition). Champaign, IL: DEF Publishers. doi:www.nobaproject.com

Gurung, R. A. R., & Schwartz, E. (2009). *Optimizing teaching and learning: Pedagogical research in practice.* Malden, MA: Blackwell.

Gurung, R. A. R., & Wilson, J. H. (Eds.). (2013). *Doing the scholarship of teaching and learning, measuring systematic changes to teaching and improvements in learning: New directions for teaching and learning* (Vol. 136). San Francisco, CA: Jossey-Bass.

Hake, R. R. (1998). Interactive-engagement versus traditional methods: A six-thousand-student survey of mechanics test data for introductory physics courses. *American Journal of Physics, 66,* 64–74.

Haladyna, T. M., Downing, S. M., & Rodriguez, M. C. (2002). A review of multiple-choice item-writing guidelines for classroom assessment. *Applied Measurement in Education, 15,* 309–333.

Halonen, J. S. (2014, October 10). *Building postmodern departments.* Meeting of Florida Council of Undergraduate Curriculum and Assessment. Tallahassee, FL.

Halpern, D. F. (2002). Teaching for critical thinking: A four-part model to enhance thinking skills. In S. F. Davis & W. Buskist (Eds.), *The teaching of psychology: Essays in honor of Wilbert J. McKeachie and Charles L. Brewer* (pp. 91–105). Mahwah, NJ: Lawrence Erlbaum Associates, Inc.

Halpern, D. F. (2010). *Halpern Critical Thinking Assessment.* Retrieved from http://www.lafayettelifesciences.com/product_detail.asp?ItemID=2050

Halpern, D. F. (2014). *Thought and knowledge: An introduction to critical thinking* (5th ed.). New York, NY: Psychology Press.

Halpern, D. F. (Ed.). (2010). *Undergraduate education in psychology: A blueprint for the future of the discipline.* Washington, DC: American Psychological Association.

Halpern, D. F., & Butler, H. A. (2011). Critical thinking and the education of psychologically literate citizens. In J. Craney & D. S. Dunn (Eds.), *Educating the psychologically literate citizen: Foundations and global perspectives* (pp. 27–40). New York, NY: Oxford University Press.

Hamilton, D. L., Sherman, S. J., Way, N., & Percy, E. J. (2015). Convergence and divergence in perceptions of persons and groups. In M. Mikulincer, P. R. Shaver, J. F. Dovidio, & J. A. Simpson (Eds.), *APA handbook of personality and social psychology, Volume 2: Group processes* (pp. 229–261). Washington, DC: American Psychological Association. doi:10.1037/14342-009

Handelsman, M. M. (2006). Teaching ethics in introductory psychology. In D. S. Dunn & S. L. Chew (Eds.), *Best practices for teaching introduction to psychology* (pp. 159–175). Mahwah, NJ: Erlbaum.

Hansen, K., Gerbasi, M., Todorov, A., Kruse, E., & Pronin, E. (2014). People claim objectivity after knowingly using biased strategies. *Personality and Social Psychology Bulletin, 40,* 691–699. doi:10.1177/0146167214523476

Hardin, E. E. (2013, March). *Teaching controversial topics.* Invited presentation at the 25th Annual Southeastern Conference on the Teaching of Psychology (SETOP), Atlanta, GA.

Hart, P. D. (2013). *It takes more than a major: Employer priorities for college learning and student success.* Report conducted on behalf of the Association of American Colleges and Universities. Retrieved from http://www.aacu.org/leap/documents/2013_ EmployerSurvey.pdf

Hastorf, A., & Cantril, H. (1954). They saw a game: A case study. *Journal of Abnormal and Social Psychology, 49,* 129–134.

Hattie, J. (2015). The applicability of visible learning to higher education. *Scholarship of Teaching and Learning in Psychology, 1,* 79–91.

Hattie, J. A. C., & Timperley, H. (2007). The power of feedback. *Review of Educational Research, 77,* 81–112. doi: 10.3102/003465430298487

Hattie, J. A. C., & Yates, G. C. R. (2014). Using feedback to promote learning. In V. A. Benassi, C. E. Overson, & C. M. Hakala (Eds.), *Applying the science of learning in education: Infusing psychological science into the curriculum* (pp. 45–58). Society for the Teaching of Psychology. Retrieved from the Society for the Teaching of Psychology website: http://teachpsych.org/ebooks/asle2014/index.php

Hendrick, B. (2010). *Family dinners reduce teen drug use: Survey shows teens who don't eat dinner with families are more likely to abuse drugs.* Retrieved from http://www.webmd .com/parenting/news/20100922/family-dinners-reduce-teen-drug-use

Henrich, J., Heine, S. J., and Norenzayan, A. (2010). The weirdest people in the world? *Behavioral and Brain Sciences, 33,* 61-83.

Heppner, F. (2007). *Teaching the large college class: A guidebook for instructors with multitudes.* San Francisco, CA: Jossey-Bass.

Herman, W. E. (2010). *How much do students remember from an introductory psychology course?* Poster presented at the Annual Conference on the Teaching of Psychology: Ideas & Innovations, Tarrytown, NY.

Hermann, A. D., & Foster, D. A. (2008). Fostering approachability and classroom participation during the first day of class: Evidence for a reciprocal interview activity. *Active Learning in Higher Education, 9,* 141–153.

Hermann, A. D., Foster, D. A., & Hardin, E. E. (2010). Does the first week of class matter? A quasi-experimental investigation of student satisfaction. *Teaching of Psychology, 37,* 79–84. doi:10.1080/00986281003609314

Hidi, S., & Renninger, K. A. (2006). The four-phase model of interest development. *Educational Psychologist, 41,* 111–127.

Hill, G. W., IV. (2006). Foreword. In D. S. Dunn & S. L. Chew (Eds.), *Best practices for teaching introduction to psychology* (pp. xiii–xiv). Mahwah, NJ: Erlbaum.

Hinds, P. J., Patterson, M., & Pfeffer, J. (2001). Bothered by abstraction: The effect of expertise on knowledge transfer and subsequent novice performance. *Journal of Applied Psychology, 86,* 1232–1243.

Hitti, M. (2005). *One drink daily may drop risk of mental decline: Moderate alcohol consumption helps women with mental skills.* Retrieved from http://www.webmd.com/mental-health/news/20050119/one-drink-daily-may-drop-risk-of-mental-decline

Hock, R., (2009). *Forty studies that changed psychology. Explorations in the history of psychological research.* Upper Saddle River, NJ: Pearson.

Hockenbury, S., Nolan, S., & Hockenbury, D. (2015). *Psychology* (7th ed.). New York, NY: Worth Publishers.

Hokayem, H., & BouJaoude, S. (2008). College students' perceptions of the theory of evolution. *Journal of Research in Science Teaching, 45,* 395–419.

Holmes, J. D., & Beins, B. C. (2009). Psychology is a science: At least some students think so. *Teaching of Psychology, 36,* 5–11.

Hom, H. L., Ciaramitaro, M., & Valentine, K. D. (2012). I knew-it-all-along, just not on my own. *Teaching of Psychology, 39,* 297–300. doi:10.1177/0098628312461483

Howell, J. L., & Shepperd, J. A. (2011). Demonstrating the correspondence bias. *Teaching of Psychology, 38,* 243–246. doi:10.1177/0098628311421320

Huba, M. E., & Freed, J. E. (2000). *Learner-centered assessment on college campuses: Shifting the focus from teaching to learning.* Needham Heights, MA: Allyn & Bacon.

Hyman, I. E., Jr., Husband, T. H., & Billings, J. F. (1995). False memories of childhood experiences. *Applied Cognitive Psychology, 9,* 181–197.

Hyman, I. Sarb, B., & Wise-Swanson B. (2014). Failure to see money on a tree: Inattentional blindness for objects that guided behavior. *Frontiers in Psychology, 5,* 356.

Insight Assessment. (2013). *California Critical Thinking Skills Test.* San Jose, CA: California Academic Press. Retrieved from http://www.insightassessment.com/Products/Products-Summary/Critical-Thinking-Skills-Tests/California-Critical-Thinking-Skills-Test-CCTST/(language)/eng-US

Ioannidis, J. P. A. (2005). Contradicted and initially stronger effects in highly cited clinical research. *Journal of the American Medical Association, 294,* 218–228.

Irons, J. (2007). On following your bliss: An interview with Jane S. Halonen. *Teaching of Psychology, 34,* 263–267.

Jackson, J. W. (2000). Demonstrating the concept of illusory correlation. *Teaching of Psychology, 27,* 273–276.

Jacowitz, K. E., & Kahneman, D. (1995). Measures of anchoring in estimation tasks. *Personality and Social Psychology Bulletin, 21,* 1161–1166. doi:10.1177/01461672952111004

James, W. (1890). *The principles of psychology* (Vol. 1). New York, NY: Henry Holt and Company.

James, W. (1890). The scope of psychology. In *The principles of psychology* (Vol. I, pp. 1–11). New York, NY: Henry Holt and Co.

Jamieson, J. P., Mendes, W. B., Blackstock, E., & Schmader, T. (2010). Turning the knots in your stomach into bows: Reappraising arousal improves performance on the GRE. *Journal of Experimental Social Psychology, 46,* 208–212.

Johnson, C., & Mullen, B. (1994). Evidence for the accessibility of paired distinctiveness in distinctiveness-based illusory correlation in stereotyping. *Personality and Social Psychology Bulletin, 20,* 65–70.

Johnson, M. K. (2007). Reality monitoring and the media. *Applied Cognitive Psychology, 21,* 981–993. doi:10.1002/acp.1393

Johnson, S. C., Dweck, C. S., & Chen, F. S. (2007). Evidence for infants' internal working models of attachment. *Psychological Science, 18*, 501–502.

Jones, E. E., & Harris, V. A. (1967). The attribution of attitudes. *Journal of Experimental Social Psychology, 3*, 1–24.

Jorgensen, T. D., & Marek, P. (2013). Workshops increase students' proficiency at identifying general and APA-style writing errors. *Teaching of Psychology, 40*, 294–299.

Jurik, V., Gröschner, A., & Seidel, T. (2014). Predicting students' cognitive learning activity and intrinsic learning motivation: How powerful are teacher statements, student profiles, and gender? *Learning and Individual Differences, 32*, 132–139. doi:10.1016/j.lindif.2014.01.005

Kahneman, D. (2011). *Thinking fast and slow.* New York, NY: Farrar, Straus, and Giroux.

Kahneman, D., & Tversky, A. (1984). Choices, values, and frames. *American Psychologist, 39*, 341–350.

Karpicke, J. D., & Roediger, H. L. (2007). Repeated retrieval during learning is the key to long-term retention. *Journal of Memory and Language, 57*, 151–162. doi:10.1016/j.jml.2006.09.004

Karpicke, J. D., & Roediger, H. L. (2008). The critical importance of retrieval for learning. *Science, 319*, 966–968.

Karpicke, J. D., Butler, A. C., & Roediger, H. L., III. (2009). Metacognitive strategies in student learning: Do students practice retrieval when they study on their own? *Memory, 17*, 471–479. doi:10.1080/09658210802647009

Kasser, T., & Sharma, Y. S. (1999). Reproductive freedom, educational equality, and females' preference for resource-acquisition characteristics in mates. *Psychological Science, 10*, 374–377.

Keith, K. D. (2011). Introduction to cross-cultural psychology. In K. D. Keith (Ed.), *Cross-cultural psychology: Contemporary themes and perspectives* (pp. 3–19). Malden, MA: Wiley-Blackwell.

Kelley, C. M., & Jacoby, L. L. (2012). Past selves and autobiographical memory. In S. Vazire, & T. D. Wilson (Eds.), *Handbook of self-knowledge* (pp. 293–309). New York, NY: Guilford Press.

Kelley, H. H. (1950). The warm-cold variable in first impressions of persons. *Journal of Personality, 18*, 431–439.

Kennedy, K. A., & Pronin, E. (2008). When disagreement gets ugly: Perceptions of bias and the escalation of conflict. *Personality and Social Psychology Bulletin, 34*, 833–848. doi:10.1177/0146167208315158

Kennedy, K. A., & Pronin, E. (2012). Bias perception and the spiral of conflict. In J. Hanson (Ed.), *Ideology, psychology, and law* (pp. 410–446). New York, NY: Oxford University Press. doi:10.1093/acprof:oso/9780199737512.003.0017

Kinkade, S. (2005). A snapshot of the status of problem-based learning in US medical schools, 2003–04. *Academic Medicine, 80*, 300–301.

Kirschner, P. A., Sweller, J., & Clark, R. E. (2006). Why minimal guidance during instruction does not work: An analysis of the failure of constructivist, discovery, problem-based, experiential, and inquiry-based teaching. *Educational Psychologist, 41*, 75–86.

Kite, M. E. (1991). Observer biases in the classroom. *Teaching of Psychology, 18*, 161–164. doi:10.1207/s15328023top1803_7

Koenig, A. M., & Dean, K. K. (2011). Cross-cultural differences and similarities in attribution. In K. D. Keith (Ed.), *Cross-cultural psychology: Contemporary themes and perspectives* (pp. 475–493). Malden, MA: Wiley-Blackwell.

Kornell, N., & Bjork, R. A. (2007). The promise and perils of self-regulated study. *Psychonomic Bulletin & Review, 14*, 219–224.

Krathwohl, D. R. (2002). A revision of Bloom's taxonomy: An overview. *Theory into Practice, 41*, 212–218.

Krull, D. S. (2001). On partitioning the fundamental attribution error: Dispositionalism and the correspondence bias. In G. B. Moskowitz (Ed.), *Cognitive social psychology: The Princeton symposium on the legacy and future of social cognition* (pp. 211–227). Mahwah, NJ: Erlbaum.

Kunda, Z. (1987). Motivation and inference: Self-serving generation and evaluation of causal theories. *Journal of Personality and Social Psychology, 53*, 636–647.

Kushlev, K., & Dunn, E. W. (2012). Affective forecasting: Knowing how we will feel in the future. In S. Vazire, & T. D. Wilson (Eds.), *Handbook of self-knowledge* (pp. 277–292). New York, NY: Guilford Press.

Kuyper, H., & Dijkstra, P. (2009). Better-than-average effects in secondary education: A 3-year follow-up. *Educational Research and Evaluation, 15*, 167–184. doi:10.1080/13803610902804416

Lambert, C. (2012). Twilight of the lecture. *Harvard Magazine, 2012.* Retrieved from http://www.harvard magazine.com/2012/03/twilight-of-the-lecture

Landrum, R. E. (2014, July). *Why skills matter: Undergraduate psychology education and a legacy at risk.* Presentation at the Stanford University Psychology One Conference, Palo Alto, CA.

Landrum, R. E., & Gurung, R. A. R. (2013). The memorability of introductory psychology revisited. *Teaching of Psychology, 40*, 222–227. doi:10.1177/009862813487417

Landrum, R. E., & Harrold, R. (2003). What employers want from psychology graduates. *Teaching of Psychology, 30*, 131–133.

Landrum, R. E., Beins, B. C., Bhalla, M., Brakke, K., Briihl, D. S., Curl-Lanager, R. M., . . . Van Kirk, J. J. (2010). Desired outcomes of an undergraduate education in psychology from departmental, student, and societal perspectives. In D. F. Halpern (Ed.), *Undergraduate education in psychology: A blueprint for the future of the discipline* (pp. 145–160). Washington, DC: American Psychological Association.

Landrum, R. E., Hettich, P. I., & Wilner, A. (2010). Alumni perceptions of workforce readiness. *Teaching of Psychology, 37*, 97–106.

Laney, C., & Loftus, E. F. (2013). Recent advances in false memory research. *South African Journal of Psychology, 43*, 137–146. doi:10.1177/0081246313484236

Lasswell, M. E., Ruch, F. L., Gorfein, D. S., & Warren, N. (1981). Person perception. In L. T. Benjamin, Jr., & K. D. Lowman (Eds.), *Activities handbook for the teaching of psychology* (pp. 185–187). Washington, DC: American Psychological Association.

Lavine, H., Jost, J. T., & Lodge, M. (2015). Political cognition and its normative implications for the "democratic experiment": Theory, evidence, and controversy. In M. Mikulincer, P. R. Shaver, E. Borgida, & J. A. Bargh (Eds.), *APA handbook of personality and social psychology, Volume 1: Attitudes and social cognition* (pp. 721–752). Washington, DC: American Psychological Association. doi:10.1037/14341-023

LaVoie, A. L. (1987). The autonomic nervous system. In V. P. Makosky, L. G. Whittemore, & A. M. Rogers (Eds.), *Activities handbook for the teaching of psychology* (Vol. 2, pp. 286–288). Washington, DC: American Psychological Association.

Lawson, T. J. (1999). Assessing psychological critical thinking as a learning outcome for psychology majors. *Teaching of Psychology, 26*, 207–209.

Lawson, T. J. (2003). A psychic-reading demonstration designed to encourage critical thinking. *Teaching of Psychology, 30*, 251–253.

Leahey, T. H. (2013). *A history of psychology: From antiquity to modernity* (7th ed.). New York, NY: Pearson.

LEAP. (2015). *Liberal education and America's promise.* Retrieved from http://www.aacu.org/leap

Leeper, R. W. (1935). A study of a neglected portion of the field of learning: The development of sensory organization. *Journal of Genetic Psychology, 46*, 41–75.

Legg, A. M., & Wilson, J. H. (2009). E-mail from professor enhances student motivation and attitudes. *Teaching of Psychology, 36*, 205–211. doi:10.1080/00986280902960034

Leight, H., Saunders, C., Calkins, R., & Withers, M. (2012). Collaborative testing improves performance but not content retention in a large-enrollment introductory biology class. *CBE-Life Sciences Education, 11*, 392–401.

Lerner, M. J., & Goldberg, J. H. (1999). When do decent people blame victims? The differing effects of the explicit/rational and implicit/experiential cognitive systems. In S. Chaiken & Y. Trope (Eds.), *Dual-process theories in social psychology.* New York, NY: Guilford Press.

Lerner, R. M. (2002). *Adolescence: Development, diversity, context, and application.* Upper Saddle River, NJ: Pearson Education, Inc.

Levine, H. G., & Forman, P. M. (1973). A study of retention of knowledge of neurosciences information. *Academic Medicine, 48*, 867–869.

Lilienfeld, S. O., Lynn, S. J., Ruscio, J., Beyerstein, B. L. (2009). *50 great myths of popular psychology: Shattering widespread misconceptions about human behavior.* Malden, MA: Wiley-Blackwell.

Lilienfeld, S. O., Lynn, S., & Namy, L. L. (2013). *Psychology: From inquiry to understanding* (3rd ed.). Boston, MA: Pearson.

Lipko-Speed, A., Dunlosky, J., & Rawson, K. A. (2014). Does testing with feedback help grade-school children learn key concepts in science? *Journal of Applied Research in Memory and Cognition, 3*, 171–176.

Little, J. L., & McDaniel, M. A. (2015). Metamemory monitoring and control following retrieval practice for text. *Memory & Cognition, 43*, 85–98. doi: 10.3758/s13421-014-0453-7

Littleford, L. N., Buskist, W., Frantz, S. M., Galvan, D. B., Hendersen, R. W., McCarthy, M. A., . . . Puente, A. E. (2010). Psychology students today and tomorrow. In D. F. Halpern (Ed.), *Undergraduate education in psychology: A blueprint for the future of the discipline* (pp. 63–79). Washington, DC: American Psychological Association. doi:10.1037/12063-004

Loewenstein, J., Thompson, L., & Gentner, D. (1999). Analogical encoding facilitates knowledge transfer in negotiation. *Psychonomic Bulletin & Review, 6*, 586–597.

Loftus, E. F. (2000). Remembering what never happened. In E. Tulving (Ed.), *Memory, consciousness, and the brain: The Tallinn conference* (pp. 106–118). Philadelphia, PA: Psychology Press.

Loftus, E. F. (2005). Planting misinformation in the human mind: A 30-year investigation of the malleability of memory. *Learning & Memory, 12*, 361–366.

Loftus, E. F., & Palmer, J. C. (1974). Reconstruction of automobile destruction: An example of the interaction between language and memory. *Journal of Verbal Learning and Verbal Behavior, 13*, 585–589.

Lom, B. (2012). Classroom activities: Simple strategies to incorporate student-centered activities within undergraduate science lectures. *Journal of Undergraduate Neuroscience Education, 11*, A64–A71.

Lowman, J. (1995). *Mastering the techniques of teaching.* San Francisco, CA: Jossey-Bass.

Lu, S. (2014). How chronic stress is harming our DNA. *APA Monitor on Psychology, 45*, 28–31.

Luborsky, L., Diguer, L., Seligman, D. A., Rosenthal, R., Krause, E. D., Johnson, S., … Schweizer, E. (1999). The researcher's own therapy allegiance: A "wild card" in comparisons of treatment efficacy. *Clinical Psychology: Science & Practice, 6*, 95–106.

Lumina Foundation for Education (2011). *The degree qualifications profile.* Retrieved from http://www.luminafoundation.org/files/resources/dqp.pdf

Lutsky, N. (2004). *10 QR Questions at the Ready.* Retrieved from http://serc.carleton.edu/quirk/CarletonResources/10questions.html

Lutsky, N. (2008). Arguing with numbers: A rationale and suggestions for teaching quantitative reasoning through argument and writing. In B. L. Madison & L. A. Steen (Eds.), *Calculation vs. context: Quantitative literacy and its implications for teacher education* (pp. 59–74). Washington, DC: Mathematics Association of America.

Lutsky, N. (2010). Teaching psychology endings: The simple gifts of a reflective close. In D. S. Dunn, B. B. Beins, M. A. McCarthy, & G. W. Hill, IV (Eds.), *Best practices for teaching beginnings and endings in the psychology major.* New York, NY: Oxford Press.

Luttrell, V. R., Bufkin, J. L., Eastman, V. J., & Miller, R. (2010). Teaching scientific writing: Measuring student learning in an intensive APA skills course. *Teaching of Psychology, 37*, 193–195. doi:10.1080/00986283.2010.488531

Macrae, C. N., & Quadflieg, S. (2010). Perceiving people. In S. T. Fiske, D. T. Gilbert, & G. Lindzey (Eds.), *Handbook of social psychology* (5th ed., Vol. 1, pp. 353–393). Hoboken, NJ: Wiley.

Madigan, R., & Brosamer, J. (1990). Improving the writing skills of students in introductory psychology. *Teaching of Psychology, 17*, 27–30.

Mager, R. F. (1962). *Preparing objectives for programmed instruction.* Palo Alto, CA: Feardon Publishers.

Maguire, E. A., Gadian, D. G., Johnsrude, I. S., Good, C. D., Ashburner, J., Frackowiak, R. S., & Frith, C. D. (2000). Navigation-related structural change in the hippocampi of taxi drivers. *Proceedings of the National Academy of Sciences, 97*, 4398–4403.

Maier, N. (1931). Reasoning in humans. *Psychological Review, 38*, 332–346.

Maisto, S., Galizio, M., & Connors, G. (2004). *Drug use and abuse.* Belmont, CA: Wadsworth.

Maki, P. L. (2004). *Assessing for learning: Building a sustainable commitment across the institution.* Sterling, VA: Stylus.

Markowitz, A. (Writer and Producer), Friedman, T. (Executive producer). (2005). *A science odyssey*. In search of ourselves [DVD]. (n.d.). WGBH Boston.

Marsh, E. J. (2007). Retelling is not the same as recalling: Implications for memory. *Current Directions in Psychological Science, 16*, 16–20.

Marsh, E. J., & Tversky, B. (2004). Spinning the stories of our lives. *Applied Cognitive Psychology, 18*, 491–503.

Martin, R., & Leventhal, H. (2004). Symptom perception and health care–seeking behavior. In J. M. Raczynski & L. C. Leviton (Eds.), *Handbook of clinical health psychology, Vol. 2: Disorders of behavior and health*. Washington, DC: American Psychological Association.

Marzano, R. J. (2009). *Designing & teaching learning goals & objectives*. Bloomington, IN: Marzano Research Laboratory.

Massar, K., & Buunk, A. P. (2009). Rivals in the mind's eye: Jealous responses after subliminal exposure to body shapes. *Personality and Individual Differences, 46*, 129–134. doi:10.1016/j.paid.2008.09.016

Matsumoto, D. (2007). Culture, context, and behavior. *Journal of Personality, 75*, 1285–1320. doi:10.1111/j.1467-6494.2007.00476.x

Matsumoto, D., & Hwang, H. S. (2011). Culture, emotion, and expression. In K. D. Keith (Ed.), *Cross-cultural psychology: Contemporary themes and perspectives* (pp. 331–343). Malden, MA: Wiley-Blackwell.

Matsumoto, D., & Juang, L. (2007). *Culture and psychology* (4th ed.). Belmont, CA: Wadsworth.

Mayer, R. E. (2008). Applying the science of learning: Evidence-based principles for the design of multimedia instruction. *American Psychologist, 63*, 760.

Mazur, E. (2009). Farewell, lecture? *Science, 323*, 50–51.

McAdam, D. (2002). Bringing psychology to life. In R. A. Griggs (Ed.), *Handbook for teaching introductory psychology* (Vol. 3, pp. 3–4) (With an emphasis on assessment). Mahwah, NJ: Erlbaum.

McDaniel, M. A., Lyle, K. B., Butler, K. M., & Dornburg, C. C. (2008). Age-related deficits in reality monitoring of action memories. *Psychology and Aging, 23*, 646–656. doi:10.1037/a0013083

McDaniel, M. A., Roediger, H. L., & McDermott, K. B. (2007). Generalizing test-enhanced learning from the laboratory to the classroom. *Psychonomic Bulletin & Review, 14*, 200–206.

McKeachie, W., & Hofer, B. W. (2001). *Teaching tips: Strategies, theories, and research for college and university teachers* (11th ed.). Boston, MA: Houghton Mifflin.

McKeachie, W., & Svinicki, M. (2013). *McKeachie's teaching tips* (14th ed.). Boston, MA: Cengage.

McKeithen, K. B., Reitman, J. S., Rueter, H. H., & Hirtle, S. C. (1981). Knowledge organization and skill differences in computer programmers. *Cognitive Psychology, 13*, 307–325.

McNally, R. J. (2012). Explaining "memories" of space alien abduction and past lives: An experimental psychopathology approach. *Journal of Experimental Psychopathology, 3*, 2–16.

McNally, R. J., & Geraerts, E. (2009). A new solution to the recovered memory debate. *Perspectives on Psychological Science, 4*, 126–134. doi:10.1111/j.1745-6924.2009.01112.x

McNamara, C. L., Williamson, A. L., & Jorgensen, T. D. (2011). Assessment of differential learning by topic in introductory psychology. *Psychology Learning & Teaching, 10,* 253–260. doi:10.2304/plat.2011.10.3.253

McTighe, J., & Wiggins, G. (1999). *Understanding by design professional development workbook.* Alexandria, VA: Association for Supervision and Curriculum Development.

McTighe, J., & Wiggins, G. P. (1999). *By design handbook.* Alexandria, VA: Association for Supervision and Curriculum Development.

Mezulis, A. H., Abramson, L. Y., Hyde, J. S., & Hankin, B. L. (2004). Is there a universal positivity bias in attributions? A meta-analytic review of individual, developmental, and cultural differences in the self-serving attributional bias. *Psychological Bulletin, 130,* 711–747. doi:10.1037/0033-2909.130.5.711.

Miller, J. E. (2004). *The Chicago guide to writing about numbers.* Chicago, IL: University of Chicago Press.

Miller, J. G. (1984). Culture and the development of everyday social explanation. *Journal of Personality and Social Psychology, 46,* 961–978.

Mitchell, G. (2012). Revisiting truth or triviality: The external validity of research in the psychological laboratory. *Perspectives on Psychological Science, 7,* 109–117.

Mitler, M. M., Guilleminault, C., Orem, J., Zarcone, V. P., & Dement, W. C. (1975). Sleeplessness, sleep attacks, and things that go wrong in the night. *Psychology Today, 9,* 45–50.

Mitterer, J. O. (2012). On the importance of discovering water: Educating psychologists for the global village. *Psychology Learning & Teaching, 11,* 326–334.

Molitor, A., & Hsu, H. (2011). Child development across cultures. In K. D. Keith (Ed.), *Cross-cultural psychology: Contemporary themes and perspectives* (pp. 75–109). Malden, MA: Wiley-Blackwell.

Molouki, S., & Pronin, E. (2015). Self and other. In M. Mikulincer, P. R. Shaver, E. Borgida, & J. A. Bargh (Eds.), *APA handbook of personality and social psychology, Volume 1: Attitudes and social cognition* (pp. 387–414). Washington, DC: American Psychological Association. doi:10.1037/14341-013

Morling, B., & Smith, C. V. (2012). *Instructor's manual and test bank for research methods in psychology: Evaluating a world of information.* New York, NY: Norton.

Mueller, P. A., & Oppenheimer, D. M. (2014). The pen is mightier than the keyboard: Advantages of longhand over laptop note taking. *Psychological Science, 25,* 1159–1168. doi:10.1177/0956797614524581

Murray, S. L., Holmes, J. G., & Griffin, D. W. (1996). The benefits of positive illusions: Idealization and the construction of satisfaction in close relationships. *Journal of Personality and Social Psychology, 70,* 79–98. doi:10.1037/0022-3514.70.1.79

Myers, D. (2014, July). *Four decades professing psychology.* Paper presented at 3rd Annual Psychology One Conference, Stanford University.

Myers, D. G. (1980). *The inflated self: Human illusions and the biblical call to hope.* New York, NY: Seabury Press.

Myers, D. G. (2011). *Myers' psychology for AP.* New York, NY: Worth Publishers.

Myers, D. G., & Dewall, C. N. (2015). *Psychology* (11th ed.). New York, NY: Worth.

Nasie, M., Bar-Tal, D., Pliskin, R., Nahhas, E., & Halperin, E. (2014). Overcoming the barrier of narrative adherence in conflicts through awareness of the psychological bias of naïve realism. *Personality and Social Psychology Bulletin, 40,* 1543–1556. doi:10.1177/0146167214551153

National Academy of Sciences. (2008). *Science, evolution, and creationism*. Washington, DC: National Academies Press.

National Center for Education Statistics. (2015). Retrieved from https://nces.ed.gov /programs/digest/d15/tables/dt15_301.20.asp?current=yes

National Numeracy Network. (2015). Retrieved from http://serc.carleton.edu/nnn /index.html

Nevid, J. S., Pastva, A., & McClelland, N. (2012). Writing-to-learn assignments in introductory psychology: Is there a learning benefit? *Teaching of Psychology, 39*, 272–275.

Neville, A. J. (2008). Problem-based learning and medical education forty years on. A review of its effects on knowledge and clinical performance. *Medical Principles and Practice: International Journal of the Kuwait University, Health Science Centre, 18*, 1–9.

Nickerson, R. S. (1998). Confirmation bias: A ubiquitous phenomenon in many guises. *Review of General Psychology, 2*, 175–220. doi:10.1037/1089-2680.2.2.175

Nier, J. A. (2004). Why does the "above average effect" exist? Demonstrating idiosyncratic trait definition. *Teaching of Psychology, 31*, 53–54.

Norman, G. (2009). Teaching basic science to optimize transfer. *Medical Teacher, 31*, 807–811.

Norman, G. R., & Schmidt, H. G. (1992). The psychological basis of problem-based learning: A review of the evidence. *Academic Medicine, 67*, 557–65.

Novotney, A. (2014). Students under pressure. *APA Monitor, 45*, 37–41.

O'Leary, K. D., Kent, R. N., & Kanowitz, J. (1975). Shaping data collection congruent with experimental hypotheses. *Journal of Applied Behavior Analysis, 8*, 43–51.

Oltmanns, T. F., & Powers, A. D. (2012). Knowing our pathology. In S. Vazire, & T. D. Wilson (Eds.), *Handbook of self-knowledge* (pp. 258–273). New York, NY: Guilford Press.

Ormrod, J. E., & Davis, K. M. (2004). *Human learning*. Upper Saddle River, NJ: Prentice Hall.

Overholser, J. C. (2007). The Boulder model in academia: Struggling to integrate the science and practice of psychology. *Journal of Contemporary Psychotherapy, 37*, 205–211. doi:10.1007/s10879-007-9055-z

Pashler, H., & Wagenmakers, E. J. (2012). Editors' introduction to the special section on replicability in psychological science: A crisis of confidence? *Perspectives on Psychological Science, 7*, 528–530.

Pavlov, I. (1927). *Conditioned reflexes*. London, UK: Oxford University Press.

Payne, B. K. (2006). Weapon bias: Split-second decisions and unintended stereotyping. *Current Directions in Psychological Science, 15*, 287–291. doi:10.1111/j.1467-8721.2006.00454.x

Pellegrino, J. W., & Hilton, M. L. (Eds.). (2012). *Education for life and work: Developing transferable knowledge and skills in the 21st century*. Washington, DC: National Research Council.

Perry, J. L., Foust, M. S., & Elicker, J. D. (2013). *Measuring the varied skills of psychology majors: A revision and update of the academic skills inventory*. Office of Teaching Resources in Psychology, Society for the Teaching of Psychology. Retrieved from http:// teachpsych.org/resources/Documents/otrp/resources/perry13.pdf

Peters, E., Västfjäll, D., Slovic, P., Mertz, C. K., Mazzocco, K., & Dickert, S. (2006). Numeracy and decision making. *Psychological Science, 17*, 407–413.

Phillips, W. L. (2011). Cross-cultural differences in visual perception of color, illusions, depth, and pictures. In K. D. Keith (Ed.), *Cross-cultural psychology: Contemporary themes and perspectives* (pp. 160–180). Malden, MA: Wiley-Blackwell.

Pierce, B. H. (1999). Effects of unconscious memory on subjective judgments: A classroom demonstration. In L. T. Benjamin, B. F. Nodine, R. M. Ernst, & C. B. Broeker (Eds.), *Activities handbook for the teaching of psychology* (Vol. 4, pp. 202–206). Washington, DC: American Psychological Association.

Pinker, S. (1997). *How the mind works.* New York, NY: W. W. Norton & Co.

Pintrich, P. R. (2003). A motivational science perspective on the role of student motivation in learning and teaching contexts. *Journal of Educational Psychology, 95,* 667–686. doi:10.1037/0022-0663.95.4.667

Plassmann, H., O'Doherty, J., Shiv, B., & Rangel, A. (2008). Marketing actions can modulate neural representations of experienced pleasantness. *Proceedings of the National Academy of Science, 105,* 1050–1054.

Pliske, R. M., Caldwell, T. L., Calin-Jageman, R. J., & Taylor-Ritzler, T. (2015). Demonstrating the effectiveness of an integrated and intensive research methods and statistics course sequence. *Teaching of Psychology, 42,* 153–156. doi:10.1177/0098628315573139

Ploeger, A., van der Maas, H. J., & Raijmakers, M. J. (2008). Is evolutionary psychology a metatheory for psychology? A discussion of four major issues in psychology from an evolutionary developmental perspective. *Psychological Inquiry, 19,* 1–18.

Popham, W. J. (2008). *Transformative assessment.* Alexandria, VA: Association for Supervision and Curriculum Development.

Popham, W. J. (2011). *Transformative assessment in action: An inside look at applying the process.* Alexandria, VA: Association for Supervision and Curriculum Development.

Prince, M. (2004). Does active learning work? A review of the research. *Journal of Engineering Education, 93,* 223–231.

Pronin, E. (2007). Perception and misperception of bias in human judgment. *Trends in Cognitive Sciences, 11,* 37–43. doi:10.1016/j.tics.2006.11.001

Pronin, E., & Schmidt, K. (2013). Claims and denials of bias and their implications for policy. In E. Shafir (Ed.), *The behavioral foundations of public policy* (pp. 195–216). Princeton, NJ: Princeton University Press.

Pronin, E., Gilovich, T., & Ross, L. (2004). Objectivity in the eye of the beholder: Divergent perceptions of bias in self versus others. *Psychological Review, 111,* 781–799. doi:10.1037/0033-295X.111.3.781

Pronin, E., Kruger, J., Savitsky, K., & Ross, L. (2001). You don't know me, but I know you: The illusion of asymmetric insight. *Journal of Personality and Social Psychology, 81,* 639–656. doi:10.1037/0022-3514.81.4.639

Pronin, E., Lin, D.Y., & Ross, L. (2002). The bias blind spot: Perceptions of bias in self versus others. *Personality and Social Psychology Bulletin, 28,* 369–381. doi:10.1177/0146167202286008

Pusateri, T. (2009, November). *The assessment cyberguide for learning goals and outcomes.* Washington, DC: American Psychological Association Education Directorate.

Puterman, E., Lin, J., Blackburn, E., O'Donovan, A., Adler, N., & Epel, E. (2010). The power of exercise: Buffering the effect of chronic stress on telomere length. *PLoS One, 5,* 1–6. doi:10.1371/journal.pone.0010837.t002

Putnam, A. L., Sungkhasettee, V. W., & Roediger, H. L. (2016). Optimizing learning in college: Tips from cognitive psychology. *Perspectives on Psychological Science, 11*(5), 652–660. doi: 10.1177/1745691616645770

Pyc, M. A., Agarwal, P. K., & Roediger, H. L. (2014). Test-enhanced learning. In V. A. Benassi, C. E. Overson, & C. M. Hakala (Eds.), *Applying the science of learning in education: Infusing psychological science into the curriculum* (pp. 78–90): Society for the Teaching of Psychology. Retrieved from the Society for the Teaching of Psychology website: http://teachpsych.org/ebooks/asle2014/index.php

Quilici, J. L., & Mayer, R. E. (1996). Role of examples in how students learn to categorize statistics word problems. *Journal of Educational Psychology, 88*, 144.

Rawson, K. A., & Dunlosky, J. (2011). Optimizing schedules of retrieval practice for durable and efficient learning: How much is enough? *Journal of Experimental Psychology: General, 140*, 283.

Rawson, K. A., Dunlosky, J., & Sciartelli, S. M. (2013). The power of successive relearning: Improving performance on course exams and long-term retention. *Educational Psychology Review, 25*, 523–548.

Ray, R. D., & Belden, N. (2007). Teaching college level content and reading comprehension skills simultaneously via an artificially intelligent adaptive computerized instructional system. *The Psychological Record, 57*, 201–218.

Riggio, H. R., & Garcia, A. L. (2009). The power of situations: Jonestown and the fundamental attribution error. *Teaching of Psychology, 36*, 108–112. doi:10.1080/00986280902739636

Ritchey, K. A., & Bott, J. P. (2010). Exploring interdisciplinary themes in introductory psychology. *Teaching of Psychology, 37*, 262–266. doi:10.1080/00986283.2010.510958

Ritsko, A., & Rawlence, C. (Directors). (2007). Secrets of the mind [Television series episode; DVD]. In E. Crichton-Miller (Producer), *NOVA*. United States: WGBH Educational Foundation.

Roberts, S. C. (2012). *Applied evolutionary psychology*. New York, NY: Oxford University Press.

Rocklin, T. (1990). A demonstration of the illusory correlation effect. In V. P. Makosky, C. C. Sileo, L. G. Whittemore, C. P. Landry, & M. L. Skutley (Eds.), *Activities handbook for the teaching of psychology* (Vol. 3, pp. 25–26). Washington, DC: American Psychological Association.

Rodgers, J. E. (1982). The malleable memory of eyewitnesses. *Science Digest, 3*, 32–35.

Roediger, H. L., & Butler, A. C. (2011). The critical role of retrieval practice in long-term retention. *Trends in Cognitive Sciences, 15*, 20–27.

Roediger, H. L., & Karpicke, J. D. (2006). Test-enhanced learning: Taking memory tests improves long-term retention. *Psychological Science, 17*, 249–255. doi: 10.1111/j.1467-9280.2006.01693.x

Rohrer, D., & Taylor, K. (2007). The shuffling of mathematics problems improves learning. *Instructional Science, 35*, 481–498.

Rosenthal, R., & Fode, K. L. (1963). Three experiments in experimenter bias. *Psychological Reports, 12*, 491–511.

Ross, L. (1977). The intuitive psychologist and his shortcomings: Distortions in the attribution process. In L. Berkowitz (Ed.), *Advances in experimental social psychology* (Vol. 10, pp. 173–220). New York, NY: Academic Press .

Ross, L., & Ward, A. (1995). Psychological barriers to dispute resolution. In M. P. Zanna (Ed.), *Advances in experimental social psychology* (Vol. 27, pp. 255–304). San Diego, CA: Academic Press. doi:10.1016/S0065-2601(08)60407-4

Ross, L., & Ward, A. (1996). Naive realism in everyday life: Implications for social conflict and misunderstanding. In E. S. Reed, E. Turiel, & T. Brown (Eds.), *Values and knowledge* (pp. 103–135). Hillsdale, NJ: Erlbaum.

Rotgans, J. I., & Schmidt, H. G. (2011a). Situational interest and academic achievement in the active-learning classroom. *Learning and Instruction, 21*, 58–67.

Rotgans, J. I., & Schmidt, H. G. (2011b). The role of teachers in facilitating situational interest in an active-learning classroom. *Teaching and Teacher Education, 27*, 37–42.

Royse, D. (Ed.). (2001). *Teaching tips for college and university instructors: A practical guide* (pp. 95–120). Boston, MA: Allyn & Bacon.

Ryan, R. M., & Deci, E. L. (2000). Intrinsic and extrinsic motivations: Classic definitions and new directions. *Contemporary Educational Psychology, 25*, 54–67. doi:10.1006/ceps.1999.1020

Sana, F., Pachai, M. V., & Kim, J. A. (2011). Training undergraduate teaching assistants in a peer mentor course. *Transformative Dialogues, 4*, 1–10.

Sana, F., Weston, T., & Cepeda, N. (2013). Laptop multitasking hinders classroom learning for both users and nearby peers. *Computers & Education, 62*, 24–31. doi:10.1016/j.compedu.2012.10.003

Schachter, S. (1959). *The psychology of affiliation.* Stanford, CA: Stanford University Press.

Schachter, S., & Singer, J. (1962). Cognitive, social, and physiological determinants of emotional state. *Psychological Review, 69*, 379–399.

Schmidt, H. G. (1983). Problem-based learning: Rationale and description. *Medical Education, 17*, 11–16.

Schmidt, H. G., Rotgans, J. I., & Yew, E. H. (2011). The process of problem-based learning: What works and why. *Medical Education, 45*, 792–806.

Schmitt, D. P., & Pilcher, J. J. (2004). Evaluating evidence of psychological adaptation: How do we know one when we see one? *Psychological Science, 15*, 643–649.

Schwarz, N., & Strack, F. (1999). Reports of subjective well-being: Judgmental processes and their methodological implications. In D. Kahneman, E. Diener, & N. Schwarz (Eds.), *Well-being: The foundations of hedonic psychology.* New York, NY: Russell Sage Foundation.

Segall, M. H., Campbell, D. T., & Herskovits, M. J. (1966). The influence of culture on visual perception. In H. Toch and C. Smith (Eds.), *Social perception* (p. 184). Indianapolis, IN: Bobbs-Merrill.

Seybert, J. A. (2002). Assessing student learning outcomes. *New Directions for Community Colleges, 117*, 55–65.

Shaffner, F. (Director). (2010). *Twelve angry men* [DVD]. Studio One.

Shepperd, J. A., & McNulty, J. K. (2002). The affective consequences of expected and unexpected outcomes. *Psychological Science, 13*, 85–88.

Sherman, D. K., Nelson, L. D., & Ross, L. D. (2003). Naïve realism and affirmative action: Adversaries are more similar than they think. *Basic and Applied Social Psychology, 25*, 275–289. doi:10.1207/S15324834BASP2504_2

Sherman, J. W., Stroessner, S. J., Conrey, F. R., & Azam, O. A. (2005). Prejudice and stereotype maintenance processes: Attention, attribution, and individuation. *Journal of Personality and Social Psychology, 89*, 607–622. doi:10.1037/0022-3514.89.4.607

Shtulman, A., & Calabi, P. (2013). Tuition vs. intuition: Effects of instruction on naïve theories of evolution. *Merrill-Palmer Quarterly, 59*, 141–167.

Shtulman, A., & Valcarcel, J. (2012). Scientific knowledge suppresses but does not supplant earlier intuitions. *Cognition, 124*, 209–215.

Shulman, L. S. (1997). Professing the liberal arts. *Education and democracy: Re-imagining liberal learning in America.* New York, NY: The College Board.

Sieck, W. R., & Arkes, H. R. (2005). The recalcitrance of overconfidence and its contribution to decision aid neglect. *Journal of Behavioral Decision Making, 18*, 29–53. doi:10.1002/bdm.486

Simons, D. J., & Chabris, C. F. (1999). Gorillas in our midst: Sustained inattentional blindness for dynamic events. *Perception, 28*, 1059–1074.

Simons, D. J., & Chabris, C. F. (2011). What people believe about how memory works: A representative survey of the US population. *PloS One, 6*, e22757. doi:10.1371/journal.pone.0022757

Simpson, J. A., Fletcher, G. J. O., & Campbell, L. (2001). The structure and function of ideal standards in close relationships. In G. J. O. Fletcher & M. S. Clark (Eds.), *Blackwell handbook of social psychology: Interpersonal processes* (pp. 86–106). Malden, MA: Blackwell.

Skinner, B. F. (1948). *Walden two.* Indianapolis, IN: Hackett Publishing.

Smith, E. E., Adams, N., & Schorr, D. (1978). Fact retrieval and the paradox of interference. *Cognitive Psychology, 10*, 438–464.

Smith, M. K., Wood, W. B., Adams, W. K., Wieman, C., Knight, J. K., Guild, N., & Su, T. T. (2009). Why peer discussion improves student performance on in-class concept questions. *Science, 323*, 122–124.

Smith, R. A., & Fineburg, A. C. (2005). Standards and outcomes: Encouraging best practices in teaching introductory psychology. In D. S. Dunn & S. L. Chew (Eds.), *Best practices for teaching introduction to psychology* (pp. 179–194). Mahwah, NJ: Erlbaum.

Society for the Teaching of Psychology. (n.d.). Office of Teaching Resources in Psychology (OTRP) Teaching of Psychology Idea Exchange (ToPIX). Retrieved from http://topix.teachpsych.org/w/page/19980993/FrontPage

Solon, T. (2007). Generic critical thinking infusion and course content learning in introductory psychology. *Journal of Instructional Psychology, 34*, 95–109.

Soppe, M., Schmidt, H. G., & Bruysten, R. J. (2005). Influence of problem familiarity on learning in a problem-based course. *Instructional Science, 33*, 271–281.

Spaulding, W. B. (1969). The undergraduate medical curriculum (1969 model): McMaster university. *Canadian Medical Association Journal, 100*, 659.

Spiegel, D. (2003). Negative and positive visual hypnotic hallucinations: Attending inside and out. *International Journal of Clinical & Experimental Hypnosis, 51*, 130–146.

Staley, C. A., & Porter, M. E. (Eds.). (2002). *Engaging large classes: Strategies and techniques for college faculty.* San Francisco, CA: Anker (Jossey-Bass).

Stanovich, K. E., & West, R. F. (2007). Natural myside bias is independent of cognitive ability. *Thinking & Reasoning, 13*, 225–247. doi:10.1080/13546780600780796

Stanovich, K. E., & West, R. F. (2008). On the relative independence of thinking biases and cognitive ability. *Journal of Personality and Social Psychology, 94*, 672–695. doi:10.1037/0022-3514.94.4.672

Stanovich, K. E., West, R. F., & Toplak, M. E. (2013). Myside bias, rational thinking, and intelligence. *Current Directions in Psychological Science, 22*, 259–264. doi:10.1177/0963721413480174

Stark, E. (2012). Enhancing and assessing critical thinking in a psychological research methods course. *Teaching of Psychology, 39,* 107–112.

Steele, C. M., & Aronson, J. (1995). Stereotype threat and the intellectual test performance of African Americans. *Journal of Personality and Social Psychology, 69,* 797.

Steen, L. A. (2001). *Mathematics and democracy: The case for quantitative literacy.* Washington, DC: Woodrow Wilson National Fellowship Foundation.

Steptoe, A. (2007). Stress effects: Overview. In G. Fink (Ed.), *Encyclopedia of stress.* San Diego, CA: Elsevier.

Sternberg, R. J., & Davidson, J. E. (1983). Insight in the gifted. *Educational Psychologist, 18,* 51–57.

Steuer, F. B., & Ham K. W., II. (2008). Psychology textbooks: Examining their accuracy. *Teaching of Psychology, 35,* 160-168. doi:10.1080/00986280802189197

Steuer, F., & Ham, K. W. (2008). Psychology textbooks: Examining their accuracy. *Teaching of Psychology, 35,* 160–168. doi:10.1080/00986280802189197

Stevens, C., & Witkow, M. (2014). Training scientific thinking skills: Evidence from an MCAT[2015]-aligned classroom module. *Teaching of Psychology, 41,* 115–121.

Stigler, S. M. (1999). *Statistics on the table.* Cambridge, MA: Harvard University Press.

Stoloff, M. L. (2010). Addressing the multiple demands of teaching introductory psychology. In D. S. Dunn, M. A. McCarthy, B. Beins, & G. W. Hill, IV (Eds.), *Best practices for teaching beginnings and endings in the psychology major: Research, cases, and recommendations* (pp. 15–29). Oxford, UK: Oxford University Press.

Stoloff, M., McCarthy, M., Keller, L., Varfolomeeva, V., Lynch, J., Makara, K., . . . Smiley, W. (2010). The undergraduate psychology major: An examination of structure and sequence. *Teaching of Psychology, 37,* 4–15. doi:10.1080/00986280903426274

Storms, M. D., & Nisbett, R. E. (1970). Insomnia and the attribution process. *Journal of Personality and Social Psychology, 16,* 319–328.

Strack, F., Martin, L. L., & Stepper, S. (1988). Inhibiting and facilitating conditions of the human smile: A nonobtrusive test of the facial feedback hypothesis. *Journal of personality and social psychology, 54,* 768.

Strobel, J., & van Barneveld, A. (2009). When is PBL more effective? A meta-synthesis of meta-analyses comparing PBL to conventional classrooms. *Interdisciplinary Journal of Problem-based Learning, 3,* 4.

Suskie, L. (2009). *Assessing student learning: A common sense guide* (2nd ed.). San Francisco, CA: Jossey-Bass/Wiley.

Suskie, L. (2010). *Assessing student learning: A common sense guide.* Hoboken, NJ: John Wiley & Sons.

Sutherland, W. J., Spiegelhalter, D., & Burgman, M. (2013). Twenty tips for interpreting scientific claims. *Nature, 503,* 335–337.

Svinicki, M. D. (2004). *Learning and motivation in the post secondary classroom.* Bolton, MA: Anker Publishing.

Svinicki, M. D., & McKeachie, W. J. (2011). *McKeachie's teaching tips: Strategies, research, and theory for college and university teachers* (13th ed.). San Francisco, CA: Wadsworth Cengage Learning.

Taylor, K., & Rohrer, D. (2010). The effects of interleaved practice. *Applied Cognitive Psychology, 24,* 837–848.

Taylor, S. E., Pham, L. B., Rivkin, I. D., & Armor, D. A. (1998). Harnessing the imagination: Mental stimulation, self-regulation, and coping. *American Psychologist, 53*, 429–439. doi:10.1037//0003-066X.53.4.429

Thaler, N., Kazemi, E., & Huscher, C. R. (2009). Developing a rubric to assess student learning outcomes using a class assignment. *Teaching of Psychology, 36*, 113–116.

Thieman, T., Clary, E., Olson, A., Dauner, R., & Ring, E. (2009). Introducing students to psychological research: General psychology as a laboratory course. *Teaching of Psychology, 36*, 160–168.

Thompson, D. W. (1951). *On growth and form*. Cambridge: The University Press.

Thompson, S. C. (1999). Illusions of control: How we overestimate our personal control. *Current Directions in Psychological Science, 8*, 187–190. doi:10.1111/1467-8721.00044

Thornhill, R. (1997). The concept of an evolved adaptation. In G. R. Bock & G. Cardew (Eds.), Characterizing human psychological adaptations (pp. 4–22). West Sussex, UK: John Wiley & Sons.

Tomcho, T. J., Rice, D., Foels, R., Folmsbee, L., Vladescu, J., Lissman, R., ... Bopp, K. (2009). APA's learning objectives for research methods and statistics in practice: A multimethod analysis. *Teaching of Psychology, 36*, 84–89.

Tourangeau, R., & Yan, T. (2007). Sensitive questions in surveys. *Psychological Bulletin, 133*, 859–883.

Trochim, W. M. K. (2006). *Research methods knowledge base: Deduction and induction*. Retrieved from http://www.socialresearchmethods.net/kb/dedind.php

Trope, Y., & Liberman, N. (2003). Temporal construal. *Psychological Review, 110*, 403–421.

Tufte, E. R. (2001). *The visual display of quantitative information*. Cheshire, CT: Graphics Press.

Tversky, A., & Kahneman, D. (1974). Judgment under uncertainty: Heuristics and biases. *Science, 185*, 1124–1131.

U.S. Department of Labor. (1991). *What work requires of schools: A SCANS report for America 2000*. The Secretary's Commission on Achieving Necessary Skills. Washington, DC: Author.

University of Minnesota Center for Teaching and Learning. (2008). *What is active learning?* Retrieved from http://www1.umn.edu/ohr/teachlearn/tutorials/active/what/index.html

Utts, J. (2003). What educated citizens should know about statistics and probability. *The American Statistician, 57*, 74–79.

van Berkel, H. J., & Schmidt, H. G. (2000). Motivation to commit oneself as a determinant of achievement in problem-based learning. *Higher Education, 40*, 231–242.

van Blankenstein, F. M., Dolmans, D. H., van der Vleuten, C. P., & Schmidt, H. G. (2011). Which cognitive processes support learning during small-group discussion? The role of providing explanations and listening to others. *Instructional Science, 39*, 189–204.

Van den Boom, D. C. (1994). The influence of temperament and mothering on attachment and exploration: An experimental manipulation of sensitive responsiveness among lower-class mothers with irritable infants. *Child Development, 65*, 1457–1477.

Van den Bos, K., & Maas, M. (2009). On the psychology of the belief in a just world: Exploring experiential and rationalistic paths to victim blaming. *Personality and Social Psychology Bulletin, 35*, 1567–1578. doi:10.1177/0146167209344628 van den Hurk, M. M., Dolmans, D. H., Wolfhagen, I. H., & van der Vleuten, C. P. (2001). Testing a causal model for learning in a problem-based curriculum. *Advances in Health Sciences Education, 6*, 141–149.

VanderStoep, S. W., Fagerlin, A., & Feenstra, J. S. (2000). What do students remember from introductory psychology? *Teaching of Psychology, 27*, 89–92.

Vescio, T. K., Sechrist, G. B., & Paolucci, M. P. (2003). Perspective taking and prejudice reduction: The mediational role of empathy arousal and situational attributions. *European Journal of Social Psychology, 33*, 455–472.

Vigorito, M. (2011). Using e-portfolios in psychology courses. In R. L. Miller, E. Amsel, B. M. Kowalewski, B. C. Beins, K. D. Keith, & B. F. Peden (Eds.), *Promoting student engagement* (Vol. 1, pp. 189–204). Retrieved from http://teachpsych.org/ebooks/pse2011/index.php

Wainright, J. L., & Patterson, C. J. (2008). Peer relations among adolescents with female same-sex parents. *Developmental Psychology, 44*, 117–126. doi:10.1037/0012-1649.44.1.117

Walton, H. J., & Matthews, M. B. (1989). Essentials of problem-based learning. *Medical Education, 23*, 542–558.

Walvoord, B. (2010). *Assessment clear and simple: A practical guide for institutions, departments, and general education.* San Francisco, CA: Jossey-Bass.

Wang, Q., Bui, V., & Song, Q. (2015). Narrative organization at encoding facilitated children's long-term episodic memory. *Memory, 23*, 602–611. doi:10.1080/09658211.2014.914229

Watson, J. B., & Rayner, R. (1920). Conditioned emotional reactions. *Journal of Experimental Psychology, 3*, 1–14. doi:10.1037/h0069608

Weimer, M. (2002). *Learner-centered teaching: Five key changes to practice.* San Francisco, CA: Jossey-Bass.

Weinberger, J., & Westen, D. (2008). RATS, we should have used Clinton: Subliminal priming in political campaigns. *Political Psychology, 29*, 631–651. doi:10.1111/j.1467-9221.2008.00658.x

Weinstein, N. D. (2003). Exploring the links between risk perceptions and preventive health behavior. In J. Suls & K. A. Wallston (Eds.), *Social psychological foundations of health and illness* (pp. 22–53). Malden, MA: Blackwell.

Weisenberg, M., Raz, T., & Hener, T. (1998). The influence of film-induced mood on pain perception. *Pain, 76*, 365–375. doi:10.1016/S0304-3959(98)00069-4

Weiten, W., & Houska, J. A. (2015). Introductory psychology: Unique challenges and opportunities. In D. S. Dunn (Ed.), *Oxford handbook of undergraduate psychology education* (pp. 289–321). New York, NY: Oxford University Press.

Wells, G. L., & Loftus, E. F. (2013). Eyewitness memory for people and events. In R. K. Otto & I. B. Weiner (Eds.), *Handbook of psychology, Vol. 11: Forensic psychology* (2nd ed., pp. 617–629). Hoboken, NJ: John Wiley & Sons.

Wells, J. K. (2009). Thrift: A guide to thrifty genes, thrifty phenotypes and thrifty norms. *International Journal of Obesity, 33*, 1331–1338.

Werker, J. F., & Tees, R. C. (1984). Cross-language speech perception: Evidence for perceptual reorganization during the first year of life. *Infant Behavior and Development, 7*, 49–63.

Westen, D., Blagov, P. S., Harenski, K., Kilts, C., & Hamann, S. (2006). Neural bases of motivated reasoning: An fMRI study of emotional constraints on partisan political judgment in the 2004 U.S. presidential election. *Journal of Cognitive Neuroscience, 18,* 1947–1958. doi:10.1162/jocn.2006.18.11.1947

Whitman, W. (1860). *Leaves of grass.* Boston, MA: Thayer and Eldridge.

Wigfield, A., & Eccles, J. S. (2000). Expectancy–value theory of achievement motivation. *Contemporary Educational Psychology, 25,* 68–81. doi:10.1006/ceps.1999.1015

Wiggins, G., & McTighe, J. (1998). *Understanding by design.* Alexandria, VA: Association for Supervision & Curriculum Development.

Wiliam, D. (2011). *Embedded formative assessment.* Bloomington, IN: Solution Tree Press.

Wilkinson, T. J., Dik, B. J., & Tix, A. P. (2008). The critical thinking lab: Developing student skills through practical application. In D. S. Dunn, J. S. Halonen, & R. A. Smith (Eds.), *Teaching critical thinking in psychology: A handbook of best practices* (pp. 263–265). Malden, MA: Wiley-Blackwell.

Williams, J.D. (2009). Belief versus acceptance: Why do people not believe in evolution? *BioEssays, 31,* 1255–1262.

Williamson, D. A., Zucker, N. L., Martin, C. K., & Smeets, M. A. M. (2001). Etiology and management of eating disorders. In P. B. Sutker & H. E. Adams (Eds.), *Comprehensive handbook of psychopathology.* New York, NY: Kluwer Academic/Plenum.

Wilson, T. D., & Gilbert, D. T. (2005). Affective forecasting: Knowing what to want. *Current Directions in Psychological Science, 14,* 131–134.

Wolpe, J. (1961). The systematic desensitization treatment of neuroses. *Journal of Nervous and Mental Disease, 132,* 180–203. doi:10.1097/00005053-196103000-00001

Zachar, P., & Leong, F. T. L. (1992). A problem of personality: Scientist and practitioner differences in psychology. *Journal of Personality, 60,* 665–677.

Zhao, X., Dowd, K., & Searcy, C. A. (2012). Assessing statistics and research methodology in the MCAT exam. *Chance, 25,* 11–17.

Zimbardo, P. G. (2004). Does psychology make a significant difference in our lives? *American Psychologist, 59,* 339–351. doi:10.1037/0003-066X.59.5.339

Zimbardo, P. G., Butler, L. D., & Wolfe, V. A. (2003). Cooperative college examinations: More gain, less pain when students share information and grades. *The Journal of Experimental Education, 71,* 101–125.

About the Editors

Dana S. Dunn is professor of psychology at Moravian College in Bethlehem, Pennsylvania. A former chair of the Department of Psychology there, he received a Ph.D. from the University of Virginia and a B.A. from Carnegie Mellon University. Dunn was president of the Society for the Teaching of Psychology in 2010. He is a fellow of Eastern Psychological Association, the Association for Psychological Science, and the American Psychological Association (APA). Dunn does research on the scholarship of teaching and learning and on the social psychology of disability. He is the author or editor of 32 books and over 150 articles, chapters, and book reviews. Dunn is the current editor-in-chief of the *Oxford Bibliographies: Psychology* and is on the editorial boards of the *Journal of Social & Clinical Psychology*, *Psychology Learning & Teaching*, and *Rehabilitation Psychology*. Dunn received the Charles L. Brewer Award for Distinguished Teaching of Psychology from the American Psychological Foundation in 2013.

Bridgette Martin Hard is a lecturer at Stanford University and coordinator for the Stanford Psychology One Program. She works with several faculty members to co-teach Stanford's introductory psychology course ("Psych One") year-round and also recruits and mentors a team of graduate and undergraduate teaching fellows who take part in the program's year-long teacher training. Her work with the Psychology One Program earned her Stanford's Lloyd L. Dinkelspiel Award in 2012 for exceptional contribution to undergraduate education. She is also the cofounder and organizer for the Stanford Psychology One Conference, an annual conference devoted to the teaching of introductory psychology. Hard received her B.S. in psychology from Furman University where she studied with Charles Brewer (namesake of APA's Charles L. Brewer Distinguished Teaching of Psychology Award) and her Ph.D. in cognitive psychology from Stanford University. She was the recipient of a National Research Service Award to pursue postdoctoral research in developmental psychology at the University of Oregon.

Index